I love *Festschrifts* and this one is a gem. It is a rich feast of essays on theology, church history, and ministerial praxis—which is quite apropos given Professor Kelly's wide range of ministry. All in all, a truly excellent way to honour his eminently faithful and spiritually profitable lifetime of teaching.

MICHAEL A. G. HAYKIN
Professor of Church History, The Southern Baptist Theological Seminary,
Louisville, Kentucky

I did not have the privilege of having Douglas Kelly as one of my seminary professors, but since moving to Charlotte it has been my privilege to work alongside and minister with many men who count Dr. Kelly as one of their formative influences. They all say the same thing about the excellence of his piety, his learning, his doctrinal fidelity, and his theological insights. As a professor at RTS Charlotte, and as a member of the same presbytery, I can now count Dr. Kelly as a friend and colleague. I'm happy to say the reports of his giftedness and godliness are true! It has also been a joy to work alongside his delightful and talented wife, Caroline. I warmly commend this volume of essays in honor of Dr. Kelly. The chapters are stimulating, learned, and edifying—a fitting tribute to Dr. Kelly's legacy inside and outside the classroom.

KEVIN DEYOUNG
Senior Pastor, Christ Covenant Church (PCA);
Associate Professor of Systematic Theology, Reformed Theological Seminary,
Charlotte, North Carolina

A humble, holy, and happy minister, Dr Kelly's life and ministry embodies the best of the Scottish, Southern, and Genevan Presbyterianism he so loves. From Caroline Kelly's mesmerizing account of Dr. Kelly's roots as a Carolina Scot, through Jonny Gibson's sterling defense of the "24 hour, ordinary day" view of creation, through Sinclair Ferguson's narrative of a forgotten Scottish pastor theologian, to an examination of the teaching of Calvin, to the piety and principles of Dr. Kelly himself, this volume provides an apt tribute. Here Dr Kelly's principal concerns are ably taken up, defended, and commended to a new generation.

DAVID STRAIN
Senior Minister, First Presbyterian Church, Jackson, Mississippi

This is no ordinary festschrift. Like any such work it honors a much loved pastor-scholar, fittingly, not by directing us to look at him, only through him and with him, at the triune God whom he confesses and adores. But by doing this in such a beautifully conceived way, using the lenses of time and place, this book is a treasure of weighty theology rooted in the winsome graciousness of personal piety and prayerful discipleship. I learnt a very great deal from these writers who have learned so much from Dr Kelly, and I thank God for him and for each of them.

DAVID GIBSON,
Minister, Trinity Church, Aberdeen, Scotland

This well-written and edited, worthy, and edifying festschrift strikes a chord of several harmonious notes—Bible, theology, history, and practical Christianity—just like the music of Douglas Kelly's life. What a friend, scholar, and faithful man of God and theologian he has been and still is! I am so grateful for him and for this excellent volume of essays.

JOEL R. BEEKE
President, Puritan Reformed Theological Seminary, Grand Rapids, Michigan

WRITINGS IN HONOR OF
Douglas F. Kelly

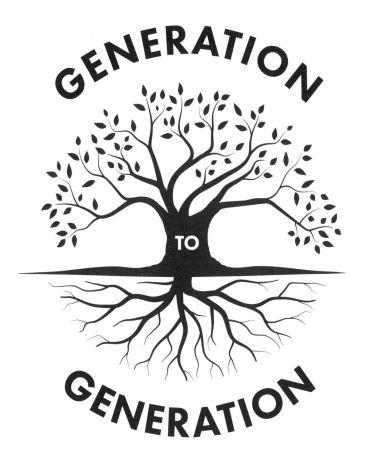

GENERATION

TO

GENERATION

EDITED BY
**Matthew S. Miller
& D. Blair Smith**

ⅢENTOR

Copyright © Matthew S. Miller & D. Blair Smith 2023

paperback ISBN 978-1-5271-1114-1
ebook ISBN 978-1-5271-1115-8

10 9 8 7 6 5 4 3 2 1

Published in 2023
in the
Mentor Imprint
by
Christian Focus Publications Ltd,
Geanies House, Fearn, Ross-shire,
IV20 1TW, Great Britain.

www.christianfocus.com

Cover design by Pete Barnsely (CreativeHoot)

Printed and bound by Bell & Bain, Glasgow

MIX
Paper | Supporting
responsible forestry
FSC® C007785

Contents

Reader of the hallowed Classics—
first the Greeks and Latins,
then the Fathers and Reformers.
Preacher of the Scriptures—

through tongues both Gaelic and Anglo,
in pulpits high and low.
Professor of Divinity—
to a generation's

ministers and missionaries,
who studied under him
in the holy seminary.
Stormer of Heaven—on

his knees for his family and
friends, for his nation and
church, the beloved Bride of Christ.
He has poured out his life

as a living sacrifice to
the Holy Trinity,
and Christo et Ecclesiae
has ordered his labors.

I give thanks to God that in him,
Dr. Douglas Kelly,
I've taken in the sweet smelling
aroma of heaven.

'Common Meter for an Uncommon Man'
—D. Blair Smith

Editor's Preface

IT is impossible to measure the impact of Douglas F. Kelly's ministry of preaching, teaching, writing, and mentoring, but this volume witnesses to that impact. In his expositional preaching as the minister of three congregations (Raeford Presbyterian Church, First Presbyterian Church in Dillon, SC, and Reedy Creek Presbyterian Church), he presented "the whole counsel of God" in a braid of exegetical depth, vivid imagery, and plainspoken language that had the characteristic effect of pulling back together the mind, heart, and will of his hearers into a more singular devotion to God. His decades of teaching as professor of Systematic Theology at Reformed Theological Seminary, Jackson, from 1983–1994, and then at Reformed Theological Seminary, Charlotte, from 1994 until his retirement in 2016, stood out for its unparalleled breadth of sources and inescapably doxological atmosphere, on account of which students were known to hasten to class so as not to miss his opening prayers. His writing moves with ease through an expanse of topics, from a pastoral emphasis on prayer (*If God Already Knows, Why Pray?*) to the political dimensions of the Reformed faith (*The Emergence of Liberty in the Modern World*) to the intersection of Scripture and science in the doctrine of creation (*Creation and Change*), culminating in his three-volume *Systematic Theology*, a work methodologically committed to beginning with exegesis, gleaning from the fields of historical theology, and making application in a post-Enlightenment culture. And at every stop along the way he has made time for others, influencing many of the men who contributed to this volume and embodying what C. S. Lewis discerned as a distinctive quality of genuinely holy people: "They will usually seem to have a lot of time: you will wonder where they get it from."[1]

One of the secrets to Dr. Kelly's remarkable ability to "find time" may lie in his uncommon respect for time—not time in terms of the minutes and seconds that mark the tyranny of the urgent, but in terms of the centuries and epochs that bear witness to lasting things. As many of the chapters in this volume attest, Dr. Kelly is unusually aware of how the past continues to shape the present, not only culturally but personally. At the personal level, this awareness has given him a deeply rooted sense of identity as one belonging to a large family stretching across the seas and back through the centuries. At the theological level, it has embedded his faith in that catholic—in terms of the church across space and across time—apprehension of the love of God that can only be known "with all the saints" (Eph. 3:18). Accordingly, his systematic theology is woven with historical theology just as his personal anecdotes are shot through with the stories of ancestors. Further evidence of his respect for time is found in the way he happily orders his days in keeping with the weekly rhythms of work and Sabbath rest established in the creation ordinance of Genesis 1:1–2:3. Douglas Kelly is, more than anyone else either of us has ever known, at peace with time—or, perhaps more fittingly, at peace with the God who, himself not subject to time,[2] made time, revealed himself through time, and accomplished our salvation "in the fullness of time" (Gal. 4:4).

For that reason, we have named this volume *Generation to Generation*,[3] a title that attests to Kelly's notable—and increasingly

---

1. C. S. Lewis, *Mere Christianity* (New York: HarperCollins, 1952), IV.11.

2. St. Augustine declares, "For God made the creatures that were to be made in the future in such a way that without Himself being subject to time He made them subject to time," to which Kelly later adds, "[God] uses time, as He uses matter and space, without in any sense being inconvenienced or hampered by it in accomplishing His chosen purposes." Douglas F. Kelly, *Creation and Change: Genesis 1.1–2.4 in the Light of Changing Scientific Paradigms*, 2nd ed. (Geanies House: Mentor, 2017), 100. The quote from Augustine comes from *The Literal Meaning of Genesis*, Vol. I: Ancient Christian Writers, No. 41, Quasten et al. editors, John H. Taylor, translator (New York: New Press, 1982), Book 4, chapter 35 (145).

3. We are thankful to contributor Rev. Mark Miller for suggesting this title.

countercultural—regard for the divinely-ordered flow of time and contentedness with his own place in it. Accordingly, the volume opens with Caroline Kelly's tracing of her husband's family history that gave rise to the man this volume honors. From that entryway it moves into Part One, which focuses on the doctrine of creation, so important in Kelly's life and thought, with chapters by John Currid, Jonny Gibson, and Alex Mark that unfold the divine creation of space and time and the blessings that come when we conform our lives to that original pattern.

In Part Two, Blair Smith, Sinclair Ferguson, and Ligon Duncan set before our eyes some of the greatest historical exemplars of piety and ministry to the end that we might still admire and imitate today what was best in them long ago. Though Kelly's acquaintance with the great lights of church history extends far and wide, his special regard for the great Reformer from Geneva, John Calvin, is undeniable, on account of which Part Three concentrates on significant episodes in Geneva from Calvin's later ministry and beyond, featuring chapters by Jon Balserak, Kirk Summers, Matthew Miller, and Christian Finnigan.

Part Four, with contributions by Mark McDowell, Mark Miller, Mantle Nance, and Gerrit Dawson, pays homage to Kelly's historical theological approach to doctrine and to his particular love for the doctrine of union with Christ. In Part Five, the volume closes with sustained consideration of Kelly's personal influence as experienced by Bill Bradford, Patrick Kelly, and Taylor Ince, each of whom vividly recounts that influence with attention to a particular facet of Kelly's teaching (dying and rising with Christ, the practice of fasting, and the place of the Psalms and prayer in the Christian life, respectively).

We wish to thank all the contributors for their participation in this project (as well as Reformed Theological Seminary, Charlotte, student Matthew Kirk for his help with the bibliography). It is a testament to Kelly's personal impact that everyone who was invited to participate agreed to do so immediately.

Matthew S. Miller and D. Blair Smith
June 2023

"He Setteth the Solitary in Families"

The Primacy of Family and Scottish Heritage in the Life of Douglas F. Kelly

Caroline Kelly

Genealogy and Family

IN September 1739, the quiet lapping of dark waters against the thickly wooded banks of the Cape Fear River would have been disturbed by the sounds of men, women, and children talking excitedly in their native Gaelic, "Feuach, 's briagha a th'ann!"(Look, isn't it lovely!).

So begins the opening chapter of Douglas Kelly's book, *Carolina Scots, An Historical and Genealogical Study of Over 100 Years of Emigration*.[1]

In many ways, these lines encapsulate central themes of his life: a deep appreciation for his Highland Scottish heritage, love of languages, enthusiasm for the Carolinas, love of family, and cheerful optimism.

---

1. Douglas Kelly with Caroline Switzer Kelly, *Carolina Scots, An Historical and Genealogical Study of Over 100 Years of Emigration* (Dillon: 1739 Publications, 1998), 3.

We can do no better than to use his own words from the Preface to that book to understand the wellspring of his view of family, and indeed of what he feels is important for life:

An eighteenth-century English traveler in the Highlands of Scotland remarked that the people had, "...a pride in their family, as almost everyone is a genealogist."[2] That was still much the case in the Cape Fear Valley region of Eastern North Carolina where I was reared in the nineteen forties and fifties. That section of the Eastern Seaboard was well aware of its Scottish roots and was also deeply marked by the Southern loyalty to the extended family. In neighborhood, church, and school, I was surrounded by people who were proud of their Scottish Highland surnames and could easily trace their pedigree back for two hundred years.

During the summers, from the time I was aged five until my last year at the University of North Carolina at Chapel Hill, I lived on the old family farm which had been granted to my father's Highland emigrant ancestors, shortly before the Revolutionary War, and had been inhabited by their descendants ever since ...

During those last years of the small family farm economy, there was still a great deal of neighborhood visiting with long conversations on the front porch, not to mention the talking that was done while working in the tobacco packhouse or in the cotton field. Most of the surrounding land holders of that section...were related by blood or marriage, being descended from the same Scottish emigrant families, and most of them tended to be members of the various Presbyterian Churches of the area ... In fact, when my bride (a native of England) came to live in these parts, she noticed how very much shared experience and history these people had, and how much they seemed to know about each other and their past. She discovered that they tended not to discuss politics in general, cultural events, and contemporary ideas but rather family concerns and interests—both current and historical—as well as church, economy, and school, and in that order. Their lives were too full of wide-ranging interesting family matters, past and present, for them to be worried with abstract discussions about ideas or culture in the broad sense.

---

2. Ian Charles Cargill Graham, *Colonists from Scotland: Emigration to North America 1707–1783* (Ithaca: Cornell University Press, 1956), 1, 2.

Thus, as I grew up, in addition to immediate relatives, many of the people who surrounded me...knew, loved, and discussed the details of the lives and times of our Carolina and Highland ancestors in a way that fascinated me, a grammar schoolboy. [We all] sat on the porch of the old Patrick Blue home in order to make the most of the shade of the tall pine trees and to catch the breeze that tended to blow on that side of the house.

They spoke of persons and events in these very fields and woods—going back to the Reconstruction, and the War Between the States and indeed the American Revolution, and the first settlement of these Sandhills—as though it were yesterday. It was almost as though our remote forefathers could be called out of the next room in the old house, or perhaps summoned from the family burial plots in Union and Bethesda Churchyards to tell their story. So, at the age of twelve, I wrote my first family history, and since then have continued to learn and collect all I could on the Scottish Highland families of Moore County and the Cape Fear Valley.

These genealogical and historical interests were greatly stimulated when I went to Edinburgh for doctoral studies ... I frequently visited my distant Kelly cousins in the Isle of Skye, who shared an appreciation of our mutual heritage as well as a strong commitment to the Christian faith.

Hand in hand with the discovery of new family connections, my understanding of Highland history was greatly expanded as I studied Gaelic under the Rev. William Matheson of the Celtic Department of Edinburgh University ... He explained the basic events and movements that were afoot during the time our Carolina ancestors emigrated from their ancient homeland ...

Then in later years, when I served as minister in the Presbyterian Churches of Raeford, North Carolina, and afterwards in Dillon, South Carolina, my congregations were largely composed of those same Highland Carolina families of which I was a part. During pastoral visitation, I learned much not only about these people and their forefathers, but my own roots since we were frequently descended from the same emigrant heads of families. Thus, an early childhood interest has been (in my view at least) providentially encouraged by the direction in which my own life and professional training and labors have flowed.[3]

---

3. Kelly, *op. cit.*

Perhaps on those hot summer evenings, when he was absorbing and storing history deep in his memory, he was in training to be a traditional 'Seanachaidh' for his Carolina Highland family—the clan antiquarian or historian, the preserver of precious oral history about the best, and sometimes the worst, of human behavior, for both example and warning. Indeed, the rehearsing of the history and stories over and over again no doubt did much both to affirm the value of memorization, and to hone and develop the prodigious memory that has served him so well over the years, not only for people and history, but for Scripture and the things of God.

Three books of genealogy and history were the mature fruit of his childhood conversations and life on that simple farm. He spent the days sometimes chopping cotton, sometimes working tobacco, with field hands—many of them black—whom he got to know well. He remembers how they, too, told him stories and also encouraged him in his calling to the ministry. He especially recalls with delight the times when they all sang hymns in four-part harmony as they moved down the rows. Since many of his extended family who gathered in the evenings on the porch were forty- or fifty-years his senior, and since family farming had changed little for generations, he was living amidst people who were really still part of the early twentieth century pre-industrial culture. For example, as a ten-year old, it was once his job to keep the outside cooking fire alight under a big cooking pot where canning jars were being processed in boiling water—and this would have been in the 1950s!

Listening to his relatives talk of their families not only opened an extraordinary window through their memories back into the early 1800s but gave him a sense that he was living in it. What must be said also is that he was the only child on the farm most of the time during the summers. He participated in a community and a lifestyle that was long gone for most people even then. The gradual mechanization of the farm economy was resulting in massive migrations from farm to city, and the increase in those earning college degrees led to opportunities to travel, perhaps far away from home and relatives.

So Douglas thought long and hard about leaving "The Old North State," and indeed he would never have moved except for his calling to the ministry. Much later, when he began to have children of his own, and especially when we lived hundreds of miles from the old home place, he realized that he needed to write down what he had absorbed as a child himself so that the memories could be handed down. He began with a short summary of the descendants of his Kelly grandfather, Malcolm (1814–1896). Then, In 1989, on the 250th anniversary of the first major settlement of the Highland Scots in North Carolina— the Argyll Colony—he completed the first draft of *Carolina Scots*, an unusual combination of history and genealogy. The first half of the book provides an illustrated history of life on both sides of the Atlantic, "to help clarify the reasons why these people—and tens of thousands of other Highland Scots—left their homeland and settled in eighteenth century Carolina." The second half is more of a typical genealogy, and it aims to provide basic information on sixty-four of the earliest immigrant families. He combines oral history with material he had read on the subject for over forty years, "to assist future genealogical research and publication on the Cape Fear Scots families by including brief genealogical notices... of as many of these families as possible."[4] The bibliography is nine pages long, but the index of names covers 71 pages, 29 of them not surprisingly given to names beginning with Mc or Mac!

In 2007 he completed an even more ambitious task: a revision of an earlier history of his paternal grandmother's family, culminating in the massive 1850-page, *The Scottish Blue Family in North America*. It includes 27,600 names, chronicles emigrations from Argyll in Scotland during the 1740s to the 1850s to North Carolina, New York, and Canada, and covers up to eleven generations of immigrants in some families. In addition to fifteen different families of Scottish emigrants, prominent

---

4. Kelly, *op. cit.*, xv.

African American families are also traced, whose ancestors were connected with the NC Blues. Again, it combines history, verified anecdotes, and pictures along with list after list of families. And the index of names in *The Blue History* covers 331 pages, 34 of them given to names beginning with Mc or Mac!

The following lengthy quotes from the section on his great-grandfather, Patrick Blue (1839–1904) also known as Peter, repeat for us the engaging stories and lessons he learned as a child:

> Character perhaps is the most important product of history, and so ... sketches may be of interest and encouragement to the generations to come. Peter Blue was a quiet, pensive person. He had a strong intellectual interest and did a good bit of reading. While he was a competent and diligent farmer, it seems his real enthusiasm and interest did not lie in that direction, but rather toward the great world of ideas – especially theology and history, and towards the "Kingdom that will not pass away." He was fond of the great Theologian John Calvin and named a son for him. Both he and his wife were diligent students of the *Westminster Confession of Faith* ... He exemplified the truest Calvinist (and Highland Scottish) spirit in his dislike of ostentation and in his refusal to put himself forward – ever ready to 'count others better than himself.' We are told he always refused to engage in derogatory talk of any who were absent – or even to allow it.[5]

> In the Eureka Community, in which the family of Patrick Blue was reared, nearly every land-owning family in the district was related by blood or marriage ... According to Mrs. Rozella McLeod [born in 1893 and who was a remarkable source of family history which she passed on to Douglas], every one of 20 or so youths [in a 1904 picture] were at least distant cousins, in that all were descended from Kenneth McIver of the Isle of Skye, who lived in the late 17th and early 18th centuries.

> These people exhibited a loyalty to Old School Presbyterianism, and a love of learning. These two things were always held together for, at Eureka, the Sunday School—and later the Church—met in the School Building for many years. As well as religious exercises, the young men of the community at this time often had meetings (for the public) and spoke on literary and

---

5. Douglas F. Kelly, *The Scottish Blue Family in North America* (Dillon: 1739 Publications, 2007), 463. A second edition and thorough revision of the 1982 *The Scottish Blue Family from Carolina to Texas.*

political topics. It is illustrative of the strong spiritual life of the Eureka Community that at the turn of the century, no less than five of its young men were preparing for the Presbyterian ministry.[6]

The State motto of North Carolina, *Esse Quam Videri*! ("To Be Rather Than to Seem"), is an apt description of the general attitude and spirit of these Sandhill folk, with their simplicity, modesty, and disdain of ostentation. They have been traditionally somewhat more reserved than most Southerners: accommodating and polite, without being overly familiar or effusive, resultant characteristics perhaps of their "plain Puritan" background. The plainness and simplicity of their life and manners is well explained in a recent article by John H. Leith:

No emphasis of the Reformed tradition is more pervasive than the advocacy of simplicity. The Reformed always opposed the pretentious, the ostentatious, the pompous, the contrived, the artificial, the redundant. They believed that such activities covered up reality. The simple was close to sincerity, for it uncovered reality. Therefore, they insisted upon simplicity in writing style, in sermon, in liturgy, in dress, in living style and in social activity.[7]

It would not be realistic in any historical account to omit the characteristic weaknesses of these Sandhills Scots and their descendants. One has only to look at the minutes of the Session of the various Presbyterian Churches of the county to see that drunkenness and fornication were not unknown vices. Gossip, rivalry, and jealousy have played their part. Stealing, however, fighting, and murder were exceedingly rare occurrences. All the vices notwithstanding, it is fair to say that a community such as Eureka around the turn of the century was a preserve of some of the finest values of Reformation Christianity and the American Constitutionalism, which it engendered.[8]

His honesty in including a paragraph like the one above no doubt arises from his own awareness that human nature does not change. It is always flawed and in need of the healing Gospel, even with the

---

6. Charles Meek et al., eds., *Eureka Presbyterian Church* (self-published), 7.

7. John H. Leith, "A Christian View of Economics," *Presbyterian Survey* 69:6 (1979), 24.

8. Kelly, *op. cit.* 475–476.

strongest families and communities, and with faithful churches. One reason why he spent so much time as a child on the family farm rather than with his parents was that World War II had left his father with a sad case of what we would now call PTSD, most likely the cause of 'self-medication' with alcohol on weekends. The young Douglas's experience of safety in the extended family helped him deal with the dislocation and pain. Perhaps in some way his exposure to the grand genealogies of the past, as well as inspiring stories about ancestors, compensated for family failings that he saw in the present. Having learned to value the past he eventually used his gifts to turn those conversations into books, preserving history that might otherwise be lost. His experiences opened up for him a view of family, and of God's redemptive plans for family, that were deeply rooted in space and time—and indeed in eternity.

The Blue History is full of obituaries which bear testimony to the 'faith of his fathers.' Here is an excerpt from the obituary of his paternal grandmother's brother, John Webster Calhoun Blue, who was killed when a frightened horse ran away with a wagon.

> The outstanding characteristics which made up his strong personality were his devotion to his home, his church, school, and community; his honor, respect and love for Christian traits and ideals, his close adherence to duty; and his eagerness and promptness to lend a helping hand to those in need of help. ...[H]e was a man whose tendency was to efface rather than emphasize his strong points. He made no claims for himself and did not need to; for his entire life, and the devotion of his neighbors and friends bespeak his true virtues of Christian grace and living.[9]

New College, Edinburgh University

The great-aunts and uncles, whose lives—except for the World Wars—had been spent almost entirely in the Sandhills of North Carolina, supported Douglas's growing interest in academics. They supported him financially as well so that while he was at UNC-Chapel Hill he was able to take advantage of the

---

9. Ibid., 478.

study-abroad year in France, and then they helped him when he won a scholarship from the St. Andrew's Society of New York for graduate studies in Edinburgh. That was when I met him, at New College, the theological faculty of the university, where I was also studying Systematic Theology and Patristics under Thomas F. Torrance.

Douglas had been quickly recognized by the younger students as a theological and biblical resource. In those days, the dining hall at New College was packed, and I often found myself at one of the long oak tables, where he would be answering question after question, particularly about Torrance's lectures. This winsome American student brought to the discussions a huge knowledge of Scripture—due in part to having followed the plan given to him by a Lumbee Indian minister (who lived near another great-aunt) to read through the Bible every year. But he also had, and has, a deep humility as a scholar. His profound grasp of and dependence on the Scriptures, along with his knowledge of the ancient languages, enabled him to understand the early church writers who were the focus of much of Torrance's work—and to unpack their insights and beauty for the rest of us.

Other topics came up too. I remember being surprised to hear him say that for a long time there had been a law on the books of North Carolina against the teaching of evolution—extraordinary to me, as someone whose first formal history lesson in elementary school was about trilobites! He went on to lay out the scientific case for a young earth, which most of us had never heard and which seemed to make a great deal of sense. And several months later, I remember the personal conviction that came upon me as I discovered Calvin's insistence that Jesus as the second Adam was the only hope for the redemption of mankind who had fallen in the sin of the first Adam, which had to mean that the first Adam was a real historical person and not a random figure along the evolutionary way. Further, if death came at a historic point with the Fall, how could we account for the 'infinite numbers' of deaths during the 'billions of years' from the trilobites to the putative evolution of a human? Humility before the Word, yes, but Douglas had the humility of conviction that caused him to resist following intellectual trends sometimes deemed necessary for intellectual promotion.

All of which brings us back to family: if Adam and Eve were, in the words of the *Westminster Confession of Faith*, our 'first parents', and it was 'not good for man to be alone', then family was central to creation, to reality, and marriage and procreation were correctly designated 'creation ordinances.' All of this was something else that I had never considered. Here we were, only a few years after the 1968 publication by Paul R. Ehrlich's *The Population Bomb*, which predicted overpopulation and mass starvation. Yet by contrast, Douglas was saying to that group of (mostly male, mostly single) theological students that, yes, Christians should not merely marry and have children, but should have large families if possible.[10] After all, not only was it a good thing to hand down family tradition and genetic qualities, but families who educated and raised children as Christians could be the best thing for a stable and morally responsible society. From those hot evenings sitting with relatives whose own grandparents were born in the early 1800s, he knew what large Christian families had done for the fledgling states of North and South Carolina in the eighteenth and nineteenth centuries. Traveling up the Cape Fear River, those Highland Scots had turned miles of land, empty of almost everything but pine trees, into productive, if modest, farms and had built churches, towns, and schools—often in that order. He described his beloved rural mid-century Eastern North Carolina as a place where nearly everyone—rich or poor—was a distant cousin, imbuing daily life with a sense of connectedness and stability. It was a place, too, where the vast majority from all walks of life were church-goers, and where almost all the churches faithfully preached the Bible.

---

10. See Psalm 127:3–5. "Children are a heritage from the Lord, offspring a reward from him. Like arrows in the hands of a warrior are children born in one's youth. Blessed is the man whose quiver is full of them. They will not be put to shame when they contend with their opponents in court."

Perhaps I should say that at this point I had no idea that I would ever be part of his life, let alone the mother of his children, living in the Carolinas surrounded by descendants of Highland emigrants! But I was intrigued with that vision. My own experience of family was in complete contrast to his: he was an only child with a couple of hundred cousins of all ages and levels of kinship living within one hundred miles. I was one of two daughters, in a decidedly nuclear family, not least because my mother's solution to difficulties in the extended family was to ignore or cut off those of whom she disapproved—which was most of them.

Sitting in class under Tom Torrance and his brother James, and under their colleague, Canon Roland Walls, we were extraordinarily blessed to witness brilliant minds grapple with the deepest truths of the faith in a spirit of devotion. They unpacked for us the attempts of the church over the centuries to understand and frame the central doctrines in such a way that we were not buried in philosophical or historical technicalities. Rather they pointed us toward God as revealed in the Scriptures, in the face of His incarnate Son, through the Holy Spirit.

How does this relate to family? On the one hand, the reality of the Incarnation validates human endeavor, for God the Son took on real human flesh, healing it and—as Torrance would say—turning it, in His very being as a man, back towards God. The Church fathers, we learned, understood that it was His entire life of obedience and not merely the sacrifice of the cross that won forgiveness for us. This means that all human life—from the racket of crying babies to the quiet of a library—has been affected and that nothing is outside the central reality of Union with Christ for the believer. We do not have to seek a kind of 'other worldly' spirituality if we belong to the one who walked the dusty roads of Galilee as a man. All daily life counts for Him. That, at least, is what I took away from those classes: the glory and hope of thinking of life as living 'in' Christ. And that would especially mean 'family life'—not just because no human exists without some experience as part of a family, but because the very being of the Triune God, in three persons, bound together in mutual love, points us to the centrality of community.

That last statement is a (highly simplified) take-away from the writings of the twelfth century Scottish monk, Richard of Saint Victor, Prior of the Abbey of Saint Victor in France. He reminds the church that when we say that God is a Trinity, we are saying that He is not a single, solitary being, cut off from others, self-dependent. Rather, the Apostle John rightly says that God is Love precisely because within Himself, being three persons, He is a community of love. Richard of Saint Victor used—perhaps coined—the Latin word, *condilectio*, (*diligere*, to love; *con*, with, together) to express the mutual cherishing of love. This truth has two implications for us: first, if we are made in His image, we are not designed to be single and solitary and cut off from others either—even if there may be times in our lives when it is so. We are designed to be in at least some kind of community. Realistically, given our degree of fallenness, that can be challenging, *but at that very point* we have access to the fruit of the Spirit—of which the first is love—to enable us to reach beyond ourselves. Second, that ability to reach beyond ourselves derives from the Trinity being a communion of love: the best kind of love, by definition, is a love that cannot be kept to oneself. So, God's very being led Him to create men and women so that He might in some way draw us into the inner love between Father, Son, and Holy Spirit.

He Setteth the Solitary in Families

As Christians, it is wonderful to know who God is, and what He has done for us and in us. Canon Walls used to speak of the Christian life as 'shot silk.' He was referring to a kind of heavy silk cloth that looks dull and dark when it is held one way, but when the angle is adjusted, and light falls on it, it shines. Without a doubt, the world we live in is fallen, but it is also true that the light of God shines through and transforms. Douglas Kelly's life is founded on the historical reality of strong, albeit flawed, Highland families and the theological apprehension of the Incarnation and the Trinity—twin foundations.

We married in 1973 and immediately moved to a small town in South Carolina. We decided to follow the example of the immigrant Scots and start a family right away. If they could do it, with limited resources but with a trust in the same God whom we serve, presumably we could! It was fun, however, to have a shared academic experience with Douglas and to be able to assist with editing his books. Of relevance to this chapter is that I was heavily involved in editing and designing *Carolina Scots*. One of my tasks was to format the lists of children. It was an eye-opening experience for this twentieth century college graduate from a small family. Here is an example from the chapter on Skye Families in Moore County:

> A second large family...was that of Daniel Kelly ... b. 1725 in Sleat, Isle of Skye, and d. 1819 in Moore County, buried at Union Church. He m. 1765 Catherine Bethune of Sleat, b.1750, d. 1795 in Skye, buried at Kilmore Church, Sleat. They had ten children ... Daniel and [nine of his] children emigrated to Moore County, N.C., in 1803. Daniel and Kate Bethune Kelly had:

> ALEXANDER b. _, m. _, d. _, in Sleat
> BARBARA b. 1767, d. 1849
> DANIEL b. 1770, d. 1829
> JAMES b. 1772, d. 1825
> DANIEL or 'DONALD' b. 1773, d. 1855
> JOHN b. 1778, d. 1836
> PETER b. 1780, d. 1853
> NANCY b. 1783, m. _ d. _?
> HUGH b. 1784, d. 1851
> JOHN BETHUNE b. 1789, d. 1847[11]

Notice their evident health and long lives in spite of rigorous travel and relocation to an entirely new place. All except the oldest were buried in the Carolinas, and it seems they all had children, though we do not know details for most of them. We do

---

11. Kelly and Kelly, *Carolina Scots*, 255–256. Dates added from pp. 256–258.

know that John and Peter each had ten children, every one of whom lived to adulthood. One of Peter's sons was single, and one son had no children. His youngest brother, John Bethune, was known in the community for building the original Carthage Court House, and the Presbyterian Church, both long replaced. But he also designed and built a house for one of Peter's sons, Alexander Kelly, 1810–1872, who had been Moore County Sheriff and also a State Senator. It is unusual for the area because it is almost a replica, in wide pine boards, of Georgian houses that he would have remembered from his native Scotland. This house is still standing and is where we now live. We consider it a wonderful blessing of God to spend the last years of our lives among memories and portraits of several who spent time in the house, including Malcolm, Peter's fourth son, who was Douglas's great-grandfather, and who was the subject of his first genealogical writings, mentioned above.

While this Kelly episode is the story of one immigrant family, similar examples can be found over and over again in the book: four, five, six children or more, almost all of whom live to adulthood. These Highland women would have been surprised that their routine lives were an inspiration to me as I struggled to handle a growing family. If they could do it, I told myself that presumably I could! And in my role as editor of the chronicle of their lives, I also became intrigued by the consistency of the spacing between their children. Almost all were two years apart, sometimes a little less, sometimes a little more. Wider spacing often happened as the parents were getting older, though one cannot know whether the increase was caused by decreased fertility or due to the task of managing a number of children! At any rate, it suggests that such natural spacing can happen when breast-feeding is the main source of nutrition until the age when babies can manage solid food.

It is easy to dismiss the large families of the Carolina Scots by pointing out that they had no choice. But biblically literate as they were, we cannot assume that they were not aware of the command of God at creation to 'Be fruitful and multiply'

(Gen. 1:28), a phrase repeated throughout Genesis and found elsewhere in the Old Testament in the context of children being a blessing. A fundamental part of having children is for the human race to continue. Indeed, there is a sense in which God is in some way dependent on humble men and women to populate both earth and heaven.

This is not said to romanticize 'pre-contraception' history, for the loss of children—more common in that era than now—is always devastating, and the physical labor involved in turning pine forest into farmland to provide for a family would have been back-breaking. Nor can we overlook the grief of those who then, as now, struggled in vain to conceive. But scanning the numerous anecdotes of those Highland women in the Blue History, not to mention finding books on housekeeping or medicine in the old Blue house that dated from the 1800s, reminded me that the basic needs for keeping body and soul together have not changed much. Families were eager then as now to make a home and build family life. They were interested in the skills needed to feed and clothe family members well, to manage a household, and to preserve food for winter. I have read Luke 12:42 many times, but it was only recently that I decided to check the Greek for the word translated as 'household' in English, and 'family' in Latin. Imagine my surprise to discover that these words were used to translate the Greek Replace with: word, *therapeia*, bringing together in one word the ideas of supporting, serving, and healing. Here is an example of the 'shot-silkness' we mentioned earlier. Family life is woven in such a way that, at its best, the mutual service between family members is designed to be restorative and health-giving.

And yet ... and yet ... The "best" does not happen all the time in any family. For some it seems that it rarely happens. I do not need to catalog for readers the endless hurt, sin, and degradation endured in broken families across our nation, worsening as the Gospel recedes. For some people, solitariness can seem attractive in comparison to the treatment they received at the hands of those who should have loved them. We are even at a point where there are attempts to obliterate the family and replace it with something else entirely because of disappointment that the inner, God-given promise of meaning through relationship has gone so wrong.

There is a further challenge to retaining and building family ties, not only horizontally among peers, but vertically as each generation is separated from the others by physical distance. This is one that the immigrants certainly knew. After all, they had left relatives in Scotland, and even after they arrived in the Carolinas, there were groups of families who, after a few years, traveled west to Tennessee, Alabama, Mississippi, and Texas. When we are around each other all the time, we often find a way just to put up with one another, and perhaps even to grow in understanding, patience and grace. And the wider the family connection in a small geographical area, the more examples there can be of ways to handle life. However, loss of physical proximity can undo all the actions—conscious and unconscious—that go into building community, into accepting any square pegs who may not naturally fit into round holes, with the sad result that many people become solitary once more. But serious geographical separation of family members can result in such different experiences that a common sense of origin is weakened and perhaps obliterated. Indeed, when families move about, there may not even be a common sense of origin at all. Is it even possible to consider that we might be able to return to something like the strong families we met above in the old genealogical lists and stories?

As a friend from Yazoo City, Mississippi, once said to me, "There is no such thing as a non-dysfunctional family." So what is the solution for families who are trying to reclaim a biblical and God-directed view of the family? It is highly ironic that warnings against change are expressed in the phrase, "Don't throw the baby out with the bath water!" Above all, a baby represents hope for the future. Speaking of a baby reminds us that the future is dependent on nurturing relationships so essential for very survival. A baby reminds us that everything, in the end, is about people and the changes that they can make together. When we think like this, we are seeing the gleam of golden threads of silk. The years of togetherness between husband and wife, between children and parents, between cousins, aunts, uncles—in other words, between the horizontal and vertical in any family—are designed to build closeness, love, and maturity. But precisely because of the physical and emotional proximity, family is also where sinfulness is inevitably experienced, whether in the realization of one's own inability to love or as the recipient of unkind or selfish behavior— or worse. Human family life, though modeled by the Creator on the mutual Trinitarian love, is desperately flawed. Just as Jesus prayed for forgiveness for those who crucified Him, He gave us a prayer that pairs a plea for forgiveness of our sins with the reminder that we ourselves must forgive. Intra-family sin can be especially painful and hard to forgive because our deep hopes for mutual love—*condilectio*—are dashed. Evangelicals are very good at preaching the need for repentance and forgiveness to enter the Kingdom of Heaven, but somehow along the way it can be easy to forget that forgiveness was won for us by the death of the Son of our Heavenly Father. The cross that struck at the heart of the Trinity is the hope for family life.

Judging by the myriad wooden churches built across the Carolinas by the immigrant Highland Scots, I believe that they knew that hope as well. Their material growth and successes were not accidental. They experienced the dull side of the silk, the hard times, the failures, the missteps, the hurts, the griefs. But they also must have glimpsed the gold threads—the joys, the sense of community, the love, the hope. They knew and lived the truth that—as it says in the King James translation, which I use here to honor Douglas's great aunts and uncles and cousins who poured out their nurturing and training into his life—"He setteth the solitary in families" (Ps. 68:6). We are designed to seek community. Deep down we know we cannot live without it. Does the fact that our society is so broken mean that we must abandon that hope? It is up to God's people to at least attempt family life, flawed or not, for we are at a stage in history where we can clearly see that the abandonment of family causes pain, not the hoped-for freedom.

The dedication of the Blue History is to 'Four Stalwart Cousins', all of whom have long gone to their reward. Douglas wrote,

> My prayer for them, and for all of us who read this story is: That the generation to come might know them, even the children which should be born; who should arise and declare them to their children: That they might set their hope in God, and not forget the works of God, but keep his commandments. (Psalm 78:7–8)[12]

May it be so for all of us reading this volume of essays dedicated to a valiant Carolina Scot.

---

12. Kelly, *op. cit.* v.

Part 1:

The Generation of Space and Time

1

The Sabbath Crescendo

Genesis 2:1–3

John Currid

Douglas Kelly, in his seminal work *Creation and Change*, underscores the importance of the Sabbath as the crescendo of the creation week in Genesis 1–2.[1] In the final chapter of the book, he poignantly says, "the very structure of the creation week orients the entire created order to the Sabbath, and thus to the remembrance of God our Creator and His relationship to us and purposes of blessing for us."[2] I could not agree more. Therefore, I want to engage with and build upon this idea by providing an exegetical analysis of the Sabbath as it first appears in Genesis 2:1–3, and then to consider how the concept of the Sabbath plays out throughout the remainder of Scripture.

---

1. It is my privilege to contribute to a volume honoring Dr. Kelly's work on creation. We have been colleagues at Reformed Theological Seminary since 1993. Not only is Dr. Kelly a fine scholar, he has also been an excellent model for other professors; his love for the Word of God is engaging and contagious.

2. Douglas. F. Kelly, *Creation and Change: Genesis 1.1–2.4 in the Light of Changing Scientific Paradigms* (Geanies House: Christian Focus, 1997), 243.

Genesis 2:1–3

> [1] Thus the heavens and the earth and all their host were completed. [2] And on the seventh day God completed his work which he had done. And on the seventh day he stopped from all his work he had done. [3] And God blessed the seventh day and he consecrated it, because on it he stopped from all his work which God had done in creation.[3]

The biblical author now records the final day of the creation week. It is the seventh day, and the number seven in Hebrew often symbolizes the completion and the fulness of a matter at hand (see, e.g., Gen. 4:15, 24; 29:18; Matt. 18:21–22). Thus, the seventh day marks the height, culmination, and climax of the creation week. There is also a sense in the original Hebrew that there is a movement from the lesser to the greater in the number seven. For example, the Hebrew Feast of Booths lasts seven days, and we read of its celebration in the New Testament. In John 7:12, the final day of the celebration is introduced as, "on the last and greatest day of the festival ..." So, the seventh day appears not merely as one of completion, but one of heightening.[4] It is important to note further that humanity, which is created on the sixth day, spends its first full day of life on the Sabbath, worshiping God and enjoying him and his creation.

Genesis 2:1

The opening verse of the section begins with a *waw* consecutive, which is the conjunction "and" prefixed to an imperfective verb. In general, the *waw* consecutive indicates "succession in time or progression as the main idea."[5] However, this mechanism can also reflect a final summation of a preceding narrative, and, so, it can be translated as "thus."[6] The reader, therefore, is being

---

3. This is the author's translation.

4. For a study of the Feast of Booths, see J.D. Currid, "Feasts and Festivals," in *Dictionary of the New Testament Use of the Old Testament*, eds. G.K. Beale, D.A. Carson, B.L. Gladd, and A.D. Naselli (Grand Rapids: Baker, 2023).

5. B.T. Arnold and J.H. Choi, *A Guide to Biblical Hebrew Syntax* (Cambridge: Cambridge University Press, 2003), 83.

6. E. Kautzsch, ed. *Gesenius' Hebrew Grammar* (Oxford: Clarendon Press, 1910), 328;

informed of a summary statement of the creation week that began in Genesis 1.[7]

The announcement of the text is that "the heavens and the earth" have been completed; this, of course, reflects Genesis 1:1, and the two physical spheres of existence. "The Hebrews had no single word to describe the universe."[8] When they desired to describe the spheres of the cosmos in their entirety they spoke of "the heavens and the earth" (Gen. 14:19). The biblical author of the text before us adds "and all their host was completed." The word "host" is a collective noun that refers to all things, animate and inanimate, that God had created on days 1–6. Sometimes in the OT the word "host" only refers to the luminaries (Deut. 4:19; 17:13), but in this verse the word is not only connected to the heavens but to the earth as well. So, this is a summary verse denoting that all the physical creation has been the work of God.

Genesis 2:2

The first line of this verse could be understood that God is yet working on the seventh day, and that his labors were not finished until sometime on that day. Numerous ancient translations recognized the issue, and so they emended the text to read "on the sixth day" (see LXX, Syriac, Samaritan Pentateuch).[9] There is, however, no need to emend the text because the Hebrew preposition "on" may simply be being used in this verse in the temporal sense of "by."[10]

---

this grammar pronounces that the *waw* consecutive in Gen 2:1 is "a final summing up of the preceding narrative." See, also, B.K. Waltke and M. O'Connor, *An Introduction to Biblical Hebrew Syntax* (Winona Lake: Eisenbrauns, 1990), 550.

7. It is unfortunate that the chapter heading of chapter 2 is located before 2:1–3 rather than after it. Gen 2:1–3 belongs with chapter 1. The chapter headings, of course, are not ancient, but much of that division work was done by Cardinal Stephen Langton, Archbishop of Canterbury, who died in AD 1228. See B. Metzger, *The Early Versions of the New Testament: Their Origin, Transmission and Limitations* (Oxford: Oxford University Press, 1977), 347.

8. J.D. Currid, *Genesis*, vol. 1 (Darlington: EP, 2003), 59.

9. See the discussion of E. Tov, *Textual Criticism of the Hebrew Bible*, 3rd ed. (Minneapolis: Fortress Press, 2012), 244–45.

10. See P. Joüon, *A Grammar of Biblical Hebrew: Part Three: Syntax* (Roma: Editrice Pontificio Instituto Biblico, 2005), 486–87.

The Hebrew verb "completed" is the same one as used in v.1, but it is in a different stem. In v.1, it appears in the pual stem, which is a passive stem that here does not indicate the subject of the verbal form. However, in v. 2 it is in the piel stem, which is active and perhaps intensive.[11] In other words, the grammar is driving home the summary point that God is the one who has done this work, and he has brought all things to completion.

This verse is structured by the use of parallelism. Using the original Hebrew word order of the verse, it looks like this:

	a	b	c	d
	And God completed	on the seventh day	his work	which he had done

	a1	b1	c1	d1
	And he stopped	on the seventh day	from all his work	which he had done

Line parallelism is repetitive for various reasons, such as ornamentation and to help the reader to memorize it. But, of course, it is principally emphatic. It highlights the finality of God's work, and that he has ceased from his labors on the seventh day.

The Hebrew verb translated as "he stopped" is šabat. The primary lexical sense of this verb is "to cease and desist."[12] The cognate noun of this verb is šabbat, which is the name signifying "Sabbath day" throughout the remainder of Scripture. In other words, it is a day of ceasing from the activities of the other six days of the creation week. This principle of the purpose of Sabbath is, therefore, a creation ordinance and it is first established in Genesis 2:1–3.[13]

---

11. Arnold and Choi, *A Guide to Biblical Hebrew Syntax*, 41–5.

12. *BDB*, 991.

13. B. Batto, "When God Sleeps," *BR* 3:4 (1987): 16–23, argues that Yahweh is perhaps like the ancient Near Eastern mythological deities who sleep or rest after performing acts of creation. The problem, of course, is the text of Genesis 2:1–3 never mentions that God was sleeping or resting, but he merely "ceased" his creative activity. There is no biblical warrant to conclude that God is asleep or inactive on the seventh day because he providentially maintains his creation at all times.

Genesis 2:3

The act of God pronouncing blessing on something he creates is a central concept in the creation account. The Hebrew verb "to bless" when used of an activity of God means that he grants an abundant and effective life on someone, such as earthly creatures (Day 5) and, especially, humans (Day 6). This type of blessing signifies that God's presence is with someone, and he bestows grace and displays keeping power. But in the verse before us, God does not bless a physical component of creation, but rather a specific time-period, that is, an on-going temporal reality. This is unusual, and it therefore demonstrates the climactic sense of the day in the creation.

In addition, God "consecrated" the seventh day. This verb derives from the basic Hebrew stem that means "to be holy." It is the first time this verb or any of its cognates are used in the Bible, and it bears the basic meaning "to be set apart/distinct/unique." This act of God again underscores the nature of the seventh day as one that is special and different from the other six days of creation. It is so described because God is the one who set it apart; this is his doing. The seventh day is, therefore, reserved by the Lord as sacred time, in contrast to the other six days which are common time.

The second half of this verse is difficult to translate well from the Hebrew. It has a choppy style. A basic, direct translation reads as follows: "because on it he ceased from all his work which God created to make." The ending of the clause contains a perfective verb ("created") followed by an infinitive ("to make"). When this happens in the Hebrew language, the second verb is elucidating the meaning of the first verb.[14] These two verbs are the ones employed by the biblical writer in Genesis 1 to describe the acts of creation: "to create" appears in vv. 1, 21, and 27, and "to make" in vv. 16, 25, and 26. The point of the biblical writer using both verbs together in 2:3 is to confirm that God is the subject of both verbs throughout the account and, therefore, the author of all that has been created.

14. Kautzsch, *Gesenius' Hebrew Grammar*, 351.

The creation account ends here in 2:3 the same way it began in 1:1, in which it is declared that "God created." This *inclusio* underscores the dominant theme of the entire creation account: the glorification of the Creator God who brought all things into existence, and that he is sovereign over all. And the Sabbath day is the consummate reminder that God is enthroned over the entire universe and everything in it points to his glory: "The heavens declare the glory of God, and the sky above proclaims his handiwork" (Ps. 19:1).

It is also important to observe that the Sabbath day, unlike the other six days of the creation week, has no ending. The first six days of creation all end with the same formulaic conclusion, "and there was evening and there was morning, the ... day" (Gen. 1:5, 8, 13, 19, 23, 31). That formula is nowhere to be found regarding the seventh day because it is on-going, continual, and never-ending. It bears an eternal significance not prescribed for the other six days of the week.

The Sabbath for Humanity

After mankind's fall into sin, the Sabbath continues as the high point or zenith of Israel's worship. For example, the cultic/worship calendar for Israel is marked out in Leviticus 23, and it is generally structured on three foundational national pilgrim festivals that the people were required to keep annually: Passover/Feast of Unleavened Bread (vv. 4–8); Feast of Weeks (vv. 15–22); and, Feast of Booths (vv. 33–43).[15] However, at the very center and heart of this worship calendar is the Sabbath. I write elsewhere that in Leviticus 23:3,

---

15. Five cultic calendars appear in the Pentateuch: Exodus 23:10–19; 34:18–26; Leviticus 23; Numbers 28–29, and Deuteronomy 16:1–17. Leviticus 23 is a systematic and standardized festal calendar, and that is one reason numerous scholars date it late in the history of Israel; see J.R. Porter, *Leviticus* (Cambridge: Cambridge University Press, 1976), 177–79. In reality, the Leviticus calendar is likely earlier than the Numbers and Deuteronomy calendars, and the latter appear to be dependent on Leviticus. For a study of all five calendars, see K. Queen-Sutherland, "Cultic Calendars in the Old Testament," *Faith and Mission* 8 (1991): 76–87.

the Sabbath is called the "Sabbath of sabbatical observance" (my translation of *šabbat šabbātôn*).[16] This construction is a superlative in Hebrew that underscores that the seventh day has been distinctly set apart from the other days of the week (cf. its usage in Exod. 31:15). Being the first festival established by God (Gen. 2:1–3), it is foundational to the Hebrew festal calendar. Its structural importance to the calendar is evident in Lev. 23 in which seven festivals are presented, and most of them appear in the seventh month of the calendar.[17] The text underscores the all-pervasive and ubiquitous nature of the command for Israel to keep the Sabbath: the phrase "wherever you live" (*bᵊkōl môšbōtêkem*) is commonly translated as "in all your dwelling places." This means that the Sabbath is not something merely to be observed in the temple or by the priests, but this weekly festival no matter where one lives binds all Israel.[18]

A second point to consider is that the Sabbath is one of the Ten Commandments (Exod. 20:8–11; Deut. 5:12–15). As an expectation for Israel, the Sabbath was already in effect in Exodus 16 regarding when the people could gather manna and quail in the wilderness. The purpose of its appearance in the Decalogue is to establish it formally into the written code of the moral, principial law of the covenant. In other words, the Sabbath was established in Genesis 2:1–3, put in effect in Exodus 16, and now inscribed in stone at Mount Sinai as prescriptive law.

In Exodus 20:9–10, the biblical writer describes how Israel is to keep the Sabbath. Six days the Israelites are to perform their ordinary labors and duties, but the Sabbath day is to be "set apart from" the usual works of the other six days. And it is to be "set apart to" the Lord, because, as the beginning of v. 10 says, "the seventh day is a Sabbath belonging to the LORD your God." It is a special, holy day and it especially and particularly belongs to God. Furthermore, this law applies to all Israel: it is for son and daughter, male slave and female slave, rich and poor, for the king and for the woman grinding at the mill. Even sojourners and animals are to have a day of ceasing from ordinary labors!

---

16. *BDB*, 992.

17. G. Wenham, *The Book of Leviticus* (Grand Rapids: Eerdmans, 1979), 301.

18. J. Currid, "Feasts and Festivals," in *Dictionary of the New Testament Use of the Old Testament*, ed. G. K. Beale, et.al. (Grand Rapids: Baker, 2023).

In the context of the escape from Egypt, we do well to consider what a great blessing the Sabbath was for the people of Israel who so recently had been enslaved in Egypt. There they had served under hard and unforgiving taskmasters and the weighty oppression of the lash. Pharaoh was harsh, cruel, and abusive. In contrast, the Lord redeems his people from the unrelentingly severe brutality of Egypt, and then he provides them with a day of ceasing, a day of rest, and a day of worship. For the Israelites, the Sabbath should have been a blessing and not a curse, a boon and not a burden.

Purposes of the Sabbath in the OT

The purposes of the Sabbath in the OT are many and varied. First, according to the fourth commandment in Exod. 20:11, the Sabbath reflects God's pattern of creation in Genesis 1–2: "For in six days the LORD made heaven and earth, the sea, and all that is in them, and rested the seventh day." Therefore, when a person observes the Sabbath, one is commemorating and imitating (*imitatio Dei*) God's creative work. Because humans are in the image of God (*imago Dei*), they should follow his prescribed pattern which brings honor to his name. It is a reminder of God's past work in creation.

In the second giving of the Decalogue in Deuteronomy 5, a different reason is given for the observance of the Sabbath.[19] Verse 15 reads, "You shall remember that you were a slave in the land of Egypt, and the LORD your God brought you out from there with a mighty hand and an outstretched arm. Therefore the LORD your God commanded you to keep the Sabbath day." Redemption from slavery in Egypt was commemorated by

---

19. These two reasons for the Sabbath are not conflicting, but they complement one another. Deuteronomy is not invalidating Exodus, but merely highlighting another reason for the Sabbath command. Interestingly, in the Dead Sea Scrolls, a fragment of Deuteronomy that includes Deuteronomy 5:15 adds the text of Exodus 20:11 right after it. The purpose of the scribal addition is to show that neither text supersedes the other: both are valid reasons for the Sabbath command given in the Decalogue. See Tov, *Textual Criticism of the Hebrew Bible*, 99.

keeping the Sabbath. And, so, the Israelite in Moab was reminded of God's recent past activity of delivering Israel out of Egypt. The Sabbath was a great day of celebration for God's salvation that had recently occurred.

The Sabbath, however, also has a present reality for the people of God: it was created as a time of rest, refreshment, and recuperation. In Exodus 23:12, the text says that mankind, by keeping the Sabbath, "may be refreshed." That same verb in Hebrew is found in Exodus 31:17, in which God made the heavens and the earth, and "on the seventh day he rested and was refreshed." The verb "refreshed" is only used three times in the entire OT; it is related to the noun *nepheš*, which means "breath/soul/life."[20] In Exodus 31:17, that verb is in the niphal pattern (passive), and it appears to mean something like "he took a breath." After his great acts of creation, God was restored in his rest. This, of course, is anthropomorphic, but it shows the benefits that mankind receives when keeping the Sabbath.

The Sabbath has another present reality for the people of God. The Lord tells Moses in Leviticus 23:3 that "[s]ix days shall work be done, but on the seventh day is a Sabbath of solemn rest, a holy convocation." The term "holy convocation" refers to religious gatherings when all the people of Israel are summoned to public worship and instruction in the Torah (Neh. 8:1–8). The assembly of the people on the Sabbath helps to bring spiritual and religious unity to the covenant people.

Another present and on-going reality for God's people is that the Sabbath serves as a sign of the covenant between God and them. In Exodus 31:16–17, God says, "the people of Israel shall keep the Sabbath, observing the Sabbath throughout their generations, as a covenant forever. It is a sign forever between me and the people of Israel that in six days the LORD made heaven and earth, and on the seventh day he rested and was refreshed." Keeping the Sabbath is a sign of the eternal covenant relationship

---

20. *LVTL*, 626–27.

between God and his people; breaking the Sabbath is tantamount to breaking the covenant.

Finally, the Sabbath has a future reality for God's people because it is a pointer to an eternal Sabbath in heaven (Heb. 4:9–10). The earthly, temporal Sabbath is, thus, a mere foretaste of the believer's final Sabbath existence in God's presence. So, in a sense, the Sabbath crescendo here on earth merely anticipates the greater Sabbath crescendo of the future, never-ending Sabbath believers will have in the heavenly temple.

Since there is one people of God throughout history (Gal. 3:28–29), then there is application of the on-going, eternal Sabbath to them.[21] So for the church today, when believers keep the Sabbath they should be reminded of God's great works of creation and redemption: believers are new creatures in Christ because they have been redeemed through Christ's work on the cross; they have been delivered from slavery to sin. For a believer, this work is a past reality secured by Christ that has an on-going reality. Second, there is a present reality because this day has been set apart for believers to gather together to worship God and to be instructed in his word. It is also a present day of refreshment and recuperation, when believers can put aside the earthly cares and concerns of the other six days of the week. As B.B. Warfield once remarked, "the Sabbath is an oasis in the desert of earthly cares." Third, Sabbath keeping has a future reality as a foretaste of the heavenly Sabbath of the believer; it points to a final Sabbath rest in heaven. Finally, believers need to understand that the Sabbath is a sign pointing to the reality that they are in covenant with God, and believers demonstrate that they are set apart from the world through Sabbath observance. The people of God are to be lights in the midst of a crooked and perverse generation (Matt. 5:14), and they are to proclaim the excellencies of him who called them out of darkness.

---

21. See, for example, A.A. Hoekema, *The Bible and the Future* (Grand Rapids: Eerdmans, 1994); and, O.P. Robertson, *The Israel of God: Yesterday, Today, Tomorrow* (Phillipsburg: Presbyterian & Reformed, 2000).

Conclusion

The Sabbath is like no other time in the world's existence. God created it prior to mankind's fall into sin; it is a creation ordinance. He set it apart as sacred time in which the people of God are, especially and uniquely, to remember God's works of creation and redemption, and to worship him with all their hearts, souls, and minds. And, as Douglas Kelly rightfully remarks, the Sabbath also "bears a profound orientation towards the future."[22] It points to the final consummation and glorification in which all the promises and purposes of God come to final fruition. This reality ought to draw the eyes of God's people toward the heavenly Sabbath, in which believers will worship God and have fellowship with him forever and ever. That is the ultimate aim of God's creation of the Sabbath in Genesis 2:1–3, and that creation text is a pointer to the eternal, final Sabbath crescendo.

There are, finally, wonderful biblical promises attached to the keeping of the Sabbath by God's people. None is more gripping that what God says to his people through the prophet Isaiah:

> If you turn back your foot from the Sabbath, from doing your pleasure on my holy day, and call the Sabbath a delight and the holy day of the Lord honorable; if you honor it, not going your own ways, or seeking your own pleasure, or talking idly; then you shall take delight in the Lord, and I will make you ride on the heights of the earth; I will feed you with the heritage of Jacob your father, for the mouth of the Lord has spoken (58:13–14).

---

22. Kelly, *Creation and Change*, 243.

2

The History of the World

Holy Space and Holy Time[1]

Jonathan Gibson

The historical was first, then the theological.
Geerhardus Vos

Introduction

In his book *Genesis in Space and Time*, Francis Schaeffer writes, "Space and time are like warp and woof. Their interwoven relationship is history."[2] This is no more true than when it comes to the prologue of the Christian Scriptures, Genesis 1:1–2:3. In it, we are presented with created space (the heavens and the earth) and ordered time (a seven-day week with a climactic Sabbath).

---

1. It is my privilege to write in honor of Douglas Kelly, a man whose commitment to Scripture, especially the account of creation, has served as an example and encouragement to many young professors like myself. I have also been the recipient of his pastoral care and encouragement. He is fondly remembered as being among that rare breed of pastor-scholars. Also, my thanks to Jonathan Brack, Jeremy Menicucci, and Peter Williams for their feedback on an earlier draft of this chapter.

2. Francis A. Schaeffer, *The Complete Works of Francis A. Schaeffer: A Christian Worldview* (Wheaton: Crossway Books, 1982), 7.

According to Schaeffer, when these two realities interweave, we get history—the history of the world. More specifically, and theologically, world history is the interweaving of *holy* space and *holy* time under the providence of a *holy* God.[3] The history of the world begins with holy, bounded space (the created heavens and earth and the Garden of Eden) in relation to holy time (the creational Sabbath); and it continues with holy, bounded space (the land of Canaan) in relation to holy time (the ceremonial Sabbath), finally consummating with holy, bounded space (the new heavens and new earth) in relation to holy time (the eternal Sabbath).

For the purposes of this chapter, we will focus on the divinely ordered Sabbath in relation to the divinely created heavens and earth as an integral component to the unfolding history of the world. The Genesis prologue presents us with two protological realities that God creates in the beginning: space and time.[4] In the beginning, God creates the heavens and the earth—protological space; he also creates a cyclical seven-day week with a climactic Sabbath—protological time. The first reality is his holy space; the second is his holy time. The first is the created theatre in which history plays out; the second is the ordered timeline along which history unfolds. This presentation will treat each of these in turn, focusing on protological time and the Sabbath Day, in particular. First, however, we turn to protological space.

God's Holy Space

The Genesis prologue begins with the protological reality of God's holy space: "In the beginning God created the heavens and the earth" (Gen. 1:1). His initial act of creation *ex nihilo* produces two physical realities: the heavens and the earth.

---

3. By holy space and holy time, I mean space and time that are set apart and consecrated to God and his purposes.

4. Protology means the study of origins or first things. In this regard, it encompasses the early chapters of Genesis and in particular the creation week (1:1–2:3).

The Heavens

The Hebrew word for heavens, שָׁמַיִם, is used throughout the prologue and forms an inclusio (Gen. 1:1; 2:1).[5] Most English Bibles translate the word as "heavens" or "heaven." A careful reading of the prologue reveals that שָׁמַיִם does not always have the same meaning. It refers to two distinct-but-related "heavens": the sky-space heavens and the supreme heavens. That these two heavens are to be differentiated is made clear by the content and flow of the prologue. In the beginning, on the first day, God creates "the heavens" (1:1). As we will see below, these are the supernatural, invisible, supreme heavens. On the second day, following the creation of the supreme heavens, God creates another heavenly realm, "an expanse" (רָקִיעַ) in the midst of the waters (1:6) on the earth. God calls this expanse "Heaven" (שָׁמַיִם; 1:8).[6] On the third day, these heavens form a canopy over the earth, below which the dry land appears as the waters are gathered together to form seas (1:9–10). On the fourth day, the two great lights of the sun and moon are placed into the expanse of these heavens (רְקִיעַ הַשָּׁמַיִם) along with the stars (1:14, 15, 17). These are the natural, visible sky-space heavens, with two regions: the lower sky heavens and the upper space heavens. The sky heavens are visible from the earth, while the space heavens are beyond the regions of this earth, what today we would call "space" or "outer space." On the fifth day, the sky-space heavens are mentioned again when God creates the birds and commands them to fly across the face of the expanse of the heavens (פְּנֵי רְקִיעַ הַשָּׁמַיִם; 1:20). The daytime and nighttime luminaries are placed in the upper space regions of these same heavens.[7]

---

5. *HALOT*, 1560. Its grammatical form (שָׁמַיִם) is a dual form, but, in reality, it is a plural form. The word occurs 11 times in Genesis 1:1–2:3; or 13 times if Genesis 2:4 is included.

6. CSB translates 1:8: "God called the expanse 'sky.'"

7. The distinction between these two regions of the one expanse of the heavens is reflected in some English Bible translations that describe the birds as the "birds of the *air*" (NKJV) or the "birds of the *sky*" (CSB) rather than the "birds of the *heavens*" (ESV) (עוֹף הַשָּׁמַיִם; 1:26, 28, 30) (italics added).

Given the content and flow of the prologue, these heavens are distinct from the heavens created in the beginning (1:1). The Genesis prologue does not explain what the first created heavens are, except to distinguish them from the natural, visible sky-space heavens created on the second day. However, while the heavens of 1:1 are distinct from the heavens of 1:8, the employment of the common term for both (שָׁמַיִם) communicates that they are related. Indeed, the relation is the location: they are "up there" above the natural, visible space heavens.

Later biblical revelation provides more insight into these heavens. Two texts in particular shed light. Isaiah 66:1:

> "Thus says the LORD:
> "Heaven is my throne,
>   and the earth is my footstool;
> what is the house that you would build for me,
>   and what is the place of my rest?"

Being the pictorial prophet that he is, Isaiah paints heaven as God's throne, the place where he dwells and from where he rules (cf. Ps. 103:19). According to Isaiah, God's house is in heaven, the place of his rest. Nehemiah provides further information on this heavenly dwelling place:

> You are the Lord, you alone. You have made heaven, the heaven of heavens, with all their host, the earth and all that is on it, the seas and all that is in them; and you preserve all of them; and the host of heaven worships you. (9:6)

We know from Isaiah's vision that this "host" is comprised of heavenly beings worshipping God and crying out, "Holy, holy, holy is the LORD of hosts; the whole earth is full of his glory!" (Isa. 6:1–3). The heavenly choir and concert are visible and audible to Isaiah in his vision, which means that they must exist somewhere beyond the expanse of the sky-space heavens. Those invited into these heavens can see and hear what is going on in them. In the New Testament, the writer to the Hebrews indicates that they exist as a physical realm when he speaks of "holy places" (τῶν ἁγίων λειτουργός) in heaven above, where Christ serves as

Minister and High Priest (8:1–2; 9:12). Christ ascended to these heavens as a physical man, so they must exist as a physical realm, albeit invisible to the human eye. They are invisible, however, not because what or who exists in them is invisible, but because they and their inhabitants are hidden from human sight, at least for now. The Apostle Paul refers to this invisible realm when he speaks of Christ as the mediated Creator of all things "in heaven and on earth, visible and invisible" (Col. 1:16).[8] Since these heavens are the dwelling place of God, we may call them the *supreme heavens*. This fits with the superlative descriptor used elsewhere: "the heaven of heavens" (שְׁמֵי הַשָּׁמַיִם; 1 Kings 8:27; 2 Chron. 6:18).[9]

Scripture thus testifies to two heavens: a *supernatural, invisible, supreme heavens*, distinct from but related to the *natural, visible, sky-space heavens*. These heavens are not an eternal realm that God has always dwelt in; rather, they are created by God in the beginning on the first day (Gen. 1:1). Although God has chosen to dwell in these heavens, he exists before and outside of them since he is eternal and infinite. In the beginning God created a supernatural, invisible realm that he chose to condescend to live in. This is where God dwells, and where he is worshipped by the heavenly hosts. These are the heavens that he created in the beginning.

So, there are two created heavenly realms: the supernatural, invisible, supreme heavens and the natural, visible, space heavens with lower and upper regions. This is the protological holy space that God creates in the beginning.

We turn now to the second physical reality that God creates in the beginning, namely, the earth.

The Earth

In the beginning God creates two heavens and one earth. As there are different "spaces" in the heavens—the invisible and visible

---

8. Syntactically, the phrase is an inverted chiasm, in which "heaven" matches "invisible."

9. ESV: "the highest heavens."

realms—so there are different spaces on the earth—the land and the sea. On the third day, God forms these earthly spaces by gathering the waters of the great deep (1:2) into seas and allowing the dry land to appear (1:9–10). God fills these two realms with living plants and creatures. On the third day, God fills the land with the vegetation of seed-bearing plants and trees. On the fifth day, he fills the waters of the seas with living creatures and the earth with flying birds (1:20–22). The two sets of creatures (fish and birds) are spoken of in relation to the distinct realms in which they perform their created activity (sea and sky).[10] The fish are the "fish of the sea," and the birds are "the birds of the sky" (1:26, 28). This filling of the land realm continues on the sixth day, as God adds to the birds on the earth livestock, and creeping things, and beasts of the earth (1:24–25). The filling of the land then climaxes in the creation of mankind, male and female, who are commanded by God to have dominion over the living creatures in the realms of sea, sky, and land (1:26–28). In this regard, man is the only living creature who is given rule; there are no "sub-rulers" under him, only rulees (cf. also Ps. 8).[11]

---

10. Note that while the birds are commanded to fly *in the sky*, they are commanded to multiply *on the earth* and not in the sky (1:22). Thus, schemes in which the creation of realms in "Days 1–3" are matched to the creation of residents in "Days 4–6" in a macro forming-filling framework are, upon close analysis, found to be wanting. They are too neat and tidy. For instance, the days do not actually match: the sun and moon created on Day 4 fill the expanse made on Day 2, not the light made on Day 1; the birds created on Day 5 fill the earth/land made on Day 3, not the expanse made on Day 2. A version of the literary framework view was first espoused by J. G. von Herder, *The Spirit of Hebrew Poetry*; trans. James Marsh; 2 vols (1st ed. in English; Burlington: Edward Smith, 1833 [German ed.: 1782–1784]), 1:58. A contemporary example is seen in Michael LeFebvre, *The Liturgy of Creation: Understanding Calendars in Old Testament Context* (Downers Grove: IVP Academic, 2019), esp. chs 8–10.

11. Contra Meredith Kline, "Space and Time in the Genesis Cosmogony," *Perspectives on Science and Christian Faith* 48:1 (1996): 1–14; Lee Irons and Meredith Kline, "The Framework View," in *The Genesis Debate* (Mission Viejo, CA: Crux Press, 2001), 217–56, who present a literary framework of created realms (Days 1–3) matched by created rulers (Days 4–6). As with the forming-filling framework, there are problems with this scheme. While the sun and moon are made on Day 4 to rule the realms of daytime and nighttime established on Day 1, the same may not be said of the creatures made on Day 5 and Day 6 ruling the respective realms made on Day 2 and Day 3. The three verbs used for ruling in Genesis 1 (רדה, משל, and כבש) are not attributed to birds ruling over the sky, or fish

Worship in Heaven and on Earth

At this point, it is appropriate to draw together these findings and make some preliminary observations. In the beginning God creates the supreme heavens and fills them with a host of heavenly creatures who worship him day and night (Neh. 9:6; Isa. 6:13). The same is true with respect to the earth. In the beginning God makes the earth and fills its two main regions of land and sea with living creatures. Psalm 148 informs us that they, along with the whole of the created order, are made to "praise the Lord." This analysis of the holy space of the heavens and the earth, created by God in the beginning, reveals how the history of the world begins. *World history begins with a holy God in his holy space of the heavens and the earth, being worshipped by angels above and creatures below.* World history continues in this same protological space of the sky-space heavens and the supreme heavens, with the sea-land earth below. God still rules from his throne in the supreme heavens with the sea-land earth as his footstool. We still live and move on the same sea-land earth under the same sky-space heavens, in which the birds fly in its lower regions while the luminaries of sun, moon, and stars shine in its upper regions. With respect to protological holy space, then, nothing has changed since the beginning of creation. It is the same heavens and the

---

over the sea, or animals over land in the prologue; indeed, they are not attributed to these creatures and realms anywhere in Scripture.

Other significant problems attend the framework interpretation. For example, when Irons and Kline posit that Day 4 is a "temporal recapitulation" of Day 1 ("The Framework View," 230), they are unable consistently to affirm that Scripture presents a "six-day" creation. On their scheme, they must affirm a "five-day" creation. To avoid the problem, any recourse to the "six-day" creation being of a purely literary/figurative nature simply ends up in nominalist exegesis, whereby the words and terms have no actual referent to which they point. For an insightful critique of the framework hypothesis in this respect, see Jean-Marc Berthoud's interaction with Henri Blocher: "What is taking place here is in fact nominalist exegesis.... For Occam, the form or the name has no real or true relation to the thing named or signified. Similarly here [in the "Framework interpretation"] literary form has no actual relation to the temporal reality of creation"; cited in Douglas F. Kelly, *Creation and Change: Genesis 1:1–2:4 in the Light of Changing Scientific Paradigms,* rev. ed. (Geanies House: Christian Focus, 2020), 160.

same earth in the same holy space. With some qualification, the same can also be said with respect to protological time.

God's Holy Time

In the beginning God creates the protological space of the heavens and the earth. He also creates protological time: the holy time of a cyclical seven-day week with a climactic Sabbath. These are the two protological realities that make up the warp and woof of history, as Schaeffer claims: holy space and holy time, interweaving under the providence of a holy God.

The rest of this chapter turns to the topic of time in the Genesis prologue, and in particular, the seventh day, commonly known as the Sabbath Day. Seven points will help to illuminate the significance of the Sabbath Day with respect to the space-time continuum of history.

The Sabbath as Chronological

Alongside the protological space that God creates in the beginning and sanctifies by his presence, there is also protological time (2:1–3). In the beginning God creates a cyclical seven-day week with a climactic, sabbatical seventh day.

To understand better the chronological nature of the Sabbath Day within the creation week, it is useful to appreciate the extent to which time in general is effused throughout the Genesis prologue.

First, there is *the beginning of time*. Genesis 1:1 presents the absolute beginning of all things. The "clock" of time only begins to tick after God's initial *ex-nihilo* creative act to bring the heavens and earth into existence. Prior to this, when God existed in his eternal, happy state, time was not in existence. Time, like everything else in the world that God makes, has a beginning. It begins when God creates the heavens and the earth. Thus, Genesis 1:1 concerns the beginning of time, as well as the absolute beginning of all things.

Second, there are *the alternating periods of time*: daytime and nighttime (1:4–5). After the initial act of creating the heavens and the earth, God creates light, separating it from the darkness. In naming the light and the darkness "Day" and "Night", respectively, God establishes alternating periods of time: daytime and nighttime. These two time periods make up the first day, and every other day afterward.

Third, there are *the boundaries of time*: evening and morning. The phrase is repeated six times for each of the first six days (1:5, 8, 13, 19, 23, 31). It could be a way of speaking about the *end points* of the main periods of a day: "and there was evening" ends the period of daytime; "and there was morning" ends the period of nighttime. Or the phrase could be a way of speaking about the *beginning points* of the main periods of a day: "and there was evening" begins the period of nighttime; "and there was morning" begins the period of daytime. The Jews began their day in the evening ("from evening until evening"; Lev. 23:32), with morning as a continuation of the day. The latter interpretation is favorable, since this is the order of time for the Jewish calendar under the first age of the world. However, regardless of what view one adopts, these rhythmic boundaries of time sound all the way through the prologue of Genesis.

Fourth, there are *the markers of time*: sun and moon. They are placed in the expanse of the space heavens to mark time (1:14–18). This is their primary purpose. They also serve to give light (1:15, 17), but only as a secondary purpose. This is seen in the allocation of purpose clauses. Five purpose clauses are allocated to the sun and moon being placed in the heavens to mark time: to separate day from night—two time references; and to mark signs and seasons, days and years—more time references (1:14, 16, 18). Only two purpose clauses are allocated to the sun and moon being placed in the heavens to give light (1:15, 17). In other words, the sun and moon are created primarily to mark time.

Fifth, there are *the registers of time*, seven in total: the first day, the second day, the third day, etc. (1:5, 8, 13, 19, 23, 31; 2:2–3). The numbers, functioning adjectivally on the Hebrew word "day" (יוֹם), are ordinal not cardinal. Hence the days are labelled first, second, third, etc., and not one, two, three, etc., as if they are mere literary constructs that can be moved around and matched with each other.[12] Rather, as ordinal registers of time they are set in a consecutive narrative, which prohibits them from being dislodged and reordered. This is reenforced by the fact that the ordinal numbers occur in an account highly structured by the Hebrew *wayyiqtol* verb (also known as the *waw* consecutive imperfect), a mainline narrative verb. Fifty-five *wayyiqtols* form the structural backbone of the narrative in an unbroken chain from 1:3–2:3.[13]

Sixth, there is *the climax of time.* The creation week rises to a crescendo on the seventh day, but the sixth day is also a precursor to the climax, indicated by several features. In the first place, there is a significant increase in the amount of divine speech compared to the other days (1:26–27, 29–30); the speech that is introduced by divine self-deliberation ("Let us...") is unlike the other speeches; the day also ends with a comprehensive assessment of everything that has been made: "And behold, it was very good." This is followed by the time register of "the sixth day," which is

---

12. Contra Kline, "Space and Time," who, in order to make his literary framework hypothesis work, has to change the ordinal numbers (first day, second day, etc.) to cardinal numbers (Day 1, Day 2, etc.) as part of his de-chronologizing, re-topicalizing scheme. A comment by Derek Kidner, Genesis, 54–55; cf. also idem, "Genesis 2:5, 6: Wet or Dry?" *Tyndale Bulletin* 17 (1966): 109–114, provides a helpful response: "Yet to the present writer the march of the days is too majestic a progress to carry no implication of ordered sequence; it also seems over-subtle to adopt a view of the passage which discounts one of the primary impressions it makes on the ordinary reader. It is a story, not only a statement." Of course, it is true that "the first day" (יוֹם אֶחָד) is spelt with the cardinal number "one" (אֶחָד) and not the expected ordinal number "first" (רִאשׁוֹן). However, this is insignificant. When אֶחָד appears in the context of other ordinal numbers, it means "first" (e.g. see 1 Sam. 1:2 and the order of Elkanah's wives: "the name of the first was Hannah [שֵׁם אַחַת חַנָּה], and the second was Peninnah [וְשֵׁם הַשֵּׁנִית פְּנִנָּה]"). The number אֶחָד is also frequently used in relation to ordinal days and years (e.g. Gen. 8:13).

13. There are three "offline" clauses that break the narrative flow but not in any significant way. The first two (*we-X-qatal*) clauses function to introduce comparative, contemporaneous action to the mainline narrative (1:5, "while the darkness he called Night"; and 1:10, "while the waters that were gathered together he called Seas"), and so they do not disrupt the temporal or logical flow of the narrative. The third clause is an "offline" simple nominal clause, functioning climactically for the sixth day (1:31, "and, behold, it was very good"). Genesis 2:1–3 then continues the narrative.

accompanied by a definite article (יוֹם הַשִּׁשִּׁי)—something lacking for the time registers of the first five days. These features of the sixth day prepare the reader for the climax of the seventh day.

The climactic nature of the seventh day is seen in the basic fact that it is the final day in a week of seven consecutive days. There are other features that point to this as well. As the closing unit of the prologue, 2:1–3 is highly stylized in a way that the material for the other days is not. The phrase "seventh day" occurs three times, each time in a sentence of seven words. The verb "finish" (כלה) occurs two times (2:1–2) and serves as an antithetical inclusio to "the beginning" of 1:1. The inversion of vocabulary from 1:1—God, heavens and earth—in 2:2—earth and heavens, God—communicates completion and crescendo, as does the twofold statement of God resting from all his work. Additionally, a definite article accompanies the ordinal number "seventh" (יוֹם הַשְּׁבִיעִי), providing stylistic climax alongside the sixth day, compared to the first five days. The day is also climactic for the simple reason that it is the recipient of God's blessing and consecration—something the other days are not, important as they are. Finally, just as the prologue moves from non-defined space in darkness (the earth covered in water, formless and empty) to defined space in light (sea and land filled with fish and birds and reptiles, livestock, and beasts), so it also moves from non-defined time ("in the beginning") to more defined time ("the first day, second day, third day," etc., up to "the seventh day").

These observations on the effusion of time in the Genesis prologue all contribute to the Sabbath Day being viewed as chronological—it is the seventh, climactic day in God's creation week.

The Sabbath as Historical

As noted, it is difficult to read the Genesis prologue and miss the effusion of time. However, what kind of time Moses intended to convey is where the debate lies. At the risk of oversimplification, there are nine main interpretations among scholars:[14] (1) instantaneous time,[15] (2) revelation time,[16] (3) indefinite/day-age time,[17] (4) gapped time,[18] (5) intermittent time,[19] (6) literary/framework time,[20] (7) analogical time,[21] (8) liturgical time,[22] and (9) historical time. Due to the limits of this chapter, we cannot engage each of these views; instead, we will present the historical view as it reflects the position of the present author as well as that of Douglas Kelly.[23]

The genre of Genesis 1:1–2:3 reveals all the characteristics of historical narrative in Hebrew prose. While the text is highly stylized in places, the classic signs of Hebrew poetry are absent: there is no parallelism and there is no paucity of prose particles.[24]

---

14. The nomenclature is my own modification of the various positions.

15. Augustine, *The Literal Meaning of Genesis,* trans. J. H. Taylor; Ancient Christian Writers: The Works of the Fathers in Translation, vol. 1 (New York: Newman Press, 1982), 29–30; 168.

16. P. J. Wiseman, *Clues to Creation in Genesis,* ed. Donald J. Wiseman (London: Marshall, Morgan & Scott, 1977).

17. J. W. Dawson, *The Origin of the World According to Revelation and Science* (New York: Harper & Brothers Publishers, 1877), 123–28.

18. Thomas Chalmers, *Natural Theology,* in *Selected Works of Thomas Chalmers,* ed. William Hanna; 12 vols (Edinburgh: Thomas Constable, 1857), 5:146. C.f. also C. I. Scofield, ed., *The Scofield Reference Bible: The Holy Bible Containing the Old and New Testaments* (London: Oxford University Press, 1917), viii–4.

19. John Lennox, *Seven Days that Divide the World: The Beginning According to Genesis and Science* (Grand Rapids: Zondervan, 2011).

20. Kline, "Space and Time"; Irons and Kline, "The Framework View"; Henri Blocher, *In the Beginning: The Opening Chapters of Genesis* (Downers Grove: IVP, 1984).

21. C. John Collins, "Reading Genesis 1:1–2:3 as an Act of Communication: Discourse Analysis and Literal Interpretation," in *Did God Create in 6 Days?,* eds Joseph A. Pipa and David W. Hall (White Hall: Tolle Lege Press, 2005), 131–150; Vern Poythress, *Redeeming Science: A God-Centered Approach* (Wheaton: Crossway, 2006), 131–47.

22. Michael LeFebvre, *The Liturgy of Creation: Understanding Calendars in Old Testament Context* (Downers Grove: IVP Academic, 2019).

23. Douglas F. Kelly, *Creation and Change.* This interpretation has the longest and widest acceptance in the history of the church. There are of course exceptions, but they are in the minority.

24. Prose particles in Hebrew poetry (definite articles, relative pronoun, direct object markers, etc.) normally comprise less than 5% of any given text; in Hebrew prose, it is normally more than 15%. In Genesis 1:1–2:3 the prose particles comprise 24.4% of the text, hence confirming its status as Hebrew prose; see Steven Boyd, "Statistical

Rather, the genre is Hebrew prose, confirmed by the unbroken fifty-five-stringed *wayyiqtol* chain that forms the structural backbone of the narrative from 1:3 to 2:3.

The interpretation of the Hebrew word יוֹם ("day") is not as straightforward. In Genesis 1:5 it refers to the period of daytime, and thus less than an ordinary day; in 2:4 it refers to a single moment in time when God created the heavens and the earth. With respect to the series of ordinal days ("the first day," "the second day," etc.), יוֹם could be real or figurative, historical or analogical, literal or literary. A few observations convince the present author that it is best read as a real, historical day.

First, when יוֹם is accompanied by an ordinal number and the phrase "evening and morning," it is hard to interpret it as anything other than an ordinary day.[25] This is especially so when the original context of Moses writing for the nation of Israel is taken into consideration. What else would an ordinal day in a seven-day week, accompanied by "evening and morning," mean to an (uneducated) Israelite coming out of Egypt?

Second, there are 205 instances of יוֹם with a numerical adjective in the Pentateuch, and in each case the uses outside of Genesis 1:1–2:3 refer to an ordinary day. If its meaning in the

---

Determination of Genre in Biblical Hebrew: Evidence for an Historical Reading of Genesis 1:1–2:3," in *Radioisotopes and the Age of the Earth: Results of a Young-Earth Creationist Research Initiative,* eds Larry Vardiman, Andrew A. Snelling, and Eugene F. Chaffin (El Cajon: Institute for Christian Research; and Chino Valley: Creation Research Society, 2005), 631–734.

25. Since the sun was not created until the fourth day, I avoid the term "24-hour day," as it can be misleading. The Genesis prologue implies that the length of the days was the same for each day; certainly, at least for the first six days. On whether the sun is needed to mark the length of a day, Geerhardus Vos, *Reformed Dogmatics: Volume One: Theology Proper*, 5 vols. (Bellingham, 2012–2014), 1:168, makes this helpful comment: "The fact that the sun and moon, as measures of time, were not present does not mean that there was no time. Already from the beginning God ordained a rhythm and created the light so that it would alternate with the darkness. When later this light was concentrated in the sun and other bodies, we are told nothing about it being only then that the 24-hour day began. There was no change at that point. Therefore, we have reason for assuming that before that time the rotation of the earth took place at the same speed and that light was so positioned as was necessary for an alternation of day and night within 24 hours."

prologue is different, this would constitute a unique use of יוֹם compared to the rest of the Pentateuch.[26] This is not impossible, but it is unlikely.

Third, Moses' later allusions back to the Genesis creation account also confirm the historical reading (Exod. 20:11; 31:17). In both texts the fronted adverbial accusative phrase "six days" (שֵׁשֶׁת־יָמִים) modifies the verb "make" (עָשׂה) with respect to time. The making of the heavens and earth and everything in them is, according to Moses, a "six-day making."[27] Again, what would this mean to an (uneducated) Israelite coming out of Egypt?

Fourth, the historical interpretation is favorable given that every alternative interpretation of the days of creation cannot give an account for the ontological origination of the ordinary day, the ordinary week, or the ordinary Sabbath. From Genesis 2:4

---

26. Of course, some may dispute that each instance in the Pentateuch refers to a *historical* day, arguing instead that, in some cases, the days could be figurative, analogical, literary, liturgical, etc. For example, LeFebvre, *Liturgy of Creation*, chapter 7, argues that the days of creation are not so much historical days as calendar days, best understood as festival "dates" in the Jewish calendar. However, this novel interpretation raises various questions: How does one discern between "historical days" and "calendar days" in the Pentateuch? What criteria does one use for each case? Are there genre indicators in the text to show when we are to read the days as liturgical rather than historical? Who decides on the criteria or genre indicators? In other words, besides the lack of historical precedence for this interpretation, it seems to depend on subjective preference as to what days are historical or liturgical.

There are more fundamental problems with LeFebvre's approach, a critique of which lies outside the remit of this chapter. However, it is worth at least flagging some concerns here. LeFebvre's hermeneutic exhibits an anti-harmonization and anachronistic approach that stands outside the bounds of the Reformed approach to scriptural harmonization and biblical theology. In relation to biblical theology, for example, LeFebvre reads the creation account in Genesis through the lens of Israel's festivals laws, laws which, for him, arose out of the *Sitz im Leben* of their agricultural and cultic life in the land. In other words, LeFebvre first begins with the experience of Israel's farming and religious life of a seven-day week with one day of rest, and then reads the creation account through this paradigm, revealing his anachronistic hermeneutic. In essence, LeFebvre's approach exhibits more affinities with higher critical scholarship than it does with Reformed biblical scholarship.

27. The phrase "in the space of six days"—first used by Archelaus, Bishop of Carrhae in A.D. 278, and later taken up by John Calvin, Archbishop Ussher, and the Westminster Divines—is thus a biblical phrase.

onwards, the text of Scripture assumes the existence of the ordinary day, week, Sabbath. This can be seen, for example, in the genealogy of Adam, the flood narrative, the patriarchal narratives, the Passover in Egypt, and the collecting of manna in the wilderness, which assumes a seven-day week with a climactic Sabbath. However, on alternative interpretations of the seven-day week of Genesis, the ordinary day, week, Sabbath just pop up in biblical history *ex nihilo-ex nowhere*, without explanation. To argue that the ordinary day begins with the creation of the sun on the fourth day is not a view accommodated by any of the alternative interpretations. To argue that it begins after the creation of man on the sixth day lacks exegetical basis, especially since the alternative interpretations (e.g. literary framework and analogical) view the next (seventh) day as eternal not ordinary. To argue that it does not really matter, or to adopt a position of agnosticism, lacks hermeneutical integrity given that the biblical text not only assumes the existence of the ordinary day, week, Sabbath, but also indicates their redemptive-historical significance. Indeed, as will be seen below, much of the drama of soteriology is built upon the foundation of protology, particularly with respect to space and time.[28]

A further point needs to be considered. Genesis 1:14 informs us that the sun and moon are created to mark days and years. The earth completes a full rotation on its axis in relation to the sun to mark a 24-hour period; the moon completes a full orbit of the earth to mark an approximate 30-day month; the earth completes a full orbit around the sun to mark the 365-day period of a year. These periods of time are marked astronomically, by the movements of sun, moon, and earth in relation to each other—but not so the week with the Sabbath as its climax. The seven-day week with a climactic Sabbath is an *arbitrary* period, *divinely imposed* on the created order. So where does the historical seven-day week and its climactic Sabbath come from, if not from the original creation week? Of course, if one holds to the historical interpretation, which

---

28. See point 3 below.

has been the dominant historical interpretation of the Christian church, at least up to the Enlightenment, then the answer is simple: the ordinary day, week, Sabbath receive their ontological origination from God at the beginning of creation (Gen. 1:1–2:3), something Moses reaffirms at Sinai (Exod. 20:11). However, if one holds to an alternative interpretation, then questions remain over the ontological origination of the ordinary day, week, Sabbath.

Fifth, the historical nature of the first Sabbath as an ordinary day is affirmed by Jesus when he says, "The Sabbath was made for man not man for the Sabbath" (Mark 2:27). Jesus is referring to the creation of man in the beginning when the first Sabbath was established. In context, Jesus is engaging the Pharisees and their view of the Sabbath as it occurs in the ordinary week. If the first Sabbath is eternal and not ordinary, then Jesus's allusion to it makes little sense since the issue at hand is not the eternal Sabbath but the ordinary Sabbath.

In sum, these points present the historical interpretation as the most persuasive reading of the days in the Genesis Prologue; as such, the Sabbath is best understood as a chronological, historical day in an ordinary seven-day week. These first two points are foundational for the next observation on the Sabbath.

The Sabbath as Redemptive-Historical

The protological space created by God in the beginning is the theatre in which history plays out, while the protological time created by God is the timeline along which history unfolds. Recall Schaeffer's comment: "Space and time are like warp and woof. Their interwoven relationship is history." This is especially so when it comes to redemptive history. God's plan of redemption plays out within the physical realm of the heavens and the earth and within the temporal realm of the cyclical seven-day week with a climactic Sabbath. In theological lingua, soteriology maps onto protology in terms of both space and time.

Two observations will help to illustrate the point.

1. Redemptive History and Protological Space

After Adam falls into sin, God does not abandon the basic structure of the created heavens and earth in his redemptive plan; rather, he operates within the protological space that he made in the beginning. An example from each of the Testaments illustrates the connection between redemptive history and protological space.

a. The Flood

Noah's flood provides a clear example of how, after the Fall, God continues to work in the world that he made as he comes in judgment and salvation. Because of the increase of sin and violence on the earth, God tells Noah that he is going to judge the world with water (Gen. 6:11–13). When God sends the flood waters upon the earth, they come from two main sources: "all the fountains of the great deep" (כָּל־מַעְיְנֹת תְּהוֹם רַבָּה; 7:11), recalling the deep waters at the initial creation over which the Spirit of God hovered (1:2); and "the windows of heaven" (וַאֲרֻבֹּת הַשָּׁמַיִם; 7:11), recalling the waters above the expanse that were separated from the waters below on the second day of creation (1:6–7). The flood is so extensive that the waters cover "all the high mountains which were under all the heavens" (כָּל־הֶהָרִים הַגְּבֹהִים אֲשֶׁר־תַּחַת כָּל־הַשָּׁמָיִם; 7:19). God's judgment thus plays out in, and by the means of, the protological space that he created in the beginning. The fact that the earth returns to its original state in the flood, a globe covered in water (1:2), reveals a connection to the original, protological space. Indeed, the whole event is presented as a decreation-recreation event akin to the first creation. In the flood waters, the earth is de-created back to its original state as a globe covered in water; then God sends a wind to blow over the earth and the waters recede, allowing the dry land to appear again. The Hebrew word for "wind" (רוּחַ) is the same as the word for "spirit" (רוּחַ); thus, the redemptive action of the wind from God (8:1) recalls the creative action of the Spirit of God at the initial creation (1:2). As a result of the waters receding, the earth is re-created back to its original state with seas and dry land and living creatures inhabiting their respective realms. The phases related to the recreation after the flood follow exactly the order of the days related to the first creation, as the table below reveals:

Genesis 1:1–2:4	Creation	Genesis 8:1–9:3, 6–7	Re-creation
Day 1 (1:2)	Earth, deep, Spirit, waters	Phase 1 (8:1b–2)	Wind, earth, waters, deep
Day 2 (1:6–8)	Waters, sky	Phase 2 (8:2b)	Windows of the heavens, sky
Day 3 (1:9)	Water, dry ground, appear	Phase 3 (8:3–5)	Water, tops of mountains, appear
Day 5 (1:20–23)	Birds, above the ground (earth)	Phase 4 (8:6–12)	Raven, dove, from the ground, vegetation
Day 6 (1:24–25)	Creatures, livestock, creatures that move along the ground, wild animals	Phase 5 (8:17–19)	Creature, birds, animals, creatures that move along the ground
Day 6 (1:26–28)	Man, image of God, male and female	Phase 6 (8:16, 18; 9:6)	Noah and his wife, man, image of God
Day 6 (1:28)	Blessed, "be fruitful, multiply, and fill the earth, and subdue it, and rule . . . [every living creature]"	Phase 7 (9:1–2, 7)	Blessed, "be fruitful, multiply and fill the earth, and subdue it. The fear of you and the dread of you shall be upon [every living creature]"

In sum, the divine judgment-salvation event of the flood plays out in the theatre of the protological space of the heavens and the earth established at the beginning of creation. After the flood, it is the same created order of space as before the flood, albeit now renewed through the cleansing of the flood-water judgment.

This mapping of redemptive history onto divinely created, protological space is demonstrated most vividly and acutely in the incarnation, life, death, burial, resurrection, and ascension of Christ.

b. Christ

In the incarnation, the Son of God comes down from heaven, "for us men and for our salvation," as the Nicene Creed affirms. Of course, since the Son is co-equal with the Father and Spirit in substance, power, and glory, he does not cease to inhabit heaven, as the omnipresent second person of the Trinity. Yet truly, and mysteriously, in the *sui generis* incarnation he does descend from the supernatural, invisible, supreme heavens, where he, along with the Father and Spirit, is worshipped by the celestial host. The Son of God comes down from the heavenly space of those supreme heavens into the earthly space of a virgin's womb, enveloping himself in darkness for nine months. In (con)descending, he assumes a human nature in the person of Jesus Christ and dwells on earth for 33 years (John 1:14). During his earthly life, he travels across the terrain of the created earth, moving from Palestine to Egypt, from Egypt to Nazareth, and back and forth from Nazareth to Jerusalem each year for the festivals. In his public ministry, he traverses the land of Palestine, north to south, east to west. He ascends and descends mountains; he crosses the seas of Galilee, even walking on its waters. Near the end of his life, he goes into a garden to pray as death begins to cast its dark shadow over him. The next day he is lifted up on a cross at Golgotha, suspended between heaven and earth, with the sky-space heavens above him and the dry land below him. After he dies, he is buried by Joseph of Arimathea in a tomb in the earth. He goes into the belly of the earth, into Sheol, the lowest part of the earth. After three days he rises from the dead out of the earth, and appears in a garden, being Replace with: mistaken for the "gardener." After forty days of travelling around the regions of Palestine—appearing before witnesses in open places, on the road to Emmaus, in a closed room, by the sea of Galilee, and on a mountain—he ascends through the sky heavens with the clouds, through the space heavens with the sun and moon and stars, into the supreme heavens with the angelic host. There he sits down on a throne. And there he is still seated in that holy space of the supreme heavens with the earth as his footstool.

As can be seen, in the events surrounding Christ's life, death, burial, resurrection, and ascension, the drama of redemptive history maps onto, and is played out in, the theatre of the protological space of the heavens and the earth established at the beginning of creation. In theological lingua, soteriology maps onto protology. The same is true with respect to protological time.

2. Redemptive History and Protological Time

An example from each of the two testaments illustrates the connection between redemptive history and protological time.

a. The Flood

As with the creation account, the flood narrative is effused with temporal markers. Three kinds of markers are employed: (1) dates in relation to Noah's age; (2) set time periods; and (3) the general categories of seasons, daytime, and nighttime. First, we are given the years of Noah's age in relation to when he begins to have children (500 years old; Gen. 5:32); when he completes the ark and the flood waters come (600 years old; Gen. 7:5–6); and the exact day when the fountains of the great deep burst forth and the windows of the heavens open and Noah enters the ark (on the seventeenth day of the second month of Noah's 600th year; Gen. 7:11). The dates of Noah's age continue to mark aspects of the flood narrative: when the ark comes to rest on the mountains of Ararat (on the seventeenth day of the seventh month of Noah's 600th year; Gen. 8:4); when the tops of the mountains are seen for the first time (on the first day of the tenth month of Noah's 600th year; Gen. 8:5); when the waters are dried from off the earth (on the first day of the first month of Noah's 601th year; Gen. 8:13); and when the earth further dries out, and Noah and his family and the animals leave the ark (on the twenty-seventh day of the second month of the same year; Gen. 8:14–19).

Second, several time periods are also mentioned throughout the flood narrative.[29] The rain falls for forty days and forty nights (7:12) and then continues to rise for another 110 days, prevailing over the earth for a total of 150 days (Gen. 7:17–24). At the end of 150 days, God sends a wind, and the waters begin to recede for a period of 74 days (Gen. 8:4).[30] Forty days after the waters recede, Noah opens the window of the ark and sends out a raven, which flies to and fro (Gen. 8:6–7). Three sets of seven days then follow where Noah sends forth a dove to search for dry land: (1) after the raven finds no resting place, Noah waits seven days and sends forth a dove, which returns to him the same day (8:8; cf. "another" in v. 10); (2) Noah waits another seven days and sends forth the dove again, which returns to him in the evening of the same day with a freshly plucked olive leaf (8:10); (3) Noah then waits another seven days and sends the dove a third time, after which it does not return (8:12). The seven-day periods recall the first creation week and thus point to the beginnings of a new creation. This is reinforced by the fact that the dove returns with a freshly plucked olive leaf on the last day of the second seven-day period "in the evening," an allusion to the boundaries of the day in the creation week ("and there was evening and there was morning"; 1:5). Indeed, if we follow the Jewish calendar of marking days from evening to evening, when the dove arrives back in the evening of the seventh day, it arrives back on the eighth day—the first day of a new week.

These temporal markers in Genesis 6–9 reveal that not only is the flood narrative connected to the timeline of Noah's age, but the time periods also recall the creation account, namely, seven days plus evening time. Near the end of the flood narrative, there

---

29. For a chronology of the flood period, amounting in total to 371 days, see Henry Morris, *The Genesis Flood: The Biblical Record and Its Scientific Implications* (Phillipsburg: Presbyterian & Reformed: 1961), 3. Morris follows a table from E. F. Kevan's commentary on Genesis in *The New Bible Commentary*, ed. F. Davidson (Grand Rapids: Eerdmans, 1953), 84–85.

30. The number 74 is derived from the time-period between the seventeenth day of the seventh month to the first day of the tenth month: 13 + 30 + 30 + 1 = 74.

is also mention of seasons ("seedtime and harvest, cold and heat") and daily order ("day and night") (8:22), both of which echo the creative activity of God in the beginning when he established day and night through the creation of light (1:5); and signs and seasons, days and years, through the creation of sun and moon (1:14). Since there is no indication to the contrary, these post-flood seasons and daily periods continue as they did before the flood.

To summarize, in the flood the drama of redemptive history plays out within the framework of protological time; in particular, it plays out in relation to the cycle of days and years of Noah's life and the cyclical seven-day period as established at the beginning of creation. In theological lingua, soteriology maps onto protology.[31]

The mapping of redemptive history onto divinely ordered, protological time is demonstrated most vividly and acutely in the circumcision, death, burial, resurrection of Christ, and the outpouring of his Spirit at Pentecost. The redemptive work of Christ plays out in relation to the seven-day period and specific days in the ordinary week.

b. Christ

The theological significance of Christ's circumcision, death, burial, resurrection, and outpouring of his Spirit at Pentecost is illuminated when we consider the days of the week on which these key events occur.

With respect to his *circumcision*, Christ receives the sign of the eternal covenant on the eighth day, in accordance with the stipulations of the Abrahamic covenant (Gen. 17:12). The cutting of his foreskin begins the shedding of blood that will bookend

---

31. The foundational significance of protological time for the flood narrative continues in the patriarchal and Passover narratives. In the former, Abraham is commanded by God to circumcise his male offspring on the eighth day (Gen. 17:12), a time marker signifying a new beginning (when set against the backdrop of a cyclical seven-day week). In the latter, the Passover is to be observed for seven days as a memorial to the night God rescued Israel out of Egypt (Exod. 12:15); it was their "new-creation" moment. These time references—the eighth day and seven days—only receive their symbolism and significance in the light of the arbitrarily, divinely imposed period of a cyclical seven-day week established at the beginning of creation.

his life. Being performed on the eighth day, it points to the new beginning that he will inaugurate for sinners through his suffering and death.

With respect to his *death*, Christ dies on a Friday, the same day of the week on which Adam was created (Gen. 1:26–28); he dies on the last day of the working week according to the cycle of time established under the first age of the world at creation (Gen. 1:31); he dies on the sixth day of the feast of unleavened bread, the day of preparation when the people ate the Passover meal (Exod. 12:15);[32] he dies at three o'clock on the Friday afternoon, the time of the evening sacrifice (Exod. 29:39), crying out in his closing moments, "It is finished!" (John 19:30).

Irenaeus, the early church father, provides an interesting take on the fact that Christ dies on a Friday—the same day Adam was created:

> The Lord, therefore, recapitulating in Himself this day, underwent His sufferings upon the day preceding the Sabbath, that is, the sixth day of the creation, on which day man was created; thus granting him a second creation by means of His passion, which is that [creation] out of death.[33]

Irenaeus also argues that Adam sinned on the day he was created, and hence why, according to him, Christ died on a Friday. Whether or not one agrees with Irenaeus on this last point, we can at least agree with him that Christ died on the same day of the week on which Adam was created. The theological significance is immediately evident: the recreation of mankind in the second Adam (through his death) occurs on the same day as the creation of mankind in the first Adam (through his life).

With respect to his *burial*, Christ is buried toward the end of the last day of the working week, just before the Sabbath. He lies buried in his grave on the Passover Sabbath, thus keeping the

---

32. Recall that the Jewish day ran from evening to evening, and so, technically, Jesus' death on the Friday is on the same day as the Passover meal the night before.

33. Irenaeus, *Against Heresies*, Book V, Chapter 23, in *Ante-Nicene Fathers, Volume I: The Apostolic Fathers with Justin Martyr and Irenaeus* (Peabody: Hendrickson, 1979), 551.

Sabbath in his death. He rests from his work on the day of rest, having cried out from the cross the day before: "It is finished!" (John 19:30) Jesus' burial confirms the completion of his work. He "sleeps" in the grave, his life's work done.[34]

With respect to his *resurrection*, Christ rises on the Sunday, the first day of a new week. This is the same day on which creation began—"the first day" (Gen. 1:5). By rising on "the first day" of a new week, Christ's resurrection indicates a "new-creation" moment in redemptive history, while also making obsolete the first age of the world in which the Sabbath was the last day of the week—"the seventh day" (Gen. 2:2–3).

Geerhardus Vos notes the epoch-defining significance of the timing of Christ's resurrection:

> It has been strikingly observed, that our Lord died on the eve of that Jewish Sabbath, at the end of one of these typical weeks of labour by which His work and its consummation were prefigured. And Christ entered upon His rest, the rest of His new, eternal life on the first day of the week, so that the Jewish Sabbath comes to lie between, was, as it were, disposed of, buried in the grave.[35]

In other words, by sleeping through the Sabbath in his death, Jesus disposes of the first (old) age of the world; and then, by rising on the Sunday, the first day of a new week, he inaugurates the second (new) age of the world. Thus, Jesus' death on the Friday is the Passover sacrifice to end all Passovers; his sleeping in death on the Saturday is the Sabbath rest to end all Sabbaths; and his resurrection on the Sunday, the first day of a new week— "the eighth day" (cf. Gen. 17:12)—serves to confirm that the old is gone and the new has come (cf. 2 Cor. 5:17). All of this is so, because the resurrection occurs a whole one day, one week, one age removed from the last Sabbath of the first (old) age of the world.

---

34. In the Jewish mindset, death and subsequent burial was viewed as a form of sleep (Job 3:11–17; Ps. 13:3; 90:5; Dan. 12:2). In burial the person slept until the resurrection. In the Gospels, Jesus himself speaks in similar terms about death (Mark 5:39; John 11:11–14).

35. Geerhardus Vos, *Biblical Theology: Old and New Testaments* (Edinburgh: Banner of Truth, 1948), 142.

This distancing from the Sabbath of the first (old) world order is made clear by how the New Testament writers refer to the "first day of the week" in the resurrection accounts (Matt. 28:1; Mark 6:2; Luke 24:1; John 20:1). As seen above, the Greek phrase "first day of the week" is more literally rendered "one day from the Sabbath" (μία τῶν σαββάτων).[36] In the new age, the day of rest, of observance, of holy convocation, is no longer the last day of the week, the Jewish Sabbath; it is now the first day of the week (Acts 20:7), what John in Revelation calls, "the Lord's Day" (Rev. 1:10).

With respect to *Pentecost*, Christ sends his Spirit upon the church fifty days after the Passover Sabbath. Fifty days is seven weeks plus one day, which means that Pentecost occurs on a Sunday—the first day of the week. The beginning of the New Testament church thus occurs at the beginning of a new week, seven weeks plus one day after the end of the first (old) age of the world. As with the day of resurrection, this is the same day of the week on which creation begins—"the first day" (Gen. 1:5). It is also the same day of the week in which the Spirit of God first hovers over the waters at the beginning of creation (1:2). By sending his Spirit on "the first day" of a new week at Pentecost, Jesus recalls the first "creation" event in history and thus indicates a "new-creation" event in redemptive history.

In the events surrounding Christ's circumcision, death, burial, resurrection, and the outpouring of his Spirit at Pentecost, the drama of redemptive history plays out within the framework of the protological time of the cyclical seven-day week with a climactic Sabbath as established at the beginning of creation. In particular, the redemptive-historical events related to Christ are illuminated by three key days in the ordinary week: Friday, as the last day of the working week; Saturday, as the climactic Sabbath

---

36. The genitive is read in an ablative sense, carrying the idea of distance from something; see Daniel B. Wallace: "The genitive substantive is that from which the verb or sometimes head noun is separated. Thus the genitive is used to indicate the point of departure"; *Greek Grammar Beyond the Basics: An Exegetical Syntax of the New Testament* (Grand Rapids: Zondervan, 1996), 107–108.

Day of the week; and Sunday, as the first day of a new week. In this sense, the Sabbath is redemptive-historical; it frames and structures God's unfolding salvation in history. In theological lingua, soteriology maps onto protology.

The Sabbath as Typological

The Sabbath is not only chronological and historical, serving as part of the temporal framework in which redemptive history plays out, it is also typological. That is, the Sabbath points beyond itself to another reality. For something in the Old Testament to constitute a type, the following characteristics must be present: (a) *historical*: the type must be a real person, place, ordinance, institution, or event in redemptive history; (b) *theological*: the type must play some part in God's redemptive dealings with his people in history; (c) *symbolical*: the type must symbolize or signify something; (d) *analogical*: the type must correspond significantly to some anti-type in the New Testament; (e) *escalation*: the type must undergo some higher development in the New Testament. In this sense, we could say that the anti-type is eschatological. The Sabbath Day meets all these requirements: (a) being a protological reality, it is a historical reality: it is the climactic day in the cyclical seven-day week; (b) the day is theological in the sense that it is blessed and sanctified by God to be a weekly day of rest and worship for his people; (c) the day symbolizes a period of rest, physically and spiritually; (d) in the New Testament, the day finds its analog in the future rest in heaven, which also entails (e) an escalation from a limited, temporary period of rest on earth to an eternal, permanent period of rest in heaven.

The foundational reason for the Sabbath to qualify as a type is its historicity. If the first Sabbath is not a real, historical day, then we return to the problem mentioned earlier regarding the ontological origination of the ordinary day, week, Sabbath. When exactly was the first Sabbath if not in the creation week? After Genesis 2:1–3, the next explicit mention of the Sabbath Day is in Exodus where Moses commands the people to collect manna for six days but not on the seventh day, "which is a Sabbath"

(Exod. 16:26). This incident precedes the giving of the law at Sinai where God commands Israel to "Remember the Sabbath day" (Exod. 20:8). Clearly, the Sabbath Day is known to the nation of Israel as they come out of Egypt and before they reach Sinai. But where did they learn of its origination and signification for their community life, if not from the creation week?[37] In terms of redemptive history, the Sabbath Day is too significant for it just to pop up *ex nihilo-ex nowhere*, without explanation. In short, the Sabbath's historicity is a *sine qua non* for its typology.

Now, in saying that the Sabbath is typological, a hermeneutical misstep must be avoided. Those who advocate for the literary framework or analogical interpretation argue that since there is no mention of evening and morning with the seventh day, the day is not a real, historical day; rather, it is an eternal day, since God rests on it and does not return to his work of creation on the next day of a new week.[38] However, the absence of the day boundaries of "evening and morning" should not be overplayed. The absence indicates that the working week *for God* has come to an end, not that the Sabbath Day *itself* does not end. To suggest so is a non-sequitur, as the following illustration indicates.

Imagine a person who has worked their whole life in a particular job, and then after 40 years, one Friday afternoon, they finish work for the last time and enter their retirement. That weekend is a very different weekend for them than for everyone else in the company. We might say that this person's weekend never ends, because they have entered the "rest" of their retirement. However,

---

37. Since Genesis may not have been written at the time of the events recorded in the book of Exodus, the people of Israel's knowledge of the Sabbath must have come from oral tradition or other written sources. The book of Exodus reveals several things from the history of revelation recorded in the book of Genesis that the Israelite community were aware of *prior* to that history being inscripturated, for example: the names of the patriarch fathers, Abraham, Isaac, and Jacob (Exod. 3:15; 6:8; cf. Genesis 12–25); the bones of Joseph needing to be carried up out of Egypt (Exod. 13:19; cf. Gen. 50:25); not working on the Sabbath (Exod. 16:22–26; cf. Gen. 2:1–3); and the six days of creation followed by a Sabbath (Exod. 20:8–11; cf. Gen. 1:1–2:3).

38. Collins, "Reading Genesis 1:1–2:3," 137–39; Poythress, *Redeeming Science*, 131–47.

Monday morning rolls around for the rest of the workers just as it always does. They go back to work, while the person who has retired does not. In both cases, the weekly cycle continues as it always does. This is the same with God: on the first Sabbath Day at the end of the creation week, God enters his rest; but the next day (and week) rolls around for Adam and Eve. They go to work in the garden on the Sunday morning of the second week of history, while God enjoys his permanent "retirement" from the work of creation. God's rest is eternal, but it does not follow that the seventh day in the creation week is eternal. As Vos states, simply and clearly, "Although God's Sabbath is certainly endless, that cannot be said of the first Sabbath (after the six-day creation) for mankind."[39]

In short, the typological nature of the Sabbath should not be pitted against the historical nature of the Sabbath. The two are related. Indeed, the historical is a *sine qua non* of the typological.

The Sabbath as Eschatological

We get the hint that the Sabbath Day in the creation week is eschatological by the way it is spoken of in 2:1–3, without the anticipated "and there was evening and there was morning." The sentence is conspicuous by its absence, suggesting that the Sabbath Day is one that never ends. In this regard, the Sabbath serves as a type of the rest to come, the rest of eternal life in a new creation. As Vos comments, "The Sabbath is not in the first place a means of advancing religion. It has its main significance apart from that, in pointing forward to the eternal issues of life and history."[40] That is, the Sabbath is eschatological as well as typological.[41]

---

39. Vos, *Reformed Dogmatics: Theology Proper*, 1:169.

40. Vos, *Biblical Theology*, 141.

41. In this respect, LeFebvre's criticism of biblical apologists is not without merit. LeFebvre, *Liturgy of Creation*, 133, notes that biblical apologists on both sides of the debate (young earth, literal days and old earth, day-age) scarcely refer to the Sabbath or its significance in their material (e.g. Ken Ham, *The Lie: Evolution/Millions of Years* [Green Forest: Master Books, 2013]; Hugh Ross, *A Matter of Days: Resolving a Creation Controversy* [Corvina: Reasons to Believe, 2015]). To miss the typological and eschatological nature of the Sabbath in the creation week is to miss the theological significance of the day for redemptive history.

Connected to this, as a day of rest that follows six days of work, the Sabbath points to the reward of eternal life in the covenant of works. Vos is helpful again:

> The Sabbath brings this principle of the eschatological structure of history to bear upon the mind of man after a symbolical and a typical fashion. It teaches its lesson through the rhythmical succession of six days of labour and one ensuing day of rest in each successive week. Man is reminded in this way that life is not an aimless existence, that a goal lies beyond. This was true before, and apart from, redemption. The eschatological is an older strand in revelation than the soteric. The so-called 'Covenant of Works' was nothing but an embodiment of the Sabbatical principle. Had its probation been successful, then the sacramental Sabbath would have passed over into the reality it typified, and the entire subsequent course of the history of the race would have been different. What now is to be expected at the end of this world would have formed the beginning of the world-course instead.[42]

According to Vos, the original Sabbath Day was symbolical of the eternal blessedness that Adam could earn in the covenant of works. Through his obedience in the covenant of works, Adam was meant to bring himself and his posterity into the eschatological rest of which the Sabbath was a sign. But because of his disobedience in the covenant of works, Adam never brought mankind into that eschatological rest. Instead, Adam brought curse and unrest *away from* the presence of God rather than blessing and rest in the presence of God. Redemptive history conveys man's pursuit of that Sabbath rest. As such, the weekly Sabbath serves as a regular reminder to man of what awaits him—the blessed, eternal rest in God's presence.

In considering the Sabbath as redemptive-historical, typological, and eschatological, discussion of its fulfillment naturally comes into play, which brings us to the sixth observation on the Sabbath.

---

42. Vos, *Biblical Theology*, 140.

The Sabbath as Christological

Since the Sabbath is redemptive-historical and typological, it is necessarily Christological. At one level, this means that the Sabbath is fulfilled in Christ, the great harbinger of eternal rest. In his person and work, Christ brings blessing and rest from the curse and unrest of sin. As he said himself, "Come to me all you who are weary and heavy-laden and I will give you rest" (Matt. 11:28). In this regard, we may say that Jesus is the Sabbath that sinners have been looking for. However, it would be overly simplistic to think that this is all there is to say about the fulfillment of the Sabbath by Christ. Indeed, the writer of Hebrews indicates that it is not as simple as making a one-dimensional type-to-anti-type connection between the Sabbath and Christ:

> For if Joshua had given them rest, God would not have spoken of another day later on. So then, there remains a Sabbath rest for the people of God, for whoever has entered God's rest has also rested from his works as God did from his. (Heb. 4:8–10)

Writing after Christ's ascension, the writer of Hebrews makes it clear that there *yet remains* a Sabbath rest for the people of God. This means that the typological has not yet become the eschatological. If so, then the typological remains; and if the typological remains, then the Sabbath remains. Thus, although it is right to say that Christ fulfils the Sabbath in his person and work—or at least earns the right to give people the rest to which the Sabbath points—this does not mean that *the type* has become obsolete. Rather, it undergoes a change. The sign is replaced with a new sign: the Sabbath is replaced with the Lord's Day. The Jewish Sabbath, as the last day of the week, gives way to the Christian Sabbath, as the first day of the week.

The same may also be illustrated by the change in sign with respect to the Old Testament sacraments of circumcision and Passover meal. As an Old Testament sign, circumcision points to Christ (Col. 2:12–13), but the sign does not become obsolete when Christ fulfils it. Rather, it undergoes a change; it is replaced with a new sign—the sign of baptism.[43] It is the same with the Passover meal: as a sign, it points to Christ and his death on the cross as our Passover Lamb (John 19:36; 1 Cor. 5:7), but the sign does not become obsolete when Christ fulfils it. Rather, it undergoes a change; it is replaced with a new sign—the sign of the Lord's Supper. Similarly, with the Sabbath: as a sign, it points to Christ who brings the eschatological rest through his redeeming work (Matt. 11:28), but the sign (type) does not become obsolete when Christ fulfils it. Rather, it undergoes a change; it is replaced with a new sign (type)—the Lord's Day.

Here we should consider again the redemptive-historical aspect of the Sabbath in relation to Christ's death and resurrection. Recall how Jesus dies on a Friday afternoon at the end of a working week, sleeps through the Sabbath, and then rises on Sunday morning. The day in which Jesus brings eschatological rest through his resurrection is not the Sabbath but the Sunday—the first day of the week, or, as we saw more literally, "one day from the Sabbath" (μία τῶν σαββάτων). It is interesting to note how each of the Gospel writers use this temporal phrase in their resurrection accounts in relation to the Sabbath.

Matthew: "Now after the Sabbath, toward the dawn of *the first day of the week* [one day from the Sabbath], Mary Magdalene and the other Mary went to see the tomb." (28:1)

Mark: "When the Sabbath was past, Mary Magdalene, Mary the mother of James, and Salome bought spices, so that they might go and anoint him. And very early on *the first day of the week* [one day from the Sabbath], when the sun had risen, they went to the tomb." (16:1–2)

Luke: "On the Sabbath they [the women] rested according to the commandment. But on *the first day of the week* [one day from the Sabbath], at early dawn, they went to the tomb, taking the spices they had prepared." (24:1–2)

---

43. For further, see David Gibson, "Sacramental Supersessionism Revisited: A Response to Martin Salter on the Relationship between Circumcision and Baptism." *Themelios* 37:2 (2012): 191–208.

John: "Now on *the first day of the week* [one day from the Sabbath] Mary Magdalene came to the tomb early, while it was still dark, and saw that the stone had been taken away from the tomb." (20:1)

Having seen how redemptive history maps onto protological time, phrases and clauses such as "after the Sabbath" or "when the Sabbath was past" can no longer be read as mere temporal markers employed to fill out a narrative. They are theologically loaded statements, conveying in shorthand how the old age was setting while a new age was dawning.

This is reinforced by what occurs in the protological space of the heavens and earth at Christ's death and resurrection. As Christ, the Second and Last Adam, hangs on the cross, the sun in the space heavens is eclipsed at midday, eliminating any light in the sky heavens above (Matt. 27:45); after he cries out and gives up his spirit, the earth begins to shake with an earthquake (Matt. 27:51). Another earthquake accompanies his resurrection three days later (Matt. 28:2). The old order of the heavens and earth was giving way to the new order of the new heavens and earth; so too in relation to protological time. By rising from the dead on the first day of a new week, Jesus retires the old order of time under the first age of the world, in which the Sabbath is the last day of the week; and in its place he inaugurates a new order of time under the second age of the world, in which the Sabbath is now the first day of the week—the Lord's Day. The Westminster divines articulate the change clearly and succinctly in the Westminster Shorter Catechism, Q&A 59:

Q. Which day of the seven has God appointed to be the weekly sabbath? *A. From the beginning of the world to the resurrection of Christ, God appointed the seventh day of the week to be the weekly sabbath; and the first day of the week ever since, to continue to the end of the world, which is the Christian Sabbath.*

It may also be argued that, as there is a change of day to mark the Sabbath in the new age, so there is also a change of period to mark the beginning of the day. Notice how each of the Gospel writers mention the period of the day on which the resurrection takes place: "at the dawn" (τῇ ἐπιφωσκούσηι; Matt. 28:1), "very early ... when the sun had risen" (λίαν πρωῒ ... ἀνατείλαντος τοῦ ἡλίου; Mark 16:2), "at early dawn" (ὄρθρου βαθέως; Luke 24:1–2), "early, while it was still dark" (πρωῒ σκοτίας ἔτι οὔσης; John 20:1). In the Jewish calendar, under the first (old) age of the world, the Sabbath day, like every day, began in the evening (cf. Lev. 23:32: "from evening until evening"). However, at Christ's resurrection, in the second (new) age of the world, the day begins in the morning, at dawn. Indeed, this eschatological reality may even be hinted at in the Genesis prologue with the day-boundary marking line "and there was evening and there was morning." The whole creation account orients us toward the morning after the evening. If this is so, then, since the Lord's Day is the Christian Sabbath in the new age of the world, it naturally, and appropriately, begins in the morning.

In summary, the Sabbath is Christological, not only in the sense that Christ fulfils it but also in the sense that it undergoes a change in light of Christ's redeeming work. As a type, the day changes from the last day of the week (the Jewish Sabbath) to the first day of the week (the Lord's Day). It is also important to note that, in the second (new) age of the world, the type (or anti-type) does not become every day of the week. To say as much would be to exhibit an over-realized eschatology in which every day is the Sabbath. Such a scenario is reserved only for the eschaton when every day will be the Sabbath, when the eschatological rest to which the protological Sabbath first pointed will have dawned in its full consummated form. In this regard, the Sabbath has two points of fulfilment in redemptive history: the "now" of the first coming of Christ; and the "not yet" of the second coming of Christ. As Christians, we live between the "now and the not yet" of Christ's two advents, between his fulfilling the Sabbath initially and partially (by offering rest for our souls through his life, death, burial, resurrection, ascension, and outpouring of his Spirit) and his fulfilling the Sabbath ultimately and fully (by offering rest for our souls *and bodies* in a new heaven and earth through his glorious return).

This brings us to the final observation on the Sabbath.

The Sabbath as Practical

The Sabbath, in its new form of the Lord's Day, continues in redemptive history as a day to be observed. That is, the Sabbath remains a day on which rest and worship are to be practiced by God's people. This point touches on the perpetuity of the Sabbath and begins to answer the question about whether the Christian church should continue to observe the Sabbath. The answer lies in recalling some of the points already made about the Sabbath Day.

The church is to observe the Christian Sabbath today because:

1. The Sabbath Is Protological.

In the beginning God made protological space and time, and neither has changed. We live in the same physical theatre of the heavens and the earth that God created in the beginning, in which he is worshipped by angels above and creatures below. And we still live in the same temporal framework of the cyclical seven-day week with the Sabbath as a sanctified day of observance in that week. In this regard, the Sabbath remains. After all, it is a creational ordinance not a ceremonial ordinance. Through Moses, God tells Israel to "*Remember* the Sabbath" (Exod. 20:8), and then points them back to the creation of the world and the first Sabbath. He does not tell them to "*Keep* the Sabbath," and then points them to the creation of the tabernacle. The creational law precedes the ceremonial law. Of course, within the theocracy of Israel, the Sabbath takes on a certain ceremonial garb in a specific culture at a particular time in history. But the Sabbath is not itself a ceremonial ordinance; it is first and foremost a creational ordinance, and thus carries abiding significance.

2. The Sabbath Is Typological and Eschatological.

As Hebrews 4:9–10 indicates, the Sabbath serves as a type of a reality yet to come. If that reality has not yet come—which the writer of Hebrews says is the case—then the type remains; and if the type remains, then so too does its observance. The type only becomes obsolete when the anti-type has *fully* dawned. In the case of the Sabbath, as a type, it still awaits its complete fulfillment in the eternal rest of the new heavens and the new earth. The typological has not yet given way to the *fully* eschatological. There *yet remains* a type to be observed for the people of God, but with a difference. This brings us to the final reason why the Sabbath is still to be observed.

3. The Sabbath Is Redemptive-Historical and Christological.

As already noted, redemptive history plays out in the theatre of the heavens and the earth as created protological space, and within the framework of the cyclical seven-day week with a climactic Sabbath as created protological time. However, with the epoch-defining events of Christ's death, burial, and resurrection, a change occurs to the Sabbath. Jesus sleeps through the Sabbath in his burial, rising the next day—the first day of a new week— and so makes the first (old) age of the world obsolete while at the same time inaugurating a second (new) age of the world. In doing so, Christ changes the Sabbath Day from the last day of the week (under the old age) to the first day of the week (under the new age).

This Christological shift in the Sabbath is seen in how the church is formed and gathered in the New Testament. The New Testament church is formed on the Day of Pentecost, a Sunday— the first day of the week in the second (new) age of the world. It is fifty days from the Passover Sabbath—the last day of the first (old) age of the world. After Pentecost Sunday, the church continues to gather on the first day of the week. In the book of Acts and the Pauline epistles, Christians are said to meet on the first day of the week (Acts 2:1; 20:7; 1 Cor. 16:1–2); in Revelation, John receives his vision on the Lord's Day (Rev. 1:10).[44] In other words, with a new age of the world comes a change to the day of observance within

---

44. Matthew Henry rightly observes that "the first day of the week is (I think) the only day of the week, or month, or year, that is ever mentioned by number in all the New Testament—and this is several times spoken of as a day religiously observed"; *Matthew Henry's Commentary on the Whole Bible: Complete and Unabridged in One Volume* (Peabody: Hendrickson, 1994), 2052.

protological time. The day of rest and worship is no longer the last day of the week but now the first day of the week. The Sabbath Day is now the Lord's Day.

The History of the World

In closing, we return to the quote by Francis Schaeffer with which this chapter began: "Space and time are like warp and woof. Their interwoven relationship is history." Understanding what history is, the warp and woof of holy space and holy time under the providence of a holy God, helps us to grasp the significance of our weekly worship. When we gather as a church each Lord's Day in a bounded holy space on earth to worship God, along with saints and angels in the bounded holy space of heaven, we are making history. Indeed, we are proclaiming to the world that one day all history will be church history,[45] and it is time people got on the right side of history. For this is what the history of the world is about: *a holy God in his holy space of the heavens and the earth, being worshipped by angels above and creatures below, as he brings his creation into his holy time of Sabbath rest.*

If this is so, then let us come and worship God on his appointed day.

> God is in his temple,
> the Almighty Father;
> round his footstool let us gather;
> him with adoration,
> serve the Lord Most Holy
> who has mercy on the lowly;
> let us raise
> hymns of praise
> beyond mortal telling:
> God is in his temple!
>
> Christ comes to his temple,
> we, his word receiving,

---

45. I am borrowing this comment from my brother, David Gibson.

are made happy in believing;
lo! from sin delivered
he has turned our sadness,
our deep gloom to light and gladness;
let us raise
hymns of praise,
for our bonds are severed:
Christ comes to his temple.

Come and claim your temple,
gracious Holy Spirit;
in our hearts your home inherit;
make in us your dwelling,
your high work fulfilling,
into ours your will instilling,
till we raise
hymns of praise
beyond mortal telling,
in th'eternal temple.

(Gerhardt Tersteegen[46])

---

46. Gerhardt Tersteegen, 'God is in His Temple' (Hymnary.org, accessed 6/21/2023).

3

Rhythms of Rest & Work
in the Ministries of
Douglas F. Kelly & William Still

Alex Mark

In my first encounter with Douglas Kelly in 2003, I was a relatively new Christian and he was a giant of the faith. Doing my best to impress him, I sought to assert how much I knew about Reformed theology. He did his best not to laugh at me.

Instead, he decided to laugh at himself as he told me the story of when he first returned to his hometown of Lumberton, North Carolina, after receiving his PhD from the University of Edinburgh in 1973. Walking down the street, he heard two men speaking: "There's that Kelly boy. Did you hear he's a doctor now?" "Yeah, I heard, but he's not the kind that helps people."

How could a man who takes God so seriously, who has accomplished so much, who is so revered in so many spheres of academia, not take himself too seriously? Over the next two decades of walking alongside him, I saw the answer: he was a man whose soul was at rest in the sufficiency of his God, and the last five decades of ministry are the fruit of that rest.

Created For Rest and Work

It may sound strange to most of us today that work is the fruit of rest, but it is profoundly biblical. God created Adam with an extraordinary job description: tend and keep the earth. And yet it is significant that Adam was created on the sixth day, meaning that Adam's first full day on earth, before he would undertake his duties, was a day of rest. Like a tourist taking in the wonders of a new city, Adam's first full day was spent thinking deeply about his God, so that his heart could be calibrated to the true north of his Heavenly Father's glory. All work would flow from that rest, upward to the glory of God.

But the evil one, jealous of God's glory, despised Adam's rest in God. Tempting Adam to question God's trustworthiness, the serpent set a trap and the man stepped in. The result was not equality with God as the serpent promised, but rather a lifetime of seeking to be his own savior, while also knowing at the deepest level he was radically unfit for that job. In an instant, work lost its transcendence and rest became an impossibility.

For this reason, most people tend to see work and rest as polar opposites, equating work with virtue and rest with laziness. Yet biblically speaking, work and rest are not opposites; they are rhythmic complements which glorify God and bless us when they are in proper balance. We were created so that our rest fuels our work, our work builds in us a healthy capacity for rest, and both are vital aspects of our worship of God.

If work is not the opposite of rest, then what is? The opposite of rest is restlessness. With the entry of sin into the world, our first parents (and all their posterity) experienced a deep sense of inadequacy and spiritual nakedness so acute that they hid themselves with fig leaves. But the makeshift coverings only heightened their workload as continual work was now needed to keep themselves hidden. The serpent's deception interjected into God's world a new rhythm: work, work, work, yet the only payment he could give was ongoing restlessness.

The effects are clear today: our workaholism, born of a tendency to seek meaning and security through the labors of our hands, all testify not to the busyness of our schedules, but the restlessness of our hearts. So much of what we call work today is really an expression of that restlessness—a desire to create identity, to find security, and to prove our sufficiency rather than resting in the sufficiency of who God is.

If rest would ever come for man's weary soul, it must come from God Himself.

Definition of Rest

In 2010, I enrolled at Reformed Theological Seminary in Charlotte, North Carolina, in order to study with Dr. Kelly. It was an extraordinary experience to study with world-class pastor-scholars and prepare for ministry. It was also an exhausting experience as I spread myself too thin with courseload, work as Dr. Kelly's teaching assistant, an internship at a local church, and pulpit supply at my home church, all on top of personal and family obligations. I already knew my diagnosis: I needed rest, and it always seemed just a semester away.

I was in my second year of seminary when Dr. Kelly introduced me to William Still's fascinating work *Rhythms of Rest and Work*. Dr. Kelly sat under Mr. Still's ministry at Gilcomston South Church in Aberdeen, and the two remained friends until Mr. Still went to be with the Lord in 1997. Not only were the two men kindred souls in their love for God, but also in their understanding of the rhythms of rest and work that God had built into His creation, which exist both for our good and His glory.

Mr. Still's words resonated with me:

> The fundamental need of humanity is rest, in the sense that man needs to submit himself to God, in order that the divine life may be poured progressively into every part of his being. This is negative in as much as it requires man to cease from himself, that the Almighty may fill him with life-giving grace, but it is replete with the positive and vibrant blessings of God and will last to all eternity.[1]

---

1. William Still, *Collected Writings of William Still: Studies in the Christian Life*, Vol 2, ed. Sinclair B. Ferguson (Edinburgh: Rutherford House Books, 1994), 295.

He was right: the only cure for human restlessness is to rest in the sufficiency of divine grace. While physical rest is certainly a necessity and one that Scripture does address, we can never get enough physical rest to calm the restlessness of the human soul as we navigate life in a sin-cursed word. The soul must come to rest securely in God, or as St. Augustine famously said, "You have made us for Yourself, and our hearts are restless till they find their rest in Thee."[2]

And mercifully, what our souls crave, our God provides. He commands us to "Be still before the Lord and wait patiently for Him" (Ps. 37:7). He bids us to come, all who are weary, and find rest for our souls (Matt. 11:28–30). He alone can provide rest, for He alone is, in Himself, perfectly at rest. To quote Mr. Still again, "When infinite intelligence finds infinite perfections in itself, infinite stability and integrity of character are assured. This integrity is simply another name for God's righteousness, or rightness."[3]

Rhythms of Rest and Work

Our need of rest is not unanticipated by God, and thus rest is woven into creation's design.

For six days, God worked. He created the Heavens and the earth. The dynamic power of God's creative activity is immeasurable by the human mind as He commanded the stars, the moon, every beast of the field, into existence that each might take its place on the stage of creation.

And at the end of those days, He rested. The significance of this is extraordinary: it is not that God was tired from His activity and needed respite; God was establishing in the created order a rhythm of work and rest, rest and work. Mr. Still says, "God intended the divine experience to be applied to man ... it was as blessed for man as it has been blessed for God Himself."[4]

---

2. Augustine, *Confessions*, 1.1.1.

3. Still, *Collected Writings of William Still* 2, 297.

4. Ibid., 300.

This rhythm extended to the entire created order: periods of rest for the land and soil (Exod. 23:10, 11; Lev. 26:34, 35) and rest for the animals (Exod. 20:10). Periods of darkness were given for rest, and periods of light for work. Seasons for planting and seasons for harvesting. The Noahic covenant reinforced that such seasonal patterns will last as long as the earth (Gen. 8:22).

None of this is mere coincidence, but a parable of God's care to ensure our rest. Dr. Kelly explains: "In God himself, in whose image we are created, we see a pattern that is in some manner to be repeated in us. We saw that He created the world in six days, and then He entered into his rest." He continues, "We are supposed to work and we are supposed to rest. There's a rhythm in life ... harmony in the natural world, the morning and the evening, the four seasons of the year."[5]

"Six Days You Shall Do All Your Work"

There is no question that Mr. Still's ideas were deeply ingrained into Dr. Kelly's soul, as this idea of rhythmic work and rest pervade several of Dr. Kelly's writings. His volume on *Creation and Change* reflects recognition of these rhythms, as does his *Deuteronomy: A Mentor Expository Commentary*. For the narrow purpose for which this chapter was written, my primary resource was a series of sermons preached on the law at First Presbyterian Church of Dillon, South Carolina, in the spring of 1975.

In his sermon on the fourth commandment, Dr. Kelly begins by emphasizing the work aspect of Exodus 20:9, "In six days you shall do all your work." Ever the diligent worker himself, Kelly states, "... there is a deep need in us to be creative, to produce, to turn out something useful and fruitful—to work!"[6]

This is not a call to drudgery, but rather a call to worshipful productivity. God has entrusted each of us with unique gifts and talents, and has afforded to us the time to steward those gifts to His glory. Yet the fourth commandment also makes clear that He

---

5. Douglas F. Kelly, *The Law* (Dillon: First Presbyterian Church, 1975), 86.
6. Ibid., 87.

has not given us more work than what we can accomplish in six days. He does not desire to make work a burden, but rather a joy. What a vital principle for 21st century Westerners: God has not assigned to us more duties in a week than can be accomplished in a six-day span, so that we might have one day in seven for rest.

"The Seventh Day is a Sabbath to the Lord Your God"

God's creative activity in Genesis concludes with Him taking a Sabbath: "And on the seventh day God finished his work that he had done, and he rested on the seventh day from all his work that he had done. So God blessed the seventh day and made it holy, because on it God rested from all his work that he had done in creation" (Gen. 2:1–3). Almighty God, who neither slumbers nor sleeps (Ps. 121:4), chose to rest after His work of creation. He did so, not out of necessity (for God needs nothing outside of Himself) but in order to mark creation's completeness (seven days) and to enjoy the satisfaction of His creative work.

God's *Sabbath* was not a one-time event, but rather a creation ordinance, woven into the fabric of God's world. The fourth commandment not only requires that we follow this work-rest rhythm but also gives us the rationale: "For in six days the LORD made heaven and earth, the sea, and all that is in them, and rested on the seventh day. Therefore the LORD blessed the Sabbath day and made it holy" (Exod. 20:11). God's pattern established creation's rhythm.

Just as God had surveyed the creation and rested satisfied in it, the Sabbath was set apart for man to rest satisfied in God. What a gift: a day to set aside all the labors of other days, and to be reminded of the truths of the nature and character of God! Dr. Kelly says that the Sabbath is, "a very positive commandment. It's intended for our good, for our blessing, for our joy, for a well-regulated and harmonious personal life and life relationships, and life in business."[7] It is no surprise then that Scripture exhorts us to call the Sabbath a delight (Isa. 58:13).

---

7. Ibid., 85.

Perhaps no people throughout history understood the necessity of the Sabbath better than the Israelites after more than 400 years in Egyptian slavery. After Joseph and his brothers settled in Egypt, the land was increasingly being filled with Israelites who had been fruitful and multiplied, echoing God's command (Gen. 1:28; 9:1) as well as his promise to Abraham and his chosen descendants (Gen. 17:6; 35:11; 47:27). As long as Pharaoh knew who Joseph was, the Israelites had permission to live freely in the land and to work it. But when a new king of Egypt arose who did not know Joseph (Exod. 1:8), he saw the people who had once saved his nation now as a threat to national security, and he established a harsh form of chattel slavery. Ruthless taskmasters heaped upon them two awful burdens: first, they must make bricks without straw (Exod. 5:10), and second, they did not have a day off. Scripture is descriptive about their experience in Egyptian slavery: their lives were "bitter" (Exod. 1:14), with "hard" (Exod. 1:14; 6:9) service resulting in "misery" and "suffering" (Exod. 3:7) and a "broken spirit" (Exod. 6:9).

Following such a miserable existence in Egypt, one can hardly imagine the joy of hearing that their new King, Yahweh, would actually require that they rest for one full day out of every seven! It was to be a vacation every single week, and more importantly, a regular reminder that the yoke of slavery had been broken.

Kelly beautifully summarizes the gift of Sabbath rest, saying, "There's nothing more beautiful, nothing more healing, nothing that will do more for family life or for an upset personality, than to observe, reverentially and respectfully, the Sabbath Day; and to let God bless you in his own special way on that day."[8]

No Rest for the Weary

If such a rhythm is baked into creation, why do most of us find ourselves so unhealthily busy? Let us return to our distinction between rest and restlessness: just as Adam and Eve were restless in their hiding and search for security and identity, so too are we. Instead of seeking these things from our Creator, we seek them

---

8. Ibid., 89.

in the creation, thereby upsetting the very rhythm by which we could otherwise find these things our souls crave.

This is why in our contemporary culture, perhaps more than in any other in history, work has become the means to secure those things. Carl Trueman addresses this difficulty well in his excellent *The Rise and Triumph of the Modern Self*: "Is job satisfaction to be found in the fact that it enables me to feed and clothe my family? Or is it to be found in the fact that the very actions involved in my work bring me a sense of inner psychological well-being?"[9]

As a result, who I am is defined by what I do. And because there is always more to do, rest seems only to get in the way. From this perspective, work is all-consuming, and rest is burdensome.

Such an attitude is deeply theological. David Murray notes several errors that we communicate when we refuse to rest as God has ordained to us:

> I don't respect how my Creator has made me. I am strong enough to cope without God's gift of sufficient daily sleep and a weekly Sabbath. I refuse to accept my creaturely limitations and bodily needs. I see myself more as a self-sufficient machine than a God-dependent creature ... I don't trust God with my work, my church, or my family. Sure, I believe God is sovereign, but he needs all the help I can give him. If I don't do the work, who will? Although Christ has promised to build his church, who's doing the night shift?[10]

Who among us cannot relate to that? Yet so often we acknowledge it like the man of James 1 who looks in the mirror and sees his face, but then walks away, forgetting what he looks like.

Mr. Still comments with surgical precision:

> The beginning of the secret of how to rest and relax is, of course, in one's attitude, and it may very well be that this is not only a psychological but

---

9. Carl R. Trueman, *The Rise and Triumph of the Modern Self: Cultural Amnesia, Expressive Individualism, and the Road to Sexual Revolution* (Wheaton: Crossway, 2020), 23.

10. David Murray, "There Are Souls to Be Saved: How Can We Rest?" 9Marks, accessed February 14, 2023, https://www.9marks.org/article/there-are-souls-to-be-saved-how-can-we-rest/.

spiritual matter. Satan's work in the human heart is largely wrought by a kind of restlessness, and therefore, the beginning of real salvation here must embody a flat contradiction of the necessity of continual activity ... Once we see that, the battle is half won. It may be that to achieve so much involves admitting with tears of sorrow that we have been too proud to admit we needed rest.[11]

"It Is Finished!"

But how can we rest from our labors when the work is never done? By resting in the One who fulfilled all that was required of us (Gal. 4:4). When the Lord Jesus hung upon the cross, His final cry was *tetélestai* ("it is finished!"), pronouncing that not only was His work finished, but so too was all that God had required of us for salvation. Without the finished work of Christ, peace is an impossibility; through Christ, peace with God is an objective reality.

In Christ crucified and risen, our souls are able to experience true rest, and the Sabbath transforms in our eyes from burden to blessing. This transformation is marked by the transition from the Sabbath coming at the end of the week to now coming on the first day of the week. Following the resurrection on the first day of the week (Matt. 28:1, Mark 16:2, Luke 24:1; John 20:1), the Church made it her rhythm to worship on the first day as well (Acts 20:7; 1 Cor. 16:1–2).

Rather than the old rhythm of working for six days and then finally receiving rest, the New Covenant brings rest first, followed by six days of work. Like the Israelites who were to be reminded every week of how they had been liberated, the New Covenant Sabbath gives us rest first, reminding us that, indeed, "It is finished." Every week begins with the poignant reminder that we can set aside one day to do no work, and yet we are still utterly loved and accepted by God.

Mr. Still called this "a clear and sweet parable of the Gospel, in which restless sinners are able to rest from their own

---

11. Still, *Collected Writings of William Still* 2, 313.

ineffectual labours in the effectual and fruitful redeeming work of God in Christ."[12]

Sinclair Ferguson, another disciple of Mr. Still, says that the Christian

> was called to live on the basis of a day when he could reflect on God's creation, God's goodness, store his mind with reflections on who God is and how great He is, and then work through the rest of the week on that basis. And that rhythm is really very important. We need that space to have our minds decluttered and to have our minds filled with the truth of God's Word. It's the day when our whole beings are intended to be recalibrated into this weekly rhythm of rest and work and rest and work.[13]

Rest and Sanctification

In one of His many engagements with Pharisees concerning right use of the Sabbath, our Lord set before us one overarching principle: "The Sabbath was made for man, not man for the Sabbath" (Mark 2:27). The Sabbath is for man's good, and what higher good does man have in this world than to grow in sanctification and in the enjoyment of God?

Yet such growth does not happen spontaneously. Mr. Still points out that while Christian conversion is instantaneous (like an earthquake), God has ordained sanctification to be by growth (slowly, requiring the right care and nurture before a harvest is reaped).[14] Sanctification is a process of growth, whereby we learn to do natural things spiritually, and spiritual things naturally.

What is the key to this process? According to both Still and Kelly, it is the product of deliberate, holy rest and contemplation of the glory of God in the face of Jesus Christ.

Mr. Still beautifully explains this truth:

---

12. Ibid., 300.

13. Sinclair Ferguson, "Sabbath Rest," Ligonier Ministries, accessed February 14, 2023, https://www.ligonier.org/learn/articles/sabbath-rest.

14. Still, *Collected Writings of William Still* 2, 326.

So great and luxuriant are the fruits of the grace of justification flowing from God's peace with us, that entrance into them has the effect of transforming our character (see 2 Cor. 3:18).[15]

To be clear, there have been many throughout history who have outwardly observed the Sabbath but have never experienced the wondrous contemplation of the face of Christ. The Pharisees were a perfect example: at least on one occasion, they spent the Sabbath plotting how to kill Christ (Matt. 12:14)! Regardless, *abusus non tollit usum*: abuse is no argument against proper use. The Sabbath is objectively a blessing to the Christian soul.

Rest Enables Us to Get More Done

One principle of rest and work that Still and Kelly both helpfully emphasize is that intentional, diligent rest actually helps us to get more done. Mr. Still says,

> To expect the delicate and sensitive human frame and mechanism to maintain constant efficiency from early morning to late at night without any definite relaxation of tension during so many hours is, it seems to me, unreasonable, and explains why we often behave badly, and act inefficiently.[16]

Dr. Kelly emphasized extensively the return on investment that we receive in Sabbath keeping:

> ... the investment that you can get from giving one day in seven to God is absolutely fantastic—it is so high and so rich and so rewarding. How much better your work goes those other six days! Oh, the blessings, the return that you get from giving God what is already his—one day in seven![17]

Both are quite right: How frequently do worry, angst, people-pleasing, and the tyranny of the urgent sap us of the very energies God has given us for the tasks to which He has called us? In a sense, working without first resting our souls in Christ is like riding a bicycle but peddling in different directions: expending much energy but getting nowhere.

---

15. Ibid., 305.
16. Ibid.
17. Kelly, *The Law*, 96.

Mr. Still stresses the importance of this rhythm for enduring faithfulness: "We therefore see that the idea of resting in God is part of a total attitude, which includes the recognition that as finite creatures we are absolutely dependent upon him—as for our creation, so for our survival and well-being."[18]

Rhythms of Rest and Work for the Busy Pastor

I suspect that many who will read this work will be among the thousands of pastors who have been impacted by Dr. Kelly during more than a half-century of ministry. We cannot help but admire a man who has remained diligent, clear of scandal, productive, and joyful for over half a century in one of the world's hardest professions.

For most of us, resting doesn't come naturally. We hear the exhortation in Hebrews to "strive to enter the rest" (Heb. 4:11) and we think "sure—once I get through with this Sunday evening's sermon, my visitation list, and prepping for this week's Session meeting!"

Sadly, rest seems like a pipe dream to most of us unless it is providentially forced upon us. Wayne Muller notes in his book on *Finding Rest, Renewal, and Delight in our Busy Lives*, "If we do not allow for a rhythm of rest in our overly busy lives, illness becomes our Sabbath—our pneumonia, our cancer, our heart attack, our accidents create Sabbath for us."[19]

Sometimes, the thing that makes our job so difficult is our own stubborn refusal to rest, and it is no wonder that so many pastors face burnout. Yet I can testify that as he continues to labor diligently, Dr. Kelly's zeal for Gospel ministry has not waned one bit.

In many ways, the secret is his commitment to rest and work. As an observer of Dr. Kelly's life for the last two decades, I've seen

---

18. Still, *Collected Writings of William Still* 2, 301.

19. Wayne Muller, *Sabbath: Finding Rest, Renewal, and Delight in Our Busy Lives*, 1st edition (New York: Random House Publishing Group, 2000), 10.

four particular components to his longevity and productivity that are vital for pastors to understand and practice:

First, pastors must prioritize time with the Lord in Bible reading and prayer. Regardless of where he is, what conference he is speaking at, or what other projects loom over his head, he always guards a substantial portion of his time to read the Bible. He describes the profound effect that our own reading can have on us as individuals: "to understand the message of the Word of God is indeed to let loose forces in our lives as powerful as a lion."[20]

Speaking with frankness, Kelly says "There is no reason why most Christians cannot read through the Bible once every year."[21] Yet with great pastoral tenderness, he recognizes that the Bible can be intimidating and thus recommends following a reading plan, which has been his pattern nearly his whole life. Believing that "Christ speaks to us in all parts of His Word," he uses a plan that ensures a varied diet from different parts of Scripture.[22]

Likewise with prayer, Dr. Kelly advocates for a structured system of planned prayer. He begins with a time of praise, which he follows with a time of waiting and being still before the Lord (Ps. 62). Following this comes confession, during which he exhorts us to be very honest and specific about our sins, that we might see how odious they are and turn from them. Next, he urges a time of applying Scripture in prayer, reminding us "God loves His Word, and when you turn His Word into prayer, He is hearing His own voice, and that voice will have a good reception in Heaven above!"[23] Next comes a time of watching, during which he considers the affairs of our world in light of the spiritual battle being waged, and then storms the gates of heaven for those issues. He continues in a time of intercession, in which he again urges specificity through use of a prayer list. Finally,

---

20. Douglas F. Kelly, *If God Already Knows, Why Pray?* (Nashville: Wolgemuth & Hyatt Publishers, 1989), 193.

21. Ibid., 193.

22. Ibid., 193–194.

23. Ibid., 209.

he concludes the time with thanksgiving, acknowledging God's mercies with specificity.

Sometimes today, Christians are concerned that such a structured rhythm of daily reading and prayer could lend itself toward legalism. This has produced in many believers such a fear of legalism that they do not engage in regular time in the Word or prayer. Yet such fear is unnecessary, as Dr. Kelly reminds us that the goal of this is not self-justification but rather "to keep in the front of our minds a vision of who God is."[24] When we are able to do that, much like the Sabbath, the work of daily Bible reading and prayer returns an investment substantially greater than what it cost us: "your perspective on life begins to change. Days no longer slip by without a thought of Jesus. You begin to pray when matters get hard to handle, instead of complaining, and you begin to recognize the hand of God at work when things do change. Praise wells up in your heart as you become increasingly alert to His blessings."[25]

Second, we must commit ourselves to the mortification of sin. Just as the disobedience of the Israelites kept them from the enjoyment of rest in the Promised Land, sin always disrupts our rest. Certainly, the consequences of sin are disruptive, but there is more to it: we cannot possibly keep our hearts and minds still upon Christ while at the same time following the devil's temptations toward disobedience. Sin always encourages restlessness unless we put it to death.

I remember one particular conversation in which we were discussing heartbreaking news of a pastor who had tragically fallen from the ministry due to moral failure. Dr. Kelly's words were simple but powerful: "Alex, you will always be presented with temptation. You must kill it. Kill it!" I did not realize at the time that he was paraphrasing John Owen but, more importantly, I was receiving advice more precious than gold on an essential aspect of longevity in ministry.

---

24. Ibid., 195.
25. Ibid., 196.

A third pattern I saw in years of watching Dr. Kelly was to resist the temptation to make a name for himself. In my three years as his teaching assistant, Dr. Kelly received countless invitations to speak, to preach, and to write, many of which came from prestigious ministries and organizations. To be in such high demand would tempt any of us to think more highly of ourselves than we ought.

Despite nearly endless opportunities for self-aggrandizement, I did not once discern that Dr. Kelly's goal in ministry was to inflate his own ego. It doesn't mean that he didn't face that temptation, but rather than letting it take root in his heart, he confessed it before the Lord and put it to death.

How can we likewise resist such a temptation? We must be at rest in Christ as our sufficiency so that we do not sense a need to seek glory for ourselves.

During the time that I have known Dr. Kelly, he has spoken at many of those prestigious events to crowds of thousands. I have also enjoyed the fruits of his weekly ministry at Reedy Creek Presbyterian Church, a small, wonderful church in rural Minturn, South Carolina, where a dozen people in worship feels like a packed house. Astoundingly to me, he prepares the same for either group, for he understands that the goal is not to impress anyone with himself, but to please the Lord Christ through faithful ministry.

A final reason he has been so effective for so long is that he knows his calling. Far from the common vision of pastors today that more resembles a CEO than a shepherd, Dr. Kelly understands that his primary calling among the people of God "is to feed the flock by leading them to green pastures."[26]

For those of us who are called to the ministry of the Word, so often we are distracted from that chief obligation by a million other lesser duties, many of which are good in themselves. At times, we compound our duties out of fear of telling others

---

26. William Still, *The Work of the Pastor*, Revised (Geanies House: Christian Focus Publications, 2010), 17.

"no" or we wear ourselves out with stress about a whole world of issues that are not central to our calling.

I can remember Dr. Kelly often lamenting that so many pastors today were so occupied with secondary obligations that they were "too busy" for things like morning and evening worship, midweek prayer meeting, and so on. During more than one of our phone calls when I began planting the church I currently pastor, he would ask the question, "Do you have a midweek prayer meeting yet? The saints must gather to pray!" I am deeply thankful that now, in great part due to his influence, we do.

I think that every pastor would profit from the words of another giant of our time, Dale Ralph Davis:

> The "busy pastor" obviously doesn't have time to ponder or think or read (or listen), because he is, well, a "busy pastor." Believe me, I know something of the load a pastor carries. But I repudiate the busy-pastor model. I don't think there should be any busy pastors. Ministerial busyness may fulfill our egos, but it empties the soul. Many of us need to join Mary at Jesus' feet if we are to be equipped for our labor.[27]

We must know our own capacities and callings, and rather than trying to do everything, we must slow down and focus on the main thing: ministering the Word and prayer.

Rest-Powered Pastoral Ministry

For those of us who have been in ministry for more than a year or two, undoubtedly we have developed bad habits and misplaced priorities. It takes work to break our bad patterns in order to get into rhythm, but consider the benefits that healthy rhythms of rest and work bring to the faithful pastor:

Perseverance in Prayer

Every pastor has likely heard the account of Luther, who once said "I have so much to do today that I'm going to need to spend

---

27. Dale Ralph Davis, *Luke 1–13: The Year of the Lord's Favor* (Geanies House: Christian Focus Publications, 2021), 192.

three hours in prayer in order to be able to get it all done."[28] We appreciate the sentiment, but so few of us can live by that saying because we're too busy. And if we're totally honest, we tend to think we can accomplish more with our hands than with our prayers, and thus we do not slow down enough to pray with perseverance.

Perhaps that is the reason we don't have more answered prayers: because we can't slow down enough to *really* pray. Dr. Kelly exhorts us that persevering prayer must be part of every believer's life: "Just as the peasant farmer has to take his ten thousand steps to sow his tens of thousands of seeds, each one a part of the preparation for the final harvest, so there is a need for often repeated persevering prayer, all working out some desired blessing."[29]

Passionate Preaching

For most of us, especially pastors who have multiple preaching and teaching obligations during a week, we can at times become more like sermon factories than men who have meditated on and marinated in God's Word before we preach it to His people. As a result, our sermons will often become superficial, because we do not have (or make) time to slow down and think deeply about God.

Proper rhythms of rest and work shut down the sermon factory, and instead allow us to follow the sort of preaching Mr. Still spoke of: "The preaching of the Word of God, when it flows through a living vessel dedicated utterly to the Master's use, is not only an event in the lives of those who hear it but becomes, first, a decisive act, and then, necessary food for their souls."[30]

---

28. Kazlitt Arvine, *Cyclopedia of Moral and Religious Anecdotes* (Charleston: Nabu Press, 2010), 303.

29. Kelly, *If God Already Knows, Why Pray?*, 163.

30. Still, *The Work of the Pastor*, 27.

Patience with Problem People

There are many professions in which hurrying to get the work done can be admirable. Assembly line workers, for example, will be rewarded for how much they can produce in a short amount of time.

In pastoral ministry, such a mindset can be detrimental because we are not manufacturing products; we are in the "business" of, by the grace of God, "warning and teaching everyone with all wisdom, that we may present everyone mature in Christ" (Col. 1:28). There are no shortcuts or hacks, and we must resist the temptation to see quick results when dealing with the souls of those whom God has entrusted to us. Mr. Still points out that right rhythms of work and rest help us to have "good-natured tolerance," "waiting with buoyant good humour and expectancy to see babes grow up into God's salvation (1 Pet. 2:2) and as living stones into Christ's church (1 Pet. 2:5) as a spiritual house."[31]

In 2012, Dr. Kelly led a group of seminary students through an extra-curricular study of Mr. Still's *The Work of the Pastor*. Of all the wonderful lessons of that book, Dr. Kelly particularly sought to ingrain in us the holiness of our calling as we work with God's people:

> God has caused you to become pastor to some souls here who are as valuable to Him as any in the world—your quiet persistence will be a sign that you believe God has a purpose of grace for this people, and that this purpose of grace will be promoted, not by gimmicks, or stunts, or new ideas, but by the Word of God released in preaching by prayer.[32]

Peace with the Outcome of Ministry

The expectations upon pastors are weighty, but of all the stresses we face, the greatest comes from within: we think we're far more important than we are. As we practice a healthy rhythm of rest

---

31. Still, *Collected Writings of William Still* 2, 326.

32. William Still, *The Work of the Pastor* (Geanies House: Christian Focus, 2010), chap. 1, Kindle.

and work, we experience the regular reminder that there is one God, and He can handle things quite well without me. Mr. Still poignantly says, "The fact that God will look after the world while you take a little time should give you a sense of real relief!"[33]

Such a disposition will not only build stamina for ministry, but it will make ministry infinitely more effective, because the in-rhythm minister understands he is but a tool, and God is the Master Craftsman.

Longing for the Future Sabbath

No discussion of Dr. Kelly's understanding and practice of "Rhythms of Rest and Work" would be complete without a glimpse into the future, final rest that believers eagerly await (Phil. 3:20). While we will never fully experience complete and perfect rest in this world, the day is coming in which we will. Today's Sabbaths are but a foretaste of that "final, perfect consummation of all the purposes of God in and through His creation, which has been washed clean through the blood of the Lamb (Rev. 5:9) for whose pleasure all things are and were created (Rev. 4:11)."[34]

I wish to conclude this chapter in the same way that Dr. Kelly concluded several of his own treatments of this topic: with an extended, wonderfully galvanizing quote by Robert Murray M'Cheyne.

> It is a type of heaven when a believer lays aside his pen or loom, brushes aside his worldly cares, leaving them behind him with his weekday clothes, and comes up to the house of God. It is like the morning of the resurrection, the day when we shall come out of great tribulation into the presence of God and the lamb, when the believer sits under the preached Word and hears the voice of the Shepherd leading and feeding his soul.
>
> It reminds him of the day when the Lamb that is in the midst of the Throne shall feed him, and lead him to living fountains of water. When he joins in the psalm of praise, it reminds him of the day when his hands shall strike

---

33. Still, *Collected Writings of William Still* 2, 314.
34. Douglas F. Kelly, *Creation And Change: Genesis 1:1–2:4 in the Light of Changing Scientific Paradigms,* Revised edition (Geanies House: Mentor, 2017), 336.

the harp of God, 'where congregations ne'er break up and Sabbaths have no end.' When he retires and meets with God in secret in his closet, or like Isaac in some favourite spot near his dwelling, it reminds him of the day when he shall be a pillar in the house of our God and go out no more.

This is the reason we love the Lord's Day. This is the reason we call the Sabbath a delight. A well spent Sabbath we feel a day of heaven upon earth. For this reason we wish our Sabbaths to be wholly given to God. We love to spend the whole time in the public and private exercises of God's worship except so much as is taken up in works of necessity and mercy. We love to rise early on that morning and to sit up late, that we may have a long day with God.[35]

Come quickly, Lord Jesus!

---

35. Andrew A Bonar, *Memoir and Remains of Robert Murray M'Cheyne* (Edinburgh; Carlisle: Banner of Truth Trust, 1995), 539.

Part 2:

Models for the Next Generation
of Pastor-Theologians

4

The "Passive Activity" of the Godward Life:

The Grace of Christ and Spiritual Progress in Athanasius of Alexandria

D. Blair Smith

Let us offer to the Lord every virtue, and that true holiness which is in Him, and in piety let us keep the feast to Him with those things which He has hallowed for us.

Athanasius of Alexandria, *Festal Letter V*

Introduction

DOUGLAS Kelly was my first teacher in theology. I caught his infectious love for the Church Fathers and their approach to theology, a love that has burned all the way through Master of Theology and Doctor of Philosophy degrees focused on the classical theology of the Fathers. I now have the astounding privilege of teaching classes once taught by Dr. Kelly at Reformed Theological

Seminary, Charlotte, where, I pray, I carry forward even a mere spark of the torch he shone on God and all things in relation to God at the seminary. The light of that torch came fundamentally from holy Scripture, yet in Kelly's hands was refracted through the doxological theology of the Fathers. This refraction was, yes, through the good professor's teachings in the classroom, but also—and maybe most persuasively—through his life.

Dr. Kelly has appropriated the spirit of the Fathers. This appropriation can be seen in his approach to theology, expressed well by the great fourth-century Father, Hilary of Poitiers, who taught that the knowledge of God must be pursued in pious humility. The form of knowledge that is appropriate to God, he writes, is according to "devotion."[1] Life and doctrine should be an intertwined pair; theology and spirituality breathe the same air. For the Fathers, as well as for Kelly, theological reflections are never disconnected from worship and a Godward life in Christ. To pray, to worship, and to do theology come from essentially the same posture.

This posture is framed by what can be called a "passive activity," which at once highlights the divine source of all spiritual vibrancy as well as the imperative for the Christian to actively appropriate that spiritual energy. The result is an upward trajectory of godliness, such that the light of Christ is more clearly seen and thus more fully able to be shared. As much as Dr. Kelly taught the Fathers, he lived this spirit of the Fathers in the very atmosphere of his life. In this chapter I will turn to one of Kelly's favorite Fathers, Athanasius of Alexandria, through a few of his underutilized writings in order to highlight the "passive activity" of a Godward life—the kind of life family, friends, colleagues, and students have observed and cherished in Douglas Floyd Kelly.

---

1. *De Trinitate* 11.44 (SC 462:372). Cf. 1.18. Using both Athanasius and Hilary, Kelly writes about the necessity for theology to be practiced in the atmosphere of prayer. See Douglas F. Kelly, *Systematic Theology, Volume One: The God Who Is: The Holy Trinity* (Geanies House: Mentor, 2008), 48–50.

Grounded in Creation

Anyone familiar with Kelly's teachings knows his concern for a proper theology of creation. Certainly, as chapters two and three of this volume show, that touches on *how* creation happened. But it also, in keeping with an overriding patristic concern, touches on the profound implications of *what* happened. Kelly's deep reading of the Fathers' theology made him keenly aware of what lay downstream from a doctrine such as creation *ex nihilo*. In this section I will briefly lay the groundwork for Athanasius's understanding of "passive activity" in a Godward life through his theology of creation.

Athanasius's first work, *Against the Heathens – On the Incarnation*[2] (hereafter either *CG* or *DI*), establishes the vision of his theology based on God's work in creation.[3] The creation, as a creation *ex nihilo*, originates in the power of God alone.[4] He is the ultimate and only Creator. A correlative is that the nature of creation is fundamentally good, since it has its origin in a good God.[5] Both of these affirmations are significant when evaluating the import of the disjunction between the Creator and creation for Athanasius's overall understanding.

First, in taking up the Creator side of things, for Athanasius it must be affirmed that creation was a work of God which took place outside of himself and, consequently, by the power of his *will*. John Meyendorff writes,

---

2. All references to this work make use of Robert W. Thompson, ed. and trans. *Contra Gentes* and *De Incarnatione* (Oxford Early Christian Texts; Oxford: Clarendon Press, 1971). Some of the research found in this chapter comes from work done for my Master of Theology thesis at Harvard University, The Divinity School, in 2007.

3. Athanasius inherits the overarching emphasis on creation and its relevance for all of his theology from Irenaeus. In particular, the significance of a sharp ontological distinction between the creator God and creation, questions of mediation between God and the world, and the immediacy of the divine persons *ad intra* and *ad extra* are retrieved by Athanasius from Irenaeus. Khaled Anatolios, "The Immediately Triune God: A Patristic Response to Schleiermacher," *Pro Ecclesia* 10/2 (2001): 168–171; John R. Meyer, "God's Trinitarian Substance in Athanasian Theology," *SJT* 59/1 (2006): 84n.14

4. *DI* 2–3.

5. *CG* 6.

For Athanasius, creation is an act of the *will* of God, and will is ontologically distinct from *nature*. By nature, the Father generates the Son – and this generation is indeed beyond time – but creation occurs through the will of God, which means that God remains absolutely free to create or not to create, and remains transcendent to the world after creating it.[6]

The nature of the creative act according to will means the creation has an entirely different nature than the Creator.[7] That difference being so, it does not mitigate the fact that the attributes of the Creator bear on his creation. That is to say, God is good and loving, so his creative act is marked by that character and his creation receives the benefits of it through his presence by his power.[8] The goodness and love of God translate into an active God who does not leave his creation alone in ruin.[9] The independence of God from his creation then is coupled in Athanasius's theology by the fact that his character governs his continual interaction with it.[10]

---

6. *Byzantine Theology: Historical Trends and Doctrinal Themes* (New York: Fordham University Press, 1974), 129 (emphasis his). The distinction between nature and will is also brought out in Georges Florovsky's article, "The Concept of Creation in St. Athanasius," *SP* IV/1 (1962): 36–57.

7. J. Rebecca Lyman makes the point that for Athanasius the stress is on the eternality of the Creator's nature, which would, of course, put God's nature in direct contrast to a nature created *ex nihilo*. *Christology and Cosmology: Models of Divine Activity in Origen, Eusebius, and Athanasius* (Oxford: Oxford University Press, 1993), 240.

8. *CG* 6; *DI* 16–17; *De Decretis* 11.

9. *Orationes contra Arianos* (hereafter *Ar.*), 2.77. Khaled Anatolios, *Athanasius: The Coherence of his Thought* (New York: Routledge, 1998), 40–41.

10. In addition to God's character marking his interaction with the creation, the actual distinction between God's external actions and internal nature serve to deepen God's loving interaction with his creation. Anatolios details how this distinction is helpful in prioritizing theology (or God's being) over economy (or God's external acts). This prioritization, though, is not simply one of two juxtaposed realms. The will by which God creates is an "essential will" and is identified with the Son as the eternal "intra-divine ground" for God's external acts. This eternal, essential will is fulfilled not in creation but in the generation of the Son from the Father. Thus, the creation is inferior to the eternal generation of the Son but it is derivative of this "divine begetting." The divine begetting is grounded in the consubstantial relationship between the Father and the Son in which they both delight. Since God's relationship with creation is derivative of the Father's generation of the Son, it is proper to speak of God's delight in the world. So, even though there is a radical ontological gulf between God and his creation, this is mitigated by both his loving and merciful character and the eternal ground for God's act

Switching to the created side of the matter, and in particular the human side, immediately there is a tension in human beings as a result of being created out of the goodness of God but also having no being to hold them in goodness within themselves and so therefore susceptible to drifting away from God into nothingness if not for God's goodness and grace.[11] (I want to be clear here that while this is Athanasius's distinct anthropology flowing from his understanding of creation *ex nihilo*, Kelly would eschew many of these elements in light of his confessionally Reformed anthropology.) The goodness of God issued in an "added grace" in creation for humanity: that of being made in God's image, which is fundamentally the image of the Son.[12] This grace allowed an original knowledge of God through "similarity" between God and human beings,[13] meaning that even though creation *ex nihilo* necessitates an entirely *active* Creator and *passive* creation, the grace instilled in a particular part of the creation, humanity, provided for receptivity and activity on the part of human beings in their original interaction with God.[14] This ability for "dialogue" was primarily through the mind (νοῦς),[15] the location within human beings where they can realize the fact that they are in God's image.[16] In humanity's original creation, then, contemplation is the primary means of communion with God and

---

of creation. Anatolios, *Athanasius*, 119–124; Anatolios, "The Immediately Triune God," 171; Peter Widdicombe, "Athanasius and the Making of the Doctrine of the Trinity," *Pro Ecclesia* 6/4 (1997): 467.

11. *DI* 4, 10, 11; *CG* 41.

12. *DI* 3; Anatolios, *Athanasius*, 55–56; Anatolios, "Athanasius's Christology Today: The Life, Death, and Resurrection of Christ in *On the Incarnation*" (unpublished paper), 13; John Behr, *Formation of Christian Theology: The Nicene Faith, Part 1* (Crestwood: St. Vladimir's Seminary Press, 2004), 188–189.

13. *CG* 2, 8, 34.

14. Anatolios, *Athanasius*, 58.

15. *DI* 3. Lyman, *Christology and Cosmology*, 141–142; Christopher Stead, "Knowledge of God in the Eusebius and Athanasius," in *The Knowledge of God in the Greco-Roman World*, ed. J. Mansfield et al (Lieden: Brill, 1989), 234; John R. Meyer, "Athanasius' Use of Paul in His Doctrine of Salvation," *VigChr* 52/2 (1998): 166.

16. Anatolios, *Athanasius*, 61; Kannengiesser, "Athanasius of Alexandria and the Foundation of Traditional Christology," *Theological Studies* 34 (1973): 109.

the fall of humanity, in addition to being the result of disobeying God's law, entails a turning away from this contemplation to an obsession with created things[17] and drifting toward "the end" of our created nature: non-being.[18] Nothing *within humanity* could curtail the slippage away from God. None but God had the power to intervene, working out of the same goodness with which he created the world in the first place.

Athanasius's dialectic between the Creator and creation provides the broad conceptual framework for the rest of his theology and even, as will be seen below, his understanding of the Christian's spiritual progress. It is proper to highlight that this dialectic is absolute and does not involve any mediating points between Creator and creation.[19] That is to say, contrary to many conceptions in his day, Athanasius's theology of creation leaves no place for any notion of a hierarchical universe where the interaction between the divine and human takes place at various points between the two.[20] The two realms are fixed and humanity is locked into the nature of its own realm unless there is some prior action on behalf of the Creator.

Thus, *activity* is the preserve of the Creator both in initial creation (as well as any re-creation), whereas *passivity* is the natural state of creation given its ontological character. Nonetheless, through the image of God humanity can engage in a Godward activity. The fall disabled this ability. In Christ, however, can the human posture of passivity also turn into a *passive activity*? Athanasius's theological writings would certainly say so as the Spirit places us in the Son so that in the Son we can live as children of God before our heavenly Father. But what does appropriating Christ in the Godward life look like in Athanasius?

---

17. *DI* 12–13.

18. *Ar.* 1.51.

19. Peter Widdicombe, *The Fatherhood of God from Origen to Athanasius*, Revised Edition (Oxford: Oxford University Press, 1994), 151.

20. Anatolios, *Athanasius*, 25; C. J. De Vogel, "Platonism and Christianity: A Mere Antagonism or a Profound Common Ground?" *VigChr* 39/1 (1985): 53.

Appropriating the Benefits of Christ in a Godward Life

Any conception of the Godward life for Athanasius starts with the incarnation itself. A main theme of his explanation of the incarnation is the Son's sanctification by the Holy Spirit on our behalf. There is a tension in Athanasius's writings between passages that speak of an immediate sanctification by the incarnation and those that speak more of sanctification dependent on individual participation.[21] Highlighting this tension is helpful in that it parses ever so slightly, without being inarticulate regarding the unity of God's actions, the work of the Son as the unique member of the Trinity who took on flesh and sanctified it, and the work of the Holy Spirit who enables individuals to appropriate the benefits won in Christ. It is by participation *in the Spirit* that we are "knit (συναπτόμεθα) into the Godhead"[22] and we share an "indwelling and intimacy (ἐνοίκησιν καὶ οἰκειότητα)" of the Spirit.[23]

This indwelling and intimacy which takes place by means of participation in the Spirit is not overtly pressed by Athanasius into practical advice in his dogmatic writings, though there are a few notable exceptions. He does speak of maintaining communion through "confession" of Jesus as the Son of God (1 John 4:15) in his *Orations against the Arians*.[24] And in *CG* and *DI*, Athanasius addresses that the moral fortitude required to be virtuous is crucial for an accurate interpretation of Scripture. This was, of course, important in the Arian debate that took up much of Athanasius's rhetorical energies, but it also was significant for all seekers of truth.[25] By modeling one's life on the saints which, for Athanasius, were found in Scripture, one could come to the truth contained in Scripture.[26] Therefore, he pointed to an interactive relationship

---

21. Frances Young, *From Nicaea to Chalcedon: A Guide to the Literature and its Background* (London: SCM, 1983), 74.

22. *Ar.* 3.24.

23. *Ar.* 1.46.

24. *Ar.* 3.24.

25. *CG* 1 and *DI* 56.

26. *DI* 57. See Anatolios, "Athanasius and the Making of the Doctrine of the Trinity," *Pro Ecclesia* 6 (2001): 461.

between the Christian's life and his or her reading of the Bible where one obtains instruction for life through observation of the saints; by imitating those lives, one can return to the Scripture with a fuller understanding of its meaning. We should press toward the Word, in particular, by "imitation", through which we become "virtuous and sons (ἐνάρετοι καὶ υἱοί)."[27] These "practical" themes intimated at in Athanasius's "doctrinal writings" are writ large in the more instructional texts to which we now turn.

In these different literary contexts we see *imitatio* carried forward as central to Athanasius's conception of appropriating the benefits won by Christ in the spiritual life. Throughout Athanasius's writings, appropriation through imitation is naturally framed in predominantly "Christocentric" terms, since the Second Person of the Trinity is the one who became human and, therefore, is the divine person able to be imitated.[28] Christ is the model Christian. If one is to live out the Christian life faithfully, *imitatio Christi* is vital as it confirms one's status as a "son." Faithful followers of Christ are worthy of emulation as well, with the goal of growing in virtue and, therefore, Christlikeness. A model of a Christ follower is provided by Athanasius in the

---

27. *Ar.* 3.19–20. Peter Brown locates the motif of imitation within the larger context of late antiquity where it was a vital element of education. "The Saint as Exemplar in Late Antiquity," in *Saints and Virtues*, ed. J. S. Hawley (Berkeley: UC Press, 1987), 3–14.

28. In *Epistle ad Marcellinum* (hereafter *Ep.Marcell.*), 13. Athanasius writes concerning the life of Christ and its service as a model and the need to appropriate it (PG 27: 24D – 25B): "Again, the same grace is from the Savior, for when he became man for us he offered his own body in dying for our sake, in order that he might set all free from death. And desiring to show us his own heavenly and well-pleasing life, he provided its type (ἐτύπωσεν) in himself, to the end that some might no more easily be deceived by the enemy, having a pledge for protection—namely, the victory he won over the devil for our sake. For this reason, indeed, he not only taught, but also accomplished what he taught, so that everyone might hear when he spoke, and seeing as in an image (ἐν εἰκόνι), receive from him the model (παράδειγμα) for acting hearing him say, 'Learn from me, for I am gentle and lowly in heart' (Mt 11:29). A more perfect instruction in virtue one could not find than that which the Lord typified (ὁ Κύριος ἐτύπωσεν) in himself ... Those legislators among the Greeks possess the grace as far as speaking goes, but the Lord, being true Lord of all and one concerned for all, performed righteous acts, and not only made laws but offered himself as a model (τύπον) for those who wish to know the power of acting."

form of a biography of the Egyptian monk Antony in *Life of Antony* (hereafter *VA*).[29]

Ostensibly, monks requested Athanasius's account so they could imitate Antony, and Athanasius concurs that Antony is worthy as a model.[30] While it is written particularly for those interested in an ascetical lifestyle, there is no great distinction for Athanasius between what Antony represents and that to which all "ordinary" Christians are called.[31] In looking at *VA*, and Athanasius's little epistle on the value of the Book of Psalms (*Ep. Marcell.*), three aspects are present which come up again and again as "tools" in living out the transformed life: (1) the internalization of virtue; (2) the reading and memorization of Scripture; and (3) prayer.

As a great Christian model, Athanasius highlights how Antony himself learned to appropriate and internalize the best of "men of zeal" with whom he came into contact:

> He observed the graciousness of one, the eagerness for prayers in another; he took careful note of one's freedom from anger, and the human concern of another. And he paid attention to one while he lived a watchful life, or one who pursued studies, as also he admired one for patience, and another for fastings ... The gentleness of one and the long-suffering of yet another he watched closely. He marked, likewise, the piety toward Christ and the mutual love of them all. And having been filled in this manner, he returned to his own place of discipline, from that time gathering the attributes of each in himself, and striving to manifest in himself what was best from all.[32]

---

29. Athanasius is "theologizing" the life of Antony in a way very consistent with Athanasius's overall theological vision. Behr, *The Nicene Faith*, 254; Anatolios, *Athanasius*, 166.

30. *VA*, Introduction.

31. Nathan Kwok-kit Ng, *The Spirituality of Athanasius: A Key for Proper Understanding of this Important Church Father* (Bern: Peter Lang, 2001), 138, 261–263. David Brakke notes that ordinary Christians, for Athanasius, are to practice renunciation that differs in degree but not in character. *Athanasius and the Politics of Asceticism* (Oxford: Oxford University Press, 1995), 144.

32. *VA* 4 (PG 26: 815AB). Antony later in the text (55) gives this admonition to other monks: "[K]eep in mind the deeds of the saints, so that the soul, ever mindful of the commandments, might be educated by their ardor" (PG 26: 921B).

The key move in Antony's observations for Athanasius is his internalization of the virtue he perceived. Taking his cue from Luke 17:21 ("behold, the kingdom of God is within you"), he asserts that the internal nature of virtue corresponds to the original and good nature which God provided in creation.[33] All that virtue needs is willing in line with the nature made "beautiful and perfectly straight." Virtue involves an internal preservation of what was originally good. This can be tied to the prelapsarian rendering of the human being's relationship to God mentioned earlier where humanity was "fully absorbed in the contemplation of God" through the mind (νοῦς), though this ability was lost in the fall, and humanity turned away from God and went "outside" itself.[34] Nevertheless, according to Athanasius, God can still be accessed through the soul in the postlapsarian state.[35] Antony is presented as one successfully making the internal journey back to God through the soul by fortifying himself from "outside" things.[36] However, the soul is still readily able to "[twist] away from what it naturally is" and so should seek that which can protect and preserve the internal way to God.[37]

What we see in the preservation of nature made "beautiful and perfectly straight" is a "give and take" process where one observes the manifestations of virtue in others, processes and internalizes these virtues, and thereby bolsters and aids the movement of the soul to God. This virtue then emanates out into the externals of the person, producing a demeanor and conduct worthy of imitation.[38] Appearances, though, return to a consideration of the soul of the "man of zeal":

---

33. *VA* 20 (PG 26: 872C – 873A).

34. Ibid. Anatolios writes, "Thus the turning away from God represents an alienation of the soul from its native dynamism through which it has ready access to the vision of God, for the soul is 'its own path, receiving the knowledge and understanding of God the Word not from outside but from itself' (οὐκ ἔξωθεν, ἀλλ' ἐξ ἑαυτῆς) [*CG*, 33]." Ibid., 188–189.

35. E.g. *CG* 34 *inter alia*.

36. As is clear throughout the *VA*, this is not done without the presence and guidance of the Word of God.

37. *VA* 20 (PG 26: 873B).

38. *VA* 46 (PG 26: 912B).

It was not his physical dimensions that distinguished him from the rest, but the stability of character and the purity of the soul. His soul being free of confusion, he held his outer senses also undisturbed, so that from the soul's joy his face was cheerful as well, and from the movements of the body it was possible to sense and perceive the stable condition of the soul.[39]

"The stable condition of the soul" where its "utter equilibrium"[40] reigns is tied to the reading and memorization of Scripture for Athanasius. This is demonstrated at the outset of Antony's ascetical life: "[Antony] paid such close attention to what was read that nothing from Scripture did he fail to take in—rather he grasped everything, and in him the memory took the place of books (τὴν μνήμην ἀντὶ βιβλίων)."[41] In his battles with spirits he would either shout or sing Scripture in order to ward off their attacks.[42] In instructing other monks, his message was "to take to heart the precepts in the Scriptures"[43] on which his own discipline was modeled.[44] Furthermore, his prayer life included the chanting of the Psalms.[45]

The special place of the book of Psalms in Athanasius's conception of the redeemed life is at the forefront of his *Letter to Marcellinus*, particularly the relationship of the Psalms to the internal appropriation of Scripture and the effects of this in the ordering of the soul. After presenting Christ as the model Christian, Athanasius writes:

---

39. *VA* 67 (PG 26: 940A). Cf. *VA*, 14 and 93.

40. *VA* 14 (PG 26: 865A).

41. *VA* 3 (PG 26: 845A).

42. *VA* 9, 13, 60–61.

43. *VA* 55 (PG 26: 921B): In his *Festal Letters*, Athanasius elaborates on the words found in 1 Tim. 4:15 thus: "'Meditate on these things: be engaged in them.' For constant meditation, and the remembrance of divine words, strengthens piety toward God, and produces a love to Him inseparable and not merely formal; as he, being of this mind, speaks about himself and others like-minded, saying boldly, 'Who shall separate us from the love of God?'" XI: 4. All references to this work use the translation found in *Athanasius: Select Words and Letters*, trans. J. H. Newman, ed. A. Robertson, NPNF, Second Series, 4 (Grand Rapids: Eerdmans, 1978).

44. *VA* 46.

45. *VA* 39.

It was indeed for this reason that [Christ] made this resound in the Psalms before his sojourn in our midst, so that just as he provided the model (τυπῶν) of the earthly and heavenly man in his own person, so also from the Psalms he who wants to do so can learn the emotions and dispositions of the souls, finding in them also the therapy and correction suited for each emotion. If the point needs to be put more forcefully, let us say that the entire Holy Scripture is a teacher of virtues and the truths of faith, while the Book of Psalms possesses somehow the perfect image (εἰκόνα) for the souls' course of life.[46]

The Psalms present a mirror by which one can construe the proper "emotions and dispositions" of the soul worthy of emulation. As much as they serve as a "perfect image," though, they are especially suited out of all of Scripture to be internalized[47] and,

---

46. *Ep. Marcell.* 13–14 (PG 27: 25BC). Cf. 10. In response to Athanasius tying together the Psalms and the life of Christ, Anatolios writes, "[I]n the same way in which the Psalms provide a 'mirror' or 'image' wherein the soul can recognize a perfect image of itself, the same is true of the act whereby the Word became flesh and 'typified in himself' human nature. Henceforth, humanity can find 'in itself' – that is, in the model of its own humanity in Christ – the perfect image of virtue. There is a mutual internality whereby the human is typified 'in Christ' in such a way that there is thus provided for humanity a model which is accessible to it 'in itself.' It is in such a context that we must place Athanasius's saying that the way of virtue is intrinsic to the soul." *Athanasius*, 198–199.

This quote by Athanasius is very similar to a later one by the Reformer John Calvin, who wrote in his preface to his commentary on the Psalms: "I have been accustomed to call this book, I think not inappropriately, The Anatomy of all the Parts of the Soul ... [T]here is not an emotion of which any one can be conscious that is not here represented as in a mirror. Or rather, the Holy Spirit has here drawn ... all the griefs, sorrows, fears, doubts, hopes, cares, perplexities, in short, all the distracting emotions with which the minds of men are wont to be agitated." *Commentary on the Book of Psalms*, trans. James Anderson (Grand Rapids: Baker, 1979), 1:xxxvi-xxxvii.

47. On the relative ease of internalizing the Psalms, Athanasius writes: "There is ... this astonishing thing in the Psalms. In the other books [of the Bible], those who read what the holy ones say, and what they might say concerning people, are relating the things that were written about those earlier people. And likewise, those who listen consider themselves to be other than those about whom the passage speaks, so that they only come to the imitation of the deeds that are told to the extent that they marvel at them and desire to emulate (μιμεῖσθαι) them. By contrast, however, he who takes up this book – the Psalter – goes through the prophecies about the Savior, as is customary in the other Scriptures, with admiration and adoration, but the other psalms he recognizes as being his own words (ἰδίους ὄντας λόγους). And the one who hears is deeply moved,

therefore, affect the soul's order in a most powerful way.[48] Athanasius believes this occurs chiefly because of their ability to be sung. In a passage which parallels Athanasius's conception of the internal life of Antony, he writes:

> In order that some such confusion not occur in us, the Word intends the soul that possesses the mind of Christ (Χριστοῦ νοῦν), as the Apostle said, to use this as a leader, and by it to be both a master of its passions and to govern the body's members, so as to comply with reason. Thus, as in music there is a plectrum [used to pluck the strings of an instrument], so the man becoming himself a stringed instrument and devoting himself completely to the Spirit may obey in all his members the emotions, and serve the will of God. The harmonious reading of the Psalms is a figure and type of such undisturbed and calm equanimity of our thoughts. For just as we discover the ideas of the soul and communicate them through the words we put forth, so also the Lord, wishing the melody of the words to be a symbol of the spiritual harmony in a soul (τῆς πνευματικῆς ἐν ψυχῇ ἁρμονίας), has ordered that the odes be chanted tunefully, and the Psalms recited with song . . . [T]he Psalms are not recited with melodies because of a desire for pleasant sounds. Rather, this is a sure sign of the harmony of the soul's reflections (τεκμήριον τῆς ἁρμονίας τῶν ἐν τῇ ψυχῇ λογισμῶν). Indeed, the melodic reading is a symbol of the mind's well-ordered and undisturbed condition. Moreover, the praising of God in well-tuned cymbals and harp and ten-stringed instrument was again a figure and sign of the parts of the body coming into natural concord like harp strings, and of the thoughts of the soul becoming like cymbals, and then all of these being moved and living through the grand sound and through the command of the Spirit so that, as it is written, the man lives in the Spirit and mortifies the deeds of the

---

as though he himself were speaking, and is affected by the words of the songs, as if they were his own (ἰδίαν ὄντων αὐτοῦ) songs." *Ep. Marcell.* 11 (PG 27: 21C).

48. Peter Brown brings out a most interesting distinction between Origin's spirituality and Athanasius's (as depicted through Antony in the *VA*). Whereas for Origen "the greatest powers of spiritual discernment" required the aid of vast learning and philological resources (found in an upper-class, urban atmosphere) so that one could arrive at the precise meaning of Scripture, for Athanasius "the monk's heart was the new book." Brown writes, "What required infinitely skilled exegesis and long spiritual experience were the 'movements of the heart,' and the strategies and snares that the Devil laid within it." It is no surprise then that Athanasius focuses on the aid the book of Psalms can bring to moving the heart into a proper harmony with God. *The Body and Society: Men, Women, and Sexual Renunciation in Early Christianity* (New York: Columbia University Press, 1988), 229.

body [Ps 38:1–2]. For thus beautifully singing praises, he brings rhythm to his soul and leads it, so to speak, from disproportion to proportion, with the result that, due to its steadfast nature, it is not frightened by something, but rather imagines positive things, even possessing a full desire for the future goods. And gaining its composure by the singing of the phrases, it becomes forgetful of the passions and, while rejoicing, sees in accordance with the mind of Christ, conceiving the most excellent thoughts.[49]

By means of chanting and singing the Psalms, a spiritual harmony is effected in the soul through being mastered by Christ as his "mind" has sway and the Spirit obeyed. The internalization of Scripture for Athanasius is appropriating the incarnation where "[t]he model provided by Christ in his earthly sojourn is … connected with the model for the disposition of the soul provided by the Psalms, for it is he who speaks through them."[50]

The internal stability, purity, and harmony of the soul are undoubtedly related to the dominant appearance of prayer in *VA*. In the buildup of Antony's discipline, Athanasius comments on how "he prayed constantly."[51] Throughout his practice of ascetical discipline, spirits of various stripes haunted him. Of the weapons Antony uses to "defeat" them, prayer was essential: "Much prayer and asceticism is needed that one who receives through the Spirit the gift of discrimination of spirits might be able to recognize their traits … and how each of them is overturned and expelled."[52] Antony's prayers also concerned others, especially those who suffered. Athanasius demonstrates how these prayers were remarkably effectual,[53] producing for Antony not pride but an abiding attitude acknowledging that God acts out of his own good prerogative whether or not he chooses to meet his requests.[54] As one resists temptation and grows in virtue, it is implicit that one's prayers are increasingly effectual, and more and more aimed outward toward objects of compassion.

---

49. *Ep. Marcell.* 28–29 (PG 27: 40B – 41B).
50. Behr, *The Nicene Faith*, 252.
51. *VA* 3 (PG 26 815A).
52. *VA* 22 (PG 26: 876B). Cf. 5, 9, 38–39.
53. *VA* 48, 54, 56, 57 and 61.
54. *VA* 56.

This increased power in prayer demonstrates for Athanasius not the elevated "human power" of Antony but, rather, the increased power of Christ through him. It is Antony's responsibility to invoke the power of Christ through prayer, but the actual working power belongs to Christ alone.[55] Why Antony is a particularly effective instrument of Christ's power is implicitly tied to his ability to ascend in the virtue of his soul as he appropriates the "mind of Christ" and lives "in the Spirit."[56]

Gathering up these three highlighted "tools"—internalization of virtue, the reading and memorization of Scripture, and prayer—it is helpful to place them in the context of Athanasius's understanding of spiritual transformation in the Godward life. It is primarily *internal* and involves the whole person. Even if external realities such as the life of saints and the biblical text are of service, they are to be internalized and woven into the inner virtue that emanates from the soul.

Consequently, we might expect to see Athanasius have a lot to say about the Holy Spirit in the *VA* since, according to Athanasius's broader theology, it is through the indwelling of the Spirit that we are redeemed and enabled to live a Godward life. This, however, would be to misunderstand the relationship of the Holy Spirit to the Son in his theology. The Spirit lifts humanity up and grants life in God, but he does this by placing us *in the Son*. The Son is the focus of the Spirit's activity. It is true that in Athanasius's Trinitarian economy the "touching point" with humanity's redemption is "in the Spirit", but this is always done "through the Son." And as the divine economy's work *ad extra* is in this manner, it works likewise in reverse: the Son becomes the focus of the Spirit's work in the individual.[57] This is clarified

---

55. *VA* 38 *inter alia*.

56. *Ep. Marcell*. 29.

57. Susanna Elm and Behr stress that just as the work of God in Christ took place through the body, so the work of God in redemption is "through the bodies" of the redeemed. The goal of redemption for Athanasius is not to transcend the body, but for the body to be put in proper subjection to the soul. The result is a "disciplined body" which signifies a stable soul. Susanna Elm, 'Virgins of God': *The Making of Asceticism*

by recalling once again Athanasius's emphasis on the perfect reception and maintaining of the Spirit in the Son's life on earth, thereby sanctifying humanity in himself and freeing it to live in accordance with its original good nature. Appropriation of Christ's life, then, becomes a life "in Christ", where the success of the individual soul is not attributed to the person; rather, every "success" is a success of the Savior. We see this in Antony's life after his first "contest against the devil" where all achievement is attributed to the Savior, since he "condemned sin in the flesh, in order that the just requirement of the Law might be fulfilled in us, who walk not according to the flesh but according to the Spirit [Rom. 8:3-4]."[58] For Athanasius, the Spirit leads to the Son as the focus of his work. To walk according to the Spirit is to walk as the Son walked. The amount of exertion an individual such as Antony puts forth in order to emulate the Son is of no weight in the matter since it is only by the Son internally severing the solidarity that sin had formed with humanity and modeling the perfect internalization of the Holy Spirit—praise is to be focused on the Word alone.[59]

Many of the dominant themes we find in the *VA* and *Ep. Marcell.* are also evident in Athanasius's *Festal Letters*. In particular, the admonition to imitation is again a significant motif. Athanasius uses the text from 1 Corinthians 4:16 where Paul says, "Be ye therefore followers of me"[60] as a broader command to emulate the "saints" who "were examples to us of conversation in Christ."[61] Of course, for Athanasius all these examples are based on the example *par excellence* and are only worthy insofar as they are examples of Christ: "Be ye followers of me, *as I also am of Christ*" (1 Cor. 11:1).[62] As in the *VA*, the goal of this imitation

---

in Late Antiquity (Oxford: Clarendon Press, 1994), 379–380; Behr, *The Nicene Faith,* 256–257 (see especially n. 124).

58. *VA* 7.

59. As Athanasius presses throughout the *Festal Letters*, the human response to this is continual gratitude.

60. *Festal Letter* II: 1. Cf. XI: 1.

61. *Festal Letter* II: 2.

62. *Festal Letter* X: 8 (emphasis mine). Cf. II: 5 and V: 4.

is internalization—internalization that has as its aim the appropriation of the things of Christ in individual believers:

> We should imitate the deeds of the saints. But we imitate them, when we acknowledge Him who died, and no longer live unto ourselves, but Christ henceforth lives in us; when we render a recompense to the Lord to the utmost of our power, though when we make a return we give nothing of our own, but those things which we have before received from Him, this being especially of His grace, that He should require, as from us, His own gifts. He bears witness to this when He says, "My offerings are My own gifts." That is, those things which you give Me are yours, as having received them from Me, but they are the gifts of God. And let us offer to the Lord every virtue, and that true holiness which is in Him, and in piety let us keep the feast to Him with those things which He has hallowed for us.[63]

What the Son received from the Father he gives to the Church so that the Church may return those gifts to the Son which he "hallowed" for her. That is to say, it is Christ who is the giver and also the "receiver" of redemption in that the living out of virtue for the believer is nothing other than living in Christ and returning to him the gifts he has given.

The trajectory of the Christian life finds its starting point in a new creation in Christ by the grace of the Spirit. According to Athanasius, the Christian must hold fast to the Spirit by the will's continual pursuance of the things of God, especially availing oneself of Scripture, prayer, and the imitation of the saints. The Godward life necessitates a continual movement "upward" lest the Spirit be quenched. As much as Athanasius warns, though, of neglecting the copious spiritual resources given by Christ in the Spirit, he upholds the overabundant grace of God and the continual availability of repentance (here in the framework of the story of the Prodigal Son):

> For this is the work of the Father's loving-kindness and goodness, that not only should He make him alive from the dead, but that He should render His grace illustrious through the Spirit. Therefore, instead of corruption, He clothes him with an incorruptible garment; instead of hunger, He kills

---

63. *Festal Letter* V: 4.

the fatted calf; instead of far journeys, [the Father] watched for his return, providing shoes for his feet; and, what is most wonderful, placed a divine signet-ring upon his hand; whilst by all these things He begat him afresh in the image of the glory of Christ. These are the gracious gifts of the Father, by which the Lord honors and nourishes those who abide with Him, and also those who return to Him and repent.[64]

Conclusion

In reflecting on and summing up Athanasius's teaching in the *VA*, *Ep. Marcell.*, and *Festal Letters*, it is beneficial to look once again to the active/passive motif in creation and the life of Christ, as it is evident in Athanasius's conception of the redeemed life of the Christian as well. The believer "passively" receives the grace of Christ so that the Christian can take no credit for redemption— it is unmerited. Yet, grace is for naught if the believer does not "actively" live it out by ascending with the upward trajectory of this grace. For this, God gives the Holy Spirit who continues to draw the believer's attention "upward" or "forward" to the life he or she should be living in the Son. To go one's own way is to quench the work of the Spirit. To live a Godward life is to "hold fast to the end the Spirit given at the beginning."[65]

For Athanasius, the life of the Christian is one where we are grounded in and strengthened through our new relation to God in Christ (passive), yet subjectively living that out in the Spirit (active). This is a recapitulation of creation itself where God is the active agent and the creature passive. Implicitly, as Widdicombe has put it concerning the work of the Holy Spirit in sanctification and perfection, "[Athanasius] seems to think of this perfection as a taking forward of the perfection effected for man in the incarnation into the present spiritual and moral experience of the individual believer."[66] This quote brings us to what is finally at issue: that is, any call to obedience or imitation in Athanasius

---

64. *Festal Letter* IX: 10.
65. *Festal Letter* III: 4.
66. Widdicombe, *The Fatherhood of God*, 246.

(active) is grounded in the perfecting work of the Son and in the indwelling of the Holy Spirit (passive). There is a priority of grace which Athanasius is at pains to demonstrate.[67] Therefore, the Christian has all the "equipment" he or she needs by being united with the Son and obtaining the indwelling of the Spirit in order to march forward in concrete acts of faith. The Holy Spirit is the one, as the "indweller", who moves the Christian to greater and greater union of act with the Son where eschatological realities exist in the existential life of the Christian. Thus, the Godward life is a life of "passive activity."

---

67. Anatolios writes, "[Athanasius] sees the human response as strictly derivative of the divine initiative." *Athanasius*, 174.

5

A Scots Worthy

The Life and Ministry of a Theology Professor
(George Lawson)

Sinclair B. Ferguson

IT is a privilege to share in honouring the gifts, graces, and ministry of Professor Douglas Kelly, and to have the opportunity to express gratitude for his long friendship.

The essay that follows draws attention to a much loved but almost entirely forgotten minister and theological educator of a bygone era in Scotland. But it is also written in the hope that in his story, readers, who have no personal acquaintance with the recipient of this festschrift, will catch a glimpse—as though in a mirror—of characteristics that have been reflected in the life and ministry of Dr. Douglas Kelly. For what was written about the subject of this essay could equally have been written of him, albeit 150 years later:

> By his students he was loved ... His qualities both of head and heart gave him an ample title to such a peculiar and affectionate regard. He was a man of the most guileless and childlike simplicity of character, and notwithstanding the remarkable gifts with which he was endowed, and his vast erudition, his humility was most conspicuous ... In short there was an

admirable consistency between his whole manner of life and his profession as a Christian minister.[1]

George Lawson—for he is the subject of this brief essay—was born to Charles and Margaret Lawson of Boghouse Farm, West Linton, Peeblesshire, Scotland, on 13 March 1749. His father was a carpenter and a tenant farmer (on aptly named unpromising land).

The Lawson family of six sons and two daughters belonged to the Secession Church of West Linton, a division from the Church of Scotland, whose roots lay in part in the Marrow Controversy (c. 1718–1723 but rumbling on long thereafter),[2] but whose occasion was an Act of the General Assembly allowing elders and heritors to settle ministers in vacant churches.[3] In protest, in 1733 Ebenezer Erskine and a small number of other ministers formed an "Associate Presbytery", which became "The Associate Synod" in 1744. Sadly, despite the emphasis of the Marrow theology on grace, the Synod split within a couple of years over the interpretation of the 1744 Burgess Oath. Some held this involved endorsing the Church of Scotland from which they had seceded.[4] The result was the formation of two connexions, The Associate Synod and The General Associate Synod, popularly known as "The Burghers" and the "Anti-Burghers."[5]

The Lawson family were Burghers, and it was within The Associate Synod that George Lawson would serve Christ all his

---

1. W.P. (presumably Dr William Peddie) in his 1878 Prefatory Note to the republication of George Lawson's *Lectures on the History of Joseph* (Edinburgh: 1807; reprinted London: Banner of Truth Trust, 1972), ix.

2. The controversy was precipitated by the republication in Scotland of the 17th century book *The Marrow of Modern Divinity* (first published in 1645). For a modern edition, see Edward Fisher, *The Marrow of Modern Divinity* (Geanies House: Christian Heritage, 2009). The history of the controversy is traced in detail in David C. Lachman, *The Marrow Controversy, 1718–1723: An Historical and Theological Analysis* (Edinburgh: Rutherford House, 1988).

3. Thus over-riding the right of a congregation to select and call its own choice of minister.

4. The oath included a commitment to "the true religion presently confessed within this realm, and authorized by the laws thereof."

5. As we shall see, further splits took place in later years over the teaching of *The Confession of Faith* on the role of the civil magistrate.

days.[6] What Calvin wrote of Timothy could equally be applied to Lawson: he drank in godliness with his mother's milk. He was reared in regular public worship and the older disciplines of family worship which were maintained among Secession Christians. As Richard Baxter was eventually able to say about Kidderminster, similarly Lawson's students would later say about Selkirk where he ministered: simply to walk down the main street in the evening was to hear the sound of praise and prayer from almost every home.

A diligent youngster, Lawson's spiritual life was also enriched beyond his immediate family by the preaching of his minister, the able but somewhat choleric, James Mair, and his gifted tutor John Johnstone who later became minister of Ecclefechan (where he left an abiding impression on the town's most famous son, Thomas Carlyle).[7]

As a child Lawson contracted smallpox and was not expected to live. An eyesight weakness which left him, at times, with discomfort in reading was attributed to this—a fact that, as we shall see, makes the extent of his learning all the more remarkable. Endearingly this learning was accompanied with a propensity to absent-mindedness, and a relative indifference to the practical aspects of life for which, apparently, he displayed little talent![8]

---

6. Dr. Lawson passed into glory shortly before the reunion he desired between the two synods took place in 1820. A fine account of this poignant event is given in chapter XVII of John McKerrow's detailed *History of the Secession Church* (Glasgow: A Fullarton & Co; 1st ed. 1839, revised edition 1841), 660–663. Lawson would have been deeply moved by the fact that his long-time friend David Greig of Lochgelly was called to the Moderator's chair of the united synods.

7. Carlyle was reputed to have said more than once "I have seen many capped and equipped bishops, and other episcopal dignitaries; but I have never seen one who more beautifully combined in himself the Christian and the Christian gentleman than did Mr Johnstone." George Macfarlane, *The Life and Times of George Lawson of Selkirk* (Edinburgh: William Oliphant & Co, 1862), 27. In a letter to David Hope on 19 December 1834, Carlyle wrote: "The venerable John Johnstone is my model of an Apostolic Priest; more Priestlike in his humble simplicity than Archbishops to me; and more *honoured* too." Accessed from *The Carlyle Letters Online*, February 23, 2023 at: https://carlyleletters.dukeupress.edu/volume/07/lt-18341219-TC-DH-01

8. Lawson is sometimes said to have been the model for the character of the

He did, however, enter the University of Edinburgh at the tender age of 15 and thereafter proceeded to the Divinity Hall of the Synod in 1766.

The Divinity Hall

Since the life of the Divinity Hall was to become such an important and strategic element in his ministry it is worth pausing here to describe its evolution. The pathway to the ministry in the Burgher Synod first brought candidates under the pastoral supervision of their local presbytery and for their theological education attendance at four or five sessions of the Theological Hall.

The Theological Hall was not a building, but the location of the single minister appointed to serve as the theological educator and tutor.[9] Students resided in the vicinity of his congregation and attended classes with him six days each week during the months of August and September. It was presupposed that candidates had already studied the classical languages (Latin, Greek, Hebrew) in their earlier education. Classes met for several hours most days, engaged in preaching exercises (some at least of which in Lawson's day were open to and well attended by members of the public). The one help that was given to the professor was that, when the students were in session, he was ordinarily relieved of preaching in his own congregation.

As the Burgher Synod grew in numbers it was inevitable that questions would be raised about the quality of the education itself (it seems not all students attended the whole of each session).[10] In addition, placing students in the care of a single working

---

Revd. Josiah Cargill in his near-neighbour Sir Walter Scott's novel *Saint Ronan's Well* (Edinburgh: 1823). It is not difficult to see many of Lawson's characteristics in Scott's portrayal of Cargill, although the whole portrait is more of a caricature than a likeness. St. Ronan's Well is situated some 15 miles from Selkirk. The book, by universal agreement, is not one of the best of the Waverley novels.

9. Unlike the Antiburgher Synod Theological Hall, the Burgher Synod made no provision for a teacher of philosophy.

10. For example, John Brown, the grandson of Lawson's predecessor, seems to have been in attendance for only six weeks one year and four weeks in another year. See John Cairns, *Memoir of John Brown, D.D.* (Edinburgh: Edmonston and Douglas, 1860), 37–38.

pastor limited their exposure to a variety of minds and also placed enormous burdens on the professor. This notwithstanding, at least in the prescribed number of class hours, the Burgher Synod theological course was more heavily weighted than the requirements of the Established Church. The timing of the sessions was arranged during the school summer vacation (August-September) so that students could support themselves by teaching school the rest of the year.

The pathway after completion of the course of study was to be licensed as a preacher and a probationer for the ministry, and to spend the next period itinerating from vacant charge to vacant charge in the denomination—receiving hospitality from one Friday to the next before moving on to another congregation. It was a pattern that had some obvious advantages in training young ministers and also in giving congregations a personal knowledge of the future ministers in their denomination, as well as enabling them to assess their potential suitability for a call. The Lawson family bought a pony for the 20-year-old George as he set out on this new stage of life.

When George Lawson first attended the Theological Hall, it was under the direction of John Swanston of Kinross and then the more famous John Brown of Haddington (creator of the Self-Interpreting Bible—and a man of whom "an infidel blade" said that he preached "as if he was conscious that the Son of God stood at his elbow").[11] During his years of attendance the Lawson family essentially provided for him, and it was in these years that he was given the opportunity to lay the intellectual foundations that served his ministry so well in later years. It was also in the Hall that enduring friendships with several of his fellow students were first cultivated. Indeed, such were these friendships with men whom he had first met in Kinross that at first he was more willing

---

11. The source of this story was Alexander Waugh. The 'infidel blade' referred to was, reputedly, David Hume. James Hay and Henry Belfrage, *Memoir of the Rev. Alexander Waugh D.D.* (Edinburgh: William Oliphant and Son, 3rd edition 1839), 39. Hay and Belfrage also provide a description of the life of the Theological Hall under John Brown, derived from his sons, (*ibid.*, 35–38).

to accept a call to Milnathort in Kinross than he was to Selkirk in the Scottish Borders. It was John Brown who, perhaps with some foresight, placed his weight on him accepting the call to Selkirk.

Lawson shone as a student, and it was in this context that his phenomenal recall ability came to the surface. On one occasion when John Brown selected him to translate a passage from the Hebrew Bible he noticed that Lawson did not have one with him. Pressed on the point he said that he simply did not have room for it in his luggage, but he knew the text, and proceeded as though it were open before him. On another occasion when Brown had left the room, Lawson rose and continued the lecture—and must have been embarrassed to discover that Brown had returned and having listened commented that, clearly, he had found his successor. There is no record of whether he was smiling or frowning as he spoke! Moments such as these led to the description of him as the Scottish "Socrates." C.H. Spurgeon would describe him as "a man of great genius." Dr. Hunter, the Divinity Professor in Edinburgh University, was not alone when he noted that "Dr. Lawson says great things, but he says them like a child."

In 1771 Lawson was settled in the Burgher congregation in the town of Selkirk, in a general area rich in the story of Scottish theology. It lies some 30 miles away from the probable birthplace of John Duns Scotus (c. 1265-1308), 35 miles away from John Knox's birthplace in Haddington, 18 miles away from the scene of Thomas Boston's ministry in Ettrick. The distinguished medieval theologian, Richard the Scot of St. Victor in Paris (d. 1173) is sometimes held to have hailed from the same Scottish Borders. Only 5 miles from Selkirk lies "Abbotsford", the magnificent home of the novelist Sir Walter Scott.

Here, in Selkirk, Lawson's predecessor was the popular Andrew Moir who had died prematurely aged 39.[12] He left a particularly memorable impression on one elderly member of the congregation who later told Lawson's grandson (a successor to

---

12. Manuscript sermons of Moir (as well as of the Lawson ministers of Selkirk) are held in The National Library of Scotland in Edinburgh.

both his grandfather and father), "Deed, sir, I mind Mr. Moir weel; he was a burning and a shining light. I can honestly assure you he was far more popular than a' you Lawsons"—obviously a hard act to follow; but, as we shall see, George Lawson senior made one major life decision that would surely have endeared him to the congregation.

The population of Selkirk ("The church in the woods") was then somewhere under 2,000 (now around 5,000). Its most famous 18th century son, Dr. Mungo Park, the explorer of the Niger River, was the second child Lawson baptised after his installation (a statue of him was erected opposite what was his manse).[13]

After several years as a bachelor, Lawson settled on proposing marriage to a Miss Rogers, the daughter of a local banker. But within a year he was alone again in the manse, now a young widower. He later married a daughter of his predecessor Andrew Moir. She was the young widow of a minister who had served in Berwick. The second marriage for both was blessed with three sons and five daughters. Of these, two daughters (Charlotte and Jane) and one son (John, a theology student) predeceased him,[14] while in a remarkable ministerial lineage his son Andrew (the twin of Charlotte) and then his eldest son George became his successors in the Selkirk congregation.

George Lawson was very much a "homebird." He was devoted to his family (an affection that appears to have been wholly

---

13. "H.B" in his *The Life of Mungo Park* (Edinburgh: Fraser & Co., 1835), 14, claims that Park's parents originally destined him for the ministry of the Church of Scotland. However that choice of denomination seems unlikely for a son baptised in a Burgher congregation and in whom Lawson maintained a keen pastoral interest. Park himself had set his heart on becoming a physician.

14. George Lawson, *Reflections on the Illness and Death of a Beloved Daughter* (First published in 1799. A new edition was published in Edinburgh by William Oliphant, in 1866). Lawson began to write these pages when Charlotte was believed to have little or no prospect of survival. Like C.S. Lewis's *A Grief Observed*, they became a meditative journal on his experience. In introducing the material to a later generation, Lawson's son, George, wrote that readers familiar with his father only by other publications would, in these pages, "find that his talents, his might in the Scriptures, and his piety, were conjoined with affections as tender and melting as probably ever dwelt in a human bosom. These affections were repeatedly, by the removal of their objects from this land of shadows, the occasion of exquisite sorrow." *Reflections*, 5.

mutual), and rarely travelled any distance. Apart from one visit to London (where he met John Newton), his travels never took him far beyond the neighbouring presbyteries where he would regularly help his brethren at the five-day long Communion Seasons, and little further north than Fife on the far side of the River Forth.

Here, then, in this small border town, week by week, members of the Burgher congregation were richly fed from God's word. Lawson clearly believed that all of God's word is for all of God's people and followed the old Scottish practice of not only preaching sermons on specific texts, but on the morning of the Lord's Day, giving "the lecture," a running exposition of entire books of the Bible. This *lectio continua* style of preaching exemplified by Augustine and John Chrysostom, employed in the medieval schools by teachers such as Thomas Aquinas, had been reintroduced as a characteristic of daily whole-church ministry by Huldrych Zwingli (who had stunned Zurich by announcing he was going to preach through the Gospel of Matthew!). It found its finest expression in Calvin's daily expositions of Scripture in Geneva. In Lawson's case, the fruit of some of these expositions would emerge in the publication of his *Discourses on the Book of Esther* (1804), *The History of Joseph* (in two volumes, 1807), *Exposition of the Book of Proverbs* (also in two volumes, 1821), and his *Discourses on the History of David* (1833).[15]

In 1787 Lawson succeeded to the role of his old professor, John Brown. The Theological Hall relocated to Selkirk, and during the next three decades he was the sole instructor of some 390 students, the vast majority of whom would go on to become ministers of the gospel. It is often the case that students retain a lifelong affection for their theological professors. What is clear in the case of George Lawson is that, with few exceptions, his students— including those whose future lay outside the Burgher Synod—

---

15. These publications post-date Lawson's appointment to serve as professor in the Theological Hall. He doubtless had an ability to "layer" his exegesis and exposition so that material that was the fruit of preparation for the Theological Hall lectern could be re-served in a way that was readily digestible by the congregation he loved.

thought of him with an appreciation that bordered on reverence. His predecessor John Brown had published his own systematic theology, *A Compendious View of Natural and Revealed Religion, reflecting his lectures to his students in a sevenfold taxonomy grounded in the covenant theology of The [Westminster] Confession of Faith.* Lawson, doubtless partly out of a sense of *pietas* for his own teacher (perhaps akin to B.B. Warfield's for Charles Hodge), seems to have employed Brown's work as a "prescribed text" from which his students could develop their systematic thinking, while he himself focused on biblical exegesis and theology. Perhaps it was the memory of Brown's impressive annual closing addresses to his students that led him, by modest contrast, to leave the students with a simple word of Scripture and prayer as the annual sessions ended—although on at least one occasion, with tears in his eyes, he read part of one of his predecessor's addresses.

Most of the year, however, Lawson was a pastor to his flock. Perhaps like other congregations whose pastors have been "giants in the land" his broader influence was of secondary concern to most of his congregation. To them Dr Lawson[16] was their minister, and what mattered most to them was his preaching of the Scriptures and his pastoral care. They recognised that he was learned; but what undoubtedly mattered to them just as much, if not more, was that they observed the consistency of his Christian faith in his home life, not least in the waves of sorrows that washed on the shore of the manse. They had been fed richly by him from the Scriptures and had often experienced his loving care and his generosity in their poverty, and his tender compassion in their grief. From this environment Lawson himself probably benefited spiritually, for in this double sphere both dimensions of his gifts and graces were given the opportunity to be in exercise. It is certain that his students were enriched by his two-fold calling of

---

16. Lawson was the first Burgher minister to be awarded a D.D. — by Marischal College in 1806. Marischal College was at that time one of the two universities then located in Aberdeen (thus allowing the city to boast that it had as many universities within its borders as the whole of England—Oxford and Cambridge being the only universities in England until later in the 19th century!).

pastor and teacher, and doubtless often asked him the "How does this apply?" as well as the "What does this mean?"

Lawson's regular focus was fourfold: loving and spiritually nurturing his family; feeding and caring for his Selkirk flock; serving his ministerial brethren in his own and neighbouring presbyteries; and preparing his students for their future ministry at home and abroad. His list of publications is dominated by ministry in these contexts, with one exception: his *Considerations on the Overture lying before the Associate Synod, on the Power of the Civil Magistrate in matters of Religion*. This work, published in 1797, was his contribution to the sharp debate in both branches of the Secession Church on the relationship between Church and State, and therefore inevitably on the interpretation and application of Chapter 23 of The [Westminster] Confession of Faith, "Of the Civil Magistrate."

Lawson's view was that some measure of "liberty of opinion" was necessary so that an office-bearer's reservations about the way *The Confession of Faith* expressed the relationship of the civil magistrate to church power should not be regarded as an abandonment of commitment to the Church's subordinate standards. His view became that of the majority, but it led to a split in the Synod—one that was mirrored in the General Associate (Antiburgher) Synod—hence the sad situation beloved of some Scottish authors as an illustration of ecclesiastical pettiness in the now four groupings of the original secession: "Auld Licht[17] Burghers" and "New Licht Burghers" as well as "Auld Licht Antiburghers" and "New Licht Antiburghers."

In George Lawson's case, hurtful things were written against him, but throughout the conflict he maintained his settled commitment to receive all those he believed Jesus Christ himself had received. That Catholicity of spirit was also evidenced in his relationship with ministers of the Established Church. That said, his advocacy of what amounted to a view that there should be liberty of opinion on an issue that should not be regarded as

---

17. i.e. "Old Light", implying the "old" view of *The Confession of Faith*, chapter XXIII.

belonging to the substance of the faith was to have an unintended future history.[18] The Burgher Synod had continued the practice of the Church of Scotland in requiring a comprehensive commitment to the subordinate standards. The gravamen of the charge against Lawson and those who agreed with him was, understandably, that they were now reneging on their past commitment to the Confession. They had answered positively the question, "Do you sincerely own and believe the whole doctrine contained in the Confession of Faith and do you acknowledge the same Confession as the confession of your faith?" Thus, issues of personal integrity were woven into the emotions of the debate.[19] The majority of the members of the Synod were with Lawson.

We must fast-forward to the closing years of George Lawson's life. While most of his longest-standing friends predeceased him, his ministry in congregation and Theological Hall continued unabated until the last year of his life, although he was increasingly hampered by physical weakness. Such was his determination to finish well that, in the tradition of the apostle John, although he needed to be carried to the church, when in the pulpit he mustered up the necessary vigour to preach. While he did not live to see the reunion of the two Secession synods, his catholic spirit desired it. Perhaps fittingly his final sermon (on Psalm 82:6–7) was preached on February 06, 1820, and in it he marked the death of George III two weeks earlier. During the service he announced and then

18. Two of Lawson's best students, John Brown and Robert Balmer, would be involved in the later controversy over the question of whether *The Confession of Faith* allowed for the view that the atonement of Christ had a general as well as a particular reference. Lawson's own approach to this question—so important in the Seceder tradition because the issue of the extent of the atonement and its relation to the free offer of the gospel had played an important role in the Marrow Controversy—was perhaps more open than some of his contemporaries. Lawson's correspondence with Balmer in 1809–1810 when the latter was struggling with the subscription Formula is illuminating. See George Macfarlane, *The Life and Times of George Lawson*, 330–334. His interest in and affection for John Brown was evident, and reciprocated. See John Cairns *Memoir of John Brown, D.D.* (Edinburgh: Edmonston and Douglas, 1860), 35–36; 46–47.

19. The story of the decline in subscription to *The Confession of Faith* is carefully documented and clearly traced in Ian Hamilton, *The Erosion of Calvinist Orthodoxy* (Geanies House; Mentor, 2010).

read the section of Psalm 90 in the Scottish Psalter, which the congregation was about to sing. The words of verse 10 must have held special poignancy for the congregation as they gazed on the 70-year-old minister who had baptized them, married them, buried their parents and, in many cases, their children too, and had cared for their families through five decades:

> Threescore and ten years do sum up
> our days and years, we see;
> Or, if, by reason of more strength,
> in some fourscore they be:
> Yet doth the strength of such old men
> but grief and labor prove;
> For it is soon cut off, and we
> fly hence, and soon remove.

In a few words to them he movingly applied the psalm to himself. He could have given no clearer signal that this was, almost certainly, the last time his congregation would hear him feed their souls from the word of life.

As family and friends gathered round him in the days that followed, two of his prayers in particular seemed to display the heart of the man. The first reflected the modesty, at times almost embarrassment, with which he carried his gifts in the realization that he possessed nothing that he had not first received from his Lord (1 Cor. 4:7): "I have done little, very little." The second—the last words heard from his lips—"Lord, take me to Paradise." The first reflected the message he had preached throughout the fifty years of his ministry—his life as a Christian was all of grace; the second reflected the promise his Saviour had given to the dying thief, "Today you will be with me in Paradise." And so he was ready for the transition from the presence of the saints on earth to the immediate presence of Christ, knowing that this would be "far better."

In view of the purpose of this essay, we turn now to illustrate a few of the impressive features of Lawson's life and ministry.[20]

---

20. In this limited selection of characteristics of Dr. Lawson's personal and public life, friends of Douglas Kelly will recognize that I have in mind ways in which they have also been reflected in his life and ministry.

Man of Learning

It was apparent during Lawson's early life that he was what Scots describe as "a lad o' pairts." In addition, he was blessed with a family that saw providing for his further education as their gift to him and to the Church they loved. They allowed him the opportunity for reading, study, and reflection. The Lawson nuclear family members were his "full scholarship." It is doubtful, however, whether the full measure of his ability flourished until his years in the Theological Hall. Perhaps John Brown senior was the first who was given the opportunity to recognize just how substantial his gifts were.

George Lawson had no interest in doctrinal originality, nor was creativity or fresh insight his genius. In the area of systematic theology he relied on his teacher, John Brown's work, and his own contribution was lending to it the strength of biblical perspectives and application. But his reading and knowledge of the field was impressive. Thus, on one occasion, discussing the biblical evidence for the Trinity, he mentioned the "Johannine Comma" in the Authorized (King James) Version of 1 John 5:7-8,[21] indicating his familiarity with the question of its authenticity. While not in itself surprising, the specific reason he gave for doubting that the words in question were part of the autographic text of 1 John is eye-opening: he had read the works of Athanasius in Greek and found no reference to this form of John's statement. He argued, therefore, that its omission from the work of the great fourth century defender of the deity of Christ in relation to the Trinity was virtually conclusive proof that the words were a later interpolation. Nor was Athanasius the only early theologian whose works (in the original languages) he had devoured. And beyond that lay his knowledge of John Calvin, John Owen, Jonathan Edwards, and other major theologians, and then, undergirding everything lay his prodigious knowledge of the Scriptures.

No doubt Lawson spoke the truth when he said that the whiteness of the pages of books irritated his eyes. But that

---

21. "For there are three that bear record in heaven, *the Father, the Word, and the Holy Ghost, and these Three are One. And there are three that bear witness on earth*, the Spirit the Water, and the Blood, and these three agree in one."

does not explain how, having read the first verse of a chapter of Scripture in class, he could turn over his Bible and exegete the whole in detail without further reference to the Book before him. This appears to have been his fixed pattern whether in the pulpit or in the classroom. And not only did he exhibit these extraordinary powers of recall; it was clear to his students and congregation that he had meditated deeply on what he had read. His was a memory of contemplative love and he seems to have had a measure of Calvin's capacity to grasp the heart of a matter almost immediately. On at least one occasion, having announced his text, and turning to it in the pulpit Bible, he realized he had announced the wrong verse. Asked what he had done in view of his mistake, he responded, "Why, what could I do but just preach from the text I had given out."[22]

Friend and Pastor

"You can tell a man by his friends" may be a truism. But it was certainly true of George Lawson and illustrated in the constancy of his appreciation of them and his love for them. In his early twenties it was friendship that increased his desire to accept a call to be settled in Milnathort in Kinross where a number of his friends from his first year in Theological Hall lived and ministered. Several of his fellow divinity students remained lifelong bosom friends and correspondents. Nor did the bonds between them depend on physical proximity or even regular epistolary contact. They sensed themselves to be equidistant from Christ and therefore brought near to one another in union together in his body. These bonds were, in the best sense, spiritual and mystical, forged by years of study and the close fellowship of the annual sessions of the Theological Hall first in Kinross and then in Haddington. His brethren were by no means an "accountability group" but men whose lives and ministries served as constant reminders to be faithful.

That same spirit of friendship and kindness extended to his students. He welcomed them into his home, cared for them, prayed

---

22. Macfarlane, *Life*, 100.

for them, and counselled them personally, as well as giving them formal instruction. It is no surprise they formed very deep bonds of affection. No doubt they knew him as "Dr. Lawson" to the end of their days. But in retrospect one imagines few if any of them would have wanted to know him or call him by any other designation, any more than they would have imagined calling their own father by his Christian name. He was a father-in-God to them.

George Lawson encouraged the weak and struggling; he was firm, but he was sympathetic. The more gifted students he challenged—none more so than the young John Brown, grandson of the professor from Haddington. He took him aside on one occasion to urge him to work harder on his preaching, telling him that not only his own reputation but his professor's was on the line(!)—for people would not only say the grandson was "nothing like his grandfather", but that Lawson was nothing like Professor Brown of Haddington either! With the less gifted and even timid he was supportive and would be protective if necessary. He defended one young man who was accused by a fellow student of plagiarising the headings of a published sermon, arguing that if the originator of them was not criticised for them why should the student be charged with error! A lesser man might have shown the student the door. Another student from Greenock in the West of Scotland, by the name of Moodie, contracted a fatal disease. Lawson wrote to him a letter he so valued that he kept it with him constantly and died with it under his pillow. Testimony after testimony from his students spoke of the indelible impression left on them by the combination of his teaching and his character.

The tenderness of his friendship and pastoral care appears in clear relief in his letters to the bereaved. He belonged to their company, having lost two daughters and a son, and so, in the most literal sense, wrote out of compassion and sympathy. The pain experienced by some of his correspondents must have required great sensitivity and even delicacy (one brother minister had lost his wife and seven children). But Lawson also sought to write words of comfort of a literal kind, words cum forte—with strength. Real and lasting succour, he well knew, could not come from the grief within but only from without, from the strength of the grace of God in the gospel. So his letters are suffused with gospel comfort, expressed in the love of one whom he trusted his correspondents knew was a fellow-sufferer. His deep sense of the Christian hope and of the reality of the world to come is palpable. To a mother who had lost her son (apparently one of Lawson's divinity students) he wrote "expressing my sympathy": "You will, while you live, mourn the loss of such a son; but you will bless God you had such a son to lose."[23] It was not until some years after his own death that his *Reflections on the Illness and Death of a Beloved Daughter* was unearthed and published. His personal reflections there went a long way to explaining the depth of his sympathy with others and the extent to which he lived in a conscious awareness of the nearness of heaven.

Family Man

George Lawson had been brought up in a family modest in material treasure but rich in spiritual things, and it is clear that he breathed out the same spirit he had breathed in. He spent time with his children and invested himself in them. For all his devotion to his congregation, his labours on behalf of both present and former students, with all the demands of regular pulpit preparation, visitation, catechizing, comforting and challenging, and much else, he had energy to devote to the family circle. It is a testimony not only to the kind of minister he was, but the kind of father his children knew, that he headed a minor dynasty of Lawson ministers.

Lawson clearly enjoyed spending time with his family, and loved sharing spiritual things with them, but was also devoted to helping them to understand the world they were entering and how to live in practical and realistic ways for Christ in it. He had a deep sense of common grace. He read the entire Shakespeare corpus to the children (minus any sentiments he regarded as offensive to the gospel). He had memorized substantial quantities of Homer's *Iliad*

---

23. Macfarlane, *Life*, 437.

(in the original Greek, of course!) and would enthral his children in the evening by reciting its gripping narratives. Simplicity and cheerfulness of spirit marked him as a father. The Lawson children were singularly blessed to witness a deep integrity between what he was in public and what he was within the family circle. His smile, his generosity with what he had, the devotion and quality of his friendships were all long remembered. Not only did a "Lawson Ministerial Lineage" develop, but perhaps an even more remarkable testimony to the affection and esteem in which his congregation held their minister and his family is seen in the fact that several of them succeeded him in the pulpit in Selkirk.

Man of Prayer

The word "simplicity" appears regularly in descriptions of George Lawson. Certainly, he loved simple reality more than showy formality. His piety was not artificial.[24] He was not a fan of over-long prayers! All this was anchored in his own life, lived in the presence of God, and overflowing in the disciplines of prayer. No doubt this had its own effect on his students—and may explain why the Theological Hall stood high in the estimation of the town. In particular, he regarded prayer as the best key to unlock the inner significance of Scripture.

The closing days of life often reveal the heart of a man, or the fact that he has been hiding its true interests for years. In Lawson's case, prayer was not only a discipline but his whole *modus vivendi*. He practised the presence of God.

Like other saints he admired, Lawson's closing days were spent in spasmodic conversation with those he loved most and in prayer. When his son George asked him directly about his hope and comfort he replied, "All my hope and comfort spring out of the mercy of God, as manifested in the mediation of his Son Jesus Christ. Here are my only stay, and strength and consolation."[25]

---

24. Delightfully illustrated in a discussion on the best preparation for preaching by his own practical response "A good sleep on Saturday night!"

25. Macfarlane, *Life*, 473.

In his last audible prayers he interceded for the concentric circles of his heart's love—for his beloved family, his congregation, his students, his brothers in the ministry—and did so as someone who was looking towards and longing for the day when the earth would be filled with the glory of the Redeemer.[26]

Some words (probably written by John Brown who knew him so well) from a review of his posthumously published volumes on Proverbs, make the best conclusion to this brief introduction to this great but forgotten Scottish pastor and teacher:

> We knew well the amiable and venerable author ...; we had full opportunity to appreciate his worth; we have never seen his equal in various respects, and cannot reasonably expect to see it now ... There was a modesty, a guileless simplicity, an abhorrence of ostentation, a sincerity, an explicitness, an unbending integrity, united to the utmost gentleness and forbearance, which characterized all his deportment.[27]

Students of theology are in safe hands when their professors are men like George Lawson. Among such professors Douglas Kelly is surely to be ranked.

---

26. Ibid., 265–6.

27. Samuel Cox, ed. *Indices to The Expositor* (Second Series, Eight Volumes; London: Hodder and Stoughton, 1885), 18.

6

Doctrine and Devotion,
Truth and Love, Faith and Practice

Witsius, Cunningham, and Warfield on Ministerial
Preparation in Seminary

J. Ligon Duncan, III

Introduction

How are ministers made? That's what seminary was invented to help do (by and alongside the Church), but theological education has lost its way in our time, and we need to return to the Scriptures and to the old paths to find our way home again.[1]

---

1. Dr. Douglas F. Kelly embodies the vision of theological education expressed in this chapter, and has devoted much of his ministerial service to preparing the next generation of Reformed pastors. Dr. Kelly was my senior colleague in Systematic Theology at Reformed Theological Seminary in Jackson from 1990 until his departure to serve at RTS Charlotte, and we served on the RTS faculty for almost three decades. I first met the Kelly family in Edinburgh, Scotland in 1987. They (and I must here mention his beloved Caroline, too) welcomed me into their home and into the deep, rich bonds of their friendship. They became a formative part of my life and ministerial preparation, and they remain precious to me and my family to this day. Dr. Kelly has been a friend, encourager, example, esteemed colleague, faithful intercessor, and a father in the faith to me. The power of his intellect, the soundness of his doctrine, the reality of his piety,

What are seminaries for? Do we still need them? There are a lot of questions swirling around theological education today, and since you are reading this, you clearly care about preparing pastors and Church leaders who believe God's word and embrace sound, biblical, Christian theology, so perhaps we should reflect together on these things. Many people are looking at other options rather than traditional seminary education in our days, for a variety of reasons: the high cost of residential theological education, the desire to stay connected to a ministry in the local church, or even the view that the very idea of seminary education is obsolete. I assure you that theological educators are thinking about these kinds of things, and hear them all the time.

I even occasionally hear people question whether "seminary" is a biblical way of preparing for the ministry! I've had people say to me 'seminary is not in the Bible,' to which I reply, 'but preparation for the ministry is.' The Bible makes it amply clear that preparation and learning are necessary for ministry. Jesus spent three years with his disciples preparing them for ministry, and it is very clear that, in addition to providing for them a perfect model of self-denying service ("not to be served but to serve," Matt. 20:28, Mark 10:45) and mentoring them in practical ministry, Jesus spent a significant amount of his time with them helping them to understand the Bible better because it was fundamental to their witness to him, the mission he was preparing them for (see, for instance, Luke 24:44-48), and the whole Bible emphasizes the importance of the pursuit of sound learning for the wise in general, and for pastors in particular.

Prov. 15:14 says that "The mind of the intelligent seeks knowledge, but the mouth of fools feeds on folly." Prov. 18:15 reiterates the principle when it says, "The mind of the prudent acquires knowledge, and the ear of the wise seeks knowledge." Prov. 24:5 adds, "A wise man is strong, and a man of knowledge

and the passion of his prayers have shaped the lives of hundreds of Gospel ministers, and my own. Thank you to all the Kellys: Doug, Caroline, Doug Jr., Martha, Angus, Daniel, and Patrick.

increases power," reminding us of the old dictum "knowledge is power." The Old Testament wisdom literature is replete with calls to the believer to pursue knowledge. But the Bible says more than this: it emphasizes that ministers need to pursue study of the truth.[2]

Ezra 7:10 describes this great Old Testament leader in this way: "Ezra had set his heart to study the law of the LORD and to practice it, and to teach His statutes and ordinances in Israel." Hosea laments the lack of spiritual leaders like Ezra when he says, "My people are destroyed for lack of knowledge. Because you have rejected knowledge, I also will reject you from being My priest. Since you have forgotten the law of your God, I also will forget your children" (4:6). The same aspiration and complaint can be found in the last book of the Old Testament: "For the lips of a priest should preserve knowledge, and men should seek instruction from his mouth; for he is the messenger of the LORD of hosts" (Mal. 2:7).

But it is in the pastoral epistles that we find some of the most direct words of instruction and exhortation regarding ministerial study. Paul can say to Timothy, "Be diligent to present yourself approved to God as a workman who does not need to be ashamed, accurately handling the word of truth" (2 Tim. 2:15). Here we have an apostolic directive for a young minister to study with the equivalent exertion and effort of a tireless day-laborer. The true minister is a workman (Paul really likes this metaphor!). He works hard at his task. The true minister is to work hard at study so as to know and preach the Truth rightly.

Furthermore, Paul gives Timothy a sterling example of studiousness from his own practice and priorities. Think of his astonishing request in 2 Timothy 4:13 where he asks, "When you come bring the cloak which I left at Troas with Carpus, and the books, especially the parchments." Now think of it. Paul is only

---

2. Some of the material in this section is adapted from a portion of a chapter I wrote for *Letters to Timothy* (Cape Coral: Founders Press, 2004 & 2016), chapter 12 "Keep Studying."

months away from death. He has written the bulk of the letters of the New Testament. He has a lifetime of ministry behind him. And what does he want to do? Study! Winter is approaching and so Paul asks for his cloak, but more importantly he asks for books and parchments. Though almost at the end of his course, Paul aims to keep learning and growing by spiritual reading. Nobody has ever uttered a more poignant pastoral meditation on this little verse than C.H. Spurgeon. Here is what he says:

> How rebuked are they by the apostle! He is inspired, and yet he wants books! He has been preaching at least for thirty years, and yet he wants books! He had seen the Lord, and yet he wants books! He had had a wider experience than most men, and yet he wants books! He had been caught up into the third heaven, and had heard things which it was unlawful for a man to utter, yet he wants books! He had written the major part of the New Testament, and yet he wants books! The apostle says to Timothy and so he says to every preacher, "GIVE THYSELF UNTO READING."
>
> The man who never reads will never be read; he who never quotes will never be quoted. He who will not use the thoughts of other men's brains, proves that he has no brains of his own. Brethren, what is true of ministers is true of all our people. YOU need to read. Renounce as much as you will all light literature, but study as much as possible sound theological works, especially the Puritanic writers, and expositions of the Bible. We are quite persuaded that the best way for you to be spending your leisure, is to be either reading or praying. You may get much instruction from books which afterwards you may use as a true weapon in your Lord and Master's service. Paul cries, "Bring the books" — join in the cry.
>
> Paul herein is a picture of industry. He is in prison; he cannot preach: WHAT will he do? As he cannot preach, he will read. As we read of the fishermen of old and their boats. The fishermen were gone out of them. What were they doing? Mending their nets. So if providence has laid you upon a sick bed, and you cannot teach your class—if you cannot be working for God in public, mend your nets by reading. If one occupation is taken from you, take another, and let the books of the apostle read you a lesson of industry."[3]

---

3. This is from Spurgeon's sermon #542 "PAUL – His Cloak And His Books" in the *Metropolitan Tabernacle Pulpit* 9 (1863): 668–669.

Paul is a lifelong learner, and we should be too. But Paul also indicates that there should be a time of preparation before ministry begins. When he says that an elder must be able to teach (1 Tim. 3:2), he assumes the prior learning necessary to that work, and the Church's right and ability to discern and make a judgment about that learning when they choose the elder in the first place. He explicitly says that of deacons: "let these also first be tested and then let them serve" (1 Tim. 3:10), and the idea there is that they are to be tested before they serve, just as the candidates for the eldership are tested before they serve. That test certainly applies to the lives and character of the elders and deacons, but because of the elder's task, to teach, it must also apply to his preparation, knowledge, and orthodoxy.

So, for Jesus and Paul, preparation for ministry is not optional. That preparation is not merely practical, but especially involves a mastery of the Scriptures. And seminary is designed to fulfill this function more efficiently and comprehensively than ministerial apprenticeships could ever do.

Seminary was invented to give future ministers a concentrated period of study with a cohort of colleagues to prepare them for a lifetime of ministry, and if seminary is adequately facilitating a biblical preparation for ministry then it is a very good thing. B.B. Warfield once said: "The entire work of the Seminary deserves to be classed in the category of means of grace."[4] Why? Because the main thing that a solid, biblical, theological education does is engage the seminarian with the study of the Word of God, as the means by which Christ communicates the benefits of his mediation (see Westminster Larger Catechism, 154). How does this work?

> The Spirit of God maketh the reading, but especially the preaching of the word, an effectual means of enlightening, convincing, and humbling sinners; of driving them out of themselves, and drawing them unto Christ; of conforming them to his image, and subduing them to his will;

---

4. B. B. Warfield, "Spiritual Culture in the Theological Seminary" in *The Princeton Theological Review* 2:1 (1904): 73.

of strengthening them against temptations and corruptions; of building them up in grace, and establishing their hearts in holiness and comfort through faith unto salvation (WLC, 155).

The Westminster Confession reminds us that "The reading of the Scriptures with godly fear; the sound preaching, and conscionable hearing of the Word, in obedience unto God with understanding, faith, and reverence" are part "of the ordinary religious worship of God" (WCF 21.5), and these things are specifically part of the worship that seminarians owe to God in their studies, but they are also the very means by which God's Spirit grows them in grace and godliness, and blesses them, in order that they might bless others.

The work of theological education in the confessional Protestant tradition thus falls in the category of sanctification—a special and specific kind of sanctification: the sanctification of the Church's present and future ministry unto the gathering and perfecting of the saints for the glorying and enjoying of God. It is thus necessarily academic and intellectual, devotional and spiritual, as well as practical and ministerial.

Both the seminary and the seminarian must endeavor to tie together in the closest of relations: doctrine and piety, learning and godliness, knowledge and conviction of the truth, with growth in and expression of the truth in love, in the service of Christ and his people. This is one reason that we often speak at Reformed Theological Seminary of wanting to cultivate in our students "a mind for truth and a heart for God."

The entire work of the theological seminary may thus be construed as serving as an instrument of the Holy Spirit in applying the Word of God as a means of grace. The entire work of the seminarian is to be undertaken as an act of worship: to study to show themselves approved in order to present their bodies as a living and holy sacrifice, acceptable to God, which is their spiritual service of worship, and not to be conformed to this world, but transformed by the renewing of their mind, so that they may prove what the will of God is, that which is good and acceptable and perfect (Rom. 12:1-2) and handle accurately the Word of truth (2 Tim. 2:15), the Holy Scriptures, which are all God-breathed, and profitable for teaching, for reproof, for correction, for training in righteousness; that the man of God may be adequate, equipped for every good work (2 Tim. 3:14-17), living a life of godliness (1 Tim. 4:7), preaching the Word (2 Tim. 4:2), fighting the good fight, keeping the faith, and finishing the race (2 Tim. 4:7).

From the standpoint of confessional, Reformed, Presbyterian principles, theological education aims to gather and prepare a cohort of those called by the Church for the Gospel ministry, so that they grow by God's grace together in faith, hope and love, come to a greater and deeper knowledge and conviction of the whole counsel of God, so are thus enabled to handle accurately and to proclaim faithfully the Word of God; to pray continuously, Scripturally, and earnestly; to minister the sacraments, the covenant signs and seals of God, rightly; and to shepherd wisely and lovingly—and who correspondingly have their own hearts filled with and faith matured by that grace and truth, so that their character, life, ministry and witness are shaped by God's lavish, gracious, loving, saving work on their behalf, in Christ, and by his written self-disclosure and revealed will.

This is what prompts John R.W. Stott to say: "the key institution in the Church is the seminary or theological college. In every country the Church is a reflection of its seminaries. All the Church's future pastors and teachers pass through a seminary. It is there that they are either made or marred, either equipped and inspired or ruined."[5]

The original plan of Old Princeton Seminary reflects these same commitments and aspirations. What was its aim?

It is to form men for the Gospel ministry, who shall truly believe, and cordially love, and therefore endeavor to propagate and defend, in its genuineness, simplicity, and fulness, that system of religious belief and practice which is set forth in the Confession of Faith, Catechisms,

---

5. John R. W. Stott, *Guard the Truth: the Message of 1 Timothy & Titus* (Downers Grove: InterVarsity Press, 1996), 184.

and Plan of Government and Discipline of the Presbyterian Church is thus to perpetuate and extend the influence of true evangelical piety, and Gospel order.

It is to provide for the Church an adequate supply and succession of able and faithful ministers of the New Testament; workmen that need not to be ashamed, being qualified rightly to divide the word of truth.

It is to unite, in those who shall sustain the ministerial office, religion and literature; that piety of the heart which is the fruit only of the renewing and sanctifying grace of God, with solid learning: believing that religion without learning, or learning without religion, in the ministers of the Gospel, must ultimately prove injurious to the Church.

It is to afford more advantages than have hitherto been usually possessed by the ministers of religion in our country, to cultivate both piety and literature in their preparatory course; piety, by placing it in circumstances favourable to its growth, and by cherishing and regulating its ardour; literature, by affording favourable opportunities for its attainment, and by making its possession indispensable.

It is to provide for the Church, men who shall be able to defend her faith against infidels, and her doctrines against heretics.

It is to furnish our congregations with enlightened, humble, zealous, laborious pastors, who shall truly watch for the good of souls, and consider it as their highest honour and happiness to win them to the Saviour, and to build up their several charges in holiness and peace.

It is to promote harmony and unity of sentiment among the ministers of our Church, by educating a large body of them under the same teachers, and in the same course of study.

It is to lay the foundation of early and lasting friendships, productive of confidence and mutual assistance in after-life among the ministers of religion; which experience shows to be conducive not only to personal happiness, but to the perfecting of inquiries, researches, and publications advantageous to religion.

152

It is to preserve the unity of our Church, by educating her ministers in an enlightened attachment, not only to the same doctrines, but to the same plan of government.

It is to bring to the service of the Church genius and talent, when united with piety, however poor or obscure may be their possessor, by furnishing, as far as possible, the means of education and support, without expense to the student.

It is to found a nursery for missionaries to the heathen, and to such as are destitute of the stated preaching of the gospel; in which youth may receive that appropriate training which may lay a foundation for their ultimately becoming eminently qualified for missionary work.

It is, finally, to endeavour to raise up a succession of men, at once qualified for and thoroughly devoted to the work of the Gospel ministry; who, with various endowments, suiting them to different stations in the Church of Christ, may all possess a portion of the spirit of the primitive propagators of the Gospel; prepared to make every sacrifice, to endure every hardship, and to render every service which the promotion of pure and undefiled religion may require.[6]

The aim of this approach to theological education is to produce and prepare shepherd-teachers for the Church who have a mind for truth, a heart for God and who will live a life of ministry. Humble, happy, faithful, brave, loving, pastoral, sturdy, gentle, godly ministers who understand, teach and embody Reformed piety, doctrine, worship, polity, and practice. We want to provide God's people with ministers who know and believe their Bible; who treasure God; who bear witness to Christ and proclaim his Gospel; who are themselves transformed by grace and truth; who love their people; who live to serve; and who have a passion for the great commission.

---

6. Plan of the Theological Seminary of the Presbyterian Church in the United States of America, 1811 (Elizabeth-Town: Kollock, 1816).

The Insights of Three Theologians

The reflections and contributions of three Reformed theologians to the vision of theological education described here enrich our understanding of how God makes ministers. In 1675, Dutch theologian, Herman Witsius (1636–1708), gave his inaugural address as a professor of theology at the university in Franeker, subsequently translated and published in the little booklet *On the Character of a True Theologian* (made widely available in Scotland in a translation by John Donaldson in 1856 and again in 1871, with a commendation by William Cunningham, and more recently edited and reprinted in Greenville, SC by Reformed Academic Press in 1994). William Cunningham (1805–1861), wrote *An Introduction to Theological Studies* (seven chapters excerpted from his *Theological Lectures* [1878], from his course for first year students at New College, and published in three editions by Reformed Academic Press in 1991, 1993, and 1994). B.B. Warfield (1851–1921) wrote two superb essays, one on the seminarian, *The Religious Life of Theological Students*, originally an address delivered at Princeton Theological Seminary on October 4, 1911, and published frequently and variously since then (e.g., Phillipsburg: Presbyterian & Reformed, 1983); and another on the seminary, "Spiritual Culture in the Theological Seminary," an address delivered to the incoming Students, Sunday afternoon, September 20, 1903, in the Oratory of Stuart Hall, Princeton Theological Seminary (one can imagine J. Gresham Machen, already a student, in attendance), and subsequently published in the *Princeton Theological Review* 2, January, 1904.

Witsius, *On the Character of a True Theologian* (1675)

Though Witsius does not claim the title for himself, William Cunningham calls him "a 'true' and consummate theologian" possessed of "talent, sound judgment, learning, orthodoxy, piety and unction."[7] Dr. Mike Honeycutt (an expert on William

---

7. Witsius, *On the Character of a True Theologian* (Greenville: Reformed Academic Press, 1994), 19.

Cunningham, who studied and introduced the modern edition of Witsius' address) comments on Witsius' "precise theological formulation and intense experiential religion."[8] You can see in these two descriptions the qualities that were appreciated and aspired to in the Church's ministry. Indeed, Witsius' own definition of a theologian evidences the same interests: "By a theologian, I mean one who, imbued with a substantial knowledge of divine things derived from the teaching of God himself, declares and extols, not in words only, but by the whole course of his life, the wonderful excellencies of God and thus lives entirely for his glory."[9]

Witsius tells us that he writes this description of a true theologian (and he is not just speaking of professional academic scholars, he is especially thinking of what all ministers should be) in order "that I may have it continually before me." He wants his "delineation of the ministerial character" to point him to his duty and to remind him of his shortcomings that "he may the better discern his own failings and learn how humbly he should think of himself."[10] Already we are seeing that a combination of aspiration and humility are a part of the soil of spiritual growth for the seminarian.

He then outlines his address in three parts. He wants to contemplate how a true theologian is made, what he is supposed to do with what he has learned, and finally what he is to be himself. He says it this way:

> Let us, in contemplating such a theologian, inquire first in what school, under what teachers, by what method, he reaches a wisdom so lofty; then into the mode in which he may most successfully communicate to others what he has been taught himself; and lastly, into the habits of soul and outward walk by which he may adorn his doctrine; or, to comprehend in three words the sum of what is to be said, let us portray the TRUE THEOLOGIAN as a STUDENT, as a TEACHER, and as a MAN. For no one teaches well unless he has first learned well; no one learns well unless

---

8. Ibid., 9.
9. Ibid., 27.
10. Ibid., 26.

he learns in order to teach. And both learning and teaching are vain and unprofitable unless accompanied by practice.[11]

The True Theologian as a Student of Scripture and Disciple of the Spirit

Witsius wants the minister to "lay the foundations of his studies" in what he calls "the lower school of nature" or the "rudiments" (the basics of logic, grammar, rhetoric, moral philosophy, the acquisition of languages, etc.).

> Whatever is sound and judicious in human arts, whatever is true and substantial in philosophy, whatever is elegant and graceful in the wide extent of polite literature, all flow from the Father of Lights, the inexhaustible Fountain of all reason, truth, and beauty; and all this, therefore, collected from every quarter, ought again to be consecrated to Him.[12]

But he is especially concerned that the true theologian devote himself to the study of Scripture as a disciple of the Spirit. He wants him to "rise from that lower and merely natural school to the higher fields of Scripture study, and sitting humbly before God, let him learn from His mouth the hidden mysteries of salvation" and " be ravished with these heavenly oracles."[13] Putting his faith in God and God alone, the true theologian is "a humble disciple of the Scriptures" and "must also be a disciple of the Spirit." Why? Because "in order to understand spiritual things, we must have a spiritual mind"[14] and only the Holy Spirit can give that to us (1 Cor. 2:12–16). What is the result of this discipleship? "He [the Spirit] imparts the mind of Christ along with the things of Christ." What things? "He who is a student in this heavenly school not only knows and believes, but has also sensible experience of, the forgiveness of sins and the privilege of adoption and intimate communion with God and the grace of the indwelling Spirit

---

11. Ibid., 27–28.
12. Ibid., 30.
13. Ibid., 30–31.
14. Ibid., 31, 35.

and the hidden manna and the sweet love of Christ."[15] Thus, our true theologian has an experiential acquaintance of the things of God, and especially the saving benefits of Christ, revealed in Holy Scripture.

The True Theologian as an Experienced and Loving Teacher

Having been taught in the school of the Spirit in Scripture, our "experienced theologian" (meaning someone possessed of a true and saving knowledge of God, through Christ, by the Spirit) teaches the truth of God from Scripture, and does so from love. That is, having experienced himself the saving and sanctifying realities that are revealed by God in Scripture, and having known himself the love of God in Christ, because of his love for God and for God's people as God's own children and his brethren in Christ, he is inexorably drawn and driven to "employ every resource and put forth every effort to win many souls" and to build them up in grace and truth.[16] And so,

> he exerts himself to cherish his spiritual children in a winning and gentle manner and with an assiduity which knows no weariness, desiring to impart unto them not the gospel of God only but, if it were possible, his own soul and still more the Spirit of Christ, teaching, admonishing, beseeching, and fashioning and forming them as it were with his own hands, that at length, full of joy, he may, after the example of Christ, present them before God ...[17]

Witsius is less focused on the theologian's cultivation of skill in the art of teaching than on the motivation of his heart in teaching. What will the love of God yield in the heart of the true theologian as a teacher?

> The same spirit of love will lead him to set forth only what is certain, sound, solid, and fitted to cherish faith, excite hope, promote piety, and preserve unity and peace; doing all without prejudice, inclining to no party, abstaining with the utmost solicitude from all novelties of expression, unprofitable speech, strifes, and curious, foolish, and unlearned questions

---

15. Ibid., 36.
16. Ibid., 40.
17. Ibid., 40.

of words, by which the minds of the simple are disturbed, the Church rent in pieces—surmisings and whisperings engendered within, while without, a spectacle is exhibited which affords gratification to its enemies and a cause of triumph to Satan himself.[18]

Thus specious speculation and doctrinal deviation are revealed to be derivative not only from pride, but also from a selfish lovelessness for God and his people. The true theologian does not diverge from the pattern of sound words (2 Tim. 1:13), precisely because of his love for God and his people.

The True Theologian as a Man whose Life corresponds to his Profession

As we have already seen, Witsius taught that "both learning and teaching are vain and unprofitable, unless accompanied by practice." He was fond of telling his students that "he alone is a true Theologian, who adds the practical to the theoretical in religion."[19] Chaucer's compliment of the Poor Parson in the Canterbury Tales, "first he practiced, then he preached" is based upon a similar conviction. Both Witsius and Petrus Van Mastricht (1630–1706) studied under Gisbert Voetius, and both of them stressed that true theology is always practical and never merely notional (hence Mastricht called his magnum opus Theoretical-Practical Theology).

And so the final section of Witsius' address to seminarians begins with a searching question: "But with what heart, with what success, will that man labor who has not first sought to be himself fashioned after the image of God?" Witsius is concerned here with the minister's "habits of soul" (his inward dispositions) and "outward walk" (his personal, familial, ecclesiastical, and social manner of life). What would the habits of soul look like in a true theologian? Witsius describes them:

> The desire of heaven, contempt of the world, unfeigned gravity, a modesty leading him to be busy with his own affairs and to abstain from meddling

---

18. Ibid., 40–41.
19. Ibid., 13 and n.24, 16.

with those of others, a humility teaching him to think soberly of himself and highly of all besides, a mind solicitous to preserve peace as well as truth, fervent zeal tempered with the blandest gentleness, long-suffering under injuries and reproaches, a prudent circumspection in regard alike to the time and manner of action, a precision the most unbending and accurate in exacting of himself, with a readiness to pardon many things in his brethren, and whatever else pertains to this august preparation—these, these are the things which do not simply adorn, but which make the theologian.[20]

These are the things that a godly minister is disposed to. And what does his life look like? Witsius answers in seven copious clauses. First, he says that the true theologian does not outwardly pretend seriousness, nor long for riches, but sets his heart on things above (Col. 3:1–2).

> Show me a man who, intently meditating on sacred realities, does not simulate gravity by his beard or dress but, panting after the things which are above and eternal, holds in low estimation the sumptuous halls of the rich and the whole earth itself, with its gold and its silver;

Second, he does not covet pleasure, wealth and honors, nor the vanities and allurements of the world, but is wholly satisfied with the grace of Christ and the fellowship of the Spirit.

> who, satisfied with the grace of Christ the Saviour and the fellowship of the Divine Spirit inhabiting his breast, looks down as from a lofty eminence upon all the vanities and allurements of the world, coveting neither pleasures, nor wealth, nor honors;

Third, he does not become entangled with worldly affairs of business or politics, nor seek after positions, nor is he a manipulator, nor does he pursue the patronage of the great. He neither grovels before superiors in the Church, nor acts superior to his own flock, but concentrates fully on the pastoral care of souls and the interests of Christ's kingdom, appropriately confining his attention to his own place of ministry.

---

20. Ibid., 45–46.

who, devoting himself wholly to the care of souls, and the defense, promotion, and enlargement of the kingdom of Christ, does not give himself up to secular business or politics, watches for no office, is no demagogue, does not pay court to the great, does not cringe to his ecclesiastical superiors, nor lord it over God's heritage, and, accurately assigning to the church, the college, and the civil power their proper relative places, confines himself to his own church or chair;

Fourth, as he grows in the things of the Lord and in the duties of the Christian life, he does not compare himself favorably to others, or even to himself, but to those who are more mature, and supremely, to the commands of God in Scripture.

who, the farther he advances in the contemplation of the things which are above and in the practice of virtue, is the less disposed to tarnish the glory of his neighbor, measuring himself not by himself, but with those who are more perfect, and above all, with the perfect law of God;

Fifth, he is zealous for God's cause (rather than his own), and careful for the salvation of sinners, the protection of Christ's Church, and sound doctrine.

who, whensoever the cause of God, the salvation of souls, the defense of the Church, and the guardianship of the heavenly doctrine call for exertion, is all on fire with zeal for God and would rather die a hundred deaths than that one jot should be yielded to the enemy in that cause which is not his, but his Lord's;

Sixth, he does not want to settle scores, he forbears personal criticisms, and doesn't insist on his own views on uncertain questions. He is immovable against vehement attacks and at the same time has a way of attracting and unifying those who are in conflict.

who, at the same time, would seek no revenge for personal injuries, would bear with moderation reproaches directed against himself, and in doubtful matters not insist on his own opinion; who, as was said of Athanasius by the ancients, stands firm as a rock against the assaults of the violent, but as a magnetic center of attraction and union to those at variance;

Seventh, he is not reckless but careful, works hard but inconspicuously, seeking sincerely and simply to serve all, not viewing himself as better than others, ready to give others credit, regarding his neighbor above himself.

> who, always exercising prudence, attempts nothing rashly, exerting himself unobtrusively even in the most difficult undertakings; who in fine, not feignedly nor lightly, but with the most unaffected simplicity, is ready to throw himself at the feet of all, preferring himself to no one, but everyone to himself, is forward to give honor to all, esteeming his neighbor more than himself ...[21]

Witsius admits this is an incomplete picture, but it is still beautiful, and humbling. Indeed, he confesses that he himself falls short of it: "How little I resemble, how very far I differ from such a one, no one knows better than myself."[22] And yet his contemporaries saw much of these characteristics in him. He once said that "the love of truth and the spirit of charity, equally cultivated, constitute the brightest ornament of a Christian mind."[23] This was on full display in what Honeycutt calls "his irenic polemics with opposing theologians."[24] Witsius gives us an example, in his teaching and conduct, of a minister made by the means of grace, equally concerned for truth and love, and able to speak the truth in love.

Witsius' model of self-giving to his students is also an inspiring example to all seminary professors. As he concludes his address, and before he closes in prayer, he exhorts and encourages them with these words:

> Whatever I can do, for you I will do it. In all that I am, I will be yours. For you I will study; for you I will labor; for you I will write. You will I set before me; you will I carry in my bosom. I shall shrink neither from the weariness nor exhaustion attendant upon study if only I can subserve your improvement.[25]

---

21. Ibid., 46–47.
22. Ibid., 47.
23. Ibid., 14.
24. Ibid.
25. Ibid., 49.

Cunningham, *An Introduction to Theological Studies* (circa 1843, published 1878)

When William Cunningham began to lecture at New College, Edinburgh in the 1840s, he developed a series of lectures for first year students that were eventually published posthumously in 1878 in a book called *Theological Lectures* ([1878], reprinted in Greenville, by A Press, 1990). I encountered the volume of those lectures when I was a postgraduate student at New College in the 1980s, had it reprinted, and eventually excerpted the first seven chapters and had them published for my new students at Reformed Theological Seminary in the 1990s. When you read them, you get a feel for the kind of wisdom Cunningham imparted to those new ministerial students.

Each of the seven lectures are worth our reflection in thinking through the work of the seminary, but this is a chapter, not a booklet. His first lecture sets out helpful explanations of the function of education in general, and definitions of religion and theology in particular. It reminds us in a very Witsius-like way of the importance of an experiential knowledge of God in theology, and of the role of the Holy Spirit in understanding the Scriptures. Lectures two through four sketch out the various branches of theological studies, their significance, and relation to one another. His divisions are: first, exegetical theology; second, systematic theology; third, historical theology; and, fourth, pastoral theology. Our attention is going to be given to what he says in lectures five and six, so we will here only note that in lecture seven he makes a case for the absolute importance of mastering the biblical languages, as well as being thoroughly familiar with our English Bibles, and reminds ministerial students of the necessity of resting from their academic studies on the Lord's Day.

Now we turn our attention to lectures five and six. His great subjects in them are prayer, meditation, and temptation (meaning the experience of resisting temptation in our trials). In these two lectures, Cunningham urges upon aspiring ministers a sense of the importance of prayer and the Holy Spirit to the attainment of true knowledge of God, he shows the importance of meditation (meaning considered, prayerful, reflection on God's Word) to the minister's growth in grace, and he indicates the vital role of Christian experience, and even temptation, in our preparation for ministry. He is, of course, borrowing his outline from Martin Luther's famous dictum that *"Oratio, meditatio, tentatio* (prayer, meditation, trials/testing/affliction) make the minister." Cunningham leans more into the idea of resisting temptation than Luther's *tentatio/Anfechtung,* which Roland Bainton describes as "all the doubt, turmoil, pang, tremor, panic, despair, desolation, and desperation which invade the spirit of man."[26]

Prayer, in Light of the Necessary Agency of the Holy Spirit in Theological Study

Cunningham begins his exhortation first with prayer (following Luther): "it is the imperative and primary duty of all who desire to become acquainted with theology, and qualified for the office of a minister of the gospel, to abound in prayer and supplication."[27] But what Cunningham labors to do in much of his treatment of prayer in this lecture is to explain why prayer is so primary and necessary. His answer, in short, is that you really cannot understand the Scripture without the direct aid of the Holy Spirit. He says:

> It is a truth clearly revealed to us in Scripture, that no man ever really attains to any such knowledge of God's revealed will as will be available for his own personal salvation, or warrant him in entertaining the expectation of being instrumental through the truth in promoting the salvation of others, except through the direct agency of the Holy Ghost.[28]

He then elaborates this point. What is the reason that "the whole of your theological studies" must be accompanied "with a spirit and habit of earnest prayer for the illuminating influences of the Holy Ghost"? The answer he gives is threefold:

---

26. *Here I Stand: A Life of Martin Luther* (Nashville: Abingdon Press, 1978), 26.

27. William Cunningham, *An Introduction to Theological Studies* (Greenville: Reformed Academic Press, 1994), 57.

28. Ibid., 57–58.

First, that all really useful and valuable knowledge of theology, or of God's revealed will, must come from God himself;

Second, that God imparts this knowledge in connection with the study of his word, and the other means of grace, through the direct agency of the Holy Ghost, the third person of the Godhead; and

Third, that prayer is the direct and appropriate means which God has appointed and promised to bless, for drawing down upon us the influences of the Holy Ghost.[29]

The only proper conclusion from this three-part argument is that the whole of ministerial studies must be attended with prayer. Cunningham again expounds the point:

If these truths are duly impressed upon your minds, and if along with these convictions you have a real, sincere, and permanent desire to know God's revealed will, with a view to the great practical ends which this revelation was intended to serve with reference to men, collectively and individually, then the natural, the necessary result will be, that you will abound in prayer and supplication for the outpouring of God's Holy Spirit, that you will earnestly and importunately seek his guidance and direction with reference to the whole of your studies, to every book which you peruse, every topic to which your attention is directed, and every attempt you make to investigate the meaning of any portion of his word.[30]

Furthermore, Cunningham will argue, prayer alone can protect us from wrong desires for theological knowledge.

It is only a desire of theological knowledge, based upon those views and motives which we have described, that will lead you to abound and to persevere in prayer for the effusion of the Holy Spirit; and if you are not fervent and frequent in your prayers for his guidance, it is the plain dictate of common sense and prudence that you are not yet influenced by a sincere and intelligent desire that God by his Spirit would guide you into all truth. You are not then to infer that you have a desire for theological knowledge of the right kind, based upon right views, unless you are habitually praying

---

29. Ibid., 58.
30. Ibid.

for the guidance of God's Spirit; and you may be assured that during the whole of your theological studies, which ought to last during your lives, the restraining of prayer, a disposition to neglect or disregard this exercise, or to perform it carelessly or perfunctorily, may be regarded as marking at once a declension in your spiritual vigour and activity, and also a diminished proficiency in the acquisition of really valuable professional knowledge.[31]

This whole section of the lecture has obvious and lifelong importance for the minister. It also reminds us again of how often we are changed by prayer.

Meditation, unto the Discernment of Scripture's Meaning and Application, and our Protection from Error

Cunningham begins this lecture with a definition of meditation, which he identifies as reflection upon our learning and reading, and especially contemplating the meaning and significance of what we have read, particularly Scripture. He says:

Meditation, as including learning, reading, and reflection, and especially reading and reflecting upon the Word of God, so as to understand the meaning of its statements and the import of its teaching, is that which in the ordinary relation of cause and effect bears most directly and immediately upon the acquisition of theological knowledge.[32]

Why is this so important? Cunningham explains:

You must read and reflect. Theological knowledge cannot be put into you, *ab extra* [from the outside], without your own faculties being called into vigorous exercise. It consists radically and essentially in the formation of correct judgments, as to the meaning and import of statements in God's word ...[33]

But Cunningham goes on to argue that neglecting to meditate and reflect can leave us open to theological error. He urges in us "the right and honest exercise of our faculties, and the faithful and conscientious improvement of our opportunities," as well as

---

31. Ibid., 62.
32. Ibid., 69.
33. Ibid., 70.

"diligence, caution, and perseverance" in their exercise, in order that we be kept from error.

> The knowledge of the truth is the gift of God, and is traceable to or connected with the right and honest exercise of our faculties, and the faithful and conscientious improvement of our opportunities, while the adoption and maintenance of error is owing universally to some failure in these respects; to the want of a sincere and honest desire to know the truth, to the operation of some perverting and misleading influence, or to some failure in the diligence, caution, and perseverance with which our faculties have been brought to bear upon the investigation.[34]

Temptation, unto Intimate Acquaintance with Divine Truth and its Application in Resisting Sin

According to Cunningham (and a little differently from Luther), *tentatio*/temptation means "experience, or the practical application of divine truth in the way of guarding against evil tendencies and results."[35] He argues that you really can't understand the meaning and significance of Scripture, or apply it to others to help them resist temptation, until you have had to do so yourself, and have thereby come to understand more deeply the truth of God's word.

> You can have no thorough and intimate acquaintance with divine truth, and especially you will be very ill fitted to explain and apply it for the benefit of others, unless you have had some practice in actually bringing it to bear upon the resistance of those temptations with which all believers are assailed in their journey towards Zion.[36]

Cunningham again explains that the experience of temptation, as we take recourse to God's Word, increases our understanding of it, and our ability to rightly apply it to others.

> The habit and exercise of applying divine truth for resisting temptation and growing in grace is indispensable to every believer, to every one who has really entered upon the way to Zion. But at present we are called upon

---

34. Ibid., 71.
35. Ibid., 63.
36. Ibid., 64.

specially to notice that it tends greatly to promote and extend men's real knowledge and intimate discernment of divine truth, and to aid them unspeakably in rightly dividing it, or applying it wisely or judiciously for the benefit of others.[37]

Indeed, Cunningham says, there is an experiential knowledge and wisdom that can only be obtained by going through such temptation, and that uniquely equips ministers of the Gospel to explain to our flock, clearly and helpfully, how to fight temptation.

> This process of actually applying the word of God and the doctrines which it contains to their great practical purpose in the formation of character and in the regulation of conduct, according to the actual circumstances in which men are in providence placed, and the temptations they are called upon to encounter, produces a clear, impressive, experimental acquaintance with divine truth, which cannot be acquired in any other way, and which peculiarly fits them for communicating clear and impressive conceptions of them to others ...[38]

So, we can see in Cunningham's exposition in these two lectures, that even though he was living and ministering in the midst of rising rationalism and infidelity of the 19th century, he fully retains the experiential emphasis in theological education and ministerial preparation that we encountered in Herman Witsius, who ministered in a very different context and time.

Warfield, *Spiritual Culture in the Theological Seminary* (1903) & *The Religious Life of Theological Students* (1911)

B.B. Warfield, who taught theology at Old Princeton Seminary from 1887 to 1921, and served as its last Principal until 1902, in his address to first year students on "Spiritual Culture in the Theological Seminary" expresses the aims and aspirations of the theological seminary and counsels seminarians on how they are to make the most of their time and studies:

---

37. Ibid., 63–64.
38. Ibid., 64–65.

How are we who teach best to fulfill the trust committed to us, of guiding others in their preparation for the high office of Minister of Grace? How are you who are here to make this preparation, so to employ your time and opportunities as to become in the highest sense true stewards of the mysteries of Christ?[39]

Warfield is balancing two concerns. The first is his assertion that the academic and intellectual work of the seminary must not displace its concerns for the spiritual, moral, and practical preparation for the ministry. He says "intellectual training alone will never make a true minister; that the heart has rights which the head must respect; and that it behooves us above everything to remember that the ministry is a spiritual office."[40] To that end he will argue that

any proper preparation for the ministry must include these three chief parts—a training of the heart, a training of the hand, a training of the head—a devotional, a practical and an intellectual training? Such a training, in a word, as that we may learn first to know Jesus, then to grasp the message He would have [us] deliver to men, and then how He would have us work for Him in His vineyard.[41]

He candidly admits: "aptness to teach is only the beginning of his fitting. All the other requirements are rooted in his moral or spiritual fitness."[42]

But the other concern he has is the prevalent rejection of the necessity of academic and intellectual study for the ministry. He means to object strongly to the idea that the seminary's plan for ministerial preparation is overly intellectual, citing Joseph T. Duryea who declared it "high time that the question whether culture and learning do not unfit preachers for the preaching of the Gospel to ordinary men and women, were

---

39. B.B. Warfield, "Spiritual Culture in the Theological Seminary," in *The Princeton Theological Review*, 2:1 (1904): 65.

40. Ibid., 65.

41. Ibid., 67–68.

42. Ibid., 68.

referred back without response to the stupidity that inspires it."[43] In particular, Warfield is concerned about three things: the failure to appreciate the importance of study and learning the ministry, the false juxtaposition of it with the practical and spiritual aspects of ministerial preparation, and neglecting to grasp the reciprocity that should exist between the intellectual and spiritual, the academic and devotional, the theological and practical.

So, the whole first section of his address aims to keep these things together. Ministerial preparation requires knowledge and devotion, head and heart, truth and practice. He explains:

> Our primary business at the Seminary is, no doubt, to obtain the intellectual fitting for our ministerial work, and nothing must be allowed to supersede that in our efforts. But neither must the collateral prosecution of the requisite training of the heart and hand be neglected, as opportunity offers. Nor will a properly guarded attention to these injure the discharge of our scholastic duties; it will, on the contrary, powerfully advance their successful performance. The student cannot too sedulously cultivate devoutness of spirit ... When the heart is thoroughly aroused, the slowest mind starts into motion and an impulse is given it which carries it triumphantly over intellectual difficulties before which it quailed afraid. And equally a proper taste of the practical work of the ministry is a great quickener of the mind for the intellectual preparation. We cannot do without these things. And the student must be very careful, therefore—even on this somewhat low ground—while not permitting any distractions to divert him from his primary task as a student, yet to take full advantage of all proper opportunities that may arise to train his heart and hand also.[44]

In other words, the preparation of our heads, hearts, and hands for ministry ought not to be opposed or put at odds. Indeed, they are inseparably connected and mutually dependent and reciprocal.

In the second section of his address, he attempts to explain how this is to be done in seminary. He outlines five ways that seminary life may serve to assist this well-rounded preparation: first, in attendance upon the public means of grace; second,

---

43. Ibid., 65.
44. Ibid., 70.

additional opportunities for social worship and voluntary association for spiritual purposes; third, understanding and undertaking the work of the seminary itself as a means of grace; fourth, approaching your seminary work as a religious duty and act of worship; and fifth, the cultivation of communal devotion, engagement in and discussion about congregational labor, theological reading, and mutual interaction and conversation.

I will concentrate our attention on two of these, the third and fourth, though the fifth also warrants extended reflection. As we have already noted in this chapter, Warfield argues that

> The entire work of the Seminary deserves to be classed in the category of means of grace; and the whole routine of work done here may be made a very powerful means of grace if we will only prosecute it in a right spirit and with due regard to its religious value. For what are we engaging ourselves with in our daily studies but just the Word of God, the history of God's dealings with His people, the great truths that He has revealed to us for the salvation of our souls? And what are we doing when we engage ourselves day after day with these topics of study and meditation, but just what every Christian man strives to do when he is seeking nutriment for his soul? The only difference is that what he does sporadically, at intervals, and somewhat primarily, it is your privilege to give yourselves to unbrokenly for a space of three whole years![45]

So, since seminary is fundamentally ministering the Word of God to future ministers so that they can minister the Word of God to others, and is thus a means of grace, how should the seminarian approach his labors and respond to these privileges? Warfield is definite in his answer and exhortation:

> I beseech you, brethren, take every item of your Seminary work as a religious duty. I am emphasizing the adjective in this. I mean do all your work religiously—that is, with a religious end in view, in a religious spirit, and with the religious side of it dominant in your mind.[46]

---

45. Ibid., 73.
46. Ibid.

In other words, as we have already said, seminarians ought to approach seminary as an act of worship.

The third section of Warfield's address treats of, not Luther's and Cunningham's trilogy of *oratio, meditatio, tentatio*, but of *lectio, meditatio, oratio* making the theologian. Warfield says:

> *Lectio, meditatio, oratio,* (reading, meditation, prayer) the old Doctors used to say, *faciunt theologum* [make the theologian]. They were right. Take the terms in the highest senses they will bear, and we shall have an admirable prescription of what we must do would we cultivate to its height the Christian life that is in us.[47]

But having given this trio, he begins with *oratio*, prayer, and we see the experiential concerns of Witsius and Cunningham alive and well at the dawn of the twentieth century in confessional Reformed theological education. "Above all else that you strive after, cultivate the grace of private prayer," Warfield says. Then he adds "Next to the prayerful spirit, the habit of reverent meditation on God's truth is useful in cultivating devoutness of life."[48] What is meditation? Warfield explains: "Meditation is an exercise which stands somewhere between thought and prayer. It must not be confounded with mere reasoning; it is reasoning transfigured by devout feeling; and it proceeds by broodingly dissolving rather than by logically analyzing the thought."[49]

And what of Bible reading? Warfield connects it to the other side of meditation:

> As meditation, then, on the one side takes hold upon prayer, so, on the other, it shades off into devotional Bible-reading, the highest exercise of which, indeed, it is. Life close to God's Word, is life close to God. When I urge you to make very much while you are in the Seminary of this kind of devotional Bible study, running up into meditation, pure and simple, I am but repeating what the General Assembly specifically requires of you. "It is expected," says the Plan of the Seminary, framed by the Assembly as our organic law, "that every student will spend a portion of time, every

---

47. Ibid., 76.
48. Ibid., 77.
49. Ibid., 78.

morning and evening, in devout meditation and self-recollection and examination; in reading the Holy Scriptures solely with a view to a personal and practical application of the passage read to his own heart, character and circumstances; and in humble, fervent prayer and praise to God in secret."[50]

We hasten on to Warfield's classic, *The Religious Life of Theological Students*. Given just over a decade after "Spiritual Culture of the Theological Seminary", "Religious Life" focuses on the student, the seminarian, and the considerations which he needs to be aware of in his ministerial preparation. Warfield starts with a familiar assertion: "A minister must be learned, on pain of being utterly incompetent for his work. But before and above being learned, a minister must be godly."[51] And just as in "Spiritual Culture," he is concerned that these not be set in opposition to one another. He will spend the whole essay urging us not to sunder or oppose godliness and learning, theology and religion, mind and heart: "Put your heart into your studies; do not merely occupy your mind with them, but put your heart into them."[52] Along the way he will give good counsel on how the student can keep learning and devotion together.

But Warfield will also sound the note that only God can make ministers. That is good for us to hear. God makes ministers. Seminary is but his tool, instrument, and means. "None but he who made the world", Warfield quotes John Newton as saying, "can make a minister."[53]

Conclusion

Perhaps it is good that we end here. What is seminary? A special and specific kind of means of grace. What does it do? Cultivate doctrine and devotion, truth and love, faith and practice, mind and heart, in the life of the seminarian. What does this kind of ministerial preparation produce? Ministers of the Gospel who

---

50. Ibid., 78.
51. B.B. Warfield, *The Religious Life of Theological Students* ([1911], repr. Phillipsburg: Presbyterian & Reformed, 1983), 1.
52. Ibid., 6.
53. Ibid., 15.

explain, enforce, and apply divine truth as contained in the sacred Scriptures, in order that by the agency of the Spirit through the instrumentality of the truth, men may be first of all turned from darkness to light, and then thereafter enabled to die more and more unto sin, and to live more and more unto righteousness.[54]

In the end, ministers are meant to do two things. Declare the Good News in calling sinners home to Christ (evangelism, "gathering") and help Christians live the Christian life better (discipleship, "perfecting"). Thus, the minister's whole life and work is wrapped up in the public and personal administration of the means of grace to these ends. That's why the Westminster Confession of Faith says that the Church has been "given the ministry, oracles, and ordinances of God, for the gathering and perfecting of the saints, in this life, to the end of the world: and does, by His own presence and Spirit, according to His promise, make them effectual thereunto" (25.3).

This is what seminary was meant to help them do. And we need it today, more than ever.

---

54. Cunningham, *An Introduction to Theological Studies*, 63.

Part 3:

The Generations of Calvinism in Geneva and Beyond

7

Devotion to God and to God's War

Calvin's 2 Samuel Sermons in the Context of the

First French War of Religion

Jon Balserak

*So today there are many who would like
to be neutral in the midst of all these troubles.*
John Calvin[1]

ONE of the great services to the church and academy our
honorandus has performed is translating Calvin's sermons.
His translation of the 2 Samuel sermons is characteristically
superb and has been praised for its faithfulness and clarity.

The picture these sermons paint of Calvin is a picture
of one utterly committed to the service of his God. This is

---

1. John Calvin, *Sermons on 2 Samuel*, trans. Douglas F. Kelly (Carlisle: The
Banner of Truth Trust, 1992), 87. These sermons exist in the critical edition found
in the *Supplementa Calviniana; Sermons inédits* (ed. Erwin Mulhaupt et al.; 11 vols.;
Neukirchen: Neukirchener, 1936–) (hereafter SC). The 2 Samuel sermons are found
in volume 1, *Predigten über das 2. Buch Samuelis. In der Ursprache nach der Genfer
Handschrift herausgegeben von Hanns Rückert*. I will cite from Dr Kelly's translation
throughout.

nicely exemplified in the quotation at the head of this chapter. This quotation is from his sermon on 2 Samuel 2:18–32. The sermon has been entitled, by Professor Kelly, as "Disunity and War," and we will return to it as well as to other portions of these sermons in the volume later.

There are, unsurprisingly, numerous references to war in these sermons. The contents of 2 Samuel make this unavoidable. But what may perhaps be more surprising is Calvin's references to war in his application of the text to his hearers in St. Pierre Cathedral. He not only mentions war when discussing the trials believers endure in this life, the ravages of sin upon human existence, and the like, but also explicitly urges his congregation to support the war going on in France at the time, namely, the first of the (so-called) French Wars of Religion. They should, to be more precise, support the Huguenots who were fighting against the French Catholics in this conflict. Calvin saw this as a war approved of by God. Indeed, he understood it to be God's war and integral to the establishing in France of "the pure religion." Recall that Calvin's dedicatory letter to his Daniel lectures published in the autumn of 1561 was addressed "to all the pious worshippers of God who desire the kingdom of Christ to be rightly established in France."[2] This work of establishing Christ's kingdom was an ongoing effort and labor of love for Calvin, Beza, and their colleagues. With respect to the war, Calvin demanded support and condemned indifference and disloyalty. Before we look more at the character of Calvin's handling of war in these sermons, let us consider the context in more detail.

Life and War in 1562

The specific day his homily on 2 Samuel 2:18–32 was preached was June 5, 1562. Calvin preached his first sermon on 2 Samuel on May 23, 1562. He would preach eighty-seven sermons on 2 Samuel, finishing on February 3, 1563, after which he would

---

2. *Ioannis Calvini opera quae supersunt omnia* (ed. Guillaume Baum, Edouard Cunitz, and Edouard Reuss; 59 vols.; Brunsvigae: Apud C. A. Schwetschke et filium, 1863–1900), 18: 614 [hereafter CO].

begin 1 Kings. These 2 Samuel sermons were the subject of his weekday sermons. Though his weekday preaching (usually on an Old Testament book) ordinarily occupied just three week-days, namely, Monday, Wednesday and Friday, Calvin preached every day except Sunday on 2 Samuel. This strongly suggests the importance of the war to Calvin and the hopes he had for his sermons on 2 Samuel to aid with the war effort. It also reveals how crucial it was that the Huguenots receive support from Geneva. The only day he diverted his attention away from 2 Samuel was on Sunday when he devoted his time to expounding Matthew's gospel in the morning and various Psalms in the afternoon.[3]

The first French civil war began on April 2, 1562, following the Vassy massacre.[4] It was on April 2 that Louis of Condé along with other nobles seized Orléans and declared their intention to free the twelve-year-old French King, Charles IX, from his body of councillors, who were all Catholic and included Catherine de' Medici and members of the House of Guise. Calvinists also seized Angers, Blois, and Tours along the Loire. Skirmishes, which had been happening since the late-1550s, continued and in some regions increased. Serious battles occurred in Rouen and Orléans. Major figures such as Antoine of Navarre and Francis, the Duke of Guise, died in this first war. Tensions increased, moving Catherine de' Medici, acting as regent, to mediate a truce. This first war was temporarily settled on March 19, 1563, with the Edict of Amboise but would experience later iterations until 1598 and the Edict of Nantes. When Calvin began preaching on 2 Samuel in late-May, his French co-religionists had been engaged in this war against their Catholic countrymen and women for roughly five weeks.

---

3. See T.H.L. Parker, *Calvin's Preaching* (Louisville: Westminster/John Knox Press, 1992), 152. On Calvin's corpus more generally, Jean-François Gilmont, *Jean Calvin et le livre imprimé* (Genève: Droz 1997); Rodolphe Peter and Jean-François, Gilmont, *Bibliotheca calviniana: les oeuvres de Jean Calvin publiées au XVIe siècle* (Genève: Droz, 1991–2000).

4. On the French Wars of Religion, see *inter alia*, Mack P. Holt, *The French Wars of Religion, 1562-1629* (Cambridge: Cambridge University Press, 2005) and R.J. Knecht, *The French Wars of Religion, 1559-1598*, third edition (London: Routledge, 2010).

Calvin, Beza, and many in Geneva supported the war effort vigorously, though Geneva's official position was one of neutrality. Their support for the war took various forms. Remember that by the 1560s, all but one of the Company of Pastors were French; thus, they had strong personal reasons for wanting to involve themselves in the conflict and see a particular outcome to it, not only on religious ground but also on national grounds.[5] We may surmise from comments made by them, particularly in their correspondences, that they knew their homeland was descending into civil war. Letters received by the Genevans from individuals like Admiral Coligny around this time also confirmed the likelihood of a coming conflict.[6] Beza, in fact, as early as March 28, 1562, wrote to Calvin to inform him that he had placed himself at the service of Louis of Condé to assist with the war effort.[7]

What becomes extremely clear upon examination is that Calvin and Beza desperately wanted the Huguenots to win this war. One might raise the question of whether Calvin and his colleagues sought in any way to push (however we may want to interpret that word) France towards civil war. It is certainly plausible that they may have sought this, though by no means guaranteed. One of the biggest reasons for thinking this is the fact that Calvin and Beza were involved in the September 1560 coup plot known as the Maligny affair.[8] In point of fact, numerous

---

5. On Calvin's managing of the Genevan company of pastors, see William Naphy, *Calvin and the Consolidation of the Genevan Reformation* (Louisville: Westminster/ John Knox Press, 2003) also Scott Manetsch, *Calvin's Company of Pastors; Pastoral Care and the Emerging Reformed Church, 1536–1609* (New York: Oxford University Press, 2012). More generally, *Brill's Companion to the Reformation in Geneva*, ed. Jon Balserak (Boston and Leiden: Brill, 2021).

6. See *inter alia, CO* 18: 230.

7. Theodore Beza, *Correspondance de Théodore de Bèze* (ed. Hippolyte Aubert et al.; 42 vols.; *Travaux d'Humanisme et Renaissance* (Geneva: Librairie Droz, 1960-), IV, 76 as mentioned in Scott Manetsch, *Theodore Beza and the Question for Peace in France, 1572–1598* (Leiden: Brill, 2000), 24 [hereafter CB].

8. Alain Dufour, "L'affaire de Maligny (Lyon, 4–5 septembre 1560) vue à travers la correspondance de Calvin et de Bèze," in *Cahiers d'Histoire* 8 (1963) 269–80. For more, see Jon Balserak, *John Calvin as Sixteenth-century Prophet* (Oxford: Oxford University Press, 2014); Philip Benedict, *Season of Conspiracy: Calvin, The French Reformed Churches, and Protestant Plotting in the Reign of Francis II (1559–1560)* (Philadelphia:

letters between Calvin, Theodore Beza, François Hotman, François Morel, John Sturm, Admiral Coligny, and others make it clear they were—especially following the ascension to the throne of King Francis II on July 10, 1559—engaged in trying to rouse Antoine of Navarre to claim his right and call the Estates General, and that their plans sometimes involved the idea of giving arms and men to Antoine of Navarre, who was a prince of the blood (i.e. a popular magistrate), for this purpose.[9] Their endeavors also often involved subterfuge and deception.[10]

Calvin and Beza were in touch and had important relationships with all the major players among the Huguenots. Kingdon rightly notes that "[o]n every phase of the war's progress Geneva kept itself well informed."[11] They were aware of the movements of the Guises and the French government. Calvin, for instance, wrote to Beza on February 11, 1562, and discussed the movements of "gradually leading troops in no small numbers out of Spain and enlisting other soldiers in Italy."[12] Kingdon notes that Calvin included in his annual exhortation to the people of Geneva in 1562 prior to the election of syndics that the people choose men who were godly and capable "especially in these times when it seems that the enemies increase, and their machinations are great."[13]

The Council received requests for help, as did Calvin, from a variety of figures, specifically from Louis of Condé, and responded positively to many of these requests. They also redoubled prayers

---

American Philosophical Society Press, 2020). Intriguingly, one scholar argued that Geneva's smuggling of ministers into France was "une revolution mal conduit" and that it might have been wiser for the Genevans to take a more aggressive approach (see Etienne Trocme, "Une Revolution mal Conduite," *Revue d'Histoire et de Philosophie Religieuses* 39 (1959): 160–168). It turns out, the Genevans did take a more aggressive approach as Dufour and others have shown.

9. See *inter alia, CO* 18: 177–180; *CO* 20: 473; and *CB* III, 63.

10. See Jon Balserak, "Geneva's Use of Lies, Deceit, and Simulation in their Efforts to Reform France, 1536–1563," in *Harvard Theological Review* 112/1 (2019): 76–100.

11. Robert Kingdon, *Geneva and the Coming of the Wars of Religion in France, 1555–1563* (Geneva: Droz, 1956), 115.

12. *CO* 19: 284.

13. Kingdon, *Geneva*, 115.

for the Huguenots.[14] They also sent money, gunpowder, and weapons to the Huguenot armies. There were people in Geneva who produced arms for export.[15] Concerning soldiers, Genevan men—many being refugees from France—volunteered to serve the Huguenot armies and some of these requests were granted by the Genevan Council, though not all.[16] But Geneva had to conceal their efforts here. This was not only because the appearance of aiding the Huguenots, if gleaned by France, would be politically dangerous but also because the city was, during this period, being threatened by Catholic armies under the Duke of Savoy— this was a threat that went back decades and was something they had to take extremely seriously. They were, then, in a rather compromised position. They simply could not send men into France to serve as soldiers without taking stock of who remained in Geneva to defend the city from the threat they faced. Be that as it may, they did (as I mentioned) send some men to fight on the Huguenots' side.

Not every Genevan supported the Huguenots. In fact, the Little Council, Calvin, Beza, and others were very concerned about traitors who were present in the city. They had to deal (for instance) with the wife and brother-in-law of Baron des Adrets, who had been accused of treason.[17] Such matters offer a glimpse of the tensions present in Geneva at this time. Nonetheless, the Genevans' commitment to the Huguenots was sizeable, as is nicely summarized by Kingdon:

> It is clear that Geneva contributed in material ways to the Huguenot armies in France. Though the appearance of neutrality was maintained, the government allowed and at times encouraged the sending of small groups of men, large sums of money, and substantial quantities of gunpowder to the forces fighting for the Calvinist faith ... Geneva became a veritable arsenal of Calvinism.[18]

---

14. Ibid., 116.
15. Ibid., 121–22.
16. Ibid., 117.
17. Ibid., 120.
18. Ibid., 127.

So then, Geneva offered fulsome support to the Huguenot cause.

Calvin, Beza, and their colleagues specifically involved themselves in supporting the war in a number of ways. As already mentioned, they knew essentially every major player involved in the conflict from the side of the Huguenots and Calvin, for instance, was contacted by Louis of Condé a number of times or on other occasions Condé asked the Genevan Council to speak with Calvin, as they were making decisions about something he had requested from them. More specifically, Calvin took it upon himself to find money to support the Huguenot armies; even money to pay mercenary soldiers. Calvin played an important role in regard to obtaining money from the Swiss.[19] The letter cited by Bruce Gordon nicely depicts Calvin's willingness to pressure others on this matter: "The point in question is to find money to support the troops which M. d'Andelot has levied. This is not the moment to enter into inquiries or disputes in order to find fault with mistakes that have been committed in times past."[20]

What becomes clear upon examination—and what our consideration of these 2 Samuel sermons will also exhibit—is that "[p]olitics and religion had become so inextricably entwined that the ecclesiastical structure built by the men of Geneva was in fact now operating on a military basis,"[21] as Kingdon remarked. Similarly, John Witte, Jr., has astutely observed concerning Calvin's later thought: "he began to blur the lines between the earthly kingdom and the heavenly kingdom, between spiritual and political life, law, and liberty."[22] Both observations are accurate and make for some intriguing results, in terms of the content of Calvin's sermons.

---

19. Ibid., 118.

20. *CO* 19: 550–551; Calvin's September 1562 letter to church in Languedoc as cited in Bruce Gordon, *Calvin* (New Haven: Yale University Press, 2009), 321–22.

21. Kingdon, *Geneva*, 116.

22. John Witte, Jr, *The Reformation of Rights: Law, Religion, and Human Rights in Early Modern Calvinism* (New York: Cambridge University Press, 2007), 56.

The War and Calvin's 2 Samuel Sermons

Given Calvin and his colleagues' support of the war, it is no surprise that we find Calvin mentioning it in his exposition of 2 Samuel. There are, of course, various themes treated here. He does not only mention battles, fighting, and bloodshed. But that said, he does turn to war often and counsels his congregation specifically on it.

Calvin laments war. He bemoans it and tells his hearers they should detest "wars that arise from religion."[23] He speaks of the danger "Christians", by which he seems surely to mean the Reformed believers in France, are under and talks of the "game" of war that is played.[24] Hating war, Calvin is not naïve. His lamentation does not move him towards passivism.[25] Rather, he insists humankind must engage in wars and he and his hearers must grapple with its presence in their lives. No one can avoid war. In fact, God "intends to prove us by them."[26] We shall have more to say on God's proving of his people and their need for trust in these circumstances later. But Calvin is adamant and says quite often that war, as horrible as it is, cannot be avoided in this life.

The themes he touches on cover the gamut, from talk of the idea of a just war, to questions of the source of victory and of defeat and the spiritual character that one ought to possess in relation to conflict. But in order to examine Calvin's handling of war further, we might look in detail at some of Calvin's sermons on it.

In his exposition of 2 Samuel 2:18–32, we find Calvin making three interrelated but distinct points concerning war. The first concerns the character of the war raging between the Huguenots and the Catholics. Calvin's specific point is that this war is God's war. The Huguenots fight under Christ's "banner."[27] The second is that those who oppose this war are traitors—traitors to God

---

23. Calvin, *2 Samuel*, 72.
24. Ibid., 71.
25. Ibid., 72–73.
26. Ibid., 72.
27. Ibid., 90.

and to true believers who follow "the pure religion."[28] The third point is this. In order to establish the two earlier points, Calvin sets down a rubric which underlies his thinking, namely, that there is such continuity between the two periods of Redemptive history that the two mirror one another. Thus, the war being fought in this text between the House of Saul and House of David mirrors the conflict between the Catholics and the Calvinists. (n.b. the text of 2 Samuel 2:18–32 concerns a battle between those defending David's kingship against those from the House of Saul who opposed it and are attacking David and his fellows). I will elaborate on these three points now.

Calvin asserts "[t]here is a double war in the Church because of religion."[29] The one kind is the battle against heresy, according to which some are put to death. The second is the development of this, namely, "[w]hen people are banded against one another in sects," as eventually "it becomes necessary to resort to arms."[30] Here Calvin has described David's era as well as his own. "Let us not be astonished," he says, "if this takes place in our own times."[31] Calvin has, then, set his entire assessment of the war raging between the Catholics and Calvinists firmly within redemptive history.

Assessing this war in both David's era and Calvin's own, he criticizes the Catholics and those of the House of Saul for their wickedness. This elicits from Calvin some trenchant observations on war. He laments the number of people who have been killed in wars and criticizes "princes" who "claim to be Christians and Catholics" yet "are killing an infinite number of people."[32] The present tense here indicates his turn to commentary on the present day. The prince, then, is plainly King Charles IX along with Catherine de' Medici and other members of the French

---

28. Ibid.
29. Ibid., 86.
30. Ibid.
31. Ibid.
32. Ibid., 85.

Catholic government, including the House of Guise.[33] Turning to the other side of the battle (i.e. the side of the righteous who fight for God's honor), Calvin argues Joab "was right … to take up arms" on this occasion. This is because his military response was good and approved by God. It would, Calvin insists, have been wrong for David to have given up his right to the crown, which God had given to him. Thus, Abner and his army had a duty to defend David, God's chosen king. Turning to apply the text to his hearers, Calvin declares:

> Now then, are we to condemn those who fight not merely under a mortal man, but for the truth of God, for his service, for the pure religion for the kingdom of our Lord Jesus Christ?[34]

Calvin is plainly referring to the Huguenots; the moral man may, it seems, be an allusion to Louis of Condé. But the basic point is, Calvin's working assumption is that the two periods of redemptive history mirror one another not only generally but specifically and with respect to the subject of war such that God's support of the House of David in their war is effectively identical to God's support for the Huguenots. There "are wars inside the Church"[35] and this current war is one of them. He inserts no qualifiers into this basic conviction and adds nothing to distance himself from the plain implication that the Huguenots are fighting God's war for the establishing of God's kingdom in France. This covers points one and three.

Calvin also addresses the idea of traitors, i.e. point number two. We noted earlier Geneva's concern about traitors and now can see it manifest in a concrete example. Calvin reminds his hearers that even though war is horrible that does not mean people should conclude both parties in a war are morally equivalent. "That," he says, "would be a failure to discern properly."[36] He continues to press the point he is making. Becoming more specific, he avers:

---

33. Ibid.
34. Ibid., 87.
35. Ibid.
36. Ibid.

> Even when there are two opposing camps in the Church, if one is opposing the truth of God in order to overthrow it and the other holds to the good so that it may always follow what is commanded, it is certain that whoever is neutral will be disloyal and a traitor.[37]

He continues to identify indifference as disloyalty before explicitly calling out those who wish to stand aloof from the war currently raging. Among his remarks is the quote at the head of this article, which I cite again here:

> So today there are many who would like to be neutral in the midst of all these troubles.[38]

He continues to urge unambiguous devotion to the Huguenot cause and identify it unequivocally with the cause of God. He acknowledges that "even when we do battle for the cause of God, we should still seek reconciliation when it is genuine and necessary, but not hollow reconciliations."[39] He is at pains here to remind his hearers that an empty peace is not to be pursued. Rather, all must engage in the service of God so that it might be "carried out in integrity, as befits pure religion."[40]

Essential to his treatment of traitors is his belief that the Huguenots represent God's church. Thus, after encouraging the idea of reconciliation briefly (as I just mentioned), Calvin notes that of course the wicked and the good are, in this life, mixed together. In his mind, this leads him to conclude:

> … so that the Church of God will always have to fight, either with weapons or with verbal disputations.[41]

His explicit assertion concerning God's church fighting "with weapons" is illuminating.

And this necessity for the church to fight has ramifications. It is, he continues, certain that "we would be traitors" if we failed

---

37. Ibid.
38. Ibid.
39. Ibid., 88.
40. Ibid.
41. Ibid., 90.

to fight both "for his name and for our salvation with those whom he has taken under his banner."[42] On this point, he warns that "the papists and enemies of God" would certainly like to make peace with us "in such a way that they would then be able to ruin us."[43] Elaborating on what that means, he points to the idea that compromise with the Catholics would end up confusing the compromiser such that they would not know "what it means to be on David's side, nor what the pure religion is."[44] He continues in this vein for another paragraph before concluding with his standard manner for ending his sermons: "Now let us prostrate ourselves ..."[45] The tone of his treatment when speaking about compromise suggests that he believed there may have been, in the congregation, some who felt tempted to pursue peace at all costs. To Calvin, such a solution is an act of betrayal of God's people and of God himself.

The sermon we just considered was preached on June 5, 1562. We might examine a later sermon, such as one on 2 Samuel 10:10-19, which he preached on August 11. Now instead of being a couple of weeks old, the war had entered its fourth month. Here we find similar notes struck, but some new ones as well.

Calvin reminds his hearers that the right attitude towards this war is one of submission and humility, both in victory and in defeat. He begins the sermon with the assertion that the two bases for a just war are "the honour and worship of God and for the safety of all the people."[46] He had in an earlier sermon (on 2 Samuel 1:1-27) spoken about the justice of war when one's enemy had wickedly attacked.[47] Several months later, in his sermon on 2 Samuel 10:1-12, he raised the question and, in answering it, mentioned specifically the honor of God as the principal cause

---

42. Ibid.
43. Ibid.
44. Ibid.
45. Ibid., 91
46. Ibid., 461.
47. Ibid., 36.

why a nation might go to war as it concerns "his being worshipped and honoured."[48] In this sermon on 2 Samuel 10:10-19, Calvin addresses the matter again and establishes one's understanding of the justice of a war in which one is engaged as the foundation for all the rest of what Calvin will say.

What is of course interesting here is that many of his hearers were not, nor would they be, actually involved in the war. Yet it seems as if Calvin wishes for them to see themselves as if they *were* involved in it, after a fashion (i.e. he wanted them to support the Huguenots and, in order to encourage them to do that, he wanted to ensure that they understood their cause to be a just one). He makes it clear here and in other sermons that the Catholic cause was unjust; that they were violators of God's honor and, as such, could not engage in the war without sinning.

Yet this wish for his hearers to see the justice of the Huguenot cause and see themselves as supporters of it does not signal the beginning of Calvin preaching a fiery sermon on the need for everyone to join the war in France against the Catholics. Rather, he focuses in this sermon on the disposition of piety that ought to characterize all whom God visits with war. He turns to discuss the Christian's humble demeanour in light of the reality of war. In this regard, he produces a brief discussion of a heroic pagan who fights bravely for a good cause but in the end "God abandoned them" because "they trusted in their own selves and did not consider that the victory came from on high."[49] They were not humble but arrogant; claiming the victory as the result of their own military prowess. He continues the description of this for several paragraphs. This idea (of the arrogant unbeliever who credits himself rather than trusting in God) is one he touches on in other sermons as well. It seems particularly pertinent in that it suggests the supremacy of one's piety here, as in all of life; even in the matter of war, godliness and trust in God are of supreme importance.

---

48. Ibid., 459.
49. Ibid., 463.

On the matter of the outcome of wars, Calvin argues that we must remember that "God does not give particular promises about this or that to his children."[50] "We must," Calvin declares, "remain in suspense about many things."[51] This does not, Calvin quickly notes, mean that one ought to feel doubt, as if God has forgotten the believer. One should feel utterly assured that God is taking care of them. So when Joab said, "The Lord will do what is good in his sight," this was not, Calvin contended, a sign of weak faith, but rather of an utter trust in God to bring about the outcome that is best. Continuing down this line of argument, Calvin discusses the fact that the principle concern for the Christian is that they take refuge in God. He notes that one does not know whether one will live today or tomorrow. It is in God's hands. And so he urges:

> Therefore, when we have a good cause, let us be ready to march forward and to lose our life in it if it pleases God.[52]

Continuing these themes of utter-trust and self-sacrifice, he reminds his hearers again that we have no promise from God concerning many specific things, but that that should not serve to weaken our resolve. We must always "hold our life in our hands in order to offer it to God as a sacrifice."[53] And, knowing our cause to be a good one, we must not lose heart. This is, he argues, of particular relevance today because of the trials that are so common in their day, alluding to the war. Continuing his thought, Calvin notes that "some poor folks ... have had their throats cut; so many horrible and bloody butcheries are happening,"[54] and continues with a litany of horrendous things that accompany the war and have brought misery to so many people. Calvin's insistence in mentioning all these things is that

---

50. Ibid., 464.
51. Ibid., 464.
52. Ibid., 467.
53. Ibid.
54. Ibid.

his hearers "always keep our minds on this conclusion, that God in the end will have pity on us as on the whole body of his Church."[55]

Taking up 2 Samuel 10:15, which mentions the enemy re-assembling, Calvin turns to the concerns of envy and confusion. When we see God sparing our enemies, we must patiently await his good will. Turning to the next two verses, Calvin discusses David winning a great victory. ("David killed seven hundred of their charioteers and forty thousand of their foot soldiers" [2 Samuel 10:17-18].) Thus, Calvin explains, the Holy Spirit wanted to set before Christians in Calvin's day the afflictions that one suffers by God's will and also the victories God eventually brings. Calvin reiterates the need not to trust in "chariots and horses" (citing Psalm 20: 7) and also reminds his hearers that these things were "written for us so that we might know that God is able to break enemies' heads and put them in confusion when it pleases him."[56]

> So, although we see so many revolutions today, let us go back to this, that just as he has upheld his own in all ages, we must conclude that he will do so to the end.[57]

This, he insists, is their comfort.

His emphasis, then, throughout the sermon is on God's people trusting God through their trials and believing that God will always care for his people. From this place of repose and with confidence concerning the justice of the Calvinists' cause, he sets his hearers on a firm foundation from which to support the Huguenots—even, possibly, volunteering themselves to go and fight, for, as he said, "let us be ready to march forward and to lose our life in it if it pleases God." We have seen earlier (of course) that many of his hearers were, in fact, Frenchmen, thus making it more likely that they may well be keen to go and fight in this conflict.

---

55. Ibid., 469.
56. Ibid., 475.
57. Ibid.

Assessing the Sermons

It likely feels awkward for the modern Christian, even if she or he is a Calvinist, to find Calvin speaking as he does in his sermon on 2 Samuel 2: 18–32. Not only might one have theological qualms to raise but also many have today become extraordinarily squeamish about claiming God is on "our side" in war or claiming that wars can today be fought with the principal aim of defending God's honor and ensuring he is worshipped rightly. I do not wish to imply here that the twenty-first century church is full of passivists but rather that many have grown so weary of war and of the claims made by a multitude of nations and individuals that they fought under the banner of God that they have moved away from such claims towards safer and more comfortable ground. I also do not wish to suggest Christians must revive Calvin's confidence when addressing the issue of war and conflict. His was an era and a theology which adhered to a much closer alignment between the church and state than do we today. In neither of these ways do I suggest the Reformed community follow him, but rather that readers might reflect on his reading towards the end that we assess our own consciences.

Regarding the academic study of Calvin, this collection of sermons certainly raises some questions for scholars of Calvin, Beza, and Geneva to ponder. It is very common to assert that Calvin was opposed to any and all forms of active resistance.[58]

---

58. See, *inter alia*, Marc-Edouard Chenevière, *La Pensée Politique de Calvin* (Paris: Editions Je Sers, 1937), 327; Josef Bohatec, *Calvins Lehre von Staat und Kirche*, (Breslau: M & H Marcus, 1937); Quentin Skinner, *The Foundations of Modern Political Thought*, 2 vols. (Cambridge: Cambridge University Press, 1978), vol. 2, 191–94; H. A. Lloyd, "Calvin and the Duty of Guardians to Resist," *The Journal of Ecclesiastical History* 32/1 (1981): 65–67; Harro Höpfl, *The Christian Polity of John Calvin* (Cambridge: Cambridge University Press, 1982), 207–217, *et passim*; Carlos Eire, *War Against the Idols. The Reformation of Worship from Erasmus to Calvin* (Cambridge: Cambridge University Press, 1986), 289; William Stephenson, *Sovereign Grace: The Place and Significance of Christian Freedom in John Calvin's Political Thought* (New York: Oxford University Press, 1999), 32–35; Paul-Alexis Mellet, *Les Traités monarchomaques. Confusion des temps, résistance armée et monarchie parfaite (1560–1600)* (Geneva: Droz, 2007), 58–61, 128–133, 159–162, *et passim*; John Witte, Jr., *The Reformation of Rights; Law, Religion, and Human Rights in Early Modern Calvinism* (New York: Cambridge University Press,

While it seems acknowledged in some quarters that Calvin and Beza supported the war once it started, this acknowledgement sits somewhat awkwardly next to the common view that Calvin opposed active resistance, recently reiterated by Scott Manetsch in his presentation at the 2018 International Congress on Calvin Research meeting.[59] This awkwardness is especially apparent when one considers their involvement in things like the Maligny affair (as mentioned earlier). I do not have space here to comment on the question but will merely note that the scholarly views on this subject developed for decades are still, in my judgment, overly dependent upon theologically biased readings of book four of Calvin's *Institutio Christianae Religionis*, specifically *Institutio* 4.20.31-32.[60]

2007), 38–54; Heiko Oberman, *John Calvin and the Reformation of the Refugees* (Geneva: Droz, 2009), 72.

59. Scott Manetsch, "John Calvin, the Monarchomachs, and the Biblical Warrant for Political Resistance," in *Calvinus frater in Domino - Papers of the Twelfth International Congress on Calvin Research* (Göttingen: Vandenhoeck & Ruprecht, 2020), 13–36.

60. *CO* 2: 1116–18. For a sampling of scholarship that diverges from the idea Calvin opposed active resistance *simpliciter*, see: Alain Dufour, "L'affaire de Maligny (Lyon, 4–5 septembre 1560) vue à travers la correspondance de Calvin et de Bèze" in *Cahiers d'Histoire* 8 (1963), 269–280; Willem Nijenhuis, "The limits of civil disobedience in Calvin's last-known sermons: development of his ideas on the right of civil resistance," in *Ecclesia Reformata: v. 2: Studies on the Reformation* (Leiden: Brill, 1994), 73–94; Max Engammare, "Calvin monarchomaque? Du soupçon à l'argument," *Archiv für Reformationsgeschichte* 89 (1998), 207–26; Philip Benedict, "The Dynamics of Protestant Militancy: France, 1555–1563," in *Reformation, Revolt and Civil War in France and the Netherlands 1555–1585*, eds. Philip Benedict et al. (Amsterdam: Royal Netherlands Academy of Arts and Sciences, 1999), 35–50; Denis Crouzet, "Calvinism and the Uses of the Political and the Religious (France, ca. 1560–ca. 1572)," in *Reformation, Revolt and Civil War*, 99–114; Robert Kingdon, "Calvin's Socio-Political Legacy: Collective Government, Resistance to Tyranny, Discipline", in *The Legacy of John Calvin; Papers Presented at the 12th Colloquium of the Calvin Studies Society, April 22–24*, 1999 (Grand Rapids: CRC Product Services, 2000), 112–23; id., "Calvin and Calvinists on Resistance to Government," in *Calvinus Evangelii Propugnator: Calvin Champion of the Gospel; Papers Presented at the International Congress on Calvin Research*, Seoul, 1998, eds David Wright, Tony Lane and Jon Balserak (Grand Rapids: CRC Product Services, 2006), 54–65; David Whitford, "Robbing Paul to Pay Peter: The Reception of Paul in Sixteenth Century Political Theology," in *A Companion to Paul in the Reformation*, ed. R. Ward Holder (Leiden: Brill, 2009), 573–606; Andrew Muttitt, "John Calvin, 2 Samuel 2:8–32 and Resistance to Civil Government: Supreme Equivocation or Mastery

The other comment that might be briefly made here concerns a reflection on Calvin's encouragement in his sermon on 2 Samuel 10:10–19 to trust God fully. He made his remarks within a context somewhat different from our own. Nonetheless, since the world today has experienced numerous wars during the past half-century, modern Christians may still listen attentively to Calvin's words here. It is refreshing to read Calvin reminding his hearers repeatedly that the predominant sensibility one ought to have in times of war is a deep and abiding trust in God's providence. It is useful to recall that by April 1562, Geneva had an enormous French refugee population. Refugees began flooding into France in the mid-1500s and by the 1550s there were hundreds coming each year. It was, Jeannine Olson has surmised, the increasing influx of refugees from France that moved Geneva to start up the *Bourse française* in 1550.[61] We have detailed records that show numbers from France coming into the city each year. In 1553, for instance, seventy-eight refugees came from France to Geneva. By 1557, 1558, and 1559, that number was 886, 632, and 1726, respectively.[62] The population of Geneva increased from between 12,400 and 13,893 in 1550 to 21,400 in 1560 and the bulk of this growth was from French émigré.[63] Given this, Calvin could have been tempted to turn these 2 Samuel sermons into nationalistic

of Contextual Exegesis?" Koers 82/2 (2017), 1–6; Jon Balserak, *John Calvin as Sixteenth-Century Prophet* (Oxford: Oxford University Press, 2014); id., "Revisiting John Calvin's hostility towards French Nicodemism," in *Learning from the Past: Essays on Reception, Catholicity, and Dialogue in Honour of Anthony N. S. Lane*, eds. Jon Balserak and Richard Snoddy (London: Bloomsbury / T & T Clark, 2015), 57–76; Philip Benedict, *Season of Conspiracy: Calvin, The French Reformed Churches, and Protestant Plotting in the Reign of Francis II (1559–1560)* (Philadelphia: American Philosophical Society Press, 2020).

61. Jeannine Olson, *Calvin and Social Welfare: Deacons and the Bourse française* (Cranbury: Susquehanna University Press, 1989). See also Henri Grandjean, "La bourse française de Genève (1550–1849)," in *Etrennes Genevoises* (Geneva: Atar, 1927): 46–60.

62. *Le Livre des Habitants de Genève*, Tome I, 1555–1572, ed. Paul-F. Giesendorf, 2 vols., Travaux d'humanisme et renaissance (Geneva: Droz, 1957–1963) 1:54–218; for some details on these numbers, see Peter Wilcox, "The lectures of John Calvin and the nature of his audience," *Archiv für Reformationsgeschichte* 87 (1996) 136–48.

63. Alfred Perrenoud, *La population de Genève du seizième au début du dix-neuvième siècle* (Geneva: A. Jullien, 1979), 24, 30, 370; as cited in Naphy, *Consolidation*, 105.

pep-rallies focused on reclaiming France for her true 'native sons.' While he plainly longed for the Huguenots to win the war, there is not a hint of nationalism in these sermons. His focus is entirely on the honor of God and on the idea that God will always care for his church. In keeping with such themes, Calvin frequently encourages his hearers to have compassion on their enemies: "We cannot exterminate all the wicked from the world … [and if we could] what would it accomplish?"[64] He urges his hearers to labor to "reform all those who are not totally incorrigible."[65] Also, "our enemies [are] so addicted to evil" but "we" ought "not to be ashamed to seek their good, as far as we can."[66] Thus Calvin encourages love and mercy for their Catholic opponents and urges confidence in God in the midst of a brutal civil war. This is, as I say, a refreshing tonic to the war-weary soul and a direction the church can embrace today.

---

64. Calvin, *2 Samuel*, 89.
65. Ibid., 90.
66. Ibid., 73; also 35–37.

8

Reconsidering Beza's Critique of Sebastian Castellio's Religious Tolerance

Kirk M. Summers

Introduction

IN 2003, Perez Zagorin included a chapter in his book on the history of religious toleration titled "The First Champion of Religious Toleration: Sebastian Castellio."[1] The title itself, as well as Zagorin's sympathetic assessment of Castellio's contributions to developing a rationale for tolerance in theological matters, reflects an ongoing rehabilitation and heroicizing of this Reformation-era Basel scholar. For Zagorin, Castellio's writings, particularly those directed against John Calvin and Theodore Beza for their handling of the Michel Servetus case, represent a "beacon pointing the way to peace" in an age of chaos and division. Castellio, in his view, possessed a moral compass and humanistic bent that moved him to resist the violence of intolerance as "contrary to the spirit of Christ." Zagorin, for his part, acknowledges his debt to Castellio's

---

1. See Perez Zagorin, *How the Idea of Religious Toleration Came to the West* (Princeton: Princeton University Press, 2003), 93–144.

primary biographer, Hans Guggisberg, who wrote a dissertation on Castellio in the 1950s at Basel and whose updated study of him was published in 1997.[2] Guggisberg himself was building on the work of Ferdinand Buisson, a winner of the Nobel Peace Prize who saw in Castellio a shining model for liberal Protestantism and irenicism.[3] Altogether, the works of Buisson, Guggisberg, and Zagorin resonate with the times. Numerous subsequent scholars assume the same hagiographic tone in their analyses of Castellio, calling him a pioneer and, as Zagorin, a champion of toleration.[4] Meanwhile, the positions of Calvin and Beza come off badly in these studies as exemplifying an authoritarian, fractious, and dogmatic attitude that cast a dark veil over the life of the church and stifled the individual's personal and direct relationship with God. In a more popular venue, one pastor-writer recently goes so far as to call for the extinction of Calvin and the revival of the spirit of Castellio in the churches.[5]

How would Calvin or Beza find a place in our own times? The two works at the center of the controversy, Castellio's *On Heretics, Whether They Should Be Punished and How They Should*

---

2. The dissertation was published as Hans Guggisberg, *Sebastian Castellio im Urteil seiner Nachwelt vom Späthumanismus bis zur Aufklärung* (Basel: Helbing & Lichtenhahn, 1956). The more recent work and its translation are as follows: Hans Guggisberg, *Sebastian Castellio, 1515–1563* (Göttingen: Vandenhoeck and Ruprecht, 1997); trans. Bruce Gordon (Aldershot: Ashgate, 2002).

3. Ferdinand Edouard Buisson, *Sébastien Castellion - Sa vie et son oeuvre (1515–1563). Étude sur les origines du protestantisme liberal Français* (Paris: Hachette, 1892). See also the edition edited by Max Engammare (Geneva: Droz, 2009).

4. The major studies are as follows: Alain Dufour, "La notion de liberté chez les Réformateurs," in Hans Guggisberg, F. Lestringant, and J. C. Margolin (eds.), *La liberté de conscience (XVIe-XVIIe siècles)* (Geneva: Droz, 1991), 15–29; Bruce Gordon, "To Kill a Heretic: John Calvin and Sebastian Castellio," in Geoff Kemp (ed.), *Censorship Moments Reading Texts in the History of Censorship and Freedom of Expression* (London: Bloomsbury, 2014), 55–62; Barbara Mahlmann-Bauer (ed.), *Sebastian Castellio (1515–1563) - Dissidenz und Toleranz* (Göttingen: Vandehoeck and Ruprecht, 2018); Uwe Plath, *Der Fall Servet und die Kontroverse um die Freiheit des Glaubens und Gewissens: Castellio, Calvin und Basel 1552–1556* (Essen: Alcorde Verlag, 2014); Mirjam van Veen, *Die Freiheit des Denkens: Sebastian Castellio - Wegbereiter der Toleranz, 1515–1563* (Essen: Alcord Verlag, 2015).

5. Frank Walker, "Sebastian Castellio the Pioneer of Toleration," *Sofia* 139 (2021), 8.

Be Treated (1554) and Beza's *A Pamphlet on the Punishing of Heretics by Civil Authorities* (1554)[6] by themselves draw a sharp distinction between the former's forbearance and the latter's impatience with regard to key doctrinal differences. For many scholars, these works show that Castellio anticipates a modern mindset of ecumenical openness while Beza defends the Genevan way and advocates for an antiquated ecclesiology weighted with moral oversight, coercion, and the exacting of corporal punishment. As products of our age and its aspirations for multiculturalism, we can see the merits in Castellio's arguments as Zagorin outlines them. He wants to give the faithful space to develop in their understanding of the character and nature of God from their perspective of their own cultural framework. I argue here, however, that the easy distinctions made between Castellio's tolerance and Beza's intolerance do not tell a nuanced enough story. Not only do they begin with anachronistic premises, as others have observed,[7] they follow Castellio in couching the contentious relationship between himself and Beza as a disagreement over the limits of tolerance. For Beza, though, it was not just an intolerance over adiaphorous dogmas or even

---

6. Castellio published the work at Basel at the press of Johannes Oporinus under the pseudonym Martin Bellius: *De haereticis, an sint persequendi, et omnino quomodo sit cum eis agendum* (Magdeburg [Basel]: George Rausch [Oporinus], 1554). See also Roland Bainton, *Concerning Heretics: An Anonymous Work Attributed to Sebastian Castellio* (NY: Columbia University Press, 1935). See also Wolfgang F. Stammler, (ed.), *Das Manifest der Toleranz* (Essen: Alcorde Verlag, 2013). Beza addressed Castellio's concerns in his own *De haereticis a civili magistratu puniendis libellus* (Geneva: R. Étienne, 1554). Castellio did respond to the pamphlet of Beza, though the unpublished text is only now published as Sebastian Castellio, *De l'Impunité des hérétiques. De haereticis non puniendis* (Geneva: Droz, 1971).

7. A few scholars have attempted to create a balanced view by considering the presuppositions of the age and then examining their thought accordingly. Castellio could not imagine toleration in the broadly ecumenical sense that it is used in the current generation, so the very definition of the word creates a disconnect. See especially the following: Stefania Salvadori, "Sebastian Castellio's Doctrine of Tolerance between Theological Debate and Modernity," in Andrea Moudarres and Christiana Purdy Moudarres (eds.), *New Worlds and the Italian Renaissance* (Leiden: Brill, 2012): 195–223; Odile Panetta, "Heresy and Authority in the Thought of Théodore de Bèze," *Renaissance and Reformation* 45 (2022): 33–72.

the question of church discipline that divided them irreparably. The question as to whether Beza possesses a spirit of Christian charity or "the spirit of Christ" that lives up to the ideals espoused by Castellio misses the mark, because Beza on his side expresses other cause for alarm. To his mind, Castellio is not defending tolerance from a secure position of orthodoxy, not even from the standpoint of the basic creeds and councils to which the Church has long adhered. Castellio himself holds heretical positions on several non-negotiable doctrines; furthermore, he hedges regarding the reliability and authority of Scripture. And not only does he hold these positions, he teaches them, writes about them, and propagates them. In Beza's view, such open heterodoxy sows confusion among the faithful and threatens to undermine the Protestant churches in their infancy. Whether or not Beza fully understood that Castellio embraced certain tenets from the mystical tradition is hard to say. He did understand, however, that Castellio was not only defending the right of individuals to hold heretical positions, but in fact held such positions himself. For Beza, in his time, to balk at this is hardly irrational, and, in fairness, we should not ignore this other side of the equation.

Castellio's Couching of the Argument

In June of 1558, Sebastian Castellio sent an agitated letter from Basel to Theodore Beza in Geneva. He had heard from a mutual acquaintance that Beza was augmenting his first edition of New Testament annotations, published in 1556, and along with it was wanting to publish Castellio's response to Beza's criticisms of his translation.[8] Beza had not mentioned Castellio by name in his

---

8. The letter can be found in Aubert, Hippolyte, Alain Dufour, Hervé Genton, and Kevin Bovier (eds.), *Correspondance de Théodore de Bèze*. 45 vols. (Geneva: Droz, 1960–2017), II (1556–1558): 201–2. Hereafter *CB*. The relevant texts of their dispute are as follows: Sebastian Castellio, *Biblia, una cum annotationibus* (Basel: J. Oporin, 1551); Castellio, *Defensio suarum translationum Bibliorum, et maxime Novi Foederis* (Basel: J. Oporin, 1562); Beza, *Responsio ad defensiones et reprehensiones Sebastiani Castellionis* (Geneva: H. Étienne, 1563) [reprinted in *Tractationes theologicae*, vol. 1 (Geneva: E. Vignon, 15762), 425–506]. All quotes in the next two sections are from *CB* II.

1556 first edition of the annotations, opting instead to call him "a certain someone." Even so, Castellio recognized himself and composed a response in 1557 that he shared with his friends in manuscript form. Now, in the 1558 letter, Castellio wants Beza to stop trying to obtain the manuscript through stealth and instead ask him directly for a copy through a letter in his own hand, person to person. If so, he will send the manuscript under the condition that Beza deal with it fairly and accurately.

Although scholars have given this letter little attention, how Castellio deals with Beza next in the letter, after setting the conditions, illustrates perfectly why some are drawn to rehabilitate Castellio and refashion him as a hero of the Reformation. Castellio seems to have a "modern" outlook while Beza appears petty and vindictive, or unbending and intolerant. Castellio writes:

> So much for the conditions. Moving beyond them now, Beza, I am going to give you some advice that is sounder than any friend will ever give you. Lay off the abusive words. I say this for your sake more than mine. Your verbal abuse does not hurt my case so much as help it. If I hated you, I would want you to continue in this nastiness, since it shows whose weapons you are wielding against me. But I tell you this for your sake. First, by being abusive you are sinning against God, whose judgment you'll not escape living or dead; second, you are making soberminded people dislike you; and last, you are hurting your own case when you take weak positions and defend them by mixing in invective. You would be better off, and prove yourself more of a gentleman, if you could contradict me without the hate and bitterness. At least you would be showing you have a zeal for the truth. You can do it if you control yourself and fix your attitude. Without an attitude change, you are faking modesty, which is worse than the verbal abuse.

Castellio goes on to urge Beza to look deep into himself to see why he is so bitter. He insists he does not hate Beza even when he disagrees with him, believing instead that Christians have a duty to be civil with each other in debate. He concludes:

> You can disagree with me, but do so with charity. You have had no more faithful friend. Find fault in my translation as you can; you will not make an enemy of me. Allow me to push back if I do not agree with your arguments;

when you are right, I am happy to admit it and correct myself. I only want us to arrive at the truth.

We should note that Castellio wrote these words *after* the falling out between himself and Calvin and Beza over the Michael Servetus affair in 1553. In that case, Calvin defended the actions against Servetus in a pamphlet early in 1554, and Castellio responded from Basel a few months later with his *On Heretics, Whether They Should Be Persecuted*. Beza reacted in the same year with his own defense of Servetus's execution in the *A Pamphlet on the Punishing of Heretics by Civil Authorities*. This sequence of writings has received the lion's share of attention in the scholarship, as well as another dispute between them on the matter of predestination. Castellio's openness to the allowance of divergent views—Bruce Gordon contends he did not *condone* Servetus's heresy—and his general call to tolerance among Christians has proven attractive to modern sensibilities and has sparked the current resurgence of interest in the Basel professor.

Beza Pinpoints Castellio's Heretical Views

The tension over the annotations hints that something deeper than mere arrogance animates Beza's resistance to Castellio's advocacy of tolerance for heretics. In the June 1558 letter just examined, Castellio imagines Beza suffers from vanity and arrogance and thus cannot tolerate being corrected over his translation. It is likely, however, that Castellio has not comprehended the full extent and rationale for Beza's contempt for him. He obviously knows that Beza responded vehemently, some might think uncharitably, against his *Concerning Heretics* (1554). Thus, to his mind, Calvin and Beza have set themselves up as tyrants in Geneva and are quashing dissent or competing viewpoints of any kind. This intolerance for criticism must have carried over to the Latin translation and annotations, reasons Castellio, with the result being that Beza will not entertain any contradiction of his own interpretations of the Greek text. In other words, the case for the punishing of heretics together with the translation of the Bible suggest to Castellio that the real issue has to do with authoritarianism within the Protestant movement. In fact, Castellio's own translation and annotations of the New Testament indicate to Beza that he held semi-Pelagian heretical views. Castellio not only had a weak opinion of Scripture as the final authority for life, he espoused deviant positions about original sin, justification, and the Trinity. Beza, therefore, saw an irony in a heretic lecturing Calvin and himself on how to handle heretics. Castellio's insistence that *Christians* deal with each other in charity would not have moved Beza given that Beza identified Castellio as an enemy of the Church rather than a member of the body. For reformers who saw themselves as tasked with defending the purity of the Church, Castellio lurked about as a wolf in sheep's clothing.

Castellio's criticisms about the intent behind Beza's New Testament translation, implying that it represents an authoritative version that no one should dare to challenge, almost certainly occasioned some of Beza's qualifications in the prefaces of later editions of his major annotations. There Beza advocates for the translation of Scriptures to be a collaborative effort, a confederacy of faithful scholars across time and space who have the linguistic and intellectual tools for carrying out the task well. He references his reliance on previous commentators and exchanges with other scholars, but also admits that he avails himself of the harsher critiques from adversaries such as Castellio. Undoubtedly, therefore, Castellio misunderstands Beza's response to his own recommendations. Subsequent editions do show an evolution and modification of his opinions and judgments. He even, as we will examine shortly, adopts some of Castellio's translations, though always quietly. He never attributes the choice of wording to Castellio himself. Perhaps, we could assume, he still harbors resentment for Castellio's plea for tolerance, but limiting their dispute to just this one dynamic may be an example of modern academic narcissism. It is true, Calvin and Beza were intolerant, but tolerance among those who held to a certain basic and long-established orthodoxy was never the question.

Beza himself makes this unambiguously clear in a letter written to Heinrich Bullinger at Zurich in March 1554, shortly after the publication of Castellio's *On Heretics*. In it, Beza includes a paragraph in which he shares his initial reaction to the newly published pamphlet of a certain Martinus Bellius at Magdeburg, which he rightly identifies as pseudonyms for Castellio at Basel. Beza raises the question to Bullinger whether what he wrote should be allowed to stand. Here Beza does not concern himself so much with the question of the right to punish heresies; this proves to be a small issue in the face of Castellio's denigration and diminishing of key, time-honored doctrines of the primary councils and creeds. What Castellio imagines for the faith, according to Beza, is no faith at all: "Tell me, my father, if we put up with the things which that impious man has spewed forth in his preface, what will remain inviolate in Christianity?"

Here Beza refers to a letter that Castellio affixed to the *On Heretics* addressed to Duke Christoph of Württemberg, in which he proposes his ideas for a minimalistic Christianity. For him, essential Christianity hinges on certain broad moral mandates that Christ shared with his followers before he ascended into heaven: live devoutly and without quarrels; love one another. Nothing more accrues to salvation or contributes to our well-being than this piety and moral correction of life. "I do not know how we can lay claim to the name 'Christian' if we do not imitate Christ." Castellio surveys the various doctrinal matters that he asserts cannot really be known and will not be known until we have a clean heart, that is, until we see God face to face, since then only will we have a clean heart. Beza repeats these very doctrines in question in his letter to Bullinger as the heart of the matter and the source of his indignation:

> The body of doctrine concerning the office of Christ, the Trinity, the Lord's Table, baptism, justification, free will, the state of souls after life is either useless or at least not at all necessary for salvation. Even the Jews and Turks believe in God. Scripture is akin to the *Ethics* of Aristotle, or certainly not much richer in its teaching, but much more uncertain. We should expect another revelation. No one should be condemned as a heretic,

but each person should be able to make their own decisions. You see, my father, to what end these things tend, that with all authority of Scripture undermined we put on the garment of Pharisaism, and become a laughing stock, not only for the papists, but also for the Turks themselves.

Beza then asks Bullinger to compare these statements with what Castellio has written in the letter affixed to his edition of the Latin Bible and he will find a man steeped in blasphemy.

For his part, Castellio turns for support in the words of Jesus, where he declares that the pure in heart will see God, as well as in Paul's caveat that knowing mysteries without exhibiting love equates to nothing. He complains that vices creep into the Church when people believe that they have superior doctrinal knowledge of unknowable mysteries and then in the name of Christ persecute those holding a divergent minority opinion. "We would do well," he says, "in the face of such a great number of sins that overwhelm us, to worry about fixing ourselves instead of others." Castellio fears that if the leaders of the Church are on the hunt for heretics, they and their parishioners will detect them everywhere, leading to bloodshed and hysteria. He insists that he himself hates heretics and is not meaning to lend them support, but fears that innocent people will be charged (as Christ himself was) or someone with aberrant views will be handled uncharitably. But Castellio does not accept the traditional or commonly used definition of a heretic, as one who believes differently about one of the mysteries of the Church—if this is the case, what is orthodox in one city is going to be heretical in another, *ad infinitum*—instead, he identifies those who stubbornly and persistently resist moral (but not doctrinal) correction as the real heretics according to the biblical interpretation. Treat them as gentiles and publicans; shake the dust from your feet and have nothing to do with them. As for those who persist in doctrinal errors even after being warned, walk away from these after a time and let God, not the magistrate, deal with them.

Such are Castellio's arguments about heresy in *On Heretics*. He claims that he himself does not adopt any doctrinal position that one could label as heretical from the standpoint of orthodox Christianity. He implies, in fact, that he remains faithful to the traditional councils and creeds of the Church through time and "hates" heretics. He does contend that many of the traditional points of theology are unknowable and thus are red herrings, so to speak, for the Christian trying to imitate Christ; in this way, therefore, he separates the work of the intellect from moral impulses; faith comes not from knowing the person of Christ and his work salvific as Scripture reveals them, but purity itself, somehow mystically, leads to knowing. In a similar vein, he does not relate correct theology to right disposition. In other words, he does not agree that the imitation of Christ and the recognition of mankind's special circumstances depends on the proper understanding of doctrines such as the offices of Christ or the means of justification. Beza, in contrast, like Calvin, maintains that right living and right piety result from a true understanding of God and man as revealed in Scripture.

Semi-Pelagianism in Castellio's Annotations

In his study of the forces at work in the French reformed movement during the sixteenth century, Michael Bruening details the theological program of Castellio that divided him from the magisterial reformers.[9] Castellio promoted tolerance of divergent views, as noted thus far, arguing that no one group holds a monopoly on the truth. As to the Scriptures, though, Castellio undercut their absolute authority by denying direct inspiration in every instance and allowing for the interference of authorial voice in the relaying of God's message. The Scriptures left plenty of room for sincere disagreement in interpretation. Thus, he encouraged the analysis of a passage, not so much by a comparison with other passages, but by an open-minded reading that accounts for reason and tenor. Additionally, he thought that predestination theology stands in opposition to God's goodness

---

9. Michael Bruening, *Refusing to Kiss the Slipper: Opposition to Calvinism in the Francophone Reformation* (Oxford: Oxford University Press, 2021), 156–79.

and mercy as exhibited in the Scriptures. And, most importantly, he rejected the traditional interpretation of the Fall and its effects on a person's nature, believing instead in the inherent goodness of mankind. Christians have wholly put on the new person and do not struggle internally with the power of sin. Bruening notes that Calvin saw in Castellio one of the gravest threats to Christianity, given that "he seemed to call into question the objective truth of Christianity itself."[10] This in itself underscores that something more serious than just the issue of tolerance stirred Calvin and Beza. The Genevan reformers detected the Basel scholar's unorthodox positions and were distressed to hear that he freely spread unsound doctrines. If unchecked, he could wreak havoc among the faithful.

One piece of evidence that Bruening did not consider supports this reading of the dynamics between them and adds yet another layer to it. While fine-tuning his own annotations and translation of the New Testament, Beza identified in the notes and wording of Castellio's competing version blatant semi-Pelagian views. When Castellio asserts that Christians by definition have wholly put on the new man, he does so because of twisted views about original sin that smack of Pelagianism, a teaching that almost all theologians at that time identified as a heresy troubling the Church. Beza decided to call attention to these positions after Castellio published the previously mentioned manuscript at Basel in 1562 defending his own translation and refuting Beza's notes. Beza responded the next year with his own defense in which he goes through all the passages where the two diverge significantly and rebuts Castellio in greater detail. For our purposes, the affixed letter to the Basel authorities contains a more coherent and systematic critique of Castellio's doctrinal views, and so that is where we will turn our attention.[11]

---

10. Bruening, *Refusing to Kiss the Slipper*, 139.

11. See *CB* IV (1563): 184–93. All quotes which follow in this section are from this letter.

In the letter, Beza begins by politely excusing the Basel authorities for allowing Castellio to publish his book at Oporin's press because they did not understand how contrary to the Holy Spirit it is. Had he argued about the meaning of words or the explication of passages according to the analogy of faith, Beza admits he would not have responded, because Castellio proves himself unlearned on that level. But because of his almost impressionistic or mystical reading of the Scriptures, Castellio is spreading doctrinal errors about "the divine decrees, free will, original sin, the Word of God, the Spirit, and justification." Castellio may claim that he is being misrepresented, but his own words convict him. And, Beza continues, all the pious know how momentous the struggle was between the Church and the Pelagians in Augustine's day, and now no one doubts that she should have resisted. Once again, the true Church is struggling against similar heresy in the form of semi-Pelagianism. "Its proponents do not consider concupiscence in the faithful to be sin," he explains, "and they think that the apostles and saints are sinless. We deny this and say that sin remains in everyone. Therefore, we rely on Christ's righteousness imputed to us for the remission of sins."

Despite the long list of erroneous doctrines that Beza perceives in Castellio, for the rest of the letter to the Basel authorities, Beza focuses on this latter issue that he judges disqualifies Castellio from teaching in the Church: Castellio does not believe that "putting off the old man and putting on the new" is a process for Christians. True believers no longer struggle with sin and no evil actions can be attributed to them. And he maintains that, if Paul were referring to himself at Romans 7:19, when he says "I do not do the good I want, but the evil I do not want is what I do," and not speaking in a persona, he would be granting cover to those wanting to sin simply because Paul does it. Could he really be an "imitator of Christ," as he tells the Corinthians, if he is doing the evil which he does not wish? Furthermore, according to Castellio, concupiscence and lust are natural creations of God in a human being, and inherently good, so Paul is challenging those who think they have the pure mental impulses of a Christian but still commit sinful actions.

Beza objects that we have no better testimony of the life-giving Spirit within our hearts than the resistant struggle of the flesh against the Spirit. Evil actions have their origins in evil desires, and to have both, a spirit that wants evil and flesh that carries it out, is to be dead in sin. Castellio, in his opinion, does not see that while the faithful still struggle with sin and are still trying to separate themselves from it like a thorn in the flesh, in salvation Christ removes guilt once and for all. Beza questions why ministers use the Scriptures to urge on Christians "whose power is perfected in weakness" to continue running the race if no one imitates Christ besides the one who mirrors him perfectly. Mingled in with such arguments, Beza quotes lengthy passages of Augustine against Castellio that were originally intended for the Pelagians.

Beza considers all such assertions trifling and ludicrous compared to Castellio's interpretation of Galatians 5 concerning the struggle of flesh and spirit. Castellio argues that there the apostle lays out for the readers two kinds of people, the spiritual and carnal, and enumerates the fruits of each so they can discern to which camp they belong. Beza calls this an unbearable monstrosity. Castellio's logic leads him to read "the spirit fights against flesh" to mean the same thing as "spiritual men are contrasted with carnal men." But Paul means, "I myself in my mind serve the will and law of God, but in my flesh I serve the law of sin." Castellio retorts that those in Christ are free from the law, and that is what Paul meant. Not wanting evil is natural. Beza rejects this, for obvious reasons, adding that only grace keeps the faithful not wanting evil, but they will not reach perfection until later. If no one pleases God except the one who no longer struggles, Beza protests, what is left but to say goodbye to Christ and faith? Should we condemn all the saints who up until their last breath prayed for the remission of sins? Castellio brings infamy to Basel and the leaders there should take some action to protect the Church. Beza concludes: "Castellio, it is true that many people are speaking and writing bad things about you. Would that they were false, because then you would not be so sullied in your reputation and the Church would have peace. But after you made it your goal to attack the truth, I made it mine to defend it."

It is important to note that Beza never expresses any concern here over his own authority or that of Calvin. He uses words such as "protect" and "defend", while stressing the importance of recognizing the purpose and nature of Christ's salvific work. His desire to keep the peace in the Church and defend its walls, so to speak, during perilous times, as well as his passion to shield the faithful from being persuaded by the rhetorically well-structured presentation of false doctrines remains clear. The evident deeply felt commitment to safeguard the true Church should stand as a counterbalance or modify or refine the characterization that the Genevan leaders clung to a seemingly arbitrary or self-serving intolerance for divergent views.

Annotations

One additional factor will shape our assessment of the interactions between Castellio and Beza. Earlier, we alluded to the preface appearing in several of Beza's major editions of the New Testament, and highlighted Beza's recognition of dependence on the insights of others. As noted, Beza even includes the insights of those with whom he is not on good terms, and here names Castellio. This is an interesting statement that deserves further attention, because it suggests that Beza, for all his resistance to anything from Castellio, did take into account Castellio's arguments to improve his translation as it evolved through the five major editions (1556, 1565, 1582, 1589, 1598). To illustrate this, we will examine the case of their exchange concerning 1 Corinthians 4:19, a passage where Paul issues a warning to teachers in the Corinthian church about their empty show of rhetoric.

For a point of reference, we note that the Geneva Bible (1599), which was heavily dependent on Beza's Latin translation and the annotations, translates the passage as follows: "But I will come to you shortly, if the Lord will, and I will know, not the words of them which are puffed up, but the power." This passage appears to have occupied and troubled Beza each time he produced a new edition, seeing that in each he wavers over his choice of words. Interestingly, this is one of the passages about which he argued with Castellio, the two of them sparring about their choices in separately published defenses of their translations and notes. All the translations with the relevant text underlined appear as follows, with Beza's italics retained (indicating Latin words with no direct parallel in the Greek text) and the words in question in bold face:

1st (1556) edition: Sed veniam brevi ad vos, si Dominus voluerit, et cognoscam non **locutionem** istorum qui inflati sunt, sed *spiritualem* **virtutem**.

Here Beza is making specific choices as to the meaning of the sentence: Paul wants to assess whether those who speak with such eloquence really are filled with the Holy Spirit. The annotations indicate that he rejects the translation of the Vulgate and Erasmus, namely *sermo*, since it can refer, not only to the eloquence of their speech (that is, its form), but to the content as well, and is thus ambiguous. At the same time, he rejects the choice of another unnamed translator—here we are talking about Castellio—*oratio*, which he considers even more ambiguous than *sermo*. As for the addition of *spiritualis* modifying *virtus*, Beza notes that Paul often uses "spiritual" or "of God" to modify this word, so he feels confident that it is meant here. Furthermore, since the Greek text has *dynamis*, the adjective clarifies that *virtus* at issue here is not morality, one of the meanings of the word, but power, another common sense of it.

2nd (1565) edition: Sed veniam brevi ad vos, si Dominus voluerit, et cognoscam non **verba** istorum qui inflati sunt, sed *spiritualem* **virtutem**.

By this point, Castellio has published his defense of his translations against Beza. This leads Beza to name Castellio openly in his notes concerning the word *oratio*, but now opting for *verba* over *locutio*. He notes,

Paul here is referencing the empty splendor and flourishes of speech of those people, and so I chose *verba* because Latin speakers used it in the same sense. Paul means to contrast it with *dynamis*, that is, those heavenly, all-powerful weapons, that is to say, a zeal for God, faith, and, in short, the gifts of the spirit."

Quietly, Beza seems to have taken to heart what Castellio says about this translation in his defenses. There Castellio reminds Beza that Paul himself employs a vague term, *logos*, but when it is contrasted with *dynamis*, power, the meaning becomes clear enough and therefore *oratio*, with its double meaning, suffices. This appears to have influenced Beza to choose a translation even closer to Paul's with the note added.

3rd (1582) and 4th (1589) editions: Sed veniam brevi ad vos, si Dominus voluerit, et cognoscam non **verba** istorum qui inflati sunt, sed *spiritualem virtutem*.

Although Beza has new texts to collate and consider, he makes no changes in his translation of this verse from the 1565 edition in his 1582 and 1589 editions. In the 1598 edition, however, one of the last works he ever produced, he makes further alterations.

5th (1598) edition: Sed veniam cito ad vos, si Dominus voluerit, et cognosam non **verba** istorum inflatorum, sed **vires**.

Here appears a major translation adjustment that Castellio advocated for in the first place: he has exchanged *spiritualis virtus* for *vires*. At the same time, he completely drops his annotation explaining the need for the additional modifier and the possible confusion with moral virtue. Castellio's comment in his defense surely lies behind the alteration, as there he argues that all ambiguity over the translation of *dynamis* along with the need for the added modifier (*spiritualis*) can be avoided simply by choosing *vires*. Castellio likely caused Beza to reconsider his original choice when he pointed out how Beza translated 2 Corinthians 10:12. In this case, Beza had no problem contrasting *verba* and *virtus* without further modification. With Castellio long passed on to the next life, Beza had no reason to shun this change or give him credit. Perhaps other friends offered the same critique. More likely, though, Beza feared that any acknowledgement of contribution or influence from Castellio would appear to be an endorsement of him, or at least a softening of his own position.

Conclusion

Both Calvin and Beza had doctrinal differences with other Protestant leaders. Bullinger's views on predestination, for example, did not perfectly synch with those of Calvin, but for the peace of the church the two kept the matter muted. In none of these cases, however, was the question of how one is saved at stake. All parties involved held to the same basic message concerning the nature of sin and salvation. In contrast, and tellingly, in the letter to the Basel authorities Beza concentrated his attention on Castellio's positions concerning original sin, regeneration, and sanctification, as well as the authority of the Scriptures themselves, seeing that these doctrines lie indisputably at the heart of the Gospel itself. Even so, in his *On Punishing Heretics*, Beza, criticizes the "Academics", that is, those who doubt whether we can know anything about God for certain, for denying that a knowledge of the Trinity is valuable for human beings. He also asserts that the positing of free will in mankind undermines the notion of God's grace. Beza cast a wide net, perhaps, but he concerned himself primarily with peace in the Church. He opposed most of all the schismatics, those who break into separate groups with themselves at the head while sowing dissension. This reveals a bad character and the work of the devil, he argues; he distinguishes them from those who hold unorthodox views but do not want to cause upheaval in the Church. Such ones, unlike Castellio, quietly study and allow themselves to be taught in their quest for the truth.

9

Geneva's First New Church After Calvin and Bénédict Pictet's Dedication Sermon (1715)

Matthew S. Miller

*For here we have the first church built since the blessed
Reformation, and its design is different from that of the
others that we have.*

Bénédict Pictet, 1715

Introduction

MANY people have received a personal tour of eastern North
Carolina with the man this volume honors as their tour guide.
Such a day includes visits not only to Dr. Kelly's ancestral homes
and lands (including traipses into the woods to see the natural
springs), but also to several churches of personal significance.

There is Raeford Presbyterian Church on Edinborough
Avenue in Raeford, NC, where Kelly served as an assistant pastor
under Rev. Cortez Cooper after completing his Bachelor of

Divinity at Union Theological Seminary. Kelly went from there to begin postgraduate study at the University of Edinburgh, but when Rev. Cooper then stepped down, the congregation asked Kelly to return as the interim pastor. Answering that call, Kelly suspended his doctoral studies for one year, returning to Raeford to spend himself in the duties of preaching thrice weekly (Sunday morning, Sunday evening, and Wednesday evening) and pastoring the congregation of six hundred souls. When the congregation had secured its next pastor, Kelly resumed his doctoral studies in Edinburgh.

There is Union Presbyterian Church in Carthage, NC, with its simple, white, wooden structure and accompanying cemetery where the bodies of many of Dr. Kelly's ancestors and family "being still united to Christ, do rest in their graves till the resurrection" (Westminster Shorter Catechism, A. 37).

Just outside of Dillon, SC, one comes to the rural antebellum Reedy Creek Presbyterian Church, surrounded by glistening fields of corn and cotton on a Sunday morning, the only time in the week its doors are open for the one or two dozen worshippers who gather to lift their hearts to the Lord and sit under Dr. Kelly's preaching. His sermons preached at Reedy Creek have since been published as *Revelation: A Mentor Expository Commentary* in 2015 and *Deuteronomy: A Mentor Expository Commentary* in 2022).[1]

In the heart of Dillon stands the stately First Presbyterian Church on the corner of E. Harrison St. and S. Second Ave, where Dr. Kelly served as the pastor for nine years after completing his PhD in Edinburgh. His preaching and prayers, resounding through that sanctuary on Sunday mornings, Sunday evenings,

---

1. Douglas F. Kelly, *Revelation: A Mentor Expository Commentary* (Geanies House: Mentor, 2015), and Douglas F. Kelly, *Deuteronomy: A Mentor Expository Commentary* (Geanies House: Mentor, 2022). The closing line of the third and final volume of Kelly's *Systematic Theology* refers the reader to his work on Revelation: "It is normal to have a concluding section on Eschatology, but I will refer the interested reader to my *Revelation: A Mentor Expository Commentary,* where most of the issues are addressed in an exegetical manner" (Kelly, *Systematic Theology,* vol. 3, "The Holy Spirit and the Church" (Geanies House: Mentor, 2021).

and Wednesday evenings, were used mightily of the Lord to deepen that congregation's faith in Christ, commitment to global mission, and bonds of love with each other.

And if you are among the many people who spent time with Dr. Kelly during one of his sabbaticals in Edinburgh, you know of his affection for Holyrood Abbey at the eastern end of the Royal Mile (just beneath the ancient hills of Holyrood Park). Though the congregation, in faithfulness to the Gospel and to the Word of God, withdrew from the Church of Scotland in 2013 and thus no longer worships there (the building now belongs to another Church of Scotland congregation), no faithlessness of man can steal the memory of the sound of the high praises of God sung from the church's floor and balcony, nor can the effectual calling of many to salvation and sanctification through the powerful proclamation of "the whole counsel of God" from its pulpit be rolled back. It was there, near the frontmost pews, that I met Douglas and Caroline Kelly for the first time in the fall of 1998, and it was outside Holyrood Abbey's doors that my friends and I would linger long to speak with them after many an evening service. It was also there that I first heard Dr. Kelly preach, expounding on the power of intercessory prayer from Exodus 17:8-16 (a message I would hear him give many more times in the decades since).

Dr. Kelly would be the first to affirm Calvin's clear statement in his *Institutes of the Christian Religion* that "not church buildings but we ourselves are the temple of God" (III.XX.30).[2] And indeed one of the biblical texts from which Dr. Kelly has most frequently preached is Hebrews 12, with its emphasis that in gathered worship we rejoice in coming not to an earthly place, but "to Mount Zion and to the city of living God, the heavenly Jerusalem ..." (12:22). Even so, as creatures in time-and-space, our lives often sojourn through those "earthly sanctuaries" where heaven draws near through the preaching of the Word of God and the praises of His

---

2. John Calvin, *Institutes of the Christian Religion*, vol. 2, trans. Ford Lewis Battles (Louisville: Westminster Press, 1960), 893.

people gathered in worship. Though such edifices of wood and stone are not in themselves sacred places, they are nonetheless among those things to be "received with thanksgiving and prayer" (1 Tim. 4:4) and indeed the memory of what first brought them into existence can sometimes renew our wonder at God's ways.

With this in mind, I wish briefly to recount the history of a church building whose story is significant to the Reformed tradition yet little known in English sources. It concerns the construction and dedication of the first new church built in Geneva as a Protestant house of worship. The name of the church when it opened was simply "Temple Neuf" (New Temple), though it became known as Temple de la Fusterie. It was opened in 1715 with a dedication service preached by Bénédict Pictet, a major Reformed theologian who arguably holds the title of "Geneva's last Calvinist." The unique story of this church building reveals much about the history of Geneva—and of neighboring France—at this critical point in her history and reminds us of unchanging truths that support us in our own earthly pilgrimage.

Geneva's Three Churches in the Time of Calvin

When John Calvin arrived in Geneva in 1536—and then returned "for good" in 1541—the city of Geneva had an estimated twelve to thirteen thousand citizens served by the city's three main churches: Saint Pierre Cathedral, Temple Saint Gervais, and Temple de la Madeleine. Dominating the city's landscape was Saint Pierre Cathedral, with its Romanesque and Gothic styles boldly announcing it as the twelfth-century medieval cathedral that it was. Its two massive bell towers ordered time in the city. Temple de la Madeleine, just a three-minute walk north of Saint Pierre down toward the lake, was built in the fifteenth century on ruins dating back to the fifth.[3] It was there that William Farel preached in Geneva for the first time. Temple de Saint Gervais, to the northeast and just across the Rhône, was also built in the

---

3. Karen Maag, *Lifting Hearts to the Lord: Worship with John Calvin in Sixteenth-Century Geneva* (Grand Rapids: Eerdmans, 2016), 201.

fifteenth century, though on the foundations of a tenth-century Romanesque church which sat atop ruins of church buildings going back to the fifth or even fourth centuries.[4]

Worship services in these three churches were more frequent than found in Reformed churches today. "By the time of Calvin's death in 1564 ... Geneva's three churches each offered between nine and thirteen services a week, including either three or four on Sundays."[5] On Wednesday mornings, for instance, the bells tolled to signal the cessation of all labor until the weekday worship service ended, just as was done on Sunday mornings.[6] But Calvin wanted to guard against any notion that the church buildings themselves, which hosted such frequent gatherings for worship, were in any sense sacred places in and of themselves. He explains in his *Institutes:*

> Now as God by his word ordains common prayers for believers, so also ought there to be public temples wherein these may be performed ... If this is the lawful use of church buildings, as it certainly is, we in turn must guard against either taking them to be God's proper dwelling places, whence he may more nearly incline his ear to us—as they began to be regarded some centuries ago—or feigning for them some secret holiness or other, which would render prayer more sacred before God.[7]

Accordingly, the doors to Geneva's churches were locked between services.

Calvin's liturgical reforms led to a reconfiguring of the interior of these three churches. Gone were the high altars for

---

4. Ibid., 44, 200.

5. Karen Maag, *Worshipping with the Reformers* (Downers Grove: IVP Academic, 2021), 22.

6. Ibid., 23, 21. We may wonder whether Calvin's reticence to regard Lord's Day worship as the primary new covenant correlate to the fourth commandment may owe, at least in part, to his concern that doing so would provide a theological rationale for Genevans to resist the imposition of weekday worship services. We agree with Kyle J. Dieleman concerning the practice in Geneva: "The establishment of church services on days other than Sunday clearly flows naturally out of Calvin's conception of the fourth commandment ... Calvin believed the Sabbath commandment demands that worship should occur as frequently as possible. Having worship services every day of the week is a natural, practical extension of Calvin's theological principle." Kyle J. Dieleman, *The Battle for the Sabbath in the Dutch Reformation: Devotion or Desecration?* (Göttingen: Vandenhoeck & Ruprecht, 2019), 67.

7. Calvin, *Institutes of the Christian Religion*, vol. 2, 893.

the Mass. A pulpit was installed on the side of the sanctuary midway down its length, along with seating that was oriented not toward the front of the church but toward the pulpit (prior to this, worshippers either stood or kneeled for the Mass, though they could bring in stools if needed).[8] To aid the hearing of the sermon in a space originally designed more for the eye than the ear, a sounding board was installed over the pulpit. And in Saint Pierre Cathedral, "the numerous side chapels that had been a prominent feature of the pre-Reformation cathedral" were removed "in favor of a singular focus on the pulpit, from which the Scriptures were expounded during each Reformed worship service."[9]

But for all of Calvin's reforms in Geneva, "no new churches were built; instead, previously Catholic spaces were turned into Reformed places of worship."[10] And though the city's population grew over the course of Calvin's lifetime as Geneva received

Pierre Escuyer, *Inside view of Temple de la Madeleine*, Geneva, 1822.
Historical Museum of the Reformation, Geneva. Exhibited at MIR, Geneva.

---

8. Maag, *Lifting Our Hearts to the Lord*, 30, 43.
9. Ibid., 43.
10. Ibid., 30.

Protestants seeking refuge from Catholic persecution, the high volume of worship services in the city's three main churches sufficed to meet the needs. But tensions in France in the early 1560's set the stage for what would become, in the late-seventeenth and early-eighteenth centuries, a dramatic surge in French Huguenot refugees that would occasion the construction of a fourth church in Geneva—one quite unlike the other three.

The Huguenots and the Great Temple de Charenton

We cannot recount here all the key moments in the history of the French Reformed Church from Calvin's day to the early eighteenth century in Geneva, but the years 1598 and 1685 mark the path that leads to Geneva's new church. After nearly three decades of on-and-off religious wars in France, King Henri IV issued the Edict of Nantes in 1598 granting official toleration to the Huguenots (French Calvinists). King Henri IV's son and heir, King Louis XIII, generally honored the Edict during his reign (1610-1643), which saw the Huguenots experience a period of relative thriving (though not without some restrictions and intermittent conflict).

Among the restrictions of the Edict of Nantes was one which forbade Huguenots from holding public worship within five leagues (approximately 15-20 miles) of Paris. However, Henri IV exercised his right as king to allow an exception. In Charenton-le-Pont, less than two leagues from Paris and situated on the north side of the confluence of the Seine and Marne rivers, a Reformed congregation established itself. With notable pastors serving Paris's Huguenot community, Charenton became "the most famous Reformed congregation" in France and boasted a newly built church that became a significant symbol for France's Protestants.[11]

---

11. Jeannine Olson, "The Edict of Nantes and Its Revocation: A Balanced Assessment?" in *The Theology of the Huguenot Refuge: From the Revocation of the Edict of Nantes to the Edict of Versailles*, ed. Martin I. Klauber (Grand Rapids: Reformation Heritage Books, 2020), 23. According to Olson, the Reformed church in Charenton also welcomed Lutherans to the Lord's Table (Ibid.).

Intermittent violence was not unknown during this time, and the church in Charenton was "burned down following anti-heretical riots" in 1623.[12] But the congregation quickly designed a new and larger church in its place near the site of the original. This new "Temple de Charenton" featured a massive floor and high ceilings, with two stories of fully encircling galleries supported by twenty pillars. Natural light streamed in through its eighteen clear (not stained glass) windows topped with two rows of dormer windows.[13] It was a Protestant church through-and-through, elegant to the eye but designed so well for the ear that up to four thousand people could gather within its walls and hear the Word of God proclaimed by a single unamplified human voice. The Temple de Charenton was a significant monument to the heights attained by the French Reformed churches and was "the largest temple in France."[14]

But, in 1685, after more than two decades of measures that effectively eroded the liberties enjoyed by the Huguenots under the terms of the Edict of Nantes, King Louis XIV—striving for "un roi, une loi, une foi" (one king, one law, one faith)—signed the Edict of Fontainebleau, which officially revoked the Edict of Nantes. Reformed pastors were given "two weeks to leave the country ... or abjure their faith."[15] Ordinary lay people, forbidden from leaving the country, were consigned either to convert to Catholicism or, like the so-called Nicodemites, keep their Reformed faith in a private and hidden manner.[16]

As for Huguenot churches, Louis XIV, convinced that these temples could not be converted to Catholic places of worship,

---

12. "French Protestant Temples Old and New," December 19, 2021, at https://www.huguenotsociety.org.uk/blog/french-protestant-temples-old-and-new. Last accessed April 10, 2023.

13. This according to "Charenton Temple: Overview", http://www.crommelin.org/history/Ancestors/Scheffer/Charenton/Charenton.htm. Last accessed April 18, 2023.

14. Ibid. See also the computer model reconstruction of the church's exterior and interior at http://www.crommelin.org/history/Ancestors/Charenton/Charenton-Model/CharentonModel.htm

15. Olson, "The Edict of Nantes and Its Revocation," 27.

16. Ibid., 29; also Duley-Haour, "The Churches of the Desert," 73, 77–78.

Interior of Temple de Charenton

ordered them to be razed.[17] In a highly symbolic act, Louis personally ordered the destruction of Charenton to follow immediately after the Revocation of the Edict of Nantes was announced. The great monument of the Huguenot religion was reduced to rubble within days to the grief of the Reformed, both in and beyond France.

For the Catholic leadership in France, the destruction of Temple de Charenton was a cause of celebration.[18] Speaking two years after, in 1687, Abbot Talemand declared to the Académie Française, "Blessed ruins, the most beautiful trophy France has ever seen. Arches of triumph and statues honouring the king will not elevate it higher than this heretic temple brought down by his piety."[19]

---

17. "Destruction of the Charenton Temples," at http://www.crommelin.org/history/Ancestors/Charenton/Charenton-Destruction/Destruction.htm. Last accessed April 10, 2023.

18. As depicted on the following page. Sebastien Leclerc (1637–1714), who served in the employ of King Louis XIV as a "graveur de Roi" (engraver of the King), was regarded as one of the best French artists of his time. We can safely assume that his engraving of the demolition of the Temple de Charenton was intended to honor Louis XIV's Edict of Fontainebleau.

19. Quoted in "Charenton (Val-de-Marne)," at https://museeprotestant.org/en/

La Démolition du Temple de Charenton
Sebastien Leclerc, 1702

Grief over the destruction of the Temple de Charenton would linger in Geneva. When Bénédict Pictet gave his "Funeral Oration" for Francis Turretin in November of 1687, he recalled the honor it was for Turretin when, in 1661, Turretin "twice spoke in Charenton to a most numerous assembly."[20] Pictet then adds, "While I remember this, my spirit shudders, my voice sticks to my throat, my eyes swell with weeping."[21] Pictet, as we will see, will go on to have a remarkable theological career, but from its beginning—he was named Turretin's successor in 1686, one year after the Revocation—Pictet's attention will be significantly devoted to aiding the Huguenots, both those who fled France

---

notice/charenton-val-de-marne-2/. Last accessed April 19, 2023. See there also the image, *Interior of Temple de Charenton*.

20. Benedict Pictet, "Funeral Oration of Benedict Pictet Concerning the Life and Death of Francis Turretin," trans. David Lillegard, in Francis Turretin, *Institutes of Elenctic Theology*, vol. 1 of 3, ed. James T. Dennison (Phillipsburg: Presbyterian & Reformed Publishing, 1997), 670.

21. Ibid.

and those who chose valiantly to stay, building "underground churches" in the face of ongoing persecution (these became known as the French "Church of the Desert").[22]

Though the Revocation of the Edict of Nantes forbade Reformed lay people to leave the country, they found ways out of France. As told by Olson:

> The number of people fleeing the country had increased radically through the 1680s, eventually becoming the largest migration in early modern Europe, estimated by Myriam Yardeni at 200,000–300,000 individuals. For those caught trying to leave France, the penalties were severe. Men were sent to be galley slaves and women were imprisoned until they recanted their faith. Rewards were given for information about planned departures, and the Huguenot community was spied on for news of possible departures from France.[23]

For thousands of Huguenots who risked their lives or the galleys to escape France, Geneva was the first stop (especially for those from the southern region of France). And while most received short-term aid before moving on to settle in Switzerland, Germany, the Netherlands, the British Isles, South Africa, and the New World, many thousands chose to make their home in the city of Calvin, Beza, Diodati, and Turretin.[24]

Geneva's Need for a New Temple

In Geneva, the growing Huguenot population put pressure on the capacity of the city's three churches. The city approved and funded the addition of a new gallery inside Saint Pierre Cathedral in 1697, but it soon became clear that small measures would be no solution.[25] The struggle to find a seat in one of Geneva's three

---

22. See Duley-Haour, "The Churches of the Desert, 1685–1789," in *The Theology of the Huguenot Refuge*, 71–90.

23. Olson, 40. Olson cites Myriam Yardeni, *Refuge protestant* (Paris: Presses Universitaires de France, 1985), 17.

24. See Jane McKee, "The Huguenot Diaspora," in *The Theology of the Huguenot Refuge*, 35–50.

25. Jérôme Sautier, "Politique et Refuge Genève Face à la Révocation de l'Édit de Nantes," in *Genève et la Révocation de l'Édit de Nantes: 1680–1705*, ed. O. Reverdin (Genève: Librairie Droz, 1985), 129.

main churches on Sunday mornings, Christmas, and Easter, was becoming a regular cause of tension among the worshippers. Moreover, the crowded churches meant more worshippers were sitting too far from the pulpit to follow the preached message in medieval buildings not designed for hearing sermons.[26] The Consistory's minutes from April 18, 1700, report: "Several people complain that they cannot find places in the temples and are forced to go without preaching and thus deprive themselves of the consolation of the hearing of the Word of God. It is necessary to remedy this situation by opening a new temple..."[27]

The idea for a new church in Geneva gained steam in 1701. Place de la Fusterie (about a five-minute walk northeast from Saint Pierre's Cathedral toward the mouth of the Rhône River) was chosen as the site with the goal of building a church capable of holding 700 to 800 worshippers. But the plan was stalled for several years over questions of funding. Eventually, through a generous donation by Jean-Antoine Lullin and the designation of public funds, Geneva's Council of Two Hundred approved the project in 1708, estimating the total cost at 144,500 florin.[28]

The work of designing the new church was entrusted to Huguenot architect, Jean Vennes. As he envisioned the first church in Geneva to be designed for Calvinist worship—and especially for use by Huguenot refugees—Vennes took none other than the Temple de Charenton for his inspiration.

Construction began in 1713 and took two years to complete. The finished "Temple Neuf"—New Temple, as it was then called—features a beautiful Baroque style façade with a single bell tower. Beneath the belltower, a rounded pediment is decorated with

---

26. Edouard de Montmollin and François Delor, *Temple de la Fusterie, Temple Neuf* (Fondation des Clefs de St-Pierre: *Genève*, 1990), 4. See also Fatio, "L'Église de Genève et La Révocation de l'Édit de Nantes," in *Genéve et la Révocation de l'Édit de Nantes: 1680–1705*, 301.

27. Quoted in Montmollin and Delor, *Temple de la Fusterie, Temple Neuf,* 26.

28. Roughly the equivalent of $10,000,000 USD at the time of this volume—a significant investment for a city of no more than 20,000 people.

Geneva's coat of arms and the city's motto traced back to the time of Calvin, *post tenebras lux* (after darkness, light). Inside, a balcony supported by thirty-two colonnades standing on limestone bases wraps fully around the church's rectangular floorplan with beveled corners. Front-and-center, for the first time in a church in Geneva's history, stands the pulpit.

One can only imagine what Geneva's Huguenot refugees who remembered worship services at Charenton thought as they, now thirty years later, walked through the doors of Venne's design. The encircling gallery, the supporting colonnades, the pews oriented toward the pulpit at the front, all "generously lit" through the forty-two windows distributed over the two floors (eighteen on the ground floor and twenty-four on the upper), would have conjured up memories of the greatest Reformed temple in the land they used to call home.[29] But perhaps a second wave of nostalgia would wash over them once the service began as they heard the preacher's voice, clear and crisp, and the undissipated sound of the congregation's singing in a building designed precisely for those acts of worship. For those refugees who had spent the last three decades worshipping in Geneva's more cavernous pre-Reformation churches, it was a distinct quality of sound they had not heard in worship since before the Revocation of the Edict of Nantes.

The city scheduled the inaugural worship service for December 15, 1715. There is no evidence of any deliberation or hesitation on the city's part concerning who should preach that first sermon.

Bénédict Pictet and the Dedication Service of Temple Neuf

Though not as well known in our day, Bénédict Pictet was one of the most famous of Geneva's theologians in his day.[30] Heir to Francis Turretin's chair of theology, Moderator of Geneva's

---

29. Swiss Art in Sounds, https://swissais.ch/point_of_interest/en/qr/k9735/excerpt. Last accessed April 19, 2023.

30. Maria-Cristina Pitassi, *De l'orthodoxie aux lumières: Genève 1670–1735* (Geneva: Labor et Fides, 1992), 72–73.

Venerable Company of Pastors, twice Rector of the Academy of Geneva (1690-94 and 1712-18), collaborator in the first revisions to the Genevan Liturgy since Calvin, member of the Berlin Academy of Sciences and correspondent for the England Society for the Propagation of the Faith, Pictet was regarded for pairing his immense learning with a pastor's heart. He wrote voluminous works of theology and ethics—*La théologie chrétienne* (1702) and *La morale chrétienne* (1696)—that established his reputation as a theologian carrying the torch of Turretin's Reformed orthodox theology in an era that was increasingly infatuated with the novelties of the Enlightenment.[31] He revised Geneva's psalter and composed fifty hymns that became a staple in the city's worship services. Finally, he had a reputation for caring deeply for the afflicted. His only biographer, Eugene de Bude, says of Pictet, "In his exercise of great Christian charity, he brought doctrine down to earth."[32]

Thus it comes as no surprise that Pictet was chosen to deliver the first sermon at Neuf Temple. Before announcing his sermon text, Pictet opened with prayer that began:

> Great God, whom the heaven of heavens cannot contain (1 Kings 8), and who does not dwell in temples made with human hands (Acts 17), but who deigns to be found in places where your Holy Name is called upon and

---

31. Most recent scholarship on Pictet has misinterpreted him as a "transitional theologian" between Turretin's high orthodoxy and Jean-Alphonse Turretin's "Enlightened Orthodoxy." This misinterpretation owes largely to mistakenly regarding Pictet's 1696 *Theologia Christianae*, which is devoid of the key elements of Reformed scholasticism, as the expression of his mature theological program. However, Pictet's mature theology is not found there, but rather in his 1702 *Théologie chrétienne*—a theological tome that is approximately eight times the length of his 1696 *Theologia Christianae* and which, apart from being written in the vernacular, exhibits the hallmarks of Reformed scholasticism, including an extensive engagement with opponents and heavy referencing of church fathers, medieval theologians, and philosophers. The 1696 *Theologia Christianae* was translated into English by Frederick Reyroux as *Christian Theology* (London: L. B. Seeley and Sons, 1834), while Pictet's 1702 *Théologie chrétienne* was translated early into Dutch as *De christelyke God-geleerdheid en kennis der zaligheid, of Verklaring der waarheden, die God aan de menschen de Heilige Schrift heeft geopenbaart, nevens de wederlegging der tegengestelde dwaalingen... Vermeerdert met een kort vertoog van't allermerkwaardigste in de... geschiedenissen* (Pieter van Thol, 1729).

32. Eugene de Budé, *Vie de Bénédict Pictet: Théologien Genevois, 1655, 1724* (Lausanne: Georges Bridel, 1874), 105.

where your Word is proclaimed: We come this morning, for the first time, to humble ourselves in this New Temple before your Sovereign Majesty, to render to you our worship, to celebrate your grandeur and your infinite perfections, to admire the riches of your patience and goodness toward us, and to consecrate this place to you by our prayers and our actions of grace.[33]

After his opening prayer, Pictet announces his sermon text for this special occasion. It is one verse, Jacob's exclamation in Genesis 28:17—"How awesome is this place! This is none other than the house of God, and this is the gate of heaven!"

Early in his sermon, Pictet calls his hearers to reflect on the great privileges Geneva has uniquely enjoyed by God's grace. It is hard not to hear the juxtaposition of the histories of the Reformed churches in Geneva and in France in these words:

Although we have neither been nor are better than several peoples whom he has stricken with his plagues, he distinguishes us from others by continual favors. He preserves our precious liberty and makes us rejoice in the sweetest peace. He makes science and commerce to flourish in our midst and makes our countryside fertile. But what is infinitely more important, he enlightens us with his light and makes us to preach his truth. And whereas so many sanctuaries remain reduced to dust, he strengthens ours and even multiplies them—giving us today the grace of dedicating a new one to him, where henceforth his Great Name will be invoked and his divine praises be heard, preached, and explained. O what graces, O God![34]

After the Revocation of the Edict of Nantes, approximately seven hundred Huguenot churches were destroyed in France, Charenton chief among them. It is easy to imagine older men and women who heard Pictet's words remembering the tragic sight of their churches in France razed to the ground thirty years earlier. That such a fate has not befallen the churches of Geneva is something Pictet ascribes to the grace of God alone.

Pictet expounds the wider context of Jacob's story before zeroing in on Jacob's exclamation, "How awesome is this place!" followed by his calling it "the gate of heaven." Pictet explains that

---

33. Bénédict Pictet, *Sermon Fait le Jour de La Dedicace du Nouveau Temple, le XV de Décembre de l'an MDCCXV* (Genève: Chez Jean Antoine Querel, 1716).

34. Ibid., 3.

"gate of heaven" aptly describes what every manifestation of God's presence truly is, whether it is the ladder revealed to Jacob, the burning bush seen by his grandfather Abraham, the tabernacle of Moses and the later temple of Solomon, or—and especially—*the Church*, "which Saint Paul calls the house of the living God."[35] The gathering of believers in God's name may properly be called "the gate of heaven" on several counts:

> ... *whether* because the assemblies of the faithful here below are an image of those assemblies in Heaven above; whether because the word that is spoken there is like the opening of heaven (to use the words of St. Chrysostom); *whether* because this same word teaches us the way to go to Heaven and, when received with faith, leads us there; *whether* because the Sacraments which we administer there are the pledges of the inheritance that awaits us in Heaven; *whether* because in order to enter Heaven, we must be in the true Church here below. Such gatherings are not only the gate of Heaven, but are like a small Paradise, where God spreads his mercy and his holiness before his faithful.[36]

In all of this, Pictet emphasizes that the assembled people worshipping, not the edifice in which they worship, is "the gate of heaven."

Pictet goes on to give a brief history of religious buildings in pre-Christian and then Christian times. This overview serves to emphasize that pagan religions regarded their temples as sacred places, whereas Christians—who in the first generations after Christ had no religious buildings of their own—have regarded the gathering in Christ's name, not the place where they gather, as holy. But if there is nothing holy about the place itself, how then does one consecrate a new church building for a holy use, as Pictet and the congregation are doing on this morning at the dedication service in Temple Neuf? Pictet traces the gradual accumulation over the centuries of pomp and circumstance that enveloped the dedication of church buildings especially in the medieval era:

---

35. Ibid., 11.
36. Ibid., 13.

In this way were the churches of the Roman Catholic Church consecrated. One encounters grand mysteries in every action that was performed. But I leave it to you to ask if these ceremonies came from the Apostles, or if they were not rather an imitation of Judaism and of Paganism, and if we have not added puerilities which bring little honor to those who invented them, much less those who practice them?[37]

By contrast, Pictet announces that a true dedication of churches is done with prayers, the singing of psalms and sacred hymns, the reading and preaching of the Word of God, and the administration of the Sacraments.[38] "These are all the ceremonies that the early Christians used, and we should not add others of our own."[39] He draws his hearers attention to the fact that they see no "flowers and garlands" nor any of the other traditional Catholic elements of a dedication service. Rather, according to the example of Solomon and of the ancient Doctors of the Church when they led such dedication services, "we will celebrate the innumerable graces of God toward us, and we will sing the holy Songs to the praise of our protector." He continues:

We will bless him because he never grows tired of doing us good and because he preserves for us the precious advantages that we enjoy from his goodness. We will celebrate his power which has protected us, his mercy which has supported us, his wisdom which has led us, his love which unceasingly spreads new favors over us, despite our unworthiness, and who has given us a grace which he did not see to give to our Fathers—that of building a new church to his honor. *For here we have the first church built since the blessed Reformation, and its design is different from that of the others that we have.*[40]

The design of Temple Neuf is indeed different from Geneva's other three churches of the pre-Reformation era—and, accordingly, its dedication service is different from theirs as well.

---

37. Pictet, *Sermon Fait le Jour de La Dedicace du Nouveau Temple*, 31.
38. Ibid., 31–32.
39. Ibid., 32.
40. Ibid., 32–33. Emphasis mine.

Pictet ends his sermon with eleven points of application emphasizing the importance of maintaining worship that is reverent, Word-centered, God-glorifying, and—we must add—well-attended.[41] "We will no longer be able to pretend that we don't have enough churches to go and hear the Word of God."[42] He also seizes the occasion to call his hearers to dedicate themselves anew to God: "May this New Temple, and the new graces that God bestows upon us, lead us to seek hearts that are wholly new—hearts in which and from which God is honored, loved, and feared much more than he has been, and where he reigns, and where all our passions are entirely submitted to him."[43] And he exhorts them to look beyond this life below to heaven above and to the life to come:

> But let us consider that if this is only the gate of Heaven, we should pant for Heaven itself, for the Temple of glory, of which God himself is the builder, where we will see Jesus Christ our Lord, who is our true Propitiation, surrounded by seraphim, cherubim, and thrones, where we will hear the Songs of Angels, and where we will join our voices to those of consecrated spirits.[44]

And after quoting from Solomon's prayer of dedication, Pictet said, "Amen," and the new church designed to amplify the preached word went, for a moment, silent, with some perhaps looking with longing eyes beyond the gate of Heaven to Heaven itself.

What Became of Bénédict Pictet

In the months that followed, Pictet worked on a nearly three-hundred-page treatise on the history of church buildings and their dedications. It was published in 1716 as *Dissertation sur les Temples, leur Dedicace, et Plusiers choses qu'on y voit* (Dissertation on Temples, Their Dedications, and Many Things Seen There).[45]

---

41. Ibid., 33ff.
42. Ibid., 39.
43. Ibid., 40.
44. Ibid., 45.
45. Pictet explains the background to this book in the preface: "The New Temple that

His career in the early eighteenth century is substantially remembered not only for the wide range of works he produced, such as that one, but also for the great battle that he lost.

In Pictet's lifetime, Geneva was turning its back on its Reformed confessional heritage—a turning tragically led by Francis Turretin's own son, Jean-Alphonse Turretin. In 1706, Turretin the son nearly succeeded in leading Geneva's Company of Pastors to abrogate the *Formula Helvetica Consensus*—a 1675 confessional document designed by Francis Turretin and two Swiss colleagues to fortify (against the softening influence of the Academy of Saumur in France) Geneva's adherence to the *Canons of Dort*. Pictet rallied a small minority against this move, appealing to the Small Council against the Company of Pastors' decision. Their appeal succeeded and thus the abrogation of the *Formula* was avoided, though at the cost of a compromise that removed the requirement for pastors in Geneva to sign their names to the Formula ("la signature").

But time was on the side of the progressive majority as "[b]etween 1706 and 1725, the minority group began to die off...".[46] Pictet died in 1724. His death effectively "eliminated the last obstacle to new ideas."[47] Thus, in 1725, Geneva's pastors voted to do entirely away with the *Formula Helvetica Consensus* and the *Canons of Dort* themselves, rendering the Genevan Church, almost two hundred years after Calvin's arrival, "confessionless."[48]

---

was completed in this city several months ago has occasioned several persons expressing a desire for a small *treatise* on *temples*, on their *dedication*, and on several *things* that one sees and does there, that contains a summary of what scholars have said on these topics that is otherwise scattered among an infinite number of books. It is to satisfy such a seemingly legitimate desire that I propose in this little work to treat these questions that one sees in the following Table of Contents." Bénédict Pictet, *Dissertation sur les Temples, leur Dedicace, et Plusiers choses qu'on y voit* (Genève: Chez Fabri et Barrillot, 1716).

46. Martin I. Klauber, "Jean-Alphonse Turretini and the Abrogation of the Formula Consensus in Geneva," *Westminster Theological Journal* 53 (1991): 336.

47. Jean-Marc Berthoud, "Bénédict Pictet (1655–1724): Le dernier héraut de l'Orthodoxie genevoise," in Bénédict Pictet, *La morale chrétienne ou l'art de bien vivre, tome premier* [1710] (Genève: Pierre Thierry Benoit, 2020), 49.

48. James I. Good, *History of the Swiss Reformed Church* (Philadelphia: Board of the Reformed Church in the U.S., 1913), 279; quoted in Klauber, "Jean-Alphonse Turretini

According to Christian Moser, "The end of late orthodoxy can be dated by the death of Bénédict Pictet (1724) and the abolition of the canons of Dordt in Geneva (1725) in the mid-1720s."[49] The nineteenth-century translator of Pictet's *Christian Theology*, Frederick Reyroux, pays tribute to Pictet as one who "may in some measure be regarded as the last of those illustrious and orthodox divines who presided over the church in Geneva ... For shortly after his death ... that highly favoured church commenced her grievous declension."[50]

In something of an irony, Geneva's first Calvinist church building was dedicated with a sermon preached by Geneva's last Calvinist.

What Became of "Temple Neuf"

The "Temple Neuf" soon became known as "Temple de la Fusterie," so named for the part of the city where wood craftsmen (known in Old French as *fustiers*) made and traded beams, planks, barrel hoops, and the like.[51] In the nineteenth century, an organ was installed in the temple, occupying the gallery space above the pulpit. Today, the temple no longer hosts a congregation but rather serves as a concert hall for theatrical and musical events. It remains highly regarded for its outstanding acoustics.

Temple de la Fusterie was closed in 2021 for a multiyear project to stabilize its sinking foundation (which lies on unstable lake silt) with an expected completion date of 2026.[52]

---

and the Abrogation of the Formula Consensus in Geneva," 336.

49. Christian Moser, "Reformed Orthodoxy in Switzerland," in *A Companion to Reformed Orthodoxy*, ed. Herman J. Selderhuis (Leiden: Brill, 2013), 197.

50. Frederick Reyroux, "Translator's Preface," in Benedict Pictet, *Christian Theology*, trans. Frederick Reyroux (Philadelphia: Presbyterian Board of Publications, [1845]), iv. In breaking up the quote in this way, I am following Joel R. Beeke, *Debated Issues in Sovereign Predestination: Early Lutheran Predestination, Calvinian Reprobation, and Variations in Genevan Lapsarianism* (Göttingen: Vandenhoeck & Ruprecht, 2017), 209.

51. Cf. Jorgen Wadum, et. al., eds., *Wooden Supports in 12th to 16th Century European Paintings: A New Translation of Jacqueline Marette's* Connaissance des Primitifs par l'étude du bois du XIIe au XVIe siècle, trans. Ted Atkins and Paul van Calster ([1961] Copenhagen: Archetype Publications), chap. 5 ("Woodworking and Trade in Medieval France"). https://marette.smk.dk/-9715.html. Accessed April 18, 2023.

52. Anne Buloz, "Temple de la Fusterie: une chantier complex," in *Reformés – Le*

Conclusion

The church of Jesus Christ endures on the basis of Jesus's promise to Peter: "You are Peter, and on this rock I will build my church, and the gates of hell shall not prevail against it" (Matt. 16:18).[53] It is evident that Jesus was not speaking here of church buildings, but of the enduring fellowship of those who confess his name. Of this enduring fellowship, Calvin's successor and indefatigable supporter of the Huguenots, Theodore Beza (1519–1605), famously said that the church "is an anvil that has worn out many a hammer."

The faith of the Huguenots outlived the hammers that fell on Temple de Charenton in 1685. The construction of the Temple Neuf in Geneva in 1715 testifies not only to the endurance of the Huguenots, but also to the theology undergirding their endurance—a theology that flows back to Calvin's ministry centered on hearing and receiving the Word of God. At the same time, the conversion of Temple de la Fusterie to a concert hall warns us that no church building, however well-designed, secures the faith of those who worship there. In the words of Calvin, "not church buildings but we ourselves are temples of God."[54]

A study of the histories of church buildings serves ultimately to remind us of the truth of Hebrews 13:14 that "here we have no lasting city, but we seek the city that is to come." So then, if we are among those who grieve the loss of a church building to natural disaster, to destruction by wicked human hands, or to an apostatizing denomination that claimed its ownership rights, let us remember, in the words of Pictet, that such buildings were never themselves "the gate to heaven." And if, on the other hand, we are among those blessed, as the people of Geneva in 1715

Journal, March 30, 2022. https://www.reformes.ch/culture/2022/03/temple-de-la-fusterie-un-chantier-complexe-architecture-geneve-patrimoine-reformes. Accessed April 25, 2022.

53. The Greek word translated as "hell" is not *gehenna* but *hades*. On the importance of this distinction, see Gerrit Dawson's chapter in this volume, "Transit of Mercy: Union with Christ in His Descent and Ascent," pp. 317–332.

54. Calvin, *Institutes*, vol. 2, 893.

and for many years to come were blessed, to gather for worship in buildings well-suited to that divine purpose, let us likewise keep in mind that such buildings can never become "the gate to heaven." Rather, that gate appears wherever God's people gather here below in the name of Christ to worship the Father in spirit and in truth (John 4:24). And of that glorious heavenly gate, we have for all time this sure and certain promise from Jesus himself: "the gates of hell shall not prevail against it."

10

The Emergence of Liberty
and History's Theo-Political Problem

Christian D. Finnigan

DOUGLAS F. Kelly's *The Emergence of Liberty in the Modern World: The Influence of Calvin on Five Governments from the 16th Through 18th Centuries* was the resulting product stemming from his involvement with the Christian Legal Society and participation in their long-running Jurisprudence Panel. Kelly's stated purpose in producing this monograph was to trace "the development of Calvinist thought on church-state relations and related subjects from the sixteenth through the eighteenth centuries in five different governments."[1] *The Emergence of Liberty* was hardly the first, nor was it the final, contribution to the scholarly literature surrounding Reformation political theology. Rather, Kelly's work reflects a growing interest in connecting the Protestant Reformation with the rise of modernity in Western Europe. While Kelly's work demonstrates an integrated approach to early modern political thought, as he intentionally engages with various disciplines of history, theology, and political

---

1. Douglas F. Kelly, *The Emergence of Liberty in the Modern World: The Influence of Calvin on Five Governments from the 16th Through 18th Centuries* (Phillipsburg: Presbyterian & Reformed, 1992), 1.

237

thought, unfortunately such a cross-disciplinary approach is exceedingly rare.

The study of Reformation political theology, has proved to be inherently fraught with difficulty, as numerous historians have attempted (and largely failed) to construct a consistent political theology from a variety of early modern sources, i.e. theological *loci*, commentaries, systematics, treatises, letters, and the retrieval of varying historical and political contexts, etc. Accordingly, differing accounts and genealogies have resulted from these intellectual enquiries. Chief among these competing narratives is the whiggish narrative.

The history of western political thought has long tended to be dominated by a decidedly whiggish narrative, with scholars within this field advocating a reading of the Protestant Reformers as proto-liberals. Intellectual historians in this tradition point to the ecclesiastical split in the sixteenth century, and more specifically the emergence of the Calvinist resistance theory, as responsible for the subsequent rise of Constitutionalism, Republicanism, Federalism, and the emergence of individual rights in Western Europe.[2] Many of these whig historians draw a line from the sixteenth century Protestant Reformation directly to John Locke (1623-1704) and even to the American founding. A prominent example of this is the quote attributed to German historian, Leopold von Ranke (1795-1886): "John Calvin was virtually the founder of America."[3] More recent examples of this genealogy of liberalism can be found in the works of Hans Baron, Michael Walzer, Quentin Skinner, Harold J. Berman, John Witte, Jr., and Brad Gregory.[4] In addition, a theological school

---

2. "The whig historian is fond of showing how much Calvinism has contributed to the development of modern liberty." Hebert Butterfield, *The Whig Interpretation of History* (1931).

3. Emile Doumergue, "Calvin a Source of Democracy," in *Calvin and Calvinism: Sources of Democracy?*, eds. Robert M. Kingdon and Robert D. Linder (Lexington: D. C. Heath, 1970), 7.

4. Hans Baron, "Calvinist Republicanism and its Historical Roots," *CH*, 8 (1939), 30–42; Michael Walzer, *The Revolution of the Saints: A Study in the Origins of Radical Politics* (Cambridge MA: Harvard University Press, 1965); Quentin Skinner,

known as Radical (or Reformed) Two Kingdom Theology has developed along similar lines. Representatives of this school, including David VanDrunen and Matthew Tuininga, have seen in the work of the Protestant Reformers, specifically John Calvin (1509-1564), a strongly modern notion of the separation between the ecclesiastical and civil spheres, bearing more than a passing similarity to the American political doctrine of the separation of Church and State.[5]

In contrast to this genealogy of liberalism, another group of scholars posit a narrative which holds to a more Magisterial Reformation. Historiographically, the term "Magisterial Reformation" is a twentieth-century construct employed by George H. Williams for the purposes of taxonomy, and denotes those Protestant Reformers that had state support for their reformations, as contrasted with those of the "Radical Reformation" who sought to establish religious communities separate from the interference of secular authorities.[6] Williams's terminology would become standard in the field, and used more broadly to refer to "wherever the Reformation was carried out with the support and under the protection of the secular authorities."[7] Thus defined, Magisterial Reformation also shares important continuities with later theories, such as the "Confessionalization

---

The Foundations of Modern Political Thought: The Age of Reformation 2 vols., vol. 2 (Cambridge: Cambridge University Press, 1978); Harold J Berman, *Law and Revolution, II: The Impact of the Protestant. Reformations on the Western Legal Tradition* (Cambridge, MA: Harvard University Press, 2003); John Witte, *Law and Protestantism: The Legal Teachings of the Lutheran Reformation* (Cambridge: Cambridge University Press, 2002); John Witte, Jr, *The Reformation of Rights: Law, Religion, and Human Rights in Early Modern Calvinism* (Cambridge: Cambridge University, 2008).

5. David VanDrunen, *Natural Law and The Two Kingdoms: A Study in the Development of Reformed Social Thought* (Grand Rapids: Eerdmans, 2010); Matthew J. Tuininga, *Calvin's Political Theology and the Public Engagement of the Church: Calvin's Two Kingdoms* (Cambridge: Cambridge University Press, 2017).

6. George H. Williams, *The Radical Reformation* (Philadelphia: The Westminster Press, 1962).

7. Janet Coleman, ed., *The Individual in Political Theory and Practice* (Oxford: Oxford University Press, 1996), 80.

Thesis" of Wolfgang Reinhard and Heinz Schilling.[8] But despite its relatively recent lexical provenance, the concept of Magisterial Reformation dates to well before the twentieth century. As Mark Goldie has argued, "Protestant Europe inherited a fundamental belief from the medieval Catholic Church: that membership of the church was coextensive with membership of the commonwealth and that it was the duty of a 'godly prince' to promote and support the true religion."[9]

These contrasting narratives surrounding Reformation political theology evidence a far greater problem within the discipline of History, and more specifically the field of the history of political thought. The problem is a bifurcation of disciplines, which has in turn created a Theo-Political problem. In essence, theologians have largely been doing historical work without employing historical methodologies and without engaging academic historians. At the same time, historians (especially those within the field of the history of political thought) have been largely ignoring the overwhelmingly theological and religious contexts of their subjects. Scholars working in Reformation political theology, therefore, must confront the issues of determining how this bifurcation emerged, and whether this Theo-Political problem can be surmounted.

The Enlightenment's Effect on Church History

Prior to the Enlightenment, the modern discipline of the history of religion, or religious studies, did not exist. Rather, the pre-Enlightenment age had the "uncritical" field of Ecclesiastical History. Up through the seventeenth century, most church history was written through a confessional lens, and the predominant taxonomy for ecclesiastical historians was orthodoxy and heresy. The Enlightenment brought with it two major changes that helped

---

8. H. Schilling, "Confessional Europe", in Tracey et al. (eds), *Handbook of European History, 1400–1600: Late Middle Ages, Renaissance and Reformation*, vol. 2 (Leiden: New York: Brill, 1995).

9. Mark Goldie, "Introduction" in John Locke, *A Letter concerning Toleration and Other Writings*, ed. Mark Goldie (Indianapolis: Liberty Fund, 2010), ix.

produce the modern fields of critical church history and the history of religion. The first change was an increased scientific interest in textual sources. The second change was the relaxation of ecclesiastical and confessional constraints, which granted historians the license to question the received tradition.[10]

In the field of Church History, these revolutions roughly followed the patterns of change occurring first in the discipline of Biblical studies. The introduction of textual critical studies in the field of Biblical Studies came out of Germany. G.E Lessing (1729-1781), one of the German Enlightenment's most prominent figures, offered the following dictum, that "accidental truths of history can never become the proof of necessary truths of reason." This was nothing less than a firm rejection of the supernatural history of the Bible and Christian tradition. For Lessing, who had embraced the Enlightenment rationality of René Descartes (1596–1650), natural, observable history was the foundation of scholarly enquiry, not the supernatural *kerygma* of theology. Lessing thus launched a wave of higher criticism in Germany that would continue employing his methodology and would further seek to demystify the Scriptures of the Christian faith.

The prominent twentieth century Reformed theologian Karl Barth (1886-1968) greatly objected to the Bible being subjected to the rules and laws of modern historiography. Barth also objected to the view which held that the Bible was nothing more than a window into the past. Barth considered Lessing's dictum to be fundamentally flawed and rejected the idea that *Historie*— denoting the scientific and empirical approach to establishing history—could be used as a reliable basis for dealing with the Bible. According to Richard Burnett, in Barth's view,

> [h]istory was not a category which could comprehend, contain, or in any way circumscribe revelation. Nor was history capable of disclosing revelation, no matter how closely examined or how broadly defined. For Barth, it was not that history was disclosive of the meaning of revelation;

---

10. James E. Bradley and Richard A. Muller, *Church History: An Introduction to Research, Reference Works and Methods* (Grand Rapids: Eerdmans,1995), 13.

it was that revelation was disclosive of the meaning of history. It was not that history established or grounded revelation; it was that revelation established and grounded history.[11]

For Barth, special revelation was the ultimate form of communication, to which there is no higher. God's condescension and revelation of Himself to man could not be divided up, nor could its veracity be verified by a human system or science. God's revelation, the Bible, must therefore be treated as *sui generis*.[12] Accordingly in Barth's mind, it was inappropriate to search for a "historical Jesus" separate from the witness of the Bible. The Jesus of Nazareth and the Jesus of faith stood not as two different and opposing persons, but rather there is one Jesus, the Jesus Christ or revelation, the very Son of God, the Logos, who is found in the Bible's history (*Geschichte*), not through scientific-historical verification (*Historie*).

While Barth undoubtedly intended to save Christian history from the higher critics, what resulted instead was the expulsion of Christian Theology from the field of history. Barth had introduced a bifurcated model for dealing with religious history. Instead of seeking a faith that was in its essence historical, this bifurcation led to a purely spiritual, ahistorical faith. The effect of this was to ghettoize Christian Theologians from engaging with academic historians, only increasing the sacred-secular divide between theology and the study of history. This sacred-secular divide is especially apparent in the history of political thought—a fact that is especially surprising, given that much of the field is devoted to the early modern period, a period that is decisively religious.

The History of Political Thought

In America, the history of ideas traces back to the figure of Arthur O. Lovejoy (1873–1962). Professor of Philosophy at Johns Hopkins University, Lovejoy founded the greatly influential *Journal of the*

---

11. Richard E. Burnett, *Karl Barth's Theological Exegesis: The Hermeneutical Principles of the Römerbrief Period* (Grand Rapids: Eerdmans, 2004), 107.

12. Karl Barth, *Church Dogmatics*, 1.1, 164.

History of Ideas in 1940. Lovejoy's desire was to transcend the boundaries of specialization that had developed in the Academy and to develop a unique field devoted to the study of great ideas. Central to Lovejoy's project was his belief that ideas have power. Lovejoy believed that single concepts could be separated from their fields and studied as individual entities.

In the very first volume of the *Journal of the History of Ideas,* Lovejoy explained that the aim of the field was

> [t]o know, so far as may be known, the thoughts that have been widely held among men on matters of common human concernment, to determine how these thoughts have arisen, combined, interacted with, or counteracted, one another, and how they have severally been related to the imagination and emotions and behavior of those who have held them.[13]

As such, Lovejoy developed his approach around the concept of "unit-ideas." Lovejoy described this "unit-idea" methodology as being analogous to analytic chemistry:

> By the history of ideas I mean something at once more specific and less restricted than the history of philosophy. It is differentiated primarily by the character of the units with which it concerns itself. Though it deals in great part with the same material as the other branches of the history of thought and depends greatly upon their prior labors, it divides that material in a special way, brings the parts into new groupings and relations, views it from the standpoint of a distinctive purpose. Its initial procedure may be said—though the parallel has its dangers—to be somewhat analogous to that of analytic chemistry. In dealing with the history of philosophical doctrines, for example, it cuts into the hard-and-fast individual systems and, for its own purposes, breaks them up into their unit-idea.[14]

While Lovejoy is largely credited as the founder of the history of ideas, its most influential German-American proponent was Leo Strauss (1899-1973). Strauss, a German born Jew, who had emigrated to the United States in 1937, served as a Professor of

---

13. Arthur O. Lovejoy, "Reflections on the History of Ideas" *Journal of the History of Ideas,* 1.1 (Jan., 1940): 3–23, 8.

14. A. O. Lovejoy, *The Great Chain of Being: A Study of the History of an Idea,* The William James Lectures (Cambridge, MA: Harvard University Press 1936), 2, 3.

Political Science at the University of Chicago from 1949–1969. Strauss, similar to Lovejoy, believed that ideas have power, but Strauss also believed that ideas had inherent value. Strauss took aim at modernity's acceptance of positivism, arguing that it was impossible to have "value-free" political philosophy.[15] Where positivists claimed that empirical knowledge was the highest form of knowledge available to humanity, Strauss preferred the idealism of the classical tradition.

Strauss viewed historicism as the enemy of political philosophy. "Historicism" Strauss argued, "rejects the question of the good society."[16] For Strauss historical inquiry was, in and of itself, insufficient. The political philosopher must search for what is good. Strauss saw the good as being modelled in classical society. Concomitantly, he viewed modern society as the antithesis of the classical ideal. From Machiavelli to Nietzsche, Strauss traced the rise of positivistic social science and pointed to its corrosive influence. Most notably, Strauss singled out the German sociologist Max Weber (1864–1920) for critique. Weber, Strauss argued, evaded any discussion of morality by "the simple device of passing them off as value problems."[17] Weber's fact-value distinction was emblematic of the empirical, positivistic social science approach. Strauss disdained this social science positivism for its attempt to be value-neutral. For Strauss morality was at the very core of the Political philosopher's project.

In the United Kingdom a markedly different tradition developed. While scholars at Oxford University concentrated on the study of Political Theory (largely divorced from historical concerns), at the University of Cambridge a new discipline began to emerge. Their methodology was as concerned about ideas as the historical contexts from which they emerged. This new discipline would come to be known as the history of political thought, tracing its origins to Cambridge professor, Peter Laslett

15. Leo Strauss, *What is Political Philosophy and Other Studies* (Chicago: University of Chicago Press 1959), 22.

16. Ibid., 26.

17. Ibid., 23.

(1915–2001).[18] Laslett's publication of Robert Filmer's (ca. 1588–1653) *Patriarcha* in 1949 and his subsequent edition of Locke's *Two Treatises of Government* in 1960 are the first expressions of this new historical approach to political thought.[19] While beginning with Laslett, the Cambridge School would continue to grow and develop, becoming a significant intellectual force. In the 1970s a wave of new works, essentially all sharing a similar methodology, hit the market: John Dunn, *The Political Thought of John Locke* (1969); Duncan Forbes, *Hume's Philosophical politics* (1975); J. G. A. Pocock, *The Machiavellian Moment* (1975); Quentin Skinner, *The Foundations of Modern Political Thought* (1978).[20] Collectively, these works helped to reshape the field of the history of political thought and established a definitive Cambridge School methodology.

The Cambridge School arose, in large part, to counter the prevailing trends in the history of ideas—specifically, it opposed the idea that "the classic texts in moral, political, religious and other such modes of thought contain a 'dateless wisdom' in the form of 'universal ideas.'"[21] In sharp distinction to the work of Lovejoy and Strauss, Cambridge School intellectuals sought to reorient the works of political philosophy back into their original, historical contexts. In this respect, the history of political thought is essentially a historical enterprise.

---

18. J. G. A. Pocock, *Political Thought and History: Essays on Theory and Method* (New York: Cambridge University Press, 2009), vii-viii.

19. Sir Robert Filmer, *Patriarcha and Other Political Writings of Sir Robert Filmer, ed. Peter Laslett* (1680; Oxford: Basil Blackwell, 1949); John Locke, *Two Treatises of Government* (1689; Cambridge: Cambridge University Press 1960).

20. John Dunn, *The Political Thought of John Locke: An Historical Account of the Argument of the "Two Treatises of Government"* (Cambridge: Cambridge University Press, 1969); Duncan Forbes, *Hume's Philosophical Politics* (Cambridge: Cambridge University Press, 1975); J. G. A. Pocock, *The Machiavellian Moment: Florentine political thought and the Atlantic republican tradition* (Princeton: Princeton University Press, 1975); Quentin Skinner, *The Foundations of Modern Political Thought, Vol 2: The Age of Reformation* (Cambridge: Cambridge University Press, 1978).

21. Quentin Skinner, *Visions of Politics, Vol 1: Regarding Method* (Cambridge: Cambridge University Press, 2010) 57.

Central to this method is approaching "the past with a willingness to listen, with a commitment to trying to see things their way." [22] In order to "see things their way," the historian's task is therefore to understand, as far as is possible, the historical and linguistic context in which the author is speaking. The history of political thought then becomes, according to Pocock, "a multiplicity of language acts performed by language users in historical contexts."[23] This contextualist approach would prove the defining characteristic of the Cambridge School methodology.

The Cambridge School's Religious Problem

Since its explosion on to the intellectual scene in the 1970s, the Cambridge School methodology had grown to enjoy a position of near hegemony over the field of history of political thought. This does not mean, however, that it is without critics. One area of criticism it is most susceptible to, particularly the work of Quentin Skinner, is in its lack of engagement with religion. While much of their work focuses on the early modern period, a period known for an intense and thorough religiosity, practitioners of the Cambridge School have largely focused their attentions on secular subjects. For example, Skinner has distinguished himself as one of the leading experts on Machiavelli and Hobbes, two of the decidedly more secular figures of the early modern period. Accordingly, the question must be asked, why does there seem to be such an aversion to religion and religious figures by the Cambridge School?

At first blush, the answer to this query may well turn out to be rather benign. Religion is simply not of any particular interest to Skinner or his colleagues. Skinner has admitted to being an atheist and, therefore, has intentionally elected to eschew religious themes in his work: "I have always kept off religious themes, and tried to write about themes that won't be skewed by that aversion."[24] Likewise, Pocock has argued that an additional

---

22. Ibid., 6

23. J. G. A. Pocock, *Political Thought and History: Essays on Theory and Method* (New York: Cambridge University Press, 2009), viii.

24. Quentin Skinner as cited in John Coffey, "Skinner and the Religious Dimension

problem inherent in the historian's interacting with religious figures of the early modern period is that "few of us know one-tenth of the theology available to competently trained divines and laymen among our predecessors." [25] The works of Skinner, Pocock, and the rest are incredibly expansive, and no historian can master every field. Therefore, specialization is a perfectly natural and understandable limitation of the historian.

However, upon further examination, the benign answer begins to look less and less credible. For one, practitioners of the Cambridge School have predominantly concentrated on the early modern period for their research. This is a period which is thoroughly saturated in, and heavily influenced by, religion. Even if a scholar desired to handpick a few of the more secular figures to research out of this religious era, he must still, if he wishes to remain true to the Cambridge methodology, endeavor to understand the religious context in which that secular figure existed. Additionally, the Cambridge School has not altogether avoided dealing with religious figures. In point of fact, when forced to engage with expressly theological historical figures, these figures are often-times approached through a decidedly secularized lens. These considerations have led some scholars to suggest that the Cambridge School does not simply wish to avoid religion altogether, but rather is openly hostile to religion. A few of these scholars have further speculated that inherent in the Cambridge School methodology is a secularizing teleology. One scholar, J.C.D. Clark has noted that "[i]n respect of religion, the contextualist school has been held to be not merely secular in its assumptions, but pragmatically secularizing in a way that has also been held to detract from historical understanding."[26]

---

of Early Modern Political Thought" in Alister Chapman, John Coffey and Brad S. Gregory, eds., *Seeing Things Their Way: Intellectual History and the Return of Religion* (Notre Dame: University of Notre Dame Press, 2009), 46–74, 52.

25. J. G. A. Pocock, "A discourse of sovereignty," in Nicholas Phillipson and Quentin Skinner, eds. *Political Discourse in Early Modern Britain* (Cambridge: Cambridge University Press, 1993), 377–428, 381.

26. J.C.D. Clark, "Barbarism, Religion and the history of Political Thought," in *The Political Imagination in History: Essays Concerning J. G. A. Pocock*, ed. D.L. DeLuna (Baltimore: Owlworks, 2006) 211–29, 217.

B.W. Young in his essay, "Enlightenment Political Thought and the Cambridge School" points to the recontextualizing of John Locke as an example of the secularizing agenda of the Cambridge School. As Locke's *Two Treatises of Government* is saturated in Calvinist natural theology, it therefore runs counter to the secular Machiavellian revision of the Cambridge School. In a very telling passage Pocock admits that "the deemphasizing of Locke is for the present a tactical necessity. The historical context must be reconstructed without him before he can be fitted back into it."[27] In removing the influence of Locke from the creation of modern liberalism, a more secularized account of modernity becomes possible. Going even further, Pocock contends that Locke's influence on the Atlantic world stems from his more secular works, *The essay concerning the human understanding* and the *Letters on toleration*, not his *Two treatises on government*.[28] This is a pronounced secular revision of the received tradition of the influence of "Lockean liberalism."

This secularizing *telos* is not limited to Pocock. If anything, it is even more prevalent in the work of Quentin Skinner. In his *Visions of Politics*, Skinner notes that

> one of the uses of the past arises from the fact that we are prone to fall under the spell of our own intellectual heritage. As we analyse and reflect on our normative concepts, it is easy to become bewitched into believing that the ways of thinking about them bequeathed to us by the mainstream of our intellectual traditions must be *the* ways of thinking about them. Given this situation, one of the contributions that historians can make is to offer us a kind of exorcism.[29]

In his *Foundations*, the demon that Skinner seeks to exorcise is the spirit of the Protestant Modernisation Thesis.

---

27. Pocock, *The Machiavellian Moment*, 424.

28. J. G. A. Pocock, "The Myth of John Locke and the Obsession with Liberalism," in *John Locke: Papers Read at a Clark Library Seminar, 10 December 1977* (Los Angeles, CA, 1980), 1–24, at p. 21. As cited in B. W. Young, "Enlightenment Political Thought and the Cambridge School," *Historical Journal* 52,1 (2009): 235–251.

29. Skinner, *Visions*, 6.

Skinner has been described by some scholars as personally "hostile to Christianity."[30] One of the ways in which this hostility supposedly manifested itself was in his desire to extricate the whiggish, Protestant modernization theory in early modern studies. In volume two of his *Foundations,* Skinner's principal target was the political philosopher Michael Walzer. Walzer's *Revolution of the Saints* traced the foundation of modern liberalism to the Calvinistic revolutionaries of the sixteenth century.[31] In contrast to Walzer, Skinner points out that the Calvinist resistance theory was not originally Protestant, but was predated by and dependent on the Catholic Conciliar movement of the fifteenth century.[32] Mark Goldie commented on this, noting that,

> [o]ne is tempted to say that Skinner recovered the Catholic political tradition in order to dispose of Protestant theories of liberal modernity. He did so not of course to recommend Catholicism, but rather to clear the ground for a quite different route into the history of concepts of liberty, a subject upon which so much of his more recent work has dwelt.[33]

Not only was Skinner's aim in the *Foundations* to exorcise the Protestant Modernization Thesis, he also endeavored to explain the emergence of the modern nation state.[34] For Skinner, the modern nation state is a welcome evolution away from the model of medieval Christendom. In responding to philosopher Charles Taylor's argument for a return to a theistically-centered polis, Skinner writes that given the background of medieval Christendom "the idea of recommending the re-adoption of the same theistic perspective is I think likely to strike anyone

---

30. Michael Printy, "Skinner and Pocock in Context: Early Modern Political Thought Today" *History and Theory* 48 (February 2009): 113–121, 116.

31. Michael Walzer, *The Revolution of the Saints: A Study in the Origins of Radical Politics* (Cambridge, MA: Harvard University Press, 1965).

32. Skinner, *Foundations*, 321–22.

33. Mark Goldie, "The context of the Foundations" in *Rethinking the Foundations of Modern Political Thought*, Annabel Brett, James Tully, Holly Hamilton-Bleakley, eds. (Cambridge: Cambridge University Press, 2006), 3–19, 16–17.

34. Skinner, *Foundations*, vol 1, ix.

familiar with the historical record as a case of offering a cure for our ills potentially worse than the disease." [35] Thus, Skinner not only wishes to extricate the Protestant Modernization thesis, he also discloses his personal dislike of a theistic-centric polity, in preference of a secularized nation state.

Problems, Solutions, Interlocutors

The Cambridge School is therefore, at least in its treatment of religion, far from contextual. Rather, it and its leading practitioners seem openly hostile to religion. Instead of value-free empirical historians, what we find is an entrenched secularizing vision of history, seeking to "exorcise" the "whiggish" demons of Christianity from the history of political thought. The question ultimately is whether a place for religion exists within the history of political thought? Two different methodologies are worth consideration here. The first school to be considered, the Post-Secularists, offers a critique of the Cambridge School from philosophers and theologians critical of the secular project. Second, a more sympathetic treatment will be examined, this coming from a group of religious historians.

Some of the most interesting and unique critiques of the Cambridge School come from a school of thought we shall label the Post-Secularists. The post-secularists consist of philosophers and theologians who are critical of modernity and post-Enlightenment rationality. Its most well-known adherents are the philosophers Alasdair MacIntyre and Charles Taylor, together with a group of theologians known as "Radical Orthodox" (most notably represented by the theologian John Milbank). Collectively, these individuals argue against the post-Enlightenment, secular project. And most relevant to our question, they argue that the history of political thought is a field built on a faulty premise. This school questions the ability of positivistic social scientists to be value-free historians, and also points out that the history of

---

35. Quentin Skinner, "Modernity and Disenchantment: Some Reflections on Charles Taylor's Diagnosis" in *The Politics of Postmodernity*, James M. M. Good and Irving Velody, eds. (Cambridge: Cambridge University Press, 1998), 49–60, 57.

political thought's quest to locate the origins of the secular state is a self-propagating mythology.

First appearing in 1981, the publication of Alasdair MacIntyre's *After Virtue* created quite a stir in intellectual circles. In *After Virtue*, MacIntyre argued that we are living in an age of "barbarism and darkness." [36] He also argued that modern liberal society has lost a bearing on morality, that the "language of morality has passed from a state of order to disorder."[37] MacIntyre cites "Emotivism" as "the doctrine that all evaluative judgments and more specifically all moral judgments are *nothing but* expressions of preference, expressions of attitude or feeling, insofar as they are moral or evaluative in character."[38] MacIntyre's critique of modern political society is that it has produced disassociated individuals, who no longer have communities which value the good and moral, nor even have the language with which to construe goodness. MacIntyre, similar to Leo Strauss, sees the solution as a return to the classical formulation. As a Thomistic-Aristotelian, MacIntyre sees the virtuous community as a necessity for the inculcation of morality in society.[39]

Following MacIntyre's critique of modernity, Charles Taylor begins his *A Secular Age* by asking the question: "why was it virtually impossible not to believe in God in, say, 1500 in our Western society, while in 2000 many of us find this not only easy, but even inescapable?"[40] In Taylor's work he outlines two opposing ideologies: one, the Christian theistic belief which finds its fulfillment in God, and the other, which finds its ultimate value in human reason. In this work Taylor offers a critique of the "Enlightenment narrative" of secularism.[41] One of Taylor's many

---

36. Alasdair MacIntyre, *After Virtue* (Notre Dame: University of Notre Dame Press, 2007), 263.

37. Ibid., 11.

38. Ibid., 11–12.

39. Ibid., 155.

40. Charles Taylor, *A Secular Age* (Cambridge, MA: The Belknap Press: An Imprint of Harvard University Press 2007), 25.

41. Ibid., 273.

critiques of the "modern moral order" is its inability to answer, and its subsequent dismissal of, the question of transcendence.

In a similar manner to both MacIntyre and Taylor, adherents of Radical Orthodoxy also reject the secular order and its foundation on the social sciences. In his work *Theology and Social Theory*, John Milbank points to the "Machiavellian Moment" as the recovery of pagan politics and philosophy. As such, Machiavellian politics stand as a secular program, in no way neutral to Christianity, but rather opposed to it.[42] For Milbank, it is in Machiavelli and Hobbes that we find the launch of the secular project, and the positivistic structures modernity is built upon.

What links the post-Secularists are their critiques of modernity's reliance upon the Enlightenment. These scholars have all questioned the value-free empiricism that is central to secular modernity. This criticism is particularly relevant in the present discussion of the Cambridge School and the history of religion. What MacIntyre, Taylor, and Milbank have done is to give an alternative history of the modern world, one not premised on post-Enlightenment assumptions. This also raises significant issues for the approach to history of political thought. For one, it argues that the historian cannot simply stand outside his subject and "bracket" off "the issue of truth."[43] Second, the post-secularists call into question the rationale of the entire history of political thought project. In using post-Enlightenment, empirical, social-scientific assumptions in an attempt to establish a secular state, the historian of political thought is not standing out of his own context at all. Rather, by seeking to find the history of the rise of the modern nation-state, the history of political thought has succumbed to a post-Enlightenment premise.[44] Its purpose therefore is little more than to perpetuate its own mythology.

---

42. John Milbank, *Theology and Social Theory: Beyond Secular Reason* (Oxford: Wiley-Blackwell, 2006), 23ff.

43. Charles Taylor, "The Hermeneutics of Conflict," in *Meaning and Context: Quentin Skinner and His Critics*, James Tully, ed. (Princeton: Princeton University Press, 1989), 218–228, 220.

44. For William T. Cavanaugh, "The City: Beyond Secular Parodies" in *Radical*

In contrast to the philosophical approach of post-secularists, a group of religious historians have argued that there is, and should be, room for a union of the history of religion and the history of political thought. In *Seeing Things Their Way: Intellectual History and the Return of Religion* (2009), a number of historians currently engaged in the history of religion have suggested a path to more interaction with the historians of political thought. In selecting their title, the editors of this work have conscientiously sought to engage the work of Quentin Skinner.

In a particularly relevant chapter, John Coffey, himself a product of Cambridge, challenges Skinner's "resolutely secular orientation," noting occasions in which it becomes a "liability" to his historical analysis.[45] Coffey's chapter is not simply a criticism, however, but a proposal for reconciliation. Coffey suggests that both historical schools can benefit from one another, and he proposes a way forward for both camps. He suggests that, for one, it is incumbent upon historians of theology to pay "more attention to the impact of political context and political ideology on the theologians."[46] Conversely, he suggests that if Cambridge School historians wish to remain true to their own methodology, they will have to begin taking religion and religious contexts seriously. In making his case, Coffey demonstrates the "inadequacy of a secularized reading of early modern political texts and the importance of the religious dimension of early modern political thought."[47]

Conclusion

As one member of the Cambridge School, John Robertson, has noted, the history of political thought now faces a "fork in the road."[48] The field has become so influential it is rapidly attracting

---

Orthodoxy: A New Theology, John Milbank, Catherine Pickstock and Graham Ward, eds. (London: Routledge, 1999) 182–200, 191.

45. Coffey, "Skinner," 53.

46. Ibid., 68.

47. Ibid., 68.

48. John Robertson, "Sacred History and Political Thought: Neapolitan Responses to the Problem of Sociability after Hobbes," *The Historical Journal*, 56 (2013): 1–29, 28.

new scholars, which shall push the field of political thought into new arenas and broaden the application of the Cambridge School's methodology. However, "the conviction often associated with the Cambridge School that the history of political thought should inform the study of problems in modern politics may now be encountering more resistance than before from the political theorists."[49] Despite this fact, Robertson posits that it is of vital importance for the connection between historians of political thought and philosophers to be preserved.

Dialogue between theologians and religious historians is, therefore, of paramount importance for those who wish to practice history along the lines of the Cambridge School, provided they wish to be consistent in their methodology. Historians of political thought must appreciate not only the political and linguistic context of a speaker, but the speaker's religious context as well. Likewise, it is of vital importance for historians of political thought to engage with the post-Secularists. Whether or not the post-secularist argument is ultimately correct, in that all of modernity is constructed on and around the false premise of Enlightenment rationality, their critiques are useful for the historian of political thought. The history of political thought, particularly that of the Cambridge School, is susceptible to the charges of contextualism and historicism, therefore remembering that the "doing" of history is not a purely positivistic, value-free endeavor is essential.

If the study of Reformation political theology is to surmount its Theo-Political problem and escape the ghettoization that has occurred as a result of the bifurcation of these disciplines, theologians must begin to employ the methodologies of the academic historians, and historians must begin to take into account the theological and religious contexts and convictions of their subjects. Given the convictions and presuppositions of both fields, however, this may prove unlikely. The only solution may instead lie in the creation of a distinct field of study, the

---

49. Ibid., 28.

history of Christian political thought, which will hold to the academic integrity and rigor of historical methodology while also preserving the theological and ecclesiastical convictions of its subject matter.

It is to this genre that Douglas F. Kelly's *The Emergence of Liberty* properly belongs. In this work Kelly traced the genealogy of liberalism through Reformed political thought, but with a robust understanding of the religious and theological issues involved, all while remaining sensitive to the larger historical context of the early modern period. Accordingly, Kelly's work demonstrates the innovative aspects of Calvin's political thought while resisting the impulse to present his subject as a radical outlier. By positioning Calvin as both "backward-looking" and "forward-looking", Kelly demonstrated the uniqueness of Calvin's thought without divorcing Calvin from his theological and cultural contexts.[50] The Calvin presented by Kelly can therefore be viewed as both one of the founders of modern political thought, and as a man who is also a product of his historical context. *The Emergence of Liberty* demonstrates that developing a history of Christian political thought is not only possible, but also may ultimately prove the discipline's only hope of surmounting its Theo-Political problem.

---

50. Kelly, *The Emergence of Liberty in the Modern World*, 31–32.

Part 4:

Doctrine through the Generations

11

John Calvin's Christology and a Politics of Virtue[1]

Mark Ian McDowell

Introduction

THE question of theology's relation to politics is not a new one but has been part of Christian reflection on Scripture from the start. Modern attempts to ignore the political implications of the gospel end up overlooking its true character. As Oliver O'Donovan has said, "Theology must be political if it is to be evangelical. Rule out the political questions and you cut short the proclamation of God's saving power; you leave people enslaved where they ought to be set free from sin – their own and others."[2] What follows is an attempt to explore the relationship between Christology and politics in the work of John Calvin to shed some light on how

---

1. The theology of Douglas F. Kelly is heard through a variety of chords. It was my privilege, as a student between 2001–2005, to learn the richness of Christology, the life and ministry of John Calvin, and the importance that our theological beliefs connect deeply with our behaviour. This chapter is an attempt to honour the teaching of Dr. Kelly who displays a profound love for Christ, a humble inhabiting of the Christian tradition, and a wise model of public engagement.

2. Oliver O'Donovan, *The Desire of the Nations: Rediscovering the Roots of Political Theology* (Cambridge: Cambridge University Press, 2003), 3.

Christians might live as disciples in society. We begin by looking at the theological resources promised in a classically-inflected Christology and how this might illumine God's relation to the world. From here, we will look at Calvin's Christology as a means for understanding God's kingly rule in the civil sphere. While Calvin does not draw explicit connections from his Christology directly to what he has to say of the civil magistrate, my aim is to map out a political corollary from Calvin's Christology.

A Christological Basis

A properly ordered systematic theology, we are told, has a double theme: "God and all things relative to God."[3] Christology fits into the overall theological framework of systematic theology by seeking to explicate the Johannine teaching that "the Word was with God and the Word was God" (John 1:2), and then tracing how the eternal Word "became flesh" (John 1:14). By keeping together these inseparable truths, the task of Christology is to explain how, without ceasing to be eternal, the Word of God has taken historical and temporal form and entered into our creaturely existence to be the "one mediator between God and man" (1 Tim. 2:5). Couched in more doctrinal terminology, Christology attempts to give a conceptual explanation of the biblical teaching of God's relation to creatures, that the second person of the triune Godhead truly enters time and space to be God with us. The task of delineating this teaching has been undertaken through the distinct themes of Christ's person and work. A well-ordered Christology, therefore, deals with the second member of the Trinity and how he turns to creation to relate to us as creatures.

By keeping accounts of Christ's being and Christ's activity in close theological proximity we are in a more confident position to make clear that the life, ministry, and earthly mission of Jesus of Nazareth is the self-same life and activity of the eternal Son who has assumed a human nature. To spell out the relation between

---

3. John Webster, *God Without Measure I: Working Papers In Christian Theology, vol.1 God and the Works of God* (London: Bloomsbury, 2016), 45.

these topics this way serves several purposes: first, it specifies the agency of the one who redeems so that any consideration of Jesus' earthly history as it is recorded in Scripture is not fully comprehended without reference to the anterior life of the Word. Here, as with recent Protestant assessments of the relation between the eternal processions and economic missions, the emphasis rests on how God's eternally perfect life turns to relate to that which is not God; so too with the doctrine of Christ's person and work. Just as an inseparable yet ordered relation between God's being and God's doing is highlighted in a treatment of processions and missions, so there exists an inseparable yet ordered relation between Christ's person and work.

A second purpose of ordering the doctrine this way is not only to ensure the identity of the Redeemer is made clear, but this doctrinal arrangement prioritizes an understanding of Christ in his eternal relations with the Father and the Spirit which helps provide a firmer explanation of the Word's saving and ruling activity. In talking of the eternal life of the Word prior to the temporal history enacted by the Word, the doctrine of Christ seeks to avoid possible misunderstandings about the subject of the one who takes on flesh and redeems fallen humanity.

Structuring the doctrine of Christ in a way that attempts to integrate both themes directs our attention to the importance of theological metaphysics and ontological categories in assisting our reading of the Gospels. An upshot of taking this approach is that it fixes our understanding on Christ's work as an extension of, and inseparably tethered to, the perfection of Christ's person. And because Christ shares the unique divine essence with the Father and the Spirit, the work that Christ undertakes in time is not his work alone but involves the agency of the entire Trinity. In other words, this move bridges theology proper and economy. So conceived, discussion about Christ's person is situated in teaching about the Trinity, and discussion about Christ's work in creation is only made intelligible in a Trinitarian setting.

From this commitment that emphasizes Christ's eternal divinity alongside that of the Father and the Spirit, a further commitment follows, which proposes that because God is one in nature, the works God performs externally reflect God's unity internally, or stated more formally, the *opera Dei essentialia* are the *opera ad extra*. This is not to overlook the manner of working or *modus agendi* that relates to each member of the Godhead, but it is to point out the commonality of God's work in creation and redemption that is linked to, and derives from, God's unity. What this means in terms of Christology is that Christ's agency spans both the work of God *ad extra* in the realm of nature (*opus naturae* or *opus creationis*) as well as the realm of grace (*opus gratiae* or *opus redemptionis*).

For our purposes, it is important to note how Christ's work consists in his redemptive mission, but not to the neglect of his providential ruling in creation. The biblical warrant for assessing God's redeeming work in Christ is rich and prevalent, but if theological consideration overlooks Christ's work of providential rule it invites the possibility of bifurcating Christ's work in the realms of nature and grace, which leads to the twin problems of secularizing the sphere of creation and minimizing an appreciation of Christ's role in the realm of nature. One way to avoid this dilemma is to offer a lens through which Christ's royal rule is seen to extend to the realm of nature and to explore the Son's continued lordly care of all people as it is mediated in the sphere of the civil arena.

To set off on the right course of approach will require an account of the continuing incarnate life of Christ in his heavenly session, through which the enthroned Son both intercedes for the redeemed while also enacting his government over all creatures in the power and presence of the Holy Spirit. Attention to Christ's ascended rule and reign holds together the reality that Christ is Lord and that Christ is present. This combination has the important role of moulding the shape of a portrayal of the continuing *opus Christi* in the spheres of redemption and creation. As the ascended and sovereign Lord, the Son is present in the midst of the fellowship of the redeemed who receive from him all the benefits of his conquering rule. Furthermore, the ascended Son exercises his kingly rule in the broad sphere of creation, to believer and unbeliever alike, though in significantly different ways.

While the doctrine of Christ's ascension has not received the kind of attention it deserves, its application in upholding and preserving the common good of humanity through the civil authorities receives even less consideration. Within the theme of Christ's kingly rule at the right hand of the Father, the exalted Christ governs his created order and mediates his rule through earthly institutions and offices. This underreported theme in Christological discussion has some profound outcomes for the importance of a Christian conception of the political order and service of believers within that order. To affirm the lordship of Christ is to affirm a vision of society as a collective within which believer and unbeliever are related to Christ in a differentiated manner and, while one is moved towards an end in Christ, both are moved together towards a temporal common good. In addition, to examine this theme is to attend to the ways Christ's mediating rule cultivates ecclesial virtues and civic virtues.

To illustrate a position that commends a more fruitful depiction of Christology as it bears on matters pertaining to the civil magistrate, we will focus on the distinctive contours of the Christology of John Calvin and explore the ways they inform his teaching on the civil magistrate. From here, I proceed by looking at some of the key features of Calvin's Christology and then turn to examine the distinctive character of Calvin's teaching on the civil magistrate.

The Christology of John Calvin

If the foregoing sketch gives us a sense of those key elements that hone a more consistent and integrated Christology, then it will be important to assess whether Calvin's Christology includes those elements, and if it does, then it will be important to see how his teaching on the person and work of Christ gives shape to his thinking of God's care in Christ through the civil magistrate.

At the heart of Calvin's Christology is his distinctive use of the threefold characterization of Christ as Prophet, Priest, and King. While Calvin does not invent the doctrine, Richard Muller emphasizes that the centrality of this doctrine in Calvin's thought "becomes for the first time in the history of dogma a strict doctrinal category and a formula determinative of the shape of Christology."[4] The technical term for this teaching is the *munus triplex*, and its content seeks to elaborate Christ's work to redeem sinners in the offices of prophet, priest, and king. By arranging the biblical material under three headings, the doctrine explores how these offices point back to the life of Old Testament Israel and find their ultimate fulfilment in Christ's unique reconciling activity in prophetic, priestly, and kingly dimensions.[5]

In the hands of Calvin, the threefold office of Christ retains its biblical texture but now finds its doctrinal grounding in the Triune God's eternal resolve to redeem estranged humanity. The implications of this move are far-reaching indeed. It means that the redeeming activity carried out by Christ must be regarded as the work of the eternal Son who is commissioned in eternity to fulfill this task in redemptive history. Calvin thus presents an account of Christ's work that relies upon the prior reality of Christ's divine identity.

Calvin's use of the tripartite division of prophet, priest, and king serves as a framework to help explain how Christ occupies the role of the threefold office and fulfils their Old Testament types. Calvin's application of the *munus* is set alongside other

---

4. Richard A. Muller, *Christ and the Decree: Christology and Predestination in Reformed Theology from Calvin to Perkins* (Grand Rapids: Baker Academic, 2008), 31. Calvin enunciates his teaching on the threefold schema in his 1559 edition of the *Institutes* as follows: "Therefore, in order that faith may find a firm basis for salvation in Christ, and thus rest in him, this principle must be laid down: the office enjoined upon Christ by the Father consists of three parts. For he was given to be prophet, king and priest" (*Inst.* II.xv.1, 494).

5. Richard Belcher's important work notes that the presence of these offices predates the establishment of Israel and are even found in the work given to Adam and Eve in the garden. See *Prophet, Priest, and King: The Roles of Christ in the Bible and Our Roles Today* (Phillipsburg: Presbyterian & Reformed, 2016), 2–16.

Christological commitments so that the threefold office of Christ is coordinated with the Mediator of this office. Taken together, they call attention back to God's dealings with Israel in the Old Testament, when the effects of the fall were everywhere evident, and foreshadows of hope were visible only to the eyes of faith. But its function extends beyond the anticipation and accomplishment of redemption in time and exerts influence in explaining Christ's present heavenly session on behalf of the church and the world. For Calvin, then, the threefold office serves the important purpose of tying together the history of Israel to the temporal career of Christ as well as underscoring the unity of Christ's person in the enactment of his singular work. Without over-schematizing the *munus*, Calvin's approach is more constrained by the biblical text, which prompts him to begin with humanity's postlapsarian condition, from which he turns to consider the necessity of the one who would save us.[6] As it relates to this study, it will be important to keep an eye on how the kingly function of Christ's work is indexed to Christ's person.

To redeem humanity from its plight, Calvin points to the unique identity of the Redeemer by echoing the Chalcedonian formula: "Now it was of the greatest importance for us that he who was to be our Mediator be both true God and true man."[7] Why? The work of the Mediator "was no uncommon thing" and none other than "the self-same Son of God become man" could accomplish the task of taking "what was ours as to impart

---

6. Calvin reasons that "it is too presumptuous to imagine another reason or another end" for the incarnation of the Word other than our redemption (*Inst.* II.xii.4, 467). Speaking against Andreas Osiander's account of supralapsarian Christology, that the Word would have taken on flesh without the fall into sin, Calvin argues that the Old Testament provides ample indications through sacrifices, the priesthood, and the shedding of blood that the Mediator was never "promised without blood" (*Inst.* II.xii.4, 467), thereby tying the incarnation to the atonement. A hallmark of Calvin's theology is that his exegetical practice of staying close to Scripture chastens his doctrinal commitments. This is seen with especial clarity in his treatment of this topic: "In short, the only reason given in Scripture that the Son of God willed to take our flesh, and accepted this commandment from the Father, is that he would be a sacrifice to appease the Father on our behalf" (*Inst.* II.xii.4, 467).

7. ibid., II.xii.1, 464.

[what] was his to us, and to make what was his by nature ours by grace."[8] Invoking elements of Anselm's satisfaction theory of the atonement, Calvin reasons that there was a desperate need for one from the side of humanity to render a righteous sacrifice to God, and yet only someone from God's side had the power to do so. Calvin writes,

> Accordingly, our Lord came forth as true man and took the person and the name of Adam in order to take Adam's place in obeying the Father, to present our flesh as the price of satisfaction to God's righteous judgement, and, in the same flesh, to pay the penalty that we deserved. In short, since neither as God alone could he feel death, nor as man alone could he overcome it, he coupled human nature with divine that to atone for sin he might submit the weakness of the one to death; and that, wrestling with death by the power of the other nature, he might win victory for us.[9]

Up to this point, then, we can say that the outline of Calvin's Christology begins with Adam's fall into sin, moves to address the need for a Mediator who is both human and divine, and then gives a description of how the two natures relate in the person of the Mediator. The logic of Calvin's argument is anchored firmly in Scripture and yields important dogmatic fruits as it pertains to reflection on the Incarnation. As such, Calvin signposts the direction his treatment of the relation of Christ's natures takes by drawing reader's minds to John 1:14, "The Word was made flesh." He insists that the Word's "becoming" should not be understood "in the sense that the Word was turned into flesh or confusedly mingled with flesh ... not by confusion of substance, but by unity of person."[10] By intonating one of Chalcedon's alpha privatives, which can only be understood with its pair, namely, *atreptos kai asynchytos* (without change and without confusion), Calvin affirms the integrity of both natures in the unity of the Person. Calvin notes how each nature "retains its distinctive nature unimpaired, and yet these two natures constitute one Christ."[11]

---

8. ibid., II.xii.2, 465.
9. ibid., II.xii.2, 466.
10. ibid., II.xii.2, 482.
11. ibid., II.xii.2, 482.

And yet, a distinctively Reformed accent on the person of the Incarnation is not far from view as is evident in his immediate appeal to John 8:58, "Before Abraham was, I am."[12] Alongside a set of other passages, Calvin's reflections point to the antecedent deity of Christ. In his commentary on John, Calvin comments, "this saying of Christ contains a remarkable statement of His divine essence."[13] In the same work, Calvin ties this thought to the union, noting:

> For it does not make sense that He who is now man should be other than He who was always very God, since it is God who is said to have become man ... it follows that when He became man Christ did not cease to be what He was before and that nothing was changed in that eternal essence of God which assumed flesh. In short, the Son of God began to be man in such a way that He is still that eternal Word who had no temporal beginning.[14]

This is an important move because Calvin wants to keep the focus on the eternal subject who assumes flesh. Calvin prioritizes the Word as the divine agent in the incarnation, which allows him to put forward an account of the natures that are asymmetrically related to each other. This stress on the Word in the incarnation is not intended to diminish the integrity of the human nature that the Word assumes but it is to underscore the primacy of the infinite in relation to the finite. For Calvin, there can be no change to the Word in the incarnation because the Word is God and God is immutable. This theological commitment is strengthened by Calvin's deployment of what would become a recognized element of his Christology, namely, the *extra calvinisticum*, to which we turn briefly.[15]

While Calvin is credited with this teaching, its initial use was as a form of critique on the part of his Lutheran opponents over his

---

12. ibid., II.xii.2, 483–4.

13. *The Gospel According to St. John 1–10*, trans. T.H.L. Parker, eds., David W. Torrance and Thomas F. Torrance (Grand Rapids: Eerdmans, 1995), 235.

14. Calvin, *The Gospel According to St. John 1–10*, 20–1.

15. For influences on Calvin's account from antecedent reformers, see K.J. Drake, *The Flesh of the Word: The Extra Calvinisticum From Zwingli to Early Orthodoxy*. Oxford Studies in Historical Theology (New York: Oxford University Press, 2021).

understanding of Christ's presence in the Lord's Supper. However, accusations that Calvin somehow introduces a theological novelty are encouraged to see the historical pedigree of the theology of which his position speaks, and perhaps refer to it instead as either the *"extra Catholicum"*, *"extra Patristicum"*[16] or even the *"extra Christianum."*[17] Calvin enunciates his teaching on the *extra* in the *Institutes* as follows: "Here is something marvelous: the Son of God descended from heaven in such a way that, without leaving heaven, he willed to be borne in the virgin's womb, to go about the earth, and to hang upon the cross; yet he continuously filled the world even as he had done from the beginning!"[18] What Calvin achieves with the *extra* is the claim that even in the incarnation, the Word remains omnipresent. Calvin is clear that the second person of the Triune Godhead does not relinquish his divine attributes in the incarnation but retains them fully.[19] Significantly, for Calvin, the antecedent life of the Word is unaltered in the hypostatic union.

The implications of Calvin's teaching on the *extra calvinisticum* bear down directly on how he conceives the relation of the two natures in the hypostatic union. By extending his emphasis on the ontological status of Christ's eternal person in the direction of the relation of Christ's natures—understood as the communication of attributes (*communicatio idiomatum*)—Calvin is able to maintain that because the Son is fully and perfectly God,

---

16. David E. Willis, *Calvin's Catholic Christology: The Function of the So-Called Extra Calvinisticum in Calvin's Theology* (Leiden: Brill, 1966), 60.

17. Heiko A. Oberman, *The Dawn of the Reformation: Essays in Late Medieval and Early Reformation Thought* (Grand Rapids: Eerdmans, 1986), 252.

18. Calvin, *Inst.* II.xiii.4, 481.

19. Karl Barth puts the matter beautifully when he writes, "God is always God even in his humiliation. The divine being does not suffer any change, any diminution, any transformation into something else, any admixture with something else, let alone any cessation. The deity of Christ is the one unaltered because [it is the] unalterable deity of God. Any subtraction or weakening of it would at once throw doubt upon the atonement made in Him. He humbled Himself, but He did not do it by ceasing to be who He is. He went into a strange land, but even there, and especially there, He never became a stranger to Himself." See *Church Dogmatics*, IV.1 eds., G.W. Bromiley and T.F. Torrance, trans, G.W. Bromiley (Edinburgh: T&T Clark, 1956), 179–80.

there can be no transference or communication of the human attributes or properties to the divine nature, just as there can be no communication of divine attributes or properties to the human nature.

Calvin's distinctive teaching about Christ's person steers reflection on Christ's salvific work in a particular direction. For Calvin, the Word remains unchanged in the union with flesh, and this claim upholds the Word's complete and perfect status. As Rowan Williams assesses Calvin's teaching on the *extra* he teases out an implication of the Reformer's thought. Williams points out that Calvin's emphasis on the Word's retention of divine perfection in the union means that "there is no sense in which the embodied humanity can exhaust the single divine agency of the Word."[20] What Williams means by this is that while the work of redemption necessarily depends upon the incarnate Mediator, the full scope of the Word's agency is not enclosed within the humanity of the Mediator. There remains a dimension of the Mediator's work *extra carnem*—outside the flesh.

This feature of Calvin's Christology casts a very different complexion when set alongside that of his Lutheran counterparts in that it does not rest on a direct communication of properties between the natures. The Lutheran construal of the Eucharist depends upon the communication of ubiquity to the human nature to render the Lord's Supper efficacious. Accordingly, the humanity of Christ is essential to Christ being present, whereas the Calvinist objection is that Christ's person does not need the communication of divine properties to the flesh to guarantee the presence of the Word. The humanity of Christ does not occupy such a determinative role in the Reformed position. In other words, the presence of the Word and the efficacy of the Word are not restricted to the humanity. Along these lines, Williams argues that we would be mistaken if we thought that "the action of the Word cannot be real without the local and material presence of

---

20. Rowan Williams, *Christ: The Heart of Creation* (London: Bloomsbury, 2018), 152.

his humanity…"[21] If we press the logic of the Lutheran position further we note how it leads to the following conclusion: that "the divine action depend[s] upon the presence of humanity."[22] Contrary to this, while Calvin understands the relation between Christ's person and work to be one in which salvation is definitively accomplished in and through the Word's assumption of his human nature—and in his human nature he experiences the ambit of creaturely existence, except sin (Heb. 4:15)— he nevertheless asserts that Christ's activity beyond the scope of redemption is not demarcated by the flesh.

We extend our argument by looking at how this point is borne out by what Calvin has to say about Christ's ascension, which he describes as "one of the chief articles of our faith."[23] One aspect of its doctrinal utility for Calvin is seen in how it frames the divine movement of the risen Mediator not as a new era in the life of the Word but a demonstration of the Word's antecedent eternal identity. While Calvin's teaching on the *extra* tells us that the eternal Son never left the right hand of the Father, the ascension instructs us that the Mediator is now exalted and enthroned as the incarnate Lord. In the ascension, Christ did not dispense with his human nature, but "withdrew his bodily presence from our sight [Acts. 1:9], not to cease to be present with believers still on their earthly pilgrimage…"[24] As the Word does not surrender his deity in the incarnation, so the Word does not surrender his humanity in the ascension. Christ's incarnate existence continues in the heavenly session, but now exalted, Christ's lordship remains what it had been in his earthly life and ministry, one in which he governed the heavens and the earth. Calvin notes, "I confess, indeed, that we may not conceive of the Son of God in any other way than as clothed with flesh. But this did not prevent him, while filling heaven and earth with his divine essence, from wearing his

---

21. Williams, *Christ The Heart of Creation*, 152.

22. ibid., 152–3.

23. Calvin, *The Acts of the Apostles* vol. 1, trans W.J.G. McDonald, eds., David W. Torrance and Thomas F. Torrance (Grand Rapids: Eerdmans, 1982), 33.

24. Calvin, *Inst.*, II. xvi. 14, 523.

flesh in the womb of his mother, on the cross, in the sepulcher."[25] Calvin's Christology holds together the eternal Son's rule in such a way that even in the incarnation he governs supremely and universally. What occurs with the ascension to the right hand of the Father is not the inauguration of an office that Christ did not previously occupy but the continued exercise of this office "with a more immediate power."[26]

The thrust of Calvin's thought concerns upholding the aseity of the Son, but this truth does not overshadow his belief that the risen and ascended Lord possesses a human body local to the right hand of the Father. Both ideas help him achieve an important theological point: Instead of relying on the flesh of the risen Christ to mediate his royal rule, Calvin appeals to the operation of the Holy Spirit to mediate this heavenly governance and to provide for his subjects the "more immediate power" that comes from his ascended kingship by virtue of the work of the Spirit.[27] Out of Christ's kingly office, then, the Holy Spirit is charged to abundantly dispense "the heavenly riches of which we are in such need…" and "believers stand unconquered through the strength of their king, and his spiritual riches abound in them."[28] Christ's universal reign is not inhibited by his human nature but is exercised in and through the Holy Spirit.

From this vantage point we turn our attention to see the theological impact this Christological teaching makes on Calvin's understanding of Christ's rule in the civil realm. Before exploring this theme, we summarize the ground already covered: Calvin holds fast to an Anselmian Soteriology in his insistence on the necessity that the Mediator be from our side to procure our redemption. Alongside this is a Chalcedonian Christology

---

25. Calvin, "Last Admonition of John Calvin to Joachim Westphal," in *John Calvin's Tracts and Treatises*, vol 2, trans. Henry Beveridge (Grand Rapids: Eerdmans, 1958), 385.

26. Calvin, *Inst.*, II. xvi. 14, 523.

27. The obvious parallel here in Calvin's thought is his position on the Lord's Supper according to which the Holy Spirit conveys the benefits of the risen Christ to the faithful at the table. See Calvin, *Inst.* IV.17.

28. ibid., II. xv. 5, 500.

that strongly accents the Word's unchangeable character which serves to uphold the Word's transcendence, which, when further explicated along with the *extra calvinisticum*, generates the attending claim that the Word's agency is also beyond the flesh. We can now pose the question: how does Calvin's Christology shape his teaching on politics?

The Christological Shape of Calvin's Politics

The first way it shapes his view on politics derives from the theme of Christ's kingship, which, we recall for Calvin, spans both the Church and the entire universe. Reflecting on Eph. 1:20, and how the Father "raised [Christ] from the dead and seated him at his right hand in the heavenly places," Calvin notes that Christ shares the Father's governing power over all things,[29] and opposes any notion that Christ's heavenly rule is "confined to heaven" because his humanity is located in heaven.[30] Christ's heavenly kingship is one that concerns "the entire command and government of the universe."[31] Christ's lordship is not restricted to the soteriological and the ecclesial, but also encompasses the social and political. Politics for Calvin falls under the Lordship of Christ and exists for the good of all people, even though believer and unbeliever experience this Lordship in differing ways. Calvin articulates his account in dialogue with the two kingdoms or governments model and affirms their distinctness,[32] but whereas Martin Luther's arrangement is too pessimistic for Calvin—in fact, it trades on a starting point that regards politics as a postlapsarian phenomenon—the Genevan Reformer, like Thomas Aquinas, views politics as a good of creation and something that can

---

29. "Since the right hand of God fills heaven and earth, it follows that the kingdom and power of Christ are everywhere diffused." See Calvin, *Galatians, Ephesians, Philippians & Colossians*. Calvin's New Testament Commentaries, eds., David W. Torrance and T.F. Torrance, trans., T.H.L. Parker (Grand Rapids: Eerdmans, 1996), Ephesians, 137.

30. Calvin, *Ephesians*, 137.

31. ibid., 138.

32. Cf. Calvin, *Inst.* III.xix.15 and IV.xx.1–2 for Calvin's direct teachings on the two governments.

contribute to human flourishing. This sentiment is expressed in a key passage:

> [C]ivil government has as its appointed end, so long as we live among men, to cherish and protect the outward worship of God, to defend sound doctrine of piety and the position in the church, to adjust our life to the society of men, to form our social behaviour to civil righteousness, to reconcile us with one another, and to promote general peace and tranquility. All of this I admit to be superfluous, if God's Kingdom, such as it is now among us, wipes out the present life. But if it is God's will that we go as pilgrims upon the earth while we aspire to the true fatherland, and if the pilgrimage requires such helps, those who take these from man deprive him of his very humanity.[33]

Important to note from this quote is Calvin's contention that Christ's lordship involves the obedience of the believer to Christ both within the church and the civil sphere. Calvin provides an example of political engagement that sees participation in the civil sphere as shaping social behaviour, as cultivating "civil righteousness" on the part of believers which in turn has the effect of serving the good of our fellow citizens.[34]

Calvin's contribution to political engagement rests on a far more positive appraisal of institutions than one finds in Luther. While Luther views civil authorities as necessary for the restraint of sin and vice, they do not have the capacity, even in a limited fashion, to inculcate civic virtue, nor can they help to form Christians as faithful citizens in common life together with their neighbours. Calvin's position derives from his belief that the rule of Christ is exerted in both the civil and the ecclesial realms, which prompts a view of the civil governing structures as mechanisms through which Christ rules his people not only to a salvific end but one that supplies an external yet provisional and proximate social well-being for all people. The church is decidedly

---

33. Calvin, *Inst.* IV.xx.2, 1487.

34. In this respect, Calvin expresses something akin to an Augustinian vision of the political community that shares things in common for a limited good for all. See Augustine, *City of God Against the Pagans*, ed., R.W. Dyson (New York: Cambridge University Press, 1998), 19, 26.

the central site of Christ's mediation where Christ's people are fed by the Word and Spirit and formed into disciples, but the church is not the only site where Christ forms his people.

Alongside the church, Calvin understands the civil sphere as a locus of Christ's mediated rule that is exercised through institutions. Before he moves to define this arrangement, Calvin opposes two wrong-headed ideas related to authority. The first concerns the belief that freedom under Christ's reign equates to freedom from all other authorities. He argues, "For certain men, when they hear that the gospel promises a freedom that acknowledges no king and no magistrate among men, but looks to Christ alone, think they cannot benefit by their freedom so long as they see any power set up over them."[35] The second mistaken belief that Calvin addresses is seen in his refusal to consider a secular vision of the political community. He says,

> it has not come about that the authority over all things on earth is in the hands of kings and other rulers, but by divine providence and holy ordinance. For God was pleased so to rule the affairs of men, inasmuch as he is present with them and also presides over the making of laws and the exercising of equity in courts of justice.[36]

To the first failure, Calvin seeks to close off the possibility that Christ's reign can be reduced to the spiritual plane and treated as though Christ's kingdom in the natural realm did not exist. To the second, Calvin promotes the political order as a dignified space with political purpose because God is "present with" those in authority and because God "presides" over those in authority.

The preceding suggests a recognition on Calvin's part that Christ's rule operates on two horizons—the ecclesial and civil—and this results in a meaningful application for Christian discipleship. By relativizing political authority, Calvin is able to uphold its necessity on the basis that it is attuned to the rule of Christ. In doing so, the political community is given integrity because it exists in a rightly ordered role to Christ's overarching

---

35. Calvin, *Inst.* IV.xx.1, 1486.
36. ibid., IV.xx.4, 1489.

reign and becomes a domain in which the believer can endeavour to glorify God and to be formed as part of a politically virtuous people for discipleship in public life. Within Christ's governing work in the political sphere, the civil magistrate serves to ensure that "men breathe, eat, drink, and are kept warm," but it does more than this, providing "that each man may keep his property safe and sound; that men may carry on blameless intercourse among themselves; that honesty and modesty may be preserved among men. In short, it provides that a public manifestation of religion may exist among Christians, and that humanity may be maintained among men."[37] In fact, the civil sphere provides the social conditions for the ecclesial sphere to flourish: "it prevents idolatry, sacrilege against God's name, blasphemies against his truth, and other public offenses against religion from arising and spreading from people; it prevents the public peace from being disturbed."[38] In this way, the civil magistrate offers three immediate purposes: first, it safeguards the social peace and cohesion of a political community, that is, it is "for the public good";[39] second, it provides the ability and opportunity for the Church to worship God rightly; and third, it maps out a social context in which Christian discipleship is fostered through participation in politics.

Calvin's teaching on the civil magistrate and civil authority is informed by his classically oriented Christology, at the heart of which sits the insight that Christ's person and work are integrated. From this vantage point, the work of Christ has its power and efficacy on the basis that it is the work of the eternal Son of God.

---

37. ibid., IV.xx.3, 1488.

38. ibid., IV.xx.3, 1488.

39. In his commentary on Romans 13:1–2, Calvin says, that "it is the will of God to govern the world in this manner...." He also says, "[A]lthough dictatorships and unjust authorities are not ordained governments, yet the right of government is ordained for the well-being of mankind." And again on 13:3 he notes, "The usefulness of rulers is that the Lord has designed by this means to provide for the peace of the good, and to restrain the waywardness of the wicked" in Calvin, *Romans and Thessalonians*, trans. Ross Mackenzie and eds., David W. Torrance and Thomas. F. Torrance (Grand Rapids: Eerdmans, 1995), 281–82.

Calvin emphasizes Christ's person is consubstantial with the Father and recognizes that the threefold office filled by Christ is occupied by one who is fully and entirely God. Christ exercises his role as king as the second person of the Triune God. This rule is expressed as his loving and all-powerful governance of all things and took place during Christ's earthly life and ministry. The consequence of Christ's ascension to the right hand of the Father is an indication of Christ's continued kingly rule that is now mediated in the realms of creation and redemption. The assumption of the flesh does not constrain Christ's mediatorial rule because, as Calvin emphasizes according to the *extra calvinisticum*, the Word transcends his human nature. The upshot of this teaching is felt in relation to the political life. Just as the humanity of Christ does not require the communication of idioms from the Word to the human nature to secure the Word's agency in creation, so Christ's enthronement does not depend upon Christ's humanity to affect Christ's kingship in the political order. Christ mediates his rule through authorities for human flourishing. Calvin grasps that political institutions have their own sense of integrity and legitimacy as sites of God's ruling care of society within which the church experiences temporal peace.

With this set of Christological instincts, Calvin conceives the relation between the political and ecclesial less in terms of two discrete precincts and more in terms of a singular rule,[40] which has the effect of focusing attention "on the manner in which God governs the conduct of believers" in both the spiritual and political arenas.[41] Where Christ is King, Christ governs, and as Christ's kingship embraces both the church and the world, conceiving of reality as a shared space in which the ecclesial and political are compatible and not at odds, Christ governs both, one by the Spirit's work in the reading and preaching of the Word and

---

40. See this in Calvin, *Inst.* III.xix.15.

41. See Cornelis Venema, "The Restoration of All Things to Proper Order: An Assessment of the 'Two Kingdoms/Natural Law' Interpretation of Calvin's Public Theology" in *Kingdoms Apart: Engaging the Two Kingdoms Perspective*, ed. Ryan C. McIlhenny (Phillipsburg: Presbyterian & Reformed, 2012), 3–32.

in the political through the oversight of the civil magistrate. As the followers of Christ submit to his rule in both areas they are formed and discipled accordingly, the Spirit cultivating ecclesial virtues in one space that issues in the cultivation of civic virtues in the other. For God's glory and the neighbour's good.

Conclusion

Calvin's position on the civil authority boils down to his Christological commitments. I have argued that a Christology that accounts properly for the person of Christ helps to instruct our apprehension of the agency of Christ. Calvin's positive insight concerning political authority rests on the preceding claim that in Christ the finite is ordered to the infinite which is not contained by the finite. Rather than driving a wedge between God and humanity, this theological affirmation blesses humanity because God is above and beyond creation and able to be present and mediate his royal and loving rule in political entities. In the same way that Christ's mediation in the believing community does not require the communication of God's ubiquity to his human nature to supply presence, but rather depends on the Spirit's conveyance of Christ's benefits to us spiritually, so too, in a similar fashion, Christ rules in the political realm through magistrates and rulers who strive for our peace, protection, and flourishing. The integrity of the political space is not undermined or diminished and nor is its status sequestered from Christ's rule in the church. It is upheld and validated, and yet this is not an instance of political Nestorianism since we are reminded that Christ exercises his singular rule in both spheres, albeit in a differentiated way, forming his people in the primary site of the church and sending them forth into the world to herald the good news and participate in political service under Christ's rule for the good of the world.

12

The Doctrine of Adoption Revisited

Developments in an Underdeveloped Heritage

Mark Miller

DOUGLAS F. Kelly wrote an article entitled "Adoption: An Underdeveloped Heritage of the Westminster Standards" in the *Reformed Theological Review* in the Fall of 1993, pointing out that the Westminster Standards have received no small amount of criticism over what may be described generally as their "tone."[1] Kelly cites Philip Schaff's comparison of the Shorter Catechism to Luther's and the Heidelberg, where Schaff says the Shorter "far surpasses them in clearness and careful wording" but that it "lacks their genial warmth, freshness, and child-like simplicity."[2]

Westminster's defenders appeal to its unique inclusion of adoption to counter these criticisms. Joel Beeke observes, "How intriguing it is that the Westminster Divines, often accused of being too harsh and rigid in their theology, provided the

---

1. Douglas F. Kelly, "Adoption: An Underdeveloped Heritage of the Westminster Standards," *Reformed Theological Review* 52.3 (1993): 110.

2. *The Creeds of Christendom: with a History and Critical Notes*, ed. Philip Schaff (1931; repr. Grand Rapids: Baker, 1998), 1:787; in Kelly, "Adoption," 110. See also Horatius Bonar, *Catechisms of the Scottish Reformation* (1886), viii; in T. F. Torrance, *The School of Faith: The Catechisms of the Reformed Church* (1959; repr. Eugene: Wipf and Stock, 1996), xvii.

Christian church's first confessional chapter and formal articles on adoption—one of the most tender doctrines of the Christian faith!"[3]

Kelly argued similarly; however, he noted that adoption "has largely been neglected" by the heirs of the Westminster tradition, and that "[t]his neglect ... has tended to be detrimental to the teaching and pastoral balance of the entire tradition."[4] Kelly's thesis was that "... followers of the Westminster Tradition have unwittingly given grounds for other Christians to think that they have an insufficient confessional grasp of familial relational themes so central to Scripture because they have neglected to make use of and develop further what Westminster itself says about Adoption."[5]

This article will revisit Kelly's concerns, focusing first on the Westminster heritage of adoption; second, a strand of its development; and third, Kelly's own contributions.

A Goodly Heritage

David Garner says adoption "is arguably the most significant contribution of the Westminster Confession of Faith (WCF) to Reformed thinking."[6] A thoroughgoing survey of adoption in the works of the Westminster divines exceeds the parameters of this study; however, the atmosphere that gave rise to this contribution deserves attention. [7] We will begin by focusing on the work of one divine in particular, Stephen Marshall (1594–1655).

---

3. Joel R. Beeke, *Heirs with Christ: The Puritans on Adoption* (Grand Rapids: Reformation Heritage Books, 2008), 36. Similarly, Sinclair Ferguson observes "that a separate exposition of adoption ... is given a place in a major Christian confession for the first time in the history of the Church" in the Westminster Standards, and that "no doctrine is less scholastic in nature." Sinclair B. Ferguson, "Westminster Assembly and Documents" in *Dictionary of Scottish Church History and Theology*, ed. Nigel M. de S. Cameron (Edinburgh: T&T Clark, 1993), 865.

4. Kelly, "Adoption," 112.

5. Kelly, "Adoption," 111. See also David B. Garner, "Adoption in Christ," (Ph.D. diss., Westminster Theological Seminary, 2002), 7–8; and Ferguson, "Westminster Assembly," 865.

6. Garner, "Adoption in Christ," 7–8.

7. See Beeke, *Heirs with Christ*, 7–9.

Stephen Marshall

Stephen Marshall, "the favorite preacher of the Long Parliament,"[8] delivered a sermon in 1654 entitled, "The High Privilege of all True Believers to be the Sons of God", which was subsequently published as a small book.[9] Marshall asks why no other privileges of receiving Christ are mentioned in the text (John 1:12-13) other than being children of God. He answers:

> … though somtimes in the holy Scriptures our Sonship is but one of our Priviledges, yet very frequently in the Scripture all that Beleevers do obtain from Christ in this world and the world to come, here and to eternity, all is comprehended in this one, That they are made the Children of God … God comprehends all other priviledges in this one; that he that hath this one, he that is made the Son of God, he hath all other that can be imagined …[10]

For Marshall, adoption can be seen to embrace all the benefits of redemption: "Al the Graces & al the Good that we enjoy from Christ, you have it in this one Sentence, God predestinated us to the adoption of Children; he hath done all when he hath done that,"[11] and, "to be made a Son of God is to have the comprehension of all that is obtained by Jesus Christ."[12]

Marshall's sermon has three divisions: (1) What is adoption? (2) What is the work of adopting, or how is it done? (3) What are the benefits of adoption?

What is Adoption?

Drawing from Roman law, Marshall describes adoption as "A lawful act imitating nature, whereby a Person or Persons who have no natural right to an inheritance, are taken in, into a lawful right."[13] Marshall develops a theological definition:

---

8. William S. Barker, *Puritan Profiles: 54 Influential Puritans at the Time When the Westminster Confession of Faith Was Written* (Geanies House: Mentor, 1996), 120. See also the brief biographical sketch of Marshall on pp. 120–127.

9. Stephen Marshall, "The High Privilege of Beleevers: They Are the Sons of God" in *The Works of Mr. Stephen Marshall* (London: Peter and Edward Cole, 1661), 35.

10. Ibid., 37.

11. Ibid., 38.

12. Ibid., 39.

13. Ibid., 41.

"a gracious work of God, whereby he doth take poor sinners who beleeve in Christ, into that Glorious Condition of being his own Children."[14]

How is it Done?

Marshall unfolds adoption as a work of "the whole Trinity."[15] He explains the Father's work as twofold: (1) choosing a people to be his children, and (2) giving them to his Son to be his brethren.[16]

Marshall considers the Son's accomplishment of adoption in two sections corresponding to (1) his Work and (2) his Person. Of his Work, Marshall says, Christ

> was to purchase their Sonship for them; for though the Father would give it them freely, it should cost them nothing, yet Christ being made their Surety he must purchase it for them, so that the Lord although he was the Heir of all things, yet he condescends by his own Blood, by his own Sufferings, by himself being made a Curse, He condescends to purchase adoption for those that were given him to bring to life. This is plain in Gal. 4. where it is said, When the fulness of time was come, God sent his own Son born of a Woman, made under the Law, that we might receive the adoption of Sons, that our Adoption as it flows from Christ is the price of his Blood, that is one of the works that Christ doth.[17]

Marshall proceeds to the Person of Christ: "as our justification ariseth from Christ's righteousness being applied to us, so our Sonship arising from Christ as the Son, (being the only begotten Son of God and our elder Brother) is applied to us."[18]

Next, Marshall explains the Spirit's work in adoption. He says:

> When the acceptable time is come, that the Lord means to make a Soul that is by nature a Child of wrath to become the Child of God, He sends the Spirit of Jesus Christ into that Soul to be a band of union betwixt Christ and that soul...and they to be mystically united unto him...this is the first work of the Spirit as he is the Spirit of Adoption.[19]

---

14. Ibid., 42.
15. Ibid., 43.
16. Ibid., 43–44.
17. Ibid., 44–45.
18. Ibid., 45.
19. Ibid., 46–47.

The last statement—that effecting the mystical union "is the first work of the Spirit as he is the Spirit of Adoption"—is particularly significant. Considering Marshall's statement that adoption can embrace every benefit of redemption, adoption can also be viewed as tantamount to union with Christ. He notes a renovative dimension of adoption: "The Spirit of God works a Child-like heart in them, framing and molding their spirits ... even in the frame and bent of their spirits."[20]

What Are the Benefits?

Marshall lists three benefits of adoption: (1) being cut off from the family of Adam, the dominion of sin, and the curse; (2) being taken into God's family; and (3) being made heirs.[21] In typical Puritan fashion, Marshall follows the exposition with "uses" (applications). His poignant conclusion challenges the notion that the Westminster divines lacked "warmth."

> [T]he meanest Beleever though (as we say in the Country) he go with his Flail, or a Rake, or (as you wil say in the City) he carries the Tankard, the meanest Beleever that hath Christ for his Lord and Savior, he is exalted to a higher condition than Ahasuerus was, when he was made the Emperor of a hundred twenty & seven Provinces; for let them take al the Pomp, Wealth, & State that is in this world, let them have it all, if they have not Christ, God looks upon them as Satans slaves, and over a few daies they wil perish among the Dogs, I mean among the Devils, & be base, and be miserable for ever; wheras the poorest servant of God that believeth in Christ, the Lord tenders him as his first born, O! I would fain (if it were Gods wil) that Gods People would lay this to heart, it would comfort them against all the Scorns and Reproaches of the world...So a poor Child of God may say, I go in a russet Coat, and have never a penny of Mony in my purse, and undergo many afflictions and troubles, Wel, but God is my Father, and the very thought of the dignity that God hath exalted him to, will make him quietly and contentedly undergo all the afflictions of this world.[22]

---

20. Ibid., 47.
21. Ibid., 50–53.
22. Ibid., 60.

Though not speaking for the Assembly, Marshall's high esteem for the doctrine of adoption can be taken as indicative of the Assembly which enshrined the first confessional statement on adoption in church history.

The Westminster Standards

From Marshall's exposition of the doctrine of adoption, we now turn to examine how the Westminster Standards treat the same.

Adoption in the Westminster Confession of Faith

WCF XII, "Of Adoption," is the earliest known confessional statement devoted to the doctrine. Chad Van Dixhoorn observes that "the most noteworthy fact about this chapter on adoption is that there is a chapter at all."[23] Consisting of one 101-word sentence, chapter XII is the shortest chapter in the Confession:[24]

> All those that are justified God vouchsafeth, in and for his only Son Jesus Christ, to make partakers of the grace of adoption; by which they are taken into the number, and enjoy the liberties and privileges of the children of God; have his name put upon them; receive the Spirit of adoption; have access to the throne of grace with boldness; are enabled to cry, Abba, Father; are pitied, protected, provided for, and chastened by him as by a father; yet never cast off, but sealed to the day of redemption, and inherit the promises, as heirs of everlasting salvation.

This short chapter highlights the Trinitarian structure of Adoption: "... *God* vouchsafeth, in and for his only *Son* Jesus Christ, to make partakers of the grace of adoption; by which they ... receive the *Spirit* of adoption ..."

Situated between justification and sanctification, WCF XII says that "partakers of adoption" are "all those that are justified." This could be interpreted to mean that "the Confession makes

---

23. Chad Van Dixhoorn, *Confessing the Faith: A Reader's Guide to the Westminster Confession of Faith* (Carlisle: Banner of Truth, 2014), 171.

24. Beeke and Van Dixhoorn offer essentially the same three explanations for its brevity: (1) limited source material, (2) lack of controversy surrounding the subject, and (3) overlap with other chapters in the Confession. Joel Beeke, *Heirs with Christ*, 37; and Van Dixhoorn, *Confessing the Faith*, 172.

adoption a consequence of justification."[25] J.V. Fesko writes, "... the key point is that Reformed theologians viewed adoption as the consequence of justification; the one produces the other and its concomitants."[26] Fesko quotes Samuel Rutherford's Catechism, in which he lists "Adoptione to certaintie of salvation and Christian libertie" as "the fruittis of our justification."[27] As a consensus document, the wording of WCF XII is likely intended to accommodate a range of views, including those of Marshall and Rutherford, on the ordering of benefits.[28] Nevertheless, the fact that adoption has its own chapter, and is not simply a subsection of WCF 11 ("On Justification"), suggests that it cannot be reduced

---

25. J.V. Fesko, *The Theology of the Westminster Standards: Historical Context and Theological Insights* (Wheaton: Crossway, 2014), 236.

26. Fesko, *Westminster Standards*, 236.

27. Samuel Rutherford, *The Soume of Christian Religion*, 23, in *Catechisms of the Second Reformation*, ed. Alexander F. Mitchell (London: James Nisbet & Co., 1886), 207; in Fesko, *Westminster Standards*, 236.

28. Although no shortage of ink has been spilled in recent decades over the precise order of benefits, the primary concerns of the Assembly were Arminianism, Roman Catholicism, and antinomianism. The non-negotiable points were that faith could not precede effectual calling (Arminianism), that justification could not precede faith (eternal justification/antinomianism), that one could not be in a justified state without sanctification (antinomianism), and that justification was an immediate act not predicated upon one's performance by renovative grace (Roman Catholicism). See Jeffrey K. Jue, "The Active Obedience of Christ and the Westminster Standards: A Historical Investigation," in *Justified in Christ: God's Plan for Us in Justification*, ed. K. Scott Oliphant (Geanies House: Mentor, 2007), 102–114; Robert J. McKelvey, "'That Error and Pillar of Antinomianism': Eternal Justification," in *Drawn into Controversie: Reformed Theological Diversity and Debates within Seventeenth-Century British Puritanism*, eds. Michael A. G. Haykin and Mark Jones (Oakville: Vandenhoeck & Ruprecht, 2011), 238; Alan D. Strange, "The Imputation of the Active Obedience of Christ at the Westminster Assembly," in Haykin and Jones, *Drawn into Controversie*, 38.

Within these parameters, there is room for nuance and disagreement over the ordering of benefits. Gaffin observes that "in distinction from positions no doubt held by a number of the framers, the Standards themselves do not spell out a particular ordo salutis (of causally concatenated acts or works of God). Within the bounds of what they do teach, an explicitly articulated ordo salutis is left an open question. The Standards do not foreclose that issue for those who subscribe to them." (Richard B. Gaffin, Jr., "Biblical Theology and the Westminster Standards," *WTJ* 65 [2003], 176.) See also Richard A. Muller, *Calvin and the Reformed Tradition: On the Work of Christ and the Order of Salvation* (Grand Rapids: Baker, 2012), 238–243.

solely to an aspect of justification. The Southern Presbyterian, Francis R. Beattie, observed:

> This comprehensive inventory of the privileges which adoption brings shows how important and precious it is. Justification could never bring these benefits, for it leaves the believer in the forum of the divine procedure, with pardon, acceptance, and a title to reward, and it can bring nothing more. But adoption takes the believer from the forum and places him in the family of God, where he may rejoice in all the privileges already mentioned. Thus adoption has its proper place as a doctrine of the Christian system, and it is a very precious practical religious experience.[29]

As far as an *ordo salutis* is concerned, Van Dixhoorn judiciously observes that "[t]he saving blessings and graces that come from Jesus Christ always come as a package."[30] The language in WCF XII that locates adoption "in and for ... Jesus Christ" defines the "package" as union with Christ.[31]

Adoption in the Westminster Larger Catechism

The Larger Catechism devotes one question to adoption. WLC 74 defines adoption as:

> ... an act of the free grace of God, in and for his only Son Jesus Christ, whereby all those that are justified are received into the number of his children, have his name put upon them, the Spirit of his Son given to them, are under his fatherly care and dispensations, admitted to all the liberties and privileges of the sons of God, made heirs of all the promises, and fellow-heirs with Christ in glory.[32]

---

29. Francis R. Beattie, *The Presbyterian Standards: An Exposition of the Westminster Confession of Faith and Catechisms* (Richmond: Presbyterian Committee of Publication, 1896), 216.

30. Van Dixhoorn, *Confessing the Faith*, 172.

31. "Union with Christ is inseparable from adoption. The sonship we receive is Christ's in the first place. Adoption transpires 'in and for His Son Jesus Christ,' so that the adopted 'have His name put upon them, the Spirit of His Son given to them' (WLC 74; WCF XII). Justification, adoption, and sanctification all flow from union with Christ (WLC 69)." Beeke, *Heirs with Christ*, 38.

32. WSC 34 is essentially an abridgement of WLC 74; therefore, we shall focus on the Larger Catechism in this section.

a. Union With Christ in the WLC

WLC 74 fits within the overarching structure of WLC 65-90, which frames redemption applied in terms of "Union and Communion with Christ in Grace and Glory," which Robert J. Cara calls "an amazingly biblical discussion of many aspects of our union with Christ."[33] WLC 66 defines union with Christ as "the work of God's grace, whereby [the elect] are spiritually and mystically, yet really and inseparably, joined to Christ as their head and husband; which is done in their effectual calling."

Communion with Christ in grace describes believers' "partaking of the virtue of his mediation, in their justification, adoption, sanctification, and whatever else, in this life, manifests their union with him." Within this structure, communion in grace is "in this life," while communion in glory is essentially (though not exclusively) in heaven (WLC 86).

Robert Letham comments, "[W]hat the Larger Catechism brings to the fore is that all these [justification, adoption, sanctification, and whatever else...] are aspects of union and communion with Christ in grace and glory. At no point should they be isolated from union with Christ."[34]

b. Historico-Redemptive Contours of Adoption in the WLC

Though grouped with "communion with Christ in grace," the last clause of WLC 74 says that the adopted are "fellow-heirs with Christ **in glory**."[35] Cara observes: "Concerning the adoption section, a future aspect is included ... This shows a now/not-yet structure to adoption."[36] Additionally, WLC 83 asks "What is the communion **in glory** which the members of the invisible church

---

33. Robert J. Cara, "Redemptive-Historical Themes in the Westminster Larger Catechism," in *The Westminster Confession into the Twenty-First Century*, ed. J. Ligon Duncan, III (Geanies House: Mentor, 2009), 3:72.

34. Letham, *Westminster Assembly*, 246.

35. Emphasis in all quotations from the Standards throughout this paper has been added by this author.

36. Cara, "R-H Themes," 72–73. See also Thomas Ridgeley, *A Body of Divinity* (New York: Robert Carter and Brothers, 1855), 2:136.

enjoy **in this life?**" The now/not yet structure manifests in the question's framing. WLC 83 answers that communion in glory extends into this life:

> The members of the invisible church have communicated to them in this life, the first-fruits of glory with Christ, as they are members of him their head, and so, in him, are interested in that glory which he is fully possessed of; and as an earnest thereof, enjoy the sense of God's love, peace of conscience, joy in the Holy Ghost, and hope of glory; as, on the contrary, the sense of God's revenging wrath, horror of conscience, and a fearful expectation of judgment, are, to the wicked, the beginning of their torments which they shall endure after death.

WLC 39 states: "It was requisite that the Mediator should be man, that he might advance our nature, perform obedience to the law, suffer and make intercession for us in our nature, have a fellow-feeling of our infirmities; **that we might receive the adoption of sons**," indicating adoption was accomplished by Christ in the *historia salutis*.[37]

c. Adoption as an Act in the WLC and WSC

In both the Larger and Shorter Catechisms, effectual calling and sanctification are defined as works (WLC 67, 75; WSC 31, 34), while justification and adoption are defined as acts (WLC 71, 74; WSC 33, 34). Effectual calling and sanctification are renovative, while justification is forensic. Does the reference to adoption as an "act," therefore, restrict it to the forensic realm? Not necessarily.[38] Beeke writes:

---

37. The Scripture referenced (Gal. 4:4) further clarifies this.

38. The commentaries on the Shorter Catechism by its nearest contemporaries place more emphasis on the "free grace" than the "act." John Flavel (1628–91) asks, "What moves God to adopt any man?" He answers: "Nothing but his free love." Later he says that adoption "is a free relation on God's part" (John Flavel, *An Exposition of the Assembly's Catechism* [Dartmouth: 1688]; orig. pub. Increase Mather [Dartmouth: 1692] in vol. 6 of *The Works of John Flavel* [London: 1820] 197, 198). These are Flavel's only comments on adoption being "an act of God's free grace." Thomas Vincent (1634–78) only comments that "there is neither beauty, nor any lovely qualification, nor any thing in the least, to move and incline God to adopt any whom he doth adopt, but it is an act only of his free grace and love" (Vincent, *An Explicatory Catechism, or An Explanation of the Assembly's Shorter Catechism* [New Haven: Walter Austin and Co., 1810], 92). And Thomas Watson

[T]he Westminster Divines harmonized the forensic and familial elements of adoption. They spoke of both the judicial pronouncement of adoption ... and the adoptive experience of sonship, referred to as the "liberties and privileges of adoption…adoption, therefore, is not exhausted by its forensic aspects; rather, the forensic aspects imply an ensuing familial life of sonship that manifests itself in the visible church, which is described as the "house and family of God (WCF XXV:ii).[39]

A. A. Hodge similarly comments: "Justification effects only a change of relations. Regeneration and sanctification effect only inherent moral and spiritual states of soul. Adoption includes both."[40]

Adoption as a Pervasive Theme in the Westminster Standards

In his article, Kelly said that WCF XII has a "humane family atmosphere."[41] The same atmosphere and familial themes extend throughout the Standards. Tim Trumper finds the Standards' statements on adoption "insufficiently pervasive." He says, "although the scholastic drive for precision lent itself to a unique creedal exposition of adoption, the tendency to allot doctrines specific theological loci created a 'pigeon-hole' effect in which recognition of the interrelatedness of the various doctrines became minimalised."[42] He argues this "unwittingly undermined their own unique creedal emphasis by largely curtailing the implications of adoption to its specific confessional and catechetical loci."[43]

(1620–1686) says that "adoption is an act of pure grace. 'Having predestinated us to the adoption of children, according to the good pleasure of his will.' Eph I 5. Adoption is a mercy spun out of the bowels of free grace. All by nature are strangers, therefore have no right to sonship" (Watson, *A Body of Divinity: Contained in Sermons Upon the Westminster Assembly's Catechism* [1692; repr. Carlisle: Banner of Truth, 2000], 232). Later, Watson appears to attribute both forensic and renovative elements to adoption, when he says that "whom God adopts, he sanctifies; he not only gives a new name but a new nature" (ibid.). However, this could also mean that Watson understands adoption (forensic) as bound to sanctification (renovative).

39. Beeke, *Heirs with Christ*, 38.

40. Hodge, *Confession of Faith*, 192.

41. Kelly, "Adoption," 112.

42. Tim J. R. Trumper, "An Historical Study of Adoption in the Calvinistic Tradition," (Ph.D. diss., University of Edinburgh, 2001), 243.

43. Trumper, "Historical Study," 244.

Tested against the Standards, Trumper's criticism seems overblown. Adoption and what Beeke calls the "ensuing life of sonship" emerge in other places throughout the Standards beyond WCF XII, WLC 74, and WSC 34, going all the way back to the eternal decree. WCF III.6 states: "... they who are elected, being fallen in Adam, are redeemed by Christ, are effectually called unto faith in Christ by His Spirit working in due season, are justified, **adopted**, sanctified, and kept by His power, through faith, unto salvation ..."

Beeke observes, "[T]he Westminster Divines were concerned to apply predestination soteriologically."[44] Election is not extracted from Union with Christ in the decree, impetration, and application of redemption manifested in the benefits of justification, adoption, and sanctification.[45]

WCF VIII.5 (Christ, the Mediator) explains the basis of the inheritance of adopted children:

> The Lord Jesus, by His perfect obedience, and sacrifice of Himself, which He through the eternal Spirit, once offered up unto God, has fully satisfied the justice of His Father: and purchased, not only reconciliation, but **an everlasting inheritance in the kingdom of heaven**, for those whom the Father has given unto Him.

This seems to root adoption in both the Person and work of Christ.

In the Standards, benefits are not abstracted from each other or from the filial relationship the sons—identified as sons—sustain to the Father in union with the Son. WLC 80 ties assurance to adoption: "Q. Can true believers be infallibly assured that they are in the estate of grace, and that they shall persevere therein unto salvation?"

---

44. Beeke, *Heirs with Christ,* 37. Ironically, Beeke draws from Trumper in this assertion.

45. The decree is treated in much the same way in both the Thirty-Nine Articles of the Church of England (XVII) and the Irish Articles of Religion (III), both of which documents were highly significant to the work of the Westminster Assembly.

A. Such as truly believe in Christ, and endeavour to walk in all good conscience before him, may, without extraordinary revelation, by faith grounded upon the truth of God's promises, and by the Spirit enabling them to discern in themselves those graces to which the promises of life are made, **and bearing witness with their spirits that they are the children of God**, be infallibly assured that they are in the estate of grace, and shall persevere therein unto salvation.

Similarly, WCF XVIII.2 describes "the testimony of the **Spirit of adoption** witnessing with our spirits that **we are the children of God**, which Spirit is the earnest of our **inheritance**, whereby we are sealed to the day of redemption" as a foundation of "an infallible assurance of faith." WCF XI.5 shows practical interaction between adoption and justification: though the justified "can never fall from the state of justification, **yet they may, by their sins, fall under God's fatherly displeasure** …"

WCF XXII.1 describes Christians' liberty as manifested "in their free access to God, and their yielding obedience unto Him, not out of slavish fear, but a **child-like love** and willing mind." WCF XXV.2 describes the church as the "**family** of God." WLC 189 says the preface of the Lord's Prayer "… teacheth us, when we pray, to draw near to God with confidence of his **fatherly** goodness, and our interest therein; with reverence, and all other **childlike dispositions** …"

WLC 27 highlights what the elect are adopted out of: "The fall brought upon mankind the loss of communion with God, his displeasure and curse; so as we **are by nature children of wrath, bond slaves to Satan**, and justly liable to all punishments in this world, and that which is to come." Thomas Watson exhorts: "Extol and magnify God's mercy, who has adopted you into his family; who, of slaves, has made you sons; of heirs of hell, heirs of the promise."[46]

When it comes to adoption, the heirs of the Westminster tradition can say, "The lines are fallen unto me in pleasant places; yea, I have a goodly heritage" (Psalm 16:6).

---

46. Watson, *Body of Divinity*, 240.

Development of the Heritage

Though he lamented the underdevelopment of that heritage, Kelly pointed out that "there were some shining exceptions to the general rule of omitting the doctrine of adoption," most prominently in the branch of southern Presbyterianism influenced by old Columbia Seminary.[47]

More recently, the Westminster heritage has seen development in the appropriation of insights from biblical theology. Richard Gaffin argues compellingly that Jesus's resurrection was his justification, adoption, and sanctification, and that they, "as applied to Christ, are not separate distinct acts. Rather, each describes a different facet or aspect of the one act of being raised from the dead."[48] Consequently,

> the notion that the believer has been raised with Christ brings into view all that now characterizes him as a result of having been joined to Christ as resurrected. It means that he has been justified, adopted, sanctified, and glorified with Christ, better, that he has been united with the Christ, who is justified, adopted, sanctified, and glorified, and so by virtue of this (existential) union shares these benefits.[49]

Building on Gaffin's work, Sinclair Ferguson says the Apostle Paul

> implies that the resurrection can be seen as Jesus's adoption. As to his human nature, Jesus was "a descendant of David" but "through the Spirit of holiness" he "was declared with power to be the Son of God, by his resurrection from the dead" (Rom. 1:4).

> Older interpreters read Romans 1:3–4 ... as a statement of the two natures of Christ. But the contrast in view is ... his humiliation and exaltation. His resurrection thus constitutes him messianic Son of God with power; in it he is adopted as the Man of the new age.[50]

---

47. Kelly, "Underdeveloped Heritage," 112.

48. Richard B. Gaffin, Jr., *Resurrection and Redemption: A Study in Paul's Soteriology*, 2nd ed. (Phillipsburg: Presbyterian and Reformed, 1987), 127.

49. Gaffin, *Resurrection and Redemption*, 129.

50. Sinclair B. Ferguson, *The Holy Spirit* (Downers Grove: InterVarsity Press, 1996), 105.

David Garner further develops this in his work, *Sons in the Son.* He writes that the

> ...*ordo salutis* must reflect how union with the adopted Son makes all those united to this Son adopted. Solidaric union is sonly union. In the believers' adoption comes the duplex gratia – justification and sanctification – because the redeeming Son has secured these in his own person and faithfully delivers both dimensions of soteric grace. That is, the manifestation of union ought not to suffer abstraction, extracting it from the filial/personal context from which it flows. Manifestation of union with Christ the Son of God is irreducibly filial because the resurrected Redeemer is the Son of God adopted. Thus, justification manifests union because the adopted sons manifest the cosmically vindicated and justified Son of God. Sanctification manifests union because the adopted sons manifest the cosmically consecrated and victorious Son of God. The believers' adoption manifests their Redeemer's adoption. Union secures justified and sanctified sons who are, in the Son, justified and sanctified. From the first moment of faith unto its consummation on the last day, adoption of the sons manifests the adoption of the Son.[51]

While the Standards do not state that Christ was adopted in His resurrection,[52] they do state that Jesus purchased an everlasting inheritance for His people (WCF VIII.5), which they receive in adoption. WLC 39 says that Jesus became man "that he might advance our nature" and "that we might receive the adoption of sons." Without teaching the adoption of Christ in the accomplishment of redemption as argued by Gaffin, Ferguson, and Garner, the Standards allow and contain the "raw materials" for its development.

This development has not been without detractors. Joshua Maurer and Ty Kieser argue that "Jesus's adoption by God rests upon unwarranted soteriological premises, implies unwanted christological implications, and is exegetically tenuous and

---

51. David B. Garner, *Sons in the Son: The Riches and Reach of Adoption in Christ* (Phillipsburg: Presbyterian & Reformed, 2016), 308–9.

52. The use of Rom 1:3–4 in WLC 52 clearly takes it as applying to the two natures of Christ rather than the two states. For an overview of the history of interpretation of Rom 1:3–4 in the Reformed tradition, see Gaffin, *Resurrection and Redemption*, 100–113.

unnecessary."[53] Their concern is likely triggered by the word "adoption," which carries unfortunate baggage of ancient Christological heresy.[54]

Maurer and Kieser do not adequately account for the contours of development within redemptive history. They argue that "this historical-redemptive movement is not properly called adoption because ... Christ's relation to God as Son did not change—and this relationship is precisely what is at issue with the language and concept of adoption, both in Paul's day and our own."[55]

In Luke 3-4, Jesus's genealogy is traced backward to "Adam, which was the Son of God" (Luke 3:38), framed by the Father's declaration, "Thou art my beloved Son; in thee I am well pleased" (Luke 3:22), and the temptations of Jesus (Luke 4:1-13). Luke draws a parallel between two sons of God— one who succumbed to temptation in a verdant garden, and the other who defeated temptation in a barren wilderness.

The final state into which Jesus brings His people is undeniably superior to the original state of Adam. As Geerhardus Vos states,

> "What we inherit in the second Adam is not restricted to what we lost in the first Adam: it is much rather the full realization of what the first Adam would have achieved for us had he remained unfallen and been confirmed in his state. Someone placed in that state can never again fall from it."[56]

Paul highlights this contrast in 1 Corinthians 15:45-49:

> And so it is written, The first man Adam was made a living soul; the last Adam was made a quickening spirit. Howbeit that was not first which is spiritual, but that which is natural; and afterward that which is spiritual.

---

53. Joshua Maurer and Ty Kieser, "Jesus, 'Adopted Son of God'? Romans 1:4, Orthodox Christology, and Concerns about a Contemporary Conclusion," *Themelios* 46.2 (2021), 320. Gaffin and Garner have defended their work aptly against these criticisms (Richard B. Gaffin Jr. and David B. Garner, "The Divine and Adopted Son of God: A Response to Joshua Maurer and Ty Kieser," *Themelios* 47.1 [2022]: 144–55).

54. See Harold O.J. Brown, *Heresies: Heresy and Orthodoxy in the History of the Church* (Peabody: Hendrickson, 1984; repr. 2003), 96–99.

55. Maurer and Kieser, "Adopted Son of God?" 334–335.

56. Geerhardus Vos, "The Doctrine of the Covenant in Reformed Theology," *Redemptive History and Biblical Interpretation: The Shorter Writings of Geerhardus Vos*, Richard B. Gaffin, Jr, ed. (Phillipsburg: Presbyterian & Reformed, 1980), 243.

The first man is of the earth, earthy; the second man is the Lord from heaven. As is the earthy, such are they also that are earthy: and as is the heavenly, such are they also that are heavenly. And as we have borne the image of the earthy, we shall also bear the image of the heavenly.

Vos points out that the comparison is not between "the original provenience of Christ from heaven" and Adam from the dust of the earth; rather, it is between the original state of Adam and the glorified state of Christ. [57] Succeeding where Adam failed, Jesus became the heavenly man, life-giving Spirit, in His resurrection. Consequently, Paul says, in the resurrection "we shall be changed" (v. 51). The logic of 1 Corinthians 15 is that we shall be changed because Christ, the firstfruits (v. 20), was changed. In class, Dr. Kelly was fond of quoting an obscure line of Watts's hymn, based loosely on Psalm 72: "In [Christ] the tribes of Adam boast more blessings than their father lost."

The Last Adam entered the world to stand parallel to the first Adam in order to do what the first Adam failed to do.[58] This is why the Son of God was "made of a woman, made under the law" (Gal. 4:4). When Jesus left the tomb, He was no longer "under the law." His work of obedience was finished (John 17:4; 19:30). The same Son was no less the Son under the law; nevertheless, He enjoys a vastly higher estate as the glorified "Son of God in power."[59]

Maurer and Kieser maintain that "[a]doption necessarily includes the notion of relational change of status between persons."[60] They argue Jesus was not adopted because the word demands that the adoptee not be a son prior to adoption. In Romans 8, however, Paul says that "as many as are led by the Spirit of God, they are the sons of God" (v. 14) and that "we are the children of God" (v. 16) now; yet, he goes on to say that

---

57. Geerhardus Vos, "The Eschatological Aspect of the Pauline Conception of the Spirit," *Redemptive History and Biblical Interpretation*, 106.

58. Although it was impossible for the Last Adam to sin since, unlike the first Adam, his human nature was personalized by the second Person of the Trinity.

59. The two estates of Christ—humiliation and exaltation—is a prominent theme throughout the Standards, especially the catechisms.

60. Maurer and Kieser, "Adopted Son of God?" 335.

"ourselves also, which have the firstfruits of the Spirit, even we ourselves groan within ourselves, waiting for the adoption, to wit, the redemption of our body" (v. 23). We are the children of God by adoption now; yet "waiting for the adoption" at the resurrection. Adoption in the Pauline corpus, therefore, does not "necessarily include...relational change of status," as Maurer and Kieser narrowly define it. Their criticism proves ill-founded.

It seems to me that the most significant and salutary contribution advanced by Gaffin, Ferguson, Garner, et al, has been to draw attention to the accomplishment of the whole of redemption—including adoption—by the Lord Jesus Christ. Simply put, Jesus accomplished our adoption. Garner writes, "What makes adoption the supreme benefit...is not first its filial assurances but its Christological substance."[61]

A major factor in adoption's neglect is a failure to connect it with the work of Christ. Within the Westminster tradition, justification is readily connected with Christ's active and passive obedience. Although every benefit of redemption applied is equally as rooted in the redemption accomplished by Christ as justification, many reformed believers have not "connected the dots" with the other benefits.

Though he held adoption to be "the ultimate state unto which we are ordained," and our "highest and most eminent" privilege, no less a theologian than the prominent Westminster divine, Thomas Goodwin, said that "adoption...was not founded upon redemption, or Christ's obedience, but on Christ's personally being God's natural Son. Our justification indeed is built upon his obedience and sufferings . . . But our adoption is through his being the natural Son of God . . ."[62] Some divines agreed; others (like Marshall) held that adoption was rooted in the work of Christ. The Standards connect adoption to "the redemption purchased by Christ."[63] Most importantly, Galatians 4:4–5 appears conclusively

---

61. Garner, *Sons in the Son*, 310.

62. Thomas Goodwin, "An Exposition of the First Chapter of the Epistle to the Ephesians," in *The Works of Thomas Goodwin* (Edinburgh: James Nichol, 1861), 1:85, 96.

63. WCF VIII.5, as noted, says that Christ purchased an everlasting inheritance for

to root adoption in the work of Christ.[64] James I. Packer states: "Were I asked to focus the New Testament message in three words, my proposal would be *adoption through propitiation*, and I do not expect ever to meet a richer or more pregnant summary of the gospel than that."[65]

Douglas Kelly's Contribution to the Doctrine of Adoption

Vos writes,

> Only when the believer understands how he has to receive and has received everything from the Mediator and how God in no way whatever deals with him except through Christ, only then does a picture of the glorious work that God wrought through Christ emerge in his consciousness, and the magnificent idea of grace begin to dominate and to form in his life. For the Reformed, therefore, the entire ordo salutis, beginning with regeneration as its first stage, is bound to the mystical union with Christ. There is no gift that has not been earned by him.[66]

That includes the gift of adoption.

A richer understanding of Jesus's work earning the gift of adoption will increase its appreciation among believers. I believe that Kelly has contributed significantly to the development of the "underdeveloped heritage" in this regard.

I was somewhat disappointed to find that adoption received only three pages in a twenty-four-page chapter entitled "Justification by Faith and Sanctification" in volume III of Kelly's *Systematic Theology*;[67] however, I would submit that one full chapter in his

---

his people, connecting the inheritance of God's adopted children to the redemption purchased by Christ. Moreover, both catechisms deal with adoption within the overarching context of the Spirit's applying the redemption purchased by Christ.

64. "The adoption of sons is here described, therefore, as the object of the great eschatological redemptive event and as the direct result of redemption." Herman Ridderbos, *Paul: An Outline of His Thought*; trans., John R. de Witt (Grand Rapids: Eerdmans, 1975), 197.

65. J. I. Packer, *Knowing God* (Downers Grove: InterVarsity Press, 1973; repr. 1993), 214.

66. Vos, "Doctrine of the Covenant," 248.

67. Chapter 7 of Douglas F. Kelly, *Systematic Theology: Grounded in Holy Scripture and Understood in Light of the Church*, vol. 3, *The Holy Spirit and the Church* (Geanies

volume II (Christology) is a veritable gold mine of material on adoption, though the word is not mentioned. In much the same way that John Owen's finest work on Christology was in his work on the Holy Spirit,[68] Kelly's most significant work on adoption may well be in his Christology.

Chapter 8 of volume II of Kelly's *Systematic Theology* is entitled "Christ's Active Obedience (His Sonship)."[69] As the title suggests, Kelly unfolds the active obedience of Christ through the lens of His sonship. He writes:

> In the beginning, God created Adam to be a loving son, and love is always shown by obedience (cf. John 15:10, 14). Adam failed to render loving obedience, and in due time, God raised up Abraham and Israel to live as his obedient sons, but they too failed. So, "in the fullness of time" (cf. Gal. 4:4), God sent his own Son to live a life of deepest and fullest loving obedience. In so doing, the Incarnate Son of God obeyed from the heart, in every thought, word, and action, all the holy will of the Heavenly Father, thereby fulfilling the original intentions of God in his creation of Adam and his posterity. By his active obedience, Christ fulfills the original purpose of the "Adamic Administration" (or, as the Puritans called it, "covenant with Adam," "covenant of life," "covenant of works").[70]

Kelly develops Christ's active obedience (or Life of Sonship) along the lines of the two Adams, tracing the theme from the first man as the son of God through Israel as son of God to Christ, the Son of God. Of the first Adam, Kelly says, "God desired a human son (and daughter), who would abide in sweet fellowship with him, loving and obeying him from the heart."[71] After the Fall, Kelly traces the "seed of the woman":

> The chosen "seed of the woman," and line of the Gospel, passed through Adam's son, Seth, through his descendant, Noah, and through Noah's son, Shem; then through his descendant, Abraham, and onwards through Isaac,

---

House: Mentor, 2021), 151–174. Adoption is treated on pp. 168–171.

68. Richard W. Daniels, *The Christology of John Owen* (Grand Rapids: Reformation Heritage, 2004), 294.

69. Douglas F. Kelly, *Systematic Theology: Grounded in Holy Scripture and Understood in Light of the Church, vol. 2, The Beauty of Christ: A Trinitarian Vision* (Geanies House: Mentor, 2014), 317–340.

70. Ibid., 317, 318.

71. Ibid., 318.

Jacob, and the twelve patriarchs, especially Judah (ancestor of David, and through David's line, of Christ himself). From this point of view one could look upon the history of Israel as the way God chose to form within a particular race a line for his Son; a way to reverse the loss suffered in Adam's rebellion from the heavenly Father.

One can look at the call of Abraham as the beginning of the covenantal process in which the Lord calls out a people to be his obedient son, where Adam failed. The grace of God will be operative in this relationship (generally called the covenant of grace), and God's grace reaches its perfect fulfillment in him as "the seed of the woman" and "the seed of Abraham."[72]

Kelly sums up the history of Israel: "The first Adam had failed to be God's loving and obedient son, and so it was with God's corporate son, Israel."[73]

On the incarnation, Kelly writes:

It should come, then, as no surprise to those familiar with the history of Israel, that after God's created son, Adam, failed (for Luke's genealogy calls Adam "the son of God" – Luke 3:38) God's adopted son, Israel, failed; Even King David, anointed though he was, was marked by many failures. Then God sent the Son of his own heart: his only begotten son in the flesh, to carry through with impeccable, obedient devotion everything that he wanted in the others; to fulfill all that he ever desired in and through the new head of the human race: the last Adam.[74]

Commenting on the Father's declarations, "This is my beloved Son, in whom I am well pleased" (Matt. 3:17; 17:5), Kelly says, "Only by means of the hypostatic union of two natures in one person was Christ able successfully to recapitulate all that sonship toward which the Old Testament was reaching forward in Adam and Israel."[75] Concerning Matthew's use of Hosea 11:1—"Out of Egypt have I called my son"—Kelly explains,

In a preliminary sense, Israel was the son of God, brought out of Egypt, but the rest of the Old Testament shows how frequently that son rebelled against the Father. Nevertheless, Israel in its historical life foreshadowed

---

72. Ibid., 320.
73. Ibid., 320.
74. Ibid., 321.
75. Ibid., 322.

the true Son of God: born of the Virgin Mary. What Israel did not carry through, Christ did carry through.[76]

Working through the temptations of Christ, Kelly concludes:

> In all of the temptations... Jesus, The Messiah of Israel, showed himself to be the obedient and loving son of God, thereby restoring our race to the Father's immediate presence, for one can only look face to face upon one who has been loved and obeyed from the heart. While the devil would have us turn our faces eternally away from God, Jesus as our messianic head has turned us to look upon our Heavenly Father forevermore. His going, in our place, through the baptism of repentance and the temptations, prepared him to stand in our place in Gethsemane and on Calvary.

> At the end of his earthly ministry, the incarnate Son, facing a substitutionary, God-forsaken death in Gethsemane, unlike the first Adam, said, "Thy will be done." (Matt. 26:42), and, unlike the complaining and distrusting Israel in the wilderness, without reserve, committed his spirit into the father's hands with his last breath (Luke 23:46). The result of that self-sacrificing will and loving trust is "writ large" in Romans 1:2–3 [sic] as the ultimate fulfillment of all the promises of the Gospel: "(...Which he had promised afore by his prophets in the holy scriptures,) Concerning his Son Jesus Christ our Lord, which was made of the seed of David according to the flesh; And declared to be the son of God with power, according to the spirit of holiness by the resurrection from the dead."[77]

Kelly describes the entire life of Christ leading up to the crucifixion:

> Christ would indeed go to Calvary, but that time was not ripe until he had obeyed the Father in his earthly life for some thirty-three years of constant filial devotion and perfect obedience from the heart. This means that a life of active obedience, a life of perfect filial Sonship, was to be lived in its fullness before that hour when the Son would be glorified by the father on the cross as he poured out his life a ransom for many.[78]

Kelly explains what Christ's active obedience accomplished and its necessity for our salvation. Kelly examines the Westminster Assembly's debate on active obedience, and its necessity for our justification. Kelly even relates Christ's active obedience to our

---

76. Ibid., 322.
77. Ibid., 326, 327.
78. Ibid., 328.

sanctification.[79] Yet, he does not mention adoption. He comes close in his discussion of the covenant of grace:

> The entire Old Testament shows us that Adam failed. Israel failed. So God, out of love to the world, (John 3:16), gave his only begotten Son to stand in for it, and do what it did not do, and now could not do. In terms of the traditional covenant theology, one could say that God's Incarnate Son came to pay the penalty of the broken relationship with God (namely, substitutionary death), and – before that supreme climax of love and grace – to keep in its fullness all the righteous requirements of the law. In a certain sense, the substitutionary death keeps us from hell, and the representative obedience takes us into heaven to live forever with God.[80]

Only through Christ's perfect life of sonship and atoning death can our relationship with the Father be restored through adoption. Jesus's active obedience accomplished our adoption as much as our justification.

Kelly has contributed a highly innovative (in the best sense) treatment of the active obedience of Christ as His life of loving sonship. Beyond that, Kelly has contributed a major development of the "underdeveloped heritage of the Westminster Standards" in this remarkably original chapter—a chapter which merits further development, itself, and is a prime example of Kelly's thoroughly integrated theology.

Recently, G. K. Beale has developed his own previous work on Adam and Israel, primarily in terms of the image of God and its eschatological restoration in Christ,[81] as it relates to adoption.[82] In his new work, Beale concludes, "Those who believe come into union with the resurrected Christ, the Son of God and true Israel,

---

79. Ibid., 334, 335.

80. Ibid., 331.

81. G. K. Beale, *A New Testament Biblical Theology: The Unfolding of the Old Testament in the New* (Grand Rapids: Baker, 2011), chapter 13 ("The Inaugurated End-Time Restoration of God's Image in Humanity: The Old Testament and the Synoptic Gospels"), 381–437.

82. G. K. Beale, *Union with the Resurrected Christ: Eschatological New Creation and New Testament Biblical Theology* (Grand Rapids, Baker: 2023), 103, n.

and so they also become 'adopted sons' and true Israel at that time."[83] I would submit that Kelly's work on the active obedience of Christ as His sonship could (and should) be further developed in relation to adoption along the same lines.[84]

In his 1993 article on Adoption, Kelly dealt with criticisms that the Westminster Standards lacked warmth. In his 2014 closing words on the active obedience of Christ, the warmth he has been zealous to guard and promote is on clear display:

> Christ has turned our nature back to God, has fulfilled every righteous requirement of God in our name, and has lived the life of perfect sonship that our Heavenly Father always wanted. In all of these blessings, the Lord has made us to share, as his Holy Spirit unites us to him who is our substitute and our representative. What a happy and loving people we are called and enabled to be![85]

---

83. Beale, *Union with the Resurrected Christ*, 127.

84. Garner has incisively explored this theme in chapter 9 of *Sons in the Son*, 254–286.

85. Kelly, *Beauty of Christ*, 340.

13

Southern Presbyterianism and the Triune God of Grace

Mantle Nance

WHEN I was a senior at Furman University, I took a class on the history of South Carolina. I had always enjoyed history, especially American and Southern history, so this class was right up my alley. As a religion major, I wanted to explore something related to church history, so, for my research paper, I settled on the topic of John L. Girardeau's ministry to the slaves in antebellum Charleston. My research led me to a book called *Preachers with Power: Four Stalwarts of the South* by Douglas Kelly. It is difficult to estimate how much reading this one book changed the trajectory of my life.

The stories of the Spirit-empowered preaching of Girardeau (1825-1898), James Henley Thornwell (1812-1862), Benjamin Morgan Palmer (1818-1902), and Daniel Baker (1791-1857) stirred my heart to want to preach the free grace of Jesus Christ and see others find eternal life in him. The way Dr. Kelly wove together spiritual lessons with historical narrative rekindled my love for history and opened my eyes to its abiding relevance. And, perhaps most importantly, *Preachers with Power* introduced me to Dr. Kelly's broader ministry. I began listening to all his sermons and lectures I could get my hands on. I read other life-changing books like *If God Already Knows, Why Pray?* and articles like "The Recovery of Christian Realism in the Scottish Expository Ministry Movement."[1]

A few years after graduating from college, as I continued to pray about full-time ministry, I came to know Dr. Kelly himself. It was at the Scottish Highland Games at Grandfather Mountain, North Carolina. My dad and I had spent the morning at the games, watching the caber toss, listening to the bagpipes, and visiting various clan tents of families to which we have familial ties. And then, mid-afternoon, we headed down Grandfather on one of the school buses that shuttled folks up and down the mountain. On the bus, we began thumbing through the program, and we saw a picture of Dr. Kelly, with a description saying that he was there at the games as chaplain. We also read that he was connected to the Kelly and Blue families of Moore County. My dad said, "Your mother is connected to the Blue family of Moore County!" Could it be that Dr. Kelly is Cousin Kelly?! I looked at my dad, and he said, "I believe we need to go back up that mountain, don't we?"

So, we hopped off one bus and stood in line to get onto another. My dad graciously paid the five-dollar shuttle fee again! I have since told him, "That was the best investment you ever made in me!" Once we were back on top of the mountain, we returned to the Blue family tent, and the kind folks there were able to help us track down Dr. Kelly and Caroline. For the rest of the afternoon, Dr. Kelly and I sat under the shade of the trees and talked. That day, he became my friend and father in the faith. My sense

---

1. See Douglas Kelly, *Preachers with Power* (Edinburgh: Banner of Truth, 1992); *If God Already Knows, Why Pray?* (Geanies House: Christian Focus Publications, 1996); "The Recovery of Christian Realism" in *Pulpit and People: Essays in Honour of William Still on his 75th Birthday* edited by Nigel M. de S. Cameron and Sinclair B. Ferguson (Edinburgh: Rutherford House Books, 1986), 17–28; "Adoption: An Underdeveloped Heritage of the Westminster Standards," The Reformed Theological Review 52, no. 3 (Sept.–Dec. 1993), 110–20; "Prayer and Union with Christ," Scottish Bulletin of Evangelical Theology 8 (1990), 109–27.

of calling into Gospel ministry and my desire to study with him at Reformed Theological Seminary in Charlotte were solidified.

His influence has touched every facet of my life for the better: family life, prayer life, work ethic, ministry, academic life. His emphasis on the Trinity and his work on Southern Presbyterianism led me to do my PhD on how three Southern Presbyterian pastor-scholars stood for the Trinity against a burgeoning Unitarian movement in the nineteenth century South.[2] As I reflect on my research into their lives and ministries, I would like to share two practical takeaways that I believe are relevant for the church today: first, an emphasis on the Trinity and, second, an emphasis on grace.

An Emphasis on the Trinity

Dr. Kelly is appreciatively known for his catholic spirit and emphasis on the essentials of the faith.[3] This was also the case with many of the Southern Presbyterians in the nineteenth century, especially those who were connected to Columbia Seminary, which, at that time, was in Columbia, South Carolina. Yes, their leaders, such as Palmer, Thornwell, and Thomas Smyth, had their distinctives, and, yes, they debated them from time to time. But those debates were largely relegated to theological journals and church courts. In their lives and from their pulpits, the emphasis was not on secondary or tertiary issues, but rather on the cardinal truths of the faith, the essentials that make Christianity Christian.

Benjamin Morgan Palmer

As Dr. Kelly once said to me about Palmer, "He preached the 'big doctrines.'" In fact, if you read Palmer's sermons, you find that he consistently brought his hearers back to the central doctrine of the faith, the *sine qua non* of Christianity: the blessed Trinity.

---

2. Mantle Nance, *The Adorable Trinity: Standing for Orthodoxy in Nineteenth-Century America* (Geanies House: Mentor, 2020).

3. See Douglas Kelly, *Systematic Theology, Volume 1: The God Who Is: The Holy Trinity* (Geanies House: Mentor, 2008), 1, 9–11; *Volume 2: The Beauty of Christ: A Trinitarian Vision* (Geanies House: Mentor, 2014), 1–4.

He preached virtually every doctrine Trinitarianly. God was not a vague generality, a proposition, or a faceless force. God was loving Father, gracious Son, gentle Spirit. Sin was not merely the infraction of a written code, but rather a failure to love the "adorable Three"—a spurning of the Father's love, ingratitude for the Son's grace, resistance to the Spirit's heart-melting fellowship. Evangelism was an invitation to come home to the adopting love of the Father through the outstretched arms of his crucified Son by the gracious ministry of the Lord and Giver of life.[4]

There are reasons why Palmer emphasised the Trinity so much; no one theologizes in a vacuum. His own family had been shaken by the increasingly popular Unitarian movement in Charleston. His uncle, Benjamin Morgan Palmer, Sr., had pastored the Circular (Congregationalist) Church, which had split when his associate became a Unitarian and started the Unitarian Church of Charleston. Because of his stand for the Trinity and the Reformed faith, Palmer Sr. became known as the "Presbyterian Pope of Charleston."

Decades after the split, by which time Palmer Jr. was pastoring at First Presbyterian Church in Columbia, members of the Circular Church noticed that Palmer Sr's daughter, well-known poet and hymnwriter Mary Palmer, had stopped singing the Doxology on Sunday mornings. Eventually, she revealed that she had become a Unitarian through the influence of Charleston's Unitarian minister, Samuel Gilman and his wife, Caroline. Mary even wrote a book about her conversion to Unitarianism called *Letters Addressed to Relatives and Friends, Chiefly in Reply to Arguments in Support of the Doctrine of the Trinity*. In fact, "Biblical Unitarians" today still esteem Mary and promote her *Letters* as a clear and forceful articulation of the Unitarian faith.

But Benjamin Morgan Palmer, Jr., whom Mary referred to as "Cousin Ben," along with the rest of the Palmers, did not give up

---

4. See, for examples, Benjamin Palmer, *A Weekly Publication Containing Sermons*, 2 vols. (New Orleans: Clark & Hofeline, 1875–1876). See also *Theology of Prayer* (Richmond: Presbyterian Committee of Publication, 1894); *The Threefold Fellowship and the Threefold Assurance* (Richmond: Presbyterian Committee of Publications, 1902).

on her. They did not shun or disown her; they loved her. They did not dismiss her; they listened. They did not hold grudges; they forgave her and prayed for her. In other words, they treated her the way the Triune God of grace had treated them. And, after several years as a Unitarian, Mary came back to the Trinitarian faith of her youth. She even married an evangelical minister.

Palmer's ministerial context also led him to emphasize the Trinity. He pastored the First Presbyterian Church of New Orleans from 1856 until his death in 1902. What is interesting about the church he pastored is that it was in fact the second First Presbyterian Church of New Orleans. The first First Presbyterian Church of New Orleans, which was founded in 1818 (the year of Palmer's birth), became the First Unitarian Church of New Orleans in 1834 after its minister, the eloquent orator Theodore Clapp, became a Unitarian. Though the presbytery deposed Clapp, the vast majority of the congregation had come to love him. They voted to keep him and their church property, communion silver and all.

A beleaguered group of exiles decided to make another go of it and planted the second First Presbyterian Church of New Orleans in 1834. But Clapp's pulpit continued to grow as the focal point of spiritual life in New Orleans. When prominent citizens from outside the state would visit the city, they would visit three places: the American Theatre, the French Opera House, and, on Sunday, "Parson Clapp's Church," where attendance swelled to over a thousand each Sunday.[5]

It was into this ministerial context that Palmer stepped in 1856. It wasn't long before members of the Unitarian Church, including former Presbyterians, started coming to hear Palmer preach. After a morning service in May of 1857, he wrote in his diary, "hall filled completely, with large attendance of Unitarians."[6]

---

5. Nance, *Adorable Trinity*, 149–202.
6. Benjamin Morgan Palmer Journal (1857), BMP Papers, C. Benton Kline, Jr. Special Collections and Archives, John Bulow Campbell Library, Columbia Theological Seminary.

Palmer patiently, prayerfully preached the grace, love, and fellowship of the Triune God over the succeeding years. He did not beat people over the head with his opinions. Rather he sought to be a channel of Trinitarian love. He knew that the power to convert sinners was not in himself; the power resides in the Gospel of free grace. So, he proclaimed it freely, lovingly, winsomely, and watched God do what only he can do. Listen to one example of how he preached to Unitarians and other seekers who were intrigued by his message:

> My unconverted friend, it is a great pleasure, even though the thing be badly done, to preach God's precious Gospel to you. I take you to record that my habit is rather to woo you, if I may, with its attractive voices, rather than to hold up the glittering sword and hurl against you the anathemas of judgment. Would to heaven, I had persuasion enough in my voice, to-day, to bring you to an acceptance with us of these immense privileges! Oh, that you with us could be made willing in this, the day of His power, to hold communion with the Father and with the Son and with the eternal Spirit! And to know, as no other can teach it to you, except the Divine Spirit Himself, what is that love of Christ to the believer, which He compares to the Father's love to Himself![7]

Many were made willing. As a newspaper article put it after Palmer's death, "The greater number of the members of the Unitarian Church, which was formed by Dr. Clapp, returned to the fold of Presbyterianism through Dr. Palmer's exposition of the real principles of Presbyterianism." This revival was,

> due to the wonderful influence and power exercised by Dr. Palmer, for his great powers of mind and gentle heart in those terrible days of doubt and upheaval in the church when he first began to work in New Orleans, quietly yet surely drew the wanderers back to the fold of their childhood. His faith strengthened the faith of the faithful and calmed the fears of the doubting. His discourses, burning with fire, thronged the church Sunday after Sunday.[8]

---

7. Palmer, "Christ's Love to His People," in *A Weekly Publication Containing Sermons*, 2.102.

8. "Dr Palmer's Career," *The Daily Picayune*, New Orleans, Louisiana, 29 May 1902.

Unitarianism receded in New Orleans and Trinitarianism rapidly expanded through Palmer's ministry. First Presbyterian Church became full to the gills and planted thirteen churches in New Orleans and the surrounding region.[9] Similar movements had already taken shape in Columbia and Charleston, South Carolina, through James Henley Thornwell and Thomas Smyth (1808-1873).[10]

James Henley Thornwell

After Thornwell's father passed away at a young age, his most influential father-figure became William Robbins, a prominent attorney in Cheraw, South Carolina. Robbins, along with James Gillespie, a wealthy planter, perceived the intellectual abilities of young Thornwell, took him under their wing, and financed his education. During his late-teenage years, Thornwell lived with and was mentored by Robbins.

Robbins had grown up in Massachusetts, was brought up in the Unitarian faith, and influenced Thornwell in that direction. He was later converted to Trinitarianism through the aforementioned evangelist Daniel Baker, and he joined Saint David's Episcopal Church in Cheraw. But before he was converted, Robbins sent Thornwell to study under another Unitarian, Thomas Cooper, the president of South Carolina College (today, the University of South Carolina). Like many of the students at the college, Thornwell became transfixed by Cooper's intellect, so much so that Thornwell professed Cooper to be his idol. But the college's professor of philosophy, Robert Henry, a "thoroughgoing advocate of the Nicene creed," challenged Thornwell to rethink the Unitarianism he had imbibed from Robbins and Cooper.[11] Eventually, Thornwell was converted to the Trinitarian faith and entered the ministry.

---

9. Ibid.

10. Nance, *Adorable Trinity*, 25–94; 95–148.

11. James Thornwell, "Memoir of Dr Henry," *Southern Quarterly Review 3*, no. 1 (April 1856), 202.

Through the influence of the Presbyterians in the state legislature, Thornwell became chaplain and then president of South Carolina College for the express purpose of undoing Cooper's work and winning back the institution, the city, and the state for the Trinitarian faith. His chief objective was "persuading others to duplicate his own personal history of conversion" and "this was to repudiate Thomas Cooper."[12] Through Thornwell's influence at the college, from the pulpit of First Presbyterian Church, and finally as professor at Columbia Seminary, the city of Columbia and the Palmetto State were turned away from Unitarianism and back to the Trinitarian faith.

Here is a sample of the type of preaching he provided to the South Carolina undergraduates—the future culture-shapers of the state—week by week at the college chapel:

> The evidence, perhaps, upon which the large majority of Christians receive [the doctrine of the Trinity] is the spiritual experience of their own hearts. They have not studied isolated texts nor collected together the names, titles and achievements which are promiscuously ascribed to each of the Persons of the Godhead; but they have been conscious of their own moral necessities – they have admired the beauty and rejoiced in the fitness of those exquisite arrangements by which their need has been relieved. They know, because they have felt, the love of the Father, the grace of the Son, and the communion of the Holy Spirit....That scheme stands like a temple of majestic proportions, and bears visibly engraved upon its portals, not only the name of God, like the ancient temple of Isis, but also the sublime mystery of His personal distinctions. In walking about Zion, telling her towers and marking well her bulwarks, we perceive the hand of the Father, the hand of the Son and the hand of the Holy Ghost. There are palaces adorned for the great King which we are exhorted to consider, for there the Trinity reigns, there God displays his mysterious personality, and the whole house is filled with His glory.[13]

---

12. Michael O'Brien, *Conjectures of Order: Intellectual Life and the American South, 1810–1860*, 2 vols. (Chapel Hill: University of North Carolina Press, 2004), 1117.

13. Thornwell, *Collected Writings*, edited by John B. Adger and John L. Girardeau, 4 vols. (Richmond: Presbyterian Committee of Publication, 1871), 2.343–45.

Through such preaching, Thornwell accomplished what he had been tasked to do by "breaking down the spirit of infidelity, which had largely taken possession of the State."[14] In his tenth year at the college, he wrote, "Under God's blessing, I have succeeded beyond what I could hope, in changing the whole current of association upon the speculative question of the truth of Christianity."[15] Contrary to Cooper's vision and confident predictions, Presbyterianism grew rapidly and Unitarianism waned in Columbia. By the early decades of the twentieth century, First Presbyterian Church had planted six more churches in Columbia, while the Unitarian movement petered out.[16]

Thomas Smyth

Similarly in Charleston, Thomas Smyth countered the Unitarian movement popularized by Samuel Gilman. Smyth, originally from Ireland, had courted a Unitarian girl in his youth, and, for that reason, had examined Unitarianism for himself. Years later, after graduating from Princeton Seminary and commencing his ministry in Charleston, Smyth was able to lead her to the Trinitarian faith. He led many others in Charleston to know the Triune God of grace, including a college student named John L. Girardeau, who sat under his preaching at Second Presbyterian Church.

Through his sermons such as "Unitarianism Not the Gospel: Occasioned by the Recent Discourse of the Rev. Samuel Gilman" and his voluminous articles in which he sought to respond to Gilman's attacks on Trinitarianism, Smyth tirelessly laboured for the soul of Charleston. He sought to show the crucial differences between Unitarianism and Trinitarianism:

---

14. Benjamin Morgan Palmer, *The Life and Letters of James Henley Thornwell* (Richmond: Whittet & Shepperson, 1875), 300.

15. Ibid.

16. David B. Calhoun, *The Glory of the Lord Risen Upon It: First Presbyterian Church Columbia, South Carolina 1795–1995* (Columbia: R.L. Bryan, 1994), 194; Nance, *Adorable Trinity*, 94.

They involve a total difference of sentiment in regard to the God we worship, the medium of worship, the nature of all true and acceptable worship, and the way by which alone any of our guilty and sinful race can ever become sanctified and acceptable worshippers in the church on earth, and in the first born in heaven. One or the other must be false. Both cannot be true.[17]

According to Smyth, the doctrine of the Trinity is the "central Sun, around which the whole system of Christianity, in all its glory, and in all its harmony, revolves."[18] The Trinity worked through Smyth to call the city of Charleston away from their enamorment with Unitarianism and back to the apostolic faith.

In 1822, Thomas Jefferson, a disciple of Unitarian Joseph Priestley and an orchestrator of the Southern Unitarian movement, had written his friend, Harvard professor Benjamin Waterhouse, "I trust that there is not a young man now living in the United States who will not die an Unitarian."[19] This vision, which was held by the majority of Unitarians in the early to mid-nineteenth century, did not materialize in large measure due to the faithfulness of Smyth, Thornwell, and Palmer and their stands for the Trinity in the three Southern cities where Unitarianism had gained its greatest momentum.

Their ministries remind us that each generation of Christian ministers must keep central the doctrine and implications of the Trinity. Trinitarianism is the Christian faith, "once for all delivered to the saints" (Jude 1:3). As Dr. Kelly likes to say, "the greatest gift we have to offer the world is the Triune God himself." Southern Presbyterians like Thornwell, Smyth, and Palmer knew this to be the case, and they offered the Trinity, prayerfully, freely, and winsomely for the salvation of souls, the preservation of the faith, the edification of the church, the transformation of the culture, and the glory of our Triune God.

---

17. Thomas Smyth, *The Complete Works of Thomas Smyth* edited by J. W. Flinn. 10 vols. (Columbia: R. L. Bryan Company, 1905–1912), 9.322.

18. Thomas Smyth, "The Doctrine of the Trinity, Not Theoretical or Speculative, but Practical in its Nature and Fundamental in its Importance," *Southern Presbyterian Review 8*, no. 2 (October 1854), 158.

19. Jefferson to Waterhouse, 26 June 1822, Thomas Jefferson Papers, Library of Congress.

An Emphasis on Grace

As we have seen, these Southern Presbyterians did not present the Trinity as a doctrinal box to be checked or a cold mathematical formula. Instead, they knew and preached the Father who says to us through the gracious Gospel of his incarnate Son and by the assurance of his indwelling Spirit of adoption, "I love you, and there is nothing you can do about it." They knew that Christianity is not another religion of do-goodism or self-salvation. They knew themselves to be sinners in need of sovereign grace. They knew something of their flesh's own pride and tendencies toward pharisaism. In his prayer journal, Thornwell asked his Heavenly Father, "Save me from a legal spirit ... May my heart be the temple of the Holy Ghost ... Reveal to me thy glory in the person of your Son ... May I see his loveliness and surrender myself unreservedly to him."[20]

When James Henley Thornwell is mentioned today, especially in the Reformed branch of the Church, such sentiments are not what first come to mind. Instead, it is Thornwell's participation in and defence of Southern slavery—race-based chattel slavery—that have taken center stage. Especially in the last few years, the understandable question has become, "Should we speak of men such as Thornwell, Palmer, and Smyth in any positive way? Given their positions on race and their defense of slavery, can't we just erase them from our spiritual heritage and remove them from our theological vocabulary?" To do so is tempting. In one sense, it is the easiest path forward: "Let's just distance ourselves from them altogether."

But is doing so Christian? Does it comport with the grace of our Triune God? In his excellent book, *ReGrace: What the Shocking Beliefs of the Great Christians Can Teach Us Today*, Frank Viola examines the flawed views and lives of such stalwarts as C. S. Lewis, Jonathan Edwards, Martin Luther, and John Calvin. But his purpose is productive rather than punitive. He writes,

---

20. James Henley Thornwell Journal, JHT Papers, C. Benton Kline, Jr. Special Collections and Archives.

[T]he purpose of this book is not to lower these individuals in your eyes. It's actually the opposite. It's to show you that despite their strange (and sometimes flawed) thinking on some issues, God still used them. Mightily, even. The lesson, of course, is that God uses His people in spite of their strange or erroneous perspectives. And since that's the case, let's have more grace whenever we disagree with one another.[21]

I believe this productive, gracious approach to church history and church life is what is needed regarding the Southern Presbyterians of the nineteenth century. This is not to minimize their racial sins. It is not to defend their flawed positions on race or downplay the harm that their decisions about race have caused. Instead, it is to say that we can learn from and even honor flawed saints who have come before us. Does not the Hall of Faith in Hebrews 11 teach us that?

We should not put anyone on a pedestal. As Dr. Kelly said when he "preached me in" at Ballantyne Presbyterian Church, "The hero of the Christian faith is none other than Jesus Christ, for 'he who is from above is above all'" (John 3:31). During their lifetimes and for years thereafter Southern leaders like Thornwell, Palmer, and Smyth were treated like celebrity pastors. They were put on pedestals. Their racism and sectionalism were reconstrued and defended. And the church was weakened in its witness because of it.

Faithful scholarship and faithful Christianity involve eschewing the tendency towards idolatry of our leaders (past and present) on the one hand and cancellation of them because of their flaws (perceived and real) on the other. Faithful scholarship and faithful Christianity involve honest appraisals and critiques, coupled with humility and grace.

As Viola reminds us,

Every follower of Jesus is a rough draft. Over time, the great Editor – the Holy Spirit – shapes our lives and views. But until we see the Lord, and we 'know even as we are known,' we are all in process. This is also true

---

21. Frank Viola, *ReGrace: What the Shocking Beliefs of the Great Christians Can Teach Us Today* (Grand Rapids: Baker Books, 2019), 19.

for the great Christians who have gone before us. Therefore, one of the mistakes we should guard against is the temptation to dismiss a person's entire contribution because they may hold (or have held) to ideas we find difficult to stomach.[22]

Navigating these waters is hard. We will not do so perfectly. But we must seek to do so in a way that comports with the Gospel of Triune grace. We must do so in a way that is honest about our flaws as the Church, past and present, but also honest about the power of the Triune God of grace to redeem and work through fallen sinners for his glory and the good of all who bear his image.

---

22. Ibid., 23.

14

The Great Transit of Mercy

Union with Christ in His Descent and Ascent

Gerrit S. Dawson

THIS essay will explore two often overlooked creedal events in the saving work of Jesus Christ: his descent to the dead in spirit and his ascent to heaven in the flesh. Focus on these expands the usual range of our consideration of his salvation. Jesus went further "down" and "up" than we normally realize. Recovering consideration of the extent of Christ's journey to redeem us can invigorate the worship of the church and build wider, stronger gospel bridges to the lost.

But first, some words about five qualities of the man this *festschrift* honors, all of which have influenced this chapter.

Douglas Kelly the Christian Pastor and Theologian

1) A Huge Vision of the Triune God

The afternoon our systematics class fell on Maundy Thursday, Dr. Kelly went off syllabus and took us to the scene of Jesus's arrest in John 18. Awe came over the class at the authority in Jesus's reply as the thugs tried to arrest him. They sneered, "We seek Jesus of Nazareth." Christ answered calmly, "I Am." The armed soldiers shrank back and fell to the ground. Then Douglas said, as he would later record in his Systematic Theology, "A beam of uncreated light suddenly streamed through the thick darkness of the Judean night; a surge of deity rushed through the manhood of our Lord, and down they all went, flat out before God Almighty!"[1] We felt as if we had been taken behind the inner curtain for a peak at the beauty and majesty of our humble King. Another time, after rather calm prayer for someone uncomfortably afflicted, Doug said, "Of course evil has to flee, for nothing is remotely as great Replace with: as the Holy Trinity." It was as simple as that. The more he has learned, the more Dr. Kelly reveres the grandeur of God.

2) Prayer Undergirds Everything

Such faith in the Trinity leads Douglas to an intentional and passionate prayer life. If you or a loved one has ever gotten on his prayer list, you *know* many effectual prayers have gone up. Years later, he asked me about a child for whom he prayed diligently for more than a decade. In his teaching days, Doug invited many students to join him for regular weekly prayer in the book-laden sanctuary of his study. In later years, to visit him in his home is synonymous with an invitation to morning or evening prayer. He enacts consistently his belief in prayer's efficacy.

3) Robust Humor

Such vision and practice leads one to so much confidence in the sovereignty of God that this grim world fails to dampen joy. Doug overflows with *bon homme*. I can hear him as he passed out an exam, "Now this will be good for your sanctification!" Or asking, after quoting a medieval theologian, "Would you like me to write that out in the Old French?" (There were never any takers). Exceedingly learned, but never stuffy, Doug's infectious good spirits render him fun to be around.

---

1. Douglas F. Kelly, *Systematic Theology, Volume Two: The Beauty of Christ: A Trinitarian Vision* (Geanies House: Mentor, 2014), 357.

4) Reformed and Catholic

Douglas Kelly has never left his roots in Scottish Presbyterianism, from the Isle of Harris to the coastal plain of eastern Carolina. Yet he knows that our stream of Reformed faith flows from and leads back to the great deep and ancient river of historic orthodoxy. So in one lecture or book chapter, he might quote from Athanasius *and* John Owen, Dumitru Staniloae *and* Willie Still, Thomas Torrance *and* Samuel Rutherford. Doug's long confidence in Westminster theology leads him peacefully to read widely and gather compatible, enriching insights from other traditions in the "one holy catholic and apostolic church."

5) Theology Serves the Church

Douglas writes and teaches under the patristic demand that the doctors of the church be filled with *eusebeia*. Such devoted piety is essential to expressing proper theology. Dr. Kelly has ever worked from the patristic understanding expressed by Torrance that "godliness and theology, worship and faith, went inseparably together ... [Theology requires] a mode of worship, behaviour and thought ... devout and worthy of God the Father, the Son, and the Holy Spirit"[2] Theological inquiry has to have a source in consecration to the triune God and a purpose in the building up of Christ's people. Theology properly undertaken always leads to doxology, which leads to mission.

The Lengths of the Journey of Jesus

As the 20th century wore on, J. I. Packer lamented the shrinking of the gospel story in many contemporary presentations. Too often, the modern church has narrowed the gospel to an easy *believism* in the efficacy of the cross. Often unwittingly, we offer a version of finding "your best life now" on the way to a personal designer heaven. Thus, the magnificence of Christ's work, the overarching purpose of the Father for his creation, and the implications for our Spirit-prompted response have grown shallow. Packer writes,

---

2. Thomas F. Torrance, *The Trinitarian Faith* (Edinburgh: T & T Clark, 1988), 17.

the whole story of the Father's Christ-exalting plan of redeeming love, from eternity to eternity, must be told, or the radical reorientation of life for which the gospel calls will not be understood, and the required total shift from man-centeredness to God-centeredness, and more specifically from self-centeredness to Christ-centeredness, will not take place.[3]

It is not enough to reduce the gospel to a transaction at the cross. There is an entire interconnected series of events through which redemption has occurred. That bigger story of Jesus vitally shapes and then energizes the church for its mission to the world.

John Calvin understood the importance of the entire incarnate life of Jesus when he considered how our salvation was accomplished. Calvin acknowledged that Scripture ascribes the mode of salvation "as peculiar and proper to Christ's death." But that sacrifice only "works" because of its larger context in Christ's life of faithfulness. Calvin thus raised and answered the question,

> How has Christ abolished sin, banished the separation between us and God, and acquired righteousness to render God favorable and kindly toward us? To this we can in general reply that he has achieved this for us by *the whole course of his obedience* ... In short, *from the time when he took on the form of a servant,* he began to pay the price of liberation in order to redeem us.[4]

From the time when "[t]he Word became flesh" (John 1:14) to when "he entered once for all into the holy places" (Heb. 9:12), Christ Jesus was effecting our redemption. In fact, by looking at these events prior to and following the cross, we can deepen our understanding of this central atoning act. In particular, we want to take up the parts of Jesus's journey along which he passed through the realm of the dead and when, resurrected, he entered heaven.

So in the spirit of Douglas Kelly's century-spanning, tradition-crossing and genre-mixing curation of true theological insights, we turn to a 21st century prayer by a Catholic scholar based on

---

3. J.I. Packer, *Affirming the Apostles' Creed* (Wheaton: Crossway, 2008), 22–23.

4. John Calvin, *Institutes of the Christian Religion*, ed. John T. McNeil, trans. Ford Lewis Battles (Philadelphia: Westminster Press, 1960), 2.16.5. Italics mine.

a 6th century homily from Gregory the Great. William Storey provides the title of this chapter when he writes,

> Lord Jesus Christ,
> From the bosom of the Father
> You descended into
> The womb of the Virgin,
> From the womb you visited the cradle,
> From the cradle you came to the cross,
> From the cross to the tomb,
> From the tomb you arose in glory
> And ascended into heaven.
>
> By this great transit of mercy—
>
> you becoming as we are
> and we becoming as you are—
> grant us, O Savior of the world,
> the fullness of our divine adoption
> as sons and daughters of the living God.[5]

Jesus engaged a transit, a passage, through and beyond our life in the world to extend God's mercy to us. By his whole journey, he saves us. Storey, as a liturgical scholar, knows that *transitus* is the Latin word used for Passover. Since the time of Augustine, the church has understood Jesus's Passover as his making the redemptive *passage* through the suffering of death into resurrection. By his Passover, Jesus is the sacrificial Lamb whose blood averts God's wrath and takes away our sins.[6] He also is the pioneer and perfecter of our faith (Heb. 12:1) who crossed death's Red Sea during his descent to the dead. In coming out from the dead, rising, and then ascending into heaven, Jesus opened up

---

5. William G. Storey, *Prayers of Christian Consolation* (Chicago: Loyola Press, 2010), 186. Interestingly, ninth-century Anglo-Saxon poet Cynewulf also built from Gregory's imagery of Christ's leaps in his poem about the ascension, "Christ II." See Eleanor Parker, *Winters in the World* (London: Reaktion Books, 2022), 163–65.

6. 1 Cor. 5:7–8. See also Raniero Cantalamessa, *The Mystery of Easter* (Collegeville: The Liturgical Press, 1993), 14–18. And Phillip Pfatteicher *Journey into the Heart of God: Living the Liturgical Year* (Oxford: Oxford University Press, 2013), 215–216.

for us the Promised Land of everlasting life in communion with God. Christ's Passover, his great transit of mercy, contains all the events, inextricably linked, from incarnation through the ascent. We turn our attention now first to the meaning, and then to the implications, of two of those events, Jesus's descent in spirit to the dead and his ascent to heaven in the flesh.

What Do We Mean by Descent to the Dead?

In his concentrated formula of the essence of the gospel, Paul writes to the Corinthians, "For I delivered to you as of first importance what I also received: that Christ died for our sins in accordance with the Scriptures, that he was buried, that he was raised on the third day ... that he appeared ..." (1 Cor. 15:3–5). Paul asserts an interval between cross and resurrection. Saturday. And the time surrounding Saturday when Jesus's body was buried and stayed buried. These were the 27 to 39 of our earthly hours during which Jesus's spirit sojourned in the realm of the dead. The Westminster Larger Catechism affirms, "Christ's humiliation after his death consisted in his being buried, and continuing in the state of the dead, and under the power of death until the third day."[7]

So Jesus was not resurrected straight from the cross. He engaged the death that all people since Adam (except Enoch and Elijah) had experienced. His spirit separated from his body and entered the realm of the dead (*Sheol* in Hebrew, *Hades* in Greek). This Dr. Kelly names as "the world of departed spirits."[8] From earliest times, humans have thought of the place of the dead as downward. We are, after all, gravity bound creatures. The vitality of life enables us to get up and work, worship, love, and play. But age and illness steal our strength and eventually cause us to fall down, not up, into death. We need not debate the differences in cosmologies across centuries and cultures. The imagery of going

---

7. The Westminster Larger Catechism, A.50. (Glasgow: The Publications Committee of the Free Presbyterian Church of Scotland, 1970), 152.

8. Kelly, *Systematic Theology* 2, 417.

downward in death resonates with us, without our necessarily believing one could spelunk down a passage and encounter souls of the dead. In the Old Testament, this spiritual world of Sheol/Hades was variously envisioned as beneath the bottom of the sea (John 2:5-6) or in the heart of the earth (Num. 16:30, cf. Matt. 12:40). The psalmist could compare Sheol to the pit (Ps. 30:3), evoking a place of discarded bodies, and souls bereft of vibrant embodied worship (Ps. 6:5). Sheol is the place of no return (Job 7:9), a tedious and shadowy existence (Eccl. 9:10), with awareness of other souls (Isa. 14:9) without the fellowship of feeling home (Ps. 49:14). Paul once likened it to the mysterious abyss (Rom. 10:7) which has no bottom. Poetic personification imagines Sheol as always hungry for more souls (Prov. 27:20, Hab. 2:5). The fact that we have to use such imagery to describe a realm we cannot enter and then return from, does not mean the reality is *less* than the symbolic. The realm of death remains beyond our description, yet it is at least as grim as our most graphic depictions.

Into this state Jesus went between cross and resurrection. The New Testament refers often to *nekron,* the place, state or company, of the dead. Their bodies decay in the world; their spirits reside in shadowy Sheol. Thirty-five times, via seven different authors the New Testament describes Jesus's resurrection in terms of his being raised *ek nekron*, literally "out from dead." His spirit transitioned away from the company he had kept with the dead. He exited the state of death and returned to an embodied life on earth. To state the obvious, to be raised *ek nekron* implies that Jesus came from some place (or state) in order to return to life in the world. For Jesus to be raised necessarily means he had previously descended to the dead. Jesus, between cross and resurrection, shared the common human experience of disembodied afterlife.

This straightforward gospel assertion, however, has been complicated by translation confusion in Scripture and the Apostles' Creed. For instance, the perennially influential Authorized Version translates *Sheol/Hades* as well as *gehenna* (the state/place of damnation) with the same word: *hell.* Similarly, the older English versions of the Apostles' Creed affirm "He descended into hell," even though the original Greek (a variant of *katotera*, Eph. 4:9) and Latin (*inferos* or *inferna*) versions use words that mean more literally "the underneath" rather than the final state of God's judgment enacted.[9] The use of *hell* rather than *the dead* in translations obscures the important clarity of Holy Saturday in Sheol/Hades[10] as a crucial stage in Jesus's transit of mercy.

What Does It Mean That Jesus Ascended in the Flesh?

Gloriously, on the third day, Jesus rose bodily from the dead. The body that was crucified and buried was the same body in which Jesus showed himself alive to his disciples. Now, of course, that body had been transformed and glorified, outfitted for an embodied eternal life in heaven. Yet Jesus was and is, still Jesus.

Forty days after his resurrection, Jesus ascended to heaven, still incarnate. Across the world, people consider the heavenly realm to be "up," even though we know that "up" is quite relative for those on a spinning Replace with: globe hurtling around the sun. The church has always understood that "space travel was never in view."[11] Indeed, Calvin quipped, "What? Do we place Christ midway among the spheres? Or do we build a cottage for him among the planets? Heaven we regard as the magnificent palace of God, far outstripping all this world's fabric"[12] Jesus returned to heaven from whence he had come in the incarnation. Only now, the eternal Son of God retained the humanity he had assumed from us. He took flesh and blood into the spiritual realm, into the very presence of God.

---

9. For further exploration, see Appendix 1 in my book, *Raising Adam: Why Jesus Descended into Hell* (Edinburgh: Handsel Press and Union: Oil Lamp Books, 2018).

10. For further discussion on the ways in which Jesus's experience in Sheol may have been hellish, see my *Raising Adam*, chapter five, as well as the discussion in chapter one on three main ways a descent into hell as the state/place of judgment has been interpreted.

11. Douglas Farrow, *Ascension and Ecclesia: On the Significance of the Doctrine of the Ascension for Ecclesiology and Christian Cosmology* (Grand Rapids: Eerdmans, 1999), 39.

12. John Calvin, *Second Defense of Pious and Orthodox Faith Concerning Sacraments* in *Selected Works of John Calvin*, vol. 2, eds Henry Beveridge and Jules Bonnet, trans. Henry Beveridge (Albany: Books for the Ages, 1998), 270.

Scripturally, we see this astounding claim in passages such as Peter's affirming the great transit of mercy "through the resurrection of Jesus Christ, who has gone into heaven and is at the right hand of God" (1 Pet. 3:21–22). Paul would frame our hope of resurrected life in terms of receiving the same kind of body Jesus has now. Jesus will "transform our lowly body to be like his glorious body, by the power that enables him even to subject all things to himself" (Phil. 3:21). On Pentecost, Peter preached the story of Jesus's journey to the startled crowd, tracing his sojourn through the realm of death back to earth and then to heaven,

> this Jesus, delivered up according to the definite plan and foreknowledge of God, you crucified and killed by the hands of lawless men. God raised him up, loosing the pangs of death, because it was not possible for him to be held by it.

> [David] foresaw and spoke about the resurrection of the Christ, that he was not abandoned to Hades, nor did his flesh see corruption. This Jesus God raised up, and of that we all are witnesses. Being therefore exalted at the right hand of God, and having received from the Father the promise of the Holy Spirit, he has poured out this that you yourselves are seeing and hearing (Acts 2:23–24, 31–33).

We have ever embraced the double paradox that 1) the eternal Son of God took up our flesh and blood when he came to earth and 2) Jesus retained his embodied humanity in his return to his Father. As nineteenth-century Scottish theologian John "Rabbi" Duncan affirmed, "The dust of the earth now sits on the throne of the universe."[13] Or, as the Larger Catechism declares, "forty days after his resurrection, he, in our nature, and as our head, triumphing over enemies, visibly went up into the highest heavens."[14]

The story of Jesus's great transit of mercy expands our awareness of reality. Much, much more exists than what we can measure or even experience in this earthly realm. There is a place of departed spirits "below." There is a "place" where God is, "above" and beyond us. The journey of Jesus has bridged these realms. By defeating sin and death, Jesus has closed the gap between us

---

13. Kelly, *Systematic Theology* 2, 511.

14. Westminster Larger Catechism, A. 53.

and God in his ascension. And his journey of mercy is not over. The angel told the startled disciples as they watched their Lord depart, "This Jesus, who was taken up from you into heaven, will come in the same way as you saw him go into heaven" (Acts 1:7). Meanwhile, by his Spirit's connecting power, Jesus the God-man continues to be the bridge for humans to reunite with the triune God who made us. So we turn to consider three implications of Jesus's descent to the dead in spirit and his ascent to heaven in body.

1) Human Destiny in Christ Both Limited and Extended

Jesus experienced dereliction on the cross. Calvin's great insight was that the descent into hell as *gehenna* punishment for sin happened spiritually to Jesus during crucifixion. He writes of "that invisible and incomprehensible judgment which he underwent in the sight of God in order to that we might know not only that Christ's body was given as the price of our redemption, but that he paid a greater and more excellent price in suffering in his soul the terrible torments of a condemned and forsaken man."[15] Dr. Kelly elaborates that Jesus experienced the second death (eternal forsakenness, Rev. 20:6, 21:8) before he experienced the first death. "Because he is an infinite person, his suffering of hell for these three hours [on the cross] have been more than sufficient to exhaust all the fires and dark horrors of the infernal realm."[16] This pioneering Reformed insight highlights how judgement occurred for Jesus on the cross.

But we have been considering how Jesus's descent of humiliation had one stage further to go. Not to punishment, but to continuing in death. When Jesus died on the cross, his spirit/soul separated from his body. His corpse resided in Joseph's tomb. His spirit went to Sheol. Both remained sundered from each other until the third day. Baptized in blood on the cross, Jesus plunged into the abyss of death to which all souls previously had gone. He did not yet enter heaven. His body lay in the grave, not expected

---

15. Calvin, *Institutes*, 2.16.10.
16. Kelly, *Systematic Theology 2*, 381.

ever to walk in the land of the living again. His soul resided in the gloomy netherworld of death. The music of life stopped for the long pause of the Saturday between Good Friday and Easter.

This leg of his transit of mercy offers great comfort to those united to Christ through the Spirit in faith. We yet must die, if the Lord tarries. But we do not go to what Shakespeare called "the undiscovered country" (*Hamlet*, III.1). Though we speak in metaphors of what we cannot yet see, we can yet apprehend the truth. Christ has explored death and exhausted its mysteries. He has by his presence lit up its dark chambers. Sheol has been traversed, subdued, and rendered obsolete for those in Christ. Our spirits, though rent from our bodies in death, will not wait in Sheol but go immediately to be with the Lord (Phil. 1:23). Though we slip away from our loved ones in our dying, we are not ever alone. For Christ has sojourned through death and illuminated its passageways all the way from earth to heaven.

Jesus altered the experience of death for all believers! The destiny of those in Christ has been limited to bodily death that sends our spirits into God's immediate presence. There, with Christ, we will await the resurrection bodies that will be like his. This is the truth hinted at in Psalm 139:8, "If I ascend to heaven, you are there! / If I make my bed in Sheol, you are there!" We cannot be parted from him to whom the Spirit has joined us. And in him, we will see our beloveds again.

Moreover (more gloriously over!), we do not fear the final judgment all humans will face. The Judge is our Redeemer. His second death on the cross has removed that as a possibility for those united to him. Our once destiny into abyss has been forever curtailed. Thus, we face death companioned by Jesus through his Holy Spirit. We step into death peacefully confident that we are joined to the journey of Jesus. He has blazed a path for us, and he will ensure we will not stray from the trail he has blazed, nor fail to follow it.

At the same time, the ascension of Jesus opens up for us a limitless upward destiny. Jesus did not shed his resurrected flesh as he ascended. He did not unzip his skin suit. He embodies our humanity into eternity. Jesus, the last Adam, is man remade. He is the restart of the human race, the fulfillment of all we were meant to be. Our creational communion with God has not merely been restored in Christ. It has been expanded to everlasting capacity to know the Triune God in always deeper, higher, more creative and expressive ways into eternity. Our destiny as adopted sons and daughters is ascension in Christ—with Christ—unto active participation in the Triune life of love.

The world may show us a fetid stream of images of humanity disgraced, suggesting we can never rise above our basest impulses. The culture may portend further descent into lawlessness. Chaos in relationships and disintegration of mind, body, and soul may seem our only future. But none of this is so! Christ Jesus ascended is our anchor in the heavenlies (Heb. 6:19). We are destined for glory. By Jesus's descent in spirit, death now has a floor. By his ascension to heaven in body, heaven now has an unlimited ceiling for his brothers and sisters.

2) Present Experience Deepened and Heightened

One of the most striking by-products of union with Christ is realism about life in the present world. Someone once said, "When I came to Christ, I realized that all along I had been seeing the world in black and white, but now I was seeing in color." This enhanced experience of life includes the sorrow as well as the pleasure.

The more we meditate on the reality that Jesus entered death and stayed in death until the third day, the more squarely we will reckon with the fact of death in this world now. Christian realists do not avoid contemplating death, nor join a post-Christian culture in pretending it won't happen to us or our loved ones. We are not surprised when we stand at graveside and weep over loss. We are aware constantly that separation is coming, sooner or later, in a world such as this. Indeed, we feel as keenly as any existentialist the sorrowful futility that all life in the world inevitably dies. We participate in the groaning of all creation that has been "subjected to futility" and placed "in bondage to corruption" (Rom. 8:20–21). Christian realists feel acutely that the world is not the way it's supposed to be.

So we willingly enter the sorrows of our Savior along the way of his great transit of mercy. We shudder at the force of temptations which came against him. Our hearts sorrow to realize we may well have turned against Jesus with the self-righteousness of Pharisees. The deeper we press into Christ, the more we watch him in Gethsemane with tears. We feel crushed under the weight of the sin of the world placed upon him. Breath catches to feel a minute fraction of his loneliness when he who loved God with full and pure heart could not find his Father. We contemplate the cross resolutely though we would rather turn away as we know more truly every year, "Ah holy Jesus ... I crucified thee." We sit in the silence of Holy Saturday imagining a world without Jesus, and tasting a drop of the despair his disciples felt.

This connection to Jesus in this dark stage of his path of redemption, in turn, makes us empathetic to those suffering loss, depression, temptation, or despair. We come awake to the fear and pain of those whom Paul described as "having no hope and without God in the world" (Eph. 2:12). We weep over all the Jerusalems of the world who do not know the possibility of Christ's consolation (Mt. 23:37). Sharply, we lament how the Father's will is not being done on earth as it is in heaven. We grow through suffering and sympathy to share Jesus's heart for the world.

At the very same time, the exaltation of Jesus refreshes our spirits. The way the world is now is not the way the world will stay. Jesus retains his humanity. He remains in flesh, and that body is no longer subject to futility. His body is glorified. The ascended Jesus is himself the pledge of our future. If some power could go to the Father's right hand and pull Jesus down, our hopes would be frail indeed. But our future is as secure as his Lordship. What's coming is as certain as Jesus's name being exalted above every name in heaven, on earth and under the earth (Phil. 2:9–11). Christ's ascension in body remains our constant, objective, source of joy.

Therefore, even as we experience the ugliness of the world more poignantly than others, we who are united to Christ see the beauty that remains with precious appreciation. We see stars shining that our evil cannot reach. We sing over spring growth pushing up through frozen ground. We bless God that new lives still get born into the world. We realistically become a contagiously joyful people.

But more. The ascension of Jesus in the flesh is the firstfruits of a restored creation. The triune God has not let his creation go down to Sheol. He closed that passage behind him. Jesus has opened the way to resew the old field of creation with the new creation he began. Feeling this joy the patristics had over the ascension's effects on creation, I once wrote,

> All that is good, all that is joyful and loving in this flesh has been taken up. So dance! Nothing good in our humanity is lost. The memory of a body that works in health is more than recollection: it is now anticipation. The ache of true love once known but now sundered will be filled with glorious reunion. The feeling of the distant memory of Beauty, the ideal of Truth in a fallen world, the longing for Goodness that surfaces amidst the choking thorns of our wickedness, all these will find fulfillment when the firstfruits [of Christ's ascension] comes to harvest.[17]

Jesus's descent in spirit to the dead directs us to see and face the death in the world resolutely. His ascension in body opens us up, even amidst so much loss and evil, to the possibility of laughing, loving, and feeling fully alive in this world. Christ's exaltation liberates us from the soul-crushing humorless conformity of the present age. Now we partake of the mirth of heaven. Embracing the deeper and higher story of Jesus makes life for those in Christ relentlessly realistic and, paradoxically, continuously joyous.

3) Worship and Mission of the Church Focused and Intensified

Jesus's descent into death and his bodily ascent to heaven shapes the worship of his church. As realists being formed by the whole course of Christ's obedience, we recover the place of Biblical lament. We cannot be content with only playing happy church. We cannot preach mere practical advice for more successful

---

17. Gerrit Scott Dawson, *Jesus Ascended: The Meaning of Christ's Continuing Incarnation* (London: T&T Clark; Phillipsburg: Presbyterian & Reformed, 2004), 113.

living. Our worship gathers up the sorrows of living in such a world. We name and express the pain of relational brokenness, long time discrimination, hatred from nonbelievers, crime, and the effects of generational poverty. We recognize in prayer, music, and preaching that Holy Saturday is a present experience for many. Our Lord knew the full stop of death. He experienced forsakenness and not being rescued immediately. Linked to his great transit of mercy, we pass with others through the seasons of sorrow and darkness. Our worship rhythms will include expressions of this realism. Thus by listening to and expressing sorrow, we will draw a weary world to its only hope.

At the very same time, our worship will exude the joy that exults in the midst of suffering. Jesus went up, bearing his rich wounds, to the right hand of the Father. He has secured our future even as he has not spared us passing through suffering and death. Worship informed by his season in death and his glory in ascending will be transformative for our congregations. We will experience "on ramps" into the vicarious pain and wounds of Jesus. Then, joined to him, we will ascend in hope to the glory he prepares for us, tasting it even now, especially gathered around the table of his Supper. The joy of our worship will be all the sweeter for its realism, both about the world and about Jesus.

Such worship, of course, energizes and influences the ministry and mission of the church. Our counselling ministries will take the long journey of hearing trauma, carrying pain, and gently offering both to the ascended Christ. Our prayers will invite the Spirit to descend to the regions of death in the hearts of broken ones. We will discern how Jesus is already shining light in these depths.

Our outreach ministries will realize that because Jesus descended to the dead, there is no place on earth, no people on earth, to whom we are not called. We will pray to discern which of our community's hells we are called to tend. Where God seems absent, as if it were Holy Saturday, we will go with the news that Jesus has passed through death to the right hand of the Father. Because he is still the same Jesus who walked among us, we know that he still has the same concern for the sinners, the outcast, the infirm and the prodigal. He is pulling this world towards himself in ascension, and we want to help untangle those he is drawing that they might joyfully arise and go to Jesus.

Conclusion

Jesus undertook a great transit of mercy for us. He sojourned through the realm of death in order to transform that passage for all who are joined to him. He went up to heaven still incarnate as the pledge of what we will receive and be in union with him. These two oft-neglected events actually reinforce one another. The ascension secures the redemptive nature of his descent to the dead. The ancient church imagined that the cross was erected over the place where Adam's skull was buried. So we might further imagine that the base of the cross is planted in the depths of Sheol, for Jesus's journey from the cross descended that low. We might also imagine that the top of the cross reaches to the throne of heaven. For the victory Jesus won in his dying lifts him through death, resurrection, and ascension to the Father. Highlighting these legs of his journey does not diminish but magnifies the cross. Rather, we see his cross now spanning death and heaven. For joined to Jesus, we participate in his passage through death to life. We may live on earth seated with Christ in the heavenly places (Eph. 2:6). In becoming what we are, even in our dying, Jesus gives us who are joined to him all that he is. For in his transit of mercy, he has undertaken to conform us to his image (Rom. 8:29) and make us like himself (1 John 3:2). In that faith we are energized to soar in worship and reach the world with the gospel.

Part 5:

Faithfulness in
Our Present Generation

15

Manifesting the Atmosphere of a Different World

An Appreciative Engagement of Douglas Kelly's

A New Life in the Wasteland

Bill Bradford

Introduction

Dr. Kelly's *New Life in the Wasteland: 2 Corinthians on the Cost and Glory of Christian Ministry*, is a collection of thirteen sermons through most of the chapters of 2 Corinthians, which he originally gave on a preaching tour through Scotland to ministers of the Gospel.[1] The manuscripts were created from the sound recordings of Dr. Kelly's sermons, and as such they effectively convey his unique preaching style. In fact, especially endearing to those privileged to have sat under his ministry, one can easily imagine listening to him preach them.

As one would expect, these sermons exhibit Dr. Kelly's depth of insight into the text, his engagement with the culture,

---

1. Douglas F. Kelly, *New Life in the Wasteland: 2 Corinthians on the Cost and Glory of the Christian Ministry* (Geanies House: Christian Focus Publications, 2003).

his breadth of reading, his stories from his own and other's ministries, his visual language, his heartfelt appeals, and his concrete applications. They also manifest that stirring quality of his preaching in which you know he's trying to move you to raise your heart up to a place with the Lord that he so regularly inhabits—to his experience of union and communion with Christ. As I read these sermons, I go back to midweek prayer meetings in a rural church we both attended, in which he would lead us up to the throne of grace.

Dr. Kelly's purpose in these sermons is to set forth and apply the truths of 2 Corinthians in order to comfort, to inspire, and to instruct the people of God and especially pastors in their Gospel ministry to their churches and to the lost within the diseased, decaying, and often hostile cultures of Britain and America.

He opens by diagnosing the root cause of our "desert-like culture." Dr. Kelly preached these sermons in 1998 (though he began working through this series back in 1984), yet his evaluation then has only proved to be even more accurate today. We minister in a culture that instead of seeking to know God, which would result in life and health, has rather given itself to idols, which inevitably results in destruction (Hosea 8:4). Instead of conforming our desires to truth, we have conformed truth to our desires, and the core desire of Western culture is sexual license, which has driven its rejection of the God of the Bible and its embrace of a host of other gods—with all kinds of devastating effects on society. And, sadly, in the face of this cultural decline the Church has shown itself largely ineffective.

Proclaiming the Gospel of Hope in a Decaying World

So, what is to be done? Do we panic, despair, and retreat from the world? Do we try to recover our standing by changing the message and accommodating to the culture? Absolutely not! The church in Corinth faced the same sorts of opposition: sexual immorality, materialism, secularism, relativism, cynicism, violence, and social disintegration. Yet God in his grace transformed their society by his Word and Spirit, operating through the Church's ministry, and he can just as assuredly do so today.

Accordingly, a recurring theme throughout these sermons is our solid hope. God is at work, even when we cannot see it or feel it; therefore, as Dr. Kelly repeats, we should not despise the day of small things (Zech. 4:10). This realism about the deep problems joined to sure hope in God and trust in his powerful working is a regular emphasis of Dr. Kelly's preaching. He has a big view of God and, therefore, a big view of the power of pastoral ministry. It comes out beautifully in these sermons. Thus, the question is: how does God tend to work? Answering that question is the burden of this book.

God uses the message of the Gospel. The Gospel is not a message of "do-good moralism", nor is it a message of love as tolerance. It is the truth that Jesus Christ is the Savior of the world, the only Savior of the world. Our culture bristles at this exclusivity, but we celebrate it, for this message alone is the power of God for salvation.

The Gospel is that the Glory came down. God the Son became flesh. This is the greatest miracle, even greater than creation. He did so to obey God's law in our place and to endure God's judgment on our sin as our substitute. Then, once he satisfied the sentence of sin, he was resurrected from the dead. Therefore, 2 Corinthians 5:21 speaks of a "wondrous exchange" in which those who are united to Jesus by faith have their sins transferred to Jesus and Jesus's righteousness credited to them. 2 Corinthians 8:9 describes this "wondrous exchange" as Jesus leaving his riches behind in heaven to become poor for us, finally enduring the utter poverty of the humiliation of the cross and the torment of hell in our place. And he did this so that he might bestow on us all the riches of heaven, the very glory of God.

In his Gospel explanation, Dr. Kelly responds to a pair of poignant objections. Regarding 2 Corinthians 5:21, he voices the question, "Why does God have to punish his Son?"[2] He answers that the seriousness of our guilt is determined by the greatness

---

2. Ibid., 107–108.

of the one sinned against. God is infinite; therefore, our guilt is infinite. Only God himself can pay such a debt. For this reason, God must punish his Son in our place. But that leads into another question. Regarding 2 Corinthians 8:9, he asks, "If God is love, why does he even need to punish sin?"[3] He answers that love must be defined as the Bible defines it, not as our culture does. Scripture says God's love has a definite character: it is tender, compassionate, and self-sacrificing; and it is also holy and just. Were God to leave sin unpunished, his whole moral universe would implode. But the good news is that what God's holiness requires, his love provides in the atoning death of his Son.

As I write this, I remember Dr. Kelly in class pressing the point by gradually rolling up his tie as he spoke of God's holy love, then letting it loose and lurching forward as he said, "Were he not to punish sin, the universe would crack and cease to exist!"

On the basis of Jesus as the God-Man, our perfect Mediator who accomplishes all this on our behalf, Dr. Kelly says concerning 2 Corinthians 1:20 that Jesus becomes God's "Amen," establishing and securing all God's wonderful covenant promises to us.

We proclaim this Gospel to each other and to the world, even when it is opposed. And the Gospel's power especially comes as it transforms us. This is a major theme throughout these sermons. The wasteland of our culture is renewed as this Gospel changes us. In 2 Corinthians 3:2, Paul tells the Corinthian believers that they themselves are his letter of recommendation. Dr. Kelly comments: "The apostle says that Christian ministry is accredited not by ink on paper, but by the Holy Spirit drawing the lineaments of the character of the Lord Jesus Christ in the responses of the men and women who give themselves to the pattern of Christian truth that is proclaimed."[4]

Gazing on the Glory of Christ in Daily Life
Even more profoundly, 2 Corinthians 1:22 and 4:8 declare that when we are united to Christ by faith, God's Spirit, his sealing,

---

3. Ibid., 129–130.
4. Ibid., 60.

his down payment of the glory of heaven, enters our hearts and brings God's glory down inside us. We understand this glory as God's marvelous perfections, as much as can be communicated to a human personality, and especially his Trinitarian love, "the blissful fellowship of love between Father, Son and Holy Spirit— now flowing down to us" (2 Cor. 4:7).[5] It is God's resplendent light, his holiness, purity, and righteousness filling us and shining through us to others. (2 Cor. 3:8ff.; 4:6). It is God's undeserved love and mercy for us in Christ moving out from us to the lives of others who are also undeserving (2 Cor. 4:1; 5:14). As important as the apologetic work of arguing the truth of Christ before an idolatrous culture is, the most effective apology is the changed lives of believers, as we become God's "Amens" to the world (2 Cor. 1:20), transformed into Jesus's image, "from one degree of glory to another" (2 Cor. 3:18), living as "new creations" (2 Cor. 5:17), expressing God's lavish generosity to others (2 Cor. 9:1).

Dr. Kelly says: "The Christian ministry's effectiveness is that the gospel becomes translated into flesh and blood, and that has a way of beginning to transform an entire society. That is how the West became Christian."[6] Or again,

> The glory of God came down and began to change an entire world one by one by one. It is the same today. The same glory can come down and work the most miraculous changes in a small community, a larger one, or a whole culture. As Jesus is lifted up, he will draw his own to himself and transform them. No culture, no matter how sophisticated its pretensions, can hold back this light."[7]

Jesus's resurrection power brings God's glory down into the life of the believer for the saving of our dying world.

2 Corinthians 3:18 urges on us our most basic means of growing. We are transformed as we gaze upon Christ. That which you behold, you become like. If we look on superficial and hollow gods, we will become superficial and hollow. If we look

---

5. Ibid., 83.
6. Ibid., 62.
7. Ibid., 79.

upon Christ, God's glory comes down, and we start looking more like him. I love how Dr. Kelly says that we begin "breathing and manifesting the atmosphere of a different world."[8]

Again, this is one of the hallmarks of Dr. Kelly's ministry effectiveness. He makes a practice of gazing upon Christ. We all sense it in his praying and preaching. Neither his exegesis in itself, nor his ability to marshal the thoughts and experiences of so many authors, nor his homespun illustrations, as integral and compelling as all that is, lie at the root of Dr. Kelly's impact. It lies, rather, in the fact he not only tells you about God but proceeds to let you into his own devotional life with God—the result of gazing upon Christ in his studies, in his praying, and in his relationships with people. We sense God's glory. His own ministry effectiveness is an outflow of his personal application of the truths about which he writes, especially concerning Jesus' resurrection power bringing God's glory down inside us as we abide in Christ.

Dr. Kelly's son, Patrick, passed along a story from Dr. Kelly's early ministry. One of his parishioners said that one day Dr. Kelly walked into a hardware store, and the love of God and the presence of the Spirit was so shining through him that it moved the cashier attending him to start weeping and ask him how to be saved.

I still remember a sermon he preached in which he kept asking, "Where are you looking?" A big part of why that simple question made such an impact on me was because I knew he was speaking from a depth of personal experience about which I was only faintly acquainted. I wanted a closeness with God that I knew he had.

I also remember one time after Dr. Kelly preached, that Mrs. Kelly said to him, "You had that face on that says, 'I want to be invisible.'" I really appreciated that. He was never promoting himself, but Christ. He didn't want us to be amazed at him but amazed at the One who amazed him. In fact, he had no personal desire to be up front, but his zeal to lift up Christ had him there. It recalls to mind Paul's words: "For what we proclaim is not ourselves, but Jesus Christ as Lord ..." (2 Cor. 4:5).

---

8. Ibid., 61; cf. p. 117.

Therefore, Dr. Kelly's counsel on 2 Corinthians 8:9 is so true and helpful. When the vitality and sweetness of Christian service has drained away and ministerial professionalism or detachment has set in, "... it's only a short step to reclaiming the fragrance and the beauty of a contagious Christian testimony. It comes back once again by a fresh and continuing look at the crucified One."[9]

Along with this are his admonitions of our need to be real with God, with all our imperfections—to be people of integrity seeking to be yielded to God in everything. What most distresses us should be our daily discovery of how unlike Christ we still are. Our prayer, accordingly, is that God would help us apply the message to ourselves before we apply it to others. We endeavor to renounce secret sin (2 Cor. 4:2). We live before our relativistic culture like there really is right and wrong (which is one of the best things we can do for the world!). We practice loving our wives and children well. We strive to forgive others. We meet our financial obligations. We resist the materialism of our culture. We put others first. We seek to be generous with what we have in order to show compassion to those in need (2 Cor. 8:1-9:15).

I always appreciate that about Dr. Kelly's preaching. He has the ability to move from meditating on the lofty wonders of Christ down to clear action items, such as, "Where are you looking? Offer what gifts you have to Christ. Tithe. Pray. Fast. Keep the Sabbath. Cut away those sinful habits." And he does so always from the motive of God's abounding grace to us, his desire for us to know him, and his love for the lost.

Making Time to Love People

This leads me to another aspect of Dr. Kelly's ministerial effectiveness. He loves people. He's spent his life engaged with people. He shares his life with people. Paul's letters over and over manifest real relationships with people. 2 Corinthians is no exception. In the first chapter of 2 Corinthians, Paul is concerned that the Corinthian church understand why he was not able to

---

9. Ibid., 125.

visit them. In 2 Corinthians 2:12-13, he cannot rest because he's worried about Titus. In 2 Corinthians 11:28, he constantly bears pressure for the wellbeing of the churches. Then the letter moves to the attention given to the collection Paul is taking up (2 Cor. 8:1-9:15). Paul's love for the people in Corinth saturates the whole letter. Even when they are difficult, even when they have caused him pain, he loves them and feels burdened to stick with them in personal ministry.

It brings to mind all the time Dr. Kelly spends with people and how that's shaped so many. On a given afternoon he might say, "We need to take a break." And that meant you needed to go over to the local pub and enjoy a glass of wine together. Other times he'd invite students to travel with him on his speaking engagements. He also organized book clubs apart from his classes. Furthermore, he and Mrs. Kelly hosted all kinds of people in their home. Of course, sometimes he had jobs he needed help with, or his old truck broke down, but even these provided good fellowship! It's amazing really, that with all he had going on, all those wanting his attention, all the stressors in his life, he was able to give that gift of unhurried time to so many.

That is also why his sermons include so many personal vignettes of people to whom he ministered as well as of people who had a big influence on him—sometimes simple, uneducated people who possessed that deep acquaintance with God Dr. Kelly so values.

Handling Criticism in Ministry

And, this points me to his insights on Chapter 10, where Paul deals with criticism. Dr. Kelly speaks of criticism of the minister regularly throughout these sermons. Criticism is part of the suffering of the Christian ministry, which we will consider in a moment. But I want to go ahead and mention it now because of Dr. Kelly's perceptive remarks on the importance of knowing who we are and how crucial that is for the ministry.

Dr. Kelly asks: "How do you handle criticism?" And he responds: "You first need to ask the question, 'What do I think of

Jesus Christ?' Then, once that all-important question is answered, you need to ask: 'What do I think of myself in Christ?'"[10] Dr. Kelly answers by referring to the statement in 2 Corinthians 10:7, where Paul says he belongs to Christ. Dr. Kelly says Paul is talking there about his identity, and the core of his identity is that he is "in Christ," robed in his righteousness. That frees Paul from being dependent on his performance and deflated by criticism. Paul knows his worth to God. He trusts he can pray and serve even though he is far from perfect because he is in union with Christ. His identity also includes his secondary identities, his existence, how God sovereignly made him, his gifts, and the family from which he came. Dr. Kelly says: "One of the greatest signs of Christian maturity is the ability to accept the way God, in his providence, has made us with both positive and negative aspects in our lives and personalities, along with growing freedom from the need to impress people."[11]

What great counsel! You cannot stay emotionally engaged with people in ministry, with all the accumulated slights and hurts that result, without a secure standing in these truths: "Jesus is my righteousness. God has providentially made me as I am."

This is another part of Dr. Kelly's ministerial effectiveness. He has a deep security and contentment in his acceptance with God. He also has a strong sense of place, his people, and his upbringing. You cannot talk to him long without his family tree and his rural upbringing coming up! It has formed him in so many ways. He cherishes its strengths and recognizes its weaknesses. This frees him to be the man—and the pastor and preacher—God designed him to be, including all his great gifts and his delightful eccentricities! He is not trying to be something he is not. He is also free to be honest and vulnerable about his shortcomings and sins. The joy, confidence, humility, and genuineness this created in Dr. Kelly has helped me and many others draw closer to Christ. This mindset not only keeps us moving toward people in ministry, but it also provides the context for people to heal and change.

---

10. Ibid., 137.
11. Ibid., 142.

Embracing God's Purposes When Suffering Finds You

Following Paul's teaching through 2 Corinthians, Dr. Kelly spends a lot of time talking about the matter of suffering: how to view it and how it is useful to our lives and ministries. One of his overall emphases is that suffering is part of the pattern of the Christian life. He especially brings this out in 2 Corinthians 4:7-5:21 (cf. also 2:14-17; 8:1-9, 15; 11:1-13:14). Jesus had to die before he was resurrected; he had to go through the cross to get the crown. For the believer the pattern is similar but also distinct. God reaches us when we are dead in sin and resurrects us to union with Christ. Then he calls us to multiple deaths and resurrections to grow in Christ's image and to reach this lost world.

One day when Dr. Kelly and I were "taking a break," we got to talking about trials and the value of suffering. It caught my attention. So, I asked him: "I don't really feel that I'm suffering. What should I do?" To this he wisely responded: "You don't need to look for it. It's going to find you as you walk with him." He was right! As he says here, suffering will come because it's part of the pattern of the Christian life.

Therefore, according to 2 Corinthians 4:7ff., we do not lose heart or faint before pressure within the church and persecution from without, because we know God has deposited his power, his eternal glory, in a surprising place—in "jars of clay," our weak, fallen personalities and bodies. Just like Gideon's men hid the torches in the clay jars and broke them to reveal their lights and route the enemy (Judges 7:1-25), even so we must be broken in order for God's light to shine through us to others.

Or, going back to 2 Corinthians 2:14ff., Paul uses the metaphor of a Roman military parade. He paints the picture of a Roman general leading his chained captives back to Rome in triumphal procession, with the people throwing flowers and burning incense in his honor, to depict the Christian ministry. King Jesus is leading his people and his pastors through the world in his triumphal procession, even dragging them along in chains—being the constraints and difficulties of the Christian life—in order that, in a mysterious way, their brokenness might produce in them and spread to others the sweet fragrance of Christ.

Trusting God through Sacrificial Generosity

In chapters 8–9 he applies this pattern to giving. We do not really lose when we give our money and possessions away, or even when we give our lives away. It is a kind of death, but in the pattern of the Christian life, it results in gain. The devil will tempt us to hold back, but in view of Christ's self-giving and the riches it accrues to us, we continue to give. In fact, as Dr. Kelly explains concerning 2 Corinthians 9:6, the law of increase will be at work. The more we give the more God blesses us: sometimes in material ways, and oftentimes in spiritual growth, answered prayers and more fruitful service.

His son Patrick tells the story from the time when Dr. Kelly was teaching at RTS Jackson. The five Kelly children were young. Finances were very tight. The Kelly's struggled to pay their bills. Then, Dr. Kelly's car broke down, and they didn't have money to repair it. Right at that time a man who had done yard work for him, who was also a drug addict, came to the house and said, "Preacher Kelly, I just need $100." Dr. Kelly knew the money would likely be misused, yet he thought: "This man knows me; he came to me, and I have enough." So he wrote the man a check that literally emptied the family's bank account.

That very night, and unbeknownst to him, God was moving in one of his students. He had come to study at RTS from an Islamic-controlled East African country, leaving his wife and children behind. When he had arrived, he determined "not to be taken in by the god of mammon," so he set himself to live at the level of his wife and children back home and to give all that remained to the ministry of the Lord.

It turned out that right when Dr. Kelly was having his car troubles and had just given all his remaining money away, this student received a check from a supporter. And he sensed the Spirit saying to him, "You know who needs this more? Dr. Kelly."

The morning after draining his account, Dr. Kelly went out to the mailbox, feeling rather burdened down. In the mailbox, he found a letter. He opened it and read this from his student: "Dr. Kelly, you need this more than I do." In the letter was a check for $10,000, which the donor had written the day before.

As Dr. Kelly exclaimed, "It was a hundred times what I gave!"

The Culture-Transforming Power of Dying and Rising with Christ

Jesus calls his people to go through deaths—suffering, pruning, denying self, sacrificing for others, giving generously, and fighting the spiritual warfare, in order that life may come to others (2 Cor. 4:4-5, 12). This is Jesus's death-to-resurrection pattern. In this way we experience something of Jesus's cross. We appreciate his redemptive sufferings more, and we make them real to others. As his love for us constrains us to count the cost, to go through testings, to die for others, it awakens the world to the beauty and necessity of Jesus's redeeming love displayed at the cross (2 Cor. 5:14). And, Dr. Kelly says, "This pattern can transform any culture."[12]

He adds another motivation to embrace this pattern of life. We can lean more into our figurative dyings for others as we consider our own literal death. Dr. Kelly finds this to be Paul's purpose for including 2 Corinthians 5:1-8 where he does in his letter. He counsels:

> ... there is nothing more liberating, uplifting or empowering for an effective, fruitful, Christian ministry than to face our own mortality. Let us look it in the eye in the light of what the Lord Jesus has done and what our position is as believers. Nothing will strengthen us more to die to self when that is called for, or to put the Lord first, as is always called for. As we confront death personally, emotionally and theologically, there is a tremendous liberating power when we see our roots in the future, seated with Christ in the heavenly places.[13]

In 2 Corinthians 1:1-11, Paul's teaching on suffering becomes even more personal. Dr. Kelly makes the point that the opening

---

12. Ibid., 103.
13. Ibid., 93.

is unusual. Ordinarily Paul speaks of what God is doing in the lives of those he writes, but here he speaks of what God is doing in his own life. He thanks "the Father of mercies and the God of all comfort" for comforting us in all our afflictions so that we might comfort others in their afflictions with the comfort we have received from God, because the Corinthians have caused him so much pain. He is saying: "You've hurt me, but I thank God for that hurt, because I know God is using it to drive me to him, to enlarge my heart, for the good of the church."[14]

Therefore, as Dr. Kelly says, when suffering comes, we do not so much ask "Why did you let this happen?" as "What are you doing? How will this further your grace in my life and the lives of others?"[15] This shift in perspective is so crucial!

Affliction has value because it helps us draw close to Jesus in his sufferings. We experience in a fresh way the cost of his suffering for us. This enlivens us to his love and so converts our suffering into a doorway for his resurrection power to enter our lives, work deep change, and move out to others. Dr. Kelly says, "Sometimes when you are feeling the nails, that may be the only way that others can see his glory."[16]

Similarly, suffering also has value because we experience God's comforts in the darkness in a way we do not in the sunshine. He sheds his tender mercies upon us in such a special way that we can even cherish our trials.

Furthermore, our suffering has value in preparing us to comfort others. We are able to sympathize with and "put strength and light" into those who suffer in a way we otherwise would not be able to. I will be eternally grateful for God's preparing Dr. Kelly so that he could comfort me when tragedy struck my family. He was one of the main people with whom I wanted to speak. Characteristically, we "took a break," and he gave me his unhurried time. He grieved with me and encouraged me in the sure hope of the resurrection. He did so only as one could who was intimately familiar with the sufferings of Christ.

---

14. Ibid., 24.
15. Ibid., 25.
16. Ibid., 26.

Finally, in 2 Corinthians 1:8-9, Paul says affliction has value in keeping us from relying on our own gifts and strengths and to put us at the end of our resources. It is at that place of weakness and emptiness that God exerts his resurrection power.

And this is also the lesson of the whole chapter in 2 Corinthians 12. The Lord refrained from removing Paul's "thorn in the flesh" in order to keep him from spiritual pride and to teach him that "my power is made perfect in weakness," that "when I am weak, then I am strong" (2 Cor. 12:9-10). Paul leaves the "thorn" unexplained in order to make it a general principle. It could be any form of weakness and brokenness, any form of suffering for our fellowship with Christ. It teaches us that when we lack the wherewithal to do anything, we offer what we do have anew to God, and this is the dynamic in which God unleashes his resurrection power into our lives, bringing down his glory, for our own growth in Jesus' image and for the renewal of our dying culture.

Thus, Dr. Kelly says,

> In verses 9–10, Paul's triumphant conclusion is that power to transform lives comes out of this experience. God puts the glory in you, then he tests you; sometimes he keeps you in the crucible and he makes it cost you something, but the next thing you have got is power: not power for yourself, but power to bless others. Ultimately a whole culture may begin to change because of this power. Our sovereign God has all power in heaven and on earth committed into the hands of the Lord Jesus Christ, but this power is not let loose in any generation or culture until the Christians offer themselves afresh to him, saying, 'Here I am, Lord. Use me, whatever it takes. You do not have to explain. I will trust in you.'[17]

I had read most of this book a while back, but in preparation for this chapter, I spent several days in it. The more I pondered the truths Dr. Kelly brings out, the more I was uplifted by them. I found myself raising my hands to heaven and saying: "Lord, please change me!" And I'm sure that is the effect Dr. Kelly would want.

17. Ibid., 157.

16

A Seven-Fold Synthesis from a Hidden Wednesday Night

Douglas Kelly's Experiential Teaching on Fasting

Patrick Kelly

Let another man praise thee, and not thine own mouth;
A stranger, and not thine own lips. (Prov. 27:2)

For we dare not make ourselves of the number, or compare
ourselves with some that commend themselves: but they
measuring themselves by themselves, and comparing
themselves among themselves, are not wise. (2 Cor. 10:12)

And I was with you in weakness, and in fear, and in much
trembling. And my speech and my preaching was not with
enticing words of man's wisdom, but in demonstration of
the Spirit and of power: That your faith should not stand in
the wisdom of men, but in the power of God. (1 Cor. 2:3-5)

The Preface

A stack of books that were by my bedside table went missing for
a number of months. Having literally no idea how they could

have disappeared, in time I simply forgot about them altogether. Then, while cleaning through an area of our room, they, as it were, "reappeared." In the middle of one of the books on *The Syriac Fathers on Prayer*, there was a folded piece of notebook paper that I had been using as a book marker.

On it was the outline to a sermon, which I very distinctly remember hearing preached in a small county church to ten people or less at a Wednesday night prayer meeting on the theme of fasting. As the talk was not being recorded (and it was before iPhones and the like), I found a scrap of paper and began taking notes since it appeared to me to be a profound Biblical synthesis that could only be derived experientially. That is to say, there appeared in it a certain authority (ἐξουσία); for the preaching appeared to arise, not out of abstracted Biblical theory and Scriptural study alone but from the experience of the Living Word that reshapes one's life.

This synthesis I present here as it has helped me over the years. Yet before I do so, it may be helpful if I make explicit my reasons for presenting it. Yes, it is, at least in my view, a profound, Biblical synthesis; but beyond the theological dimensions of Biblical exegesis, I believe it offers three biographical insights into the life and ministry of Douglas F. Kelly.

A. *The Synthesis displays the rare combination of an uncommon brilliance together with a deep inner life.*

As to the former, as many of us have already come to realize, Dr. Kelly has an extraordinary mind. One of his former students took me aside at one point many years ago and asked me,

"Do you know how brilliant your dad is?"

"Not sure," I replied, being a sixteen-year-old, caught up in the short-sighted realities of high school, where my father's pathway into ministry meant we would always have broken down cars and struggle financially.

"Well, do you know of ETS, the Evangelical Theological Society conference?"

"No."

"It's probably the biggest conference in a given year for people like your dad. At any rate, he was asked to speak at it a few years back and at the end of the talk someone in the audience pretty forcefully disagreed with him on one of his points about Irenaeus of Lyon.

"And what did your dad do?"

"Well, he closed his eyes and began speaking.

"A few minutes later, reopening them, he looked out on the audience, which was in total silence, completely dumbfounded.

"Realizing what he had done, he muttered out loud, 'I guess I better translate.'

"So, closing his eyes again, he translated the quote he had just recited in Latin back into English, which, of course, directly contradicted the man's point word-for-word."

Suffice it to say, the man who had disagreed with him backed down as the translated portion of Irenaeus perfectly answered his position.

As his son (now entering my fourth decade of life), it has been very rare that I have seen such displays of brilliance in my father. In fact, I have more often witnessed the opposite. When he would come home from a day of teaching, it was as if his ability to articulate was somehow spent.

"Um, could you pass me the uh, thing by the uh, thing," he might ask pointing to a spoon and a bowl.

When I finished university, however, and began attending some of his classes (Systematic Theology II, Medieval Theology, The Trinity, etc.), I saw his ability to articulate complex spiritual realities on full display to a classroom of students hanging on his every word (especially when he would stand up from the front desk and begin walking around the front of the room, which signaled that he was about to drive his points home with an experience or an anecdote from ministry, or a biographical or historical excerpt from the life of his parishioners or extended family).

The brilliance, it seemed to me, was always hidden in a certain conscious way. So too his "deep inner life", about which my father simply doesn't reveal much. And there are many reasons for this: a different generation (being born during WWII); a different upbringing; a particular understanding of what should be kept "private" or put out in the public space, all of which are very different from my millennial, psychotherapeutic context where it's pretty acceptable, even desirable, to put my whole life and history and emotional processing on display for all to see.

My father has never done that. But, interestingly enough, he has kept a diary for the past 50 years and at very rare points, he will show me an excerpt. Two of those I present to you.

The first occurred during his ministry in Dillon when, in the words of Rev. James Philip of Edinburgh in his book, *Christian Warfare and Armour*, the life of his early ministry was marked by such continual, embattled resistance that it seemed like a "relative Hell." So it was in Dillon with things happening in the Church that, in Paul's words, would not even be "named among the pagans" (1 Cor 5:1). In the midst of these hardships and burdens, my father mentioned that sometimes when he would walk down the stairs from his upstairs study, he would experience a different type of burden—one of being so overwhelmed by the Presence of Christ that the Glory of God would literally press down upon him (in sense of spiritual weight and heaviness conveyed by the Hebrew word *kabod*), that he would have to stop on the landing of the stairs and sit by the grandfather clock until the weight would release enough for him to continue down to the first floor.

The spiritual world was very near in both the demonic struggles and the Divine Presence.

***

The second story occurred the night before his mother was scheduled for an operation. Having found a mass on CT imaging of her large intestines, the physicians believed it to be cancerous. My father, still a minister in Dillon, had introduced into the church a time where people could come up and be anointed with oil (not in some crazy charismatic way, but in the simple, Biblical sense of James 5:13-16). And so, he took some of the elders to the hospital in Lumberton, anointed my grandmother with oil and prayed.

That night, he awoke to his room being filled, in his own words,

"with the holy angels singing praises to God."

The next afternoon he went back to the hospital to hear the surgeon say,

"Well, we can't explain this medically but we did the surgery and we couldn't find the mass. It's like it disappeared."

The spiritual world is present in a way that actually effects real change.

Could that explain to a certain degree why his students seemed to say that his teaching brought them in touch with the spiritual world? That his words somehow made it real to them? That they came to apprehend the presence of the spiritual world as a reality able to break into our lives here-and-now and actually change things?

And is this what is happening in a faithful Gospel ministry?

***

To answer very briefly those who may be suspect of the orthodoxy of such happenings, I will relay a third story that is not in his diaries.

This was related to me by one of his favorite teaching assistants in the Charlotte days and concerns his time in Edinburgh. When studying with my mother under Thomas F. Torrance, they used to go to the library together nearly every day. When he would be reading Calvin's *Institutes*, my mother said that he would take his eyes off the page and for seconds to minutes look up sometimes with his eyes open, other times with them closed.

"It was only later that I found out that he was praying through each section that he read."

This was how he read John Calvin (whom, lest we reduce down to some sort of wooden figure that only scribed systematic, reformation formulations for the modern evangelical church, was actually spoken of in his day as the "theologian of the Holy Spirit"). So my father, we might say, got in touch with this side of Calvin, who saw much powerful working of the Spirit in his own time.

And with that, we move to the next point, which could be described as taking hold of the "common means of Grace."

B. The Synthesis reveals a lifelong commitment to Holy Scripture
I believe my father began systematically reading through the Scriptures once a year in his early twenties, having been deeply influenced by an old Lumbee Indian preacher, whom he used to speak of as "the most spiritual man" he ever knew—which meant that "he knew the Scriptures inside and out" (Josh. 1:8; Ps. 1:2-3, 119:97; Ezek. 19:10-11) and that "whatever he had, he gave away" (cf. Luke 3:10-11; Ezek. 18:5-9, 16, 31-32). Word and Spirit were held together in this man's life. And it was he who directed my father to read three chapters of the Scriptures a day from Monday through Saturday, then five Psalms on Sunday (which reading plan he incorporated into the appendix of *If God Already Knows Why Pray?*). So he has done this for now the past 60 years such that, as one of his students said,

"I've never been able to quote a line of Scripture which your dad can't finish."

And this daily discipline, as he more recently related to me, has been the basis of the stability in his Christian life.

"How do we stay close to Jesus? How do we endure? How do we persevere? Very simple, read three chapters a day then five on Sunday."

To this, however, given the theme of the Word being vitally combined with the Spirit, I would add that he makes it abundantly clear that the way we incorporate the Word into our life is through the Spirit of prayer. And this insight, to a certain degree, laid the foundation for his recommendations in *If God Already Knows*, to include in our prayers a time of praise and waiting and confession and praying scripture and watching before moving to intercession and closing with thanksgiving.

The Word, in short, had to be prayed into one's life, not abstracted out into the disembodied realm of theological theory, where it had no power to actually effect change.

Such vital union of Scripture and prayer, Word and Spirit, may be the "secret" to much of my father's productivity over the decades. And even more, the discipline of keeping himself "under" the Word has, in my belief, kept him humble (in the Latin sense of humilis—being "of" or "close to" the "ground"). In his own words,

> "I mean, how could a man be filled up with pride, when he's coming into the Presence of the Holy God in prayer throughout the day?"

C. The Synthesis derives from the centrality of faithful, weekly preaching operating as the leaven in the bread.

If you look back on my father's ministry—literally from the time of his early 20's when he went from University of North Carolina-Chapel Hill to Union Seminary in Richmond, VA; then to Edinburgh for his PhD under Torrance; then to the struggling town of Dillon, SC, to minister; then to Northern California for two years before being called to Reformed Theological Seminary in Jackson, MS, as a professor of Systematic Theology (a call he had turned down twice before finally accepting it the third time); to his final years of teaching at RTS in Charlotte—through the whole of it he was literally always preaching Sunday to Sunday. And for the past thirty years this has been in a small, ante-bellum country Church in Minturn, SC, by the name of Reedy Creek Presbyterian Church.

And here he preaches to maybe five or ten or, at the most, twenty people.

But it is not uncommon for him to preach to ten people at Reedy Creek in the morning then to a thousand at a larger church elsewhere that evening. Yet what I have seen over the years is that the number of people does not influence his preaching style nor communication of divine truths (1 Cor. 2:1-13)—he just preaches faithfully week by week, whether to a few at Reedy Creek or to more at Independent Presbyterian Church in Savannah, or at First Presbyterian Church in Jackson or First Presbyterian in Augusta, or Christ Presbyterian Church in New Haven, or in the former Holyrood Abbey Church in Edinburgh, or at L'Église Réformée Baptiste in Lausanne, Switzerland (preaching in French), or one of the churches on the Isle of Lewis (preaching in Gaelic).

I would also add here that he has mentioned to me that when he was in his early ministry in Jackson, it became clear to him that there were those in the PCA that were "trying to make [him] a figure." That is to say, getting him to preach at big national conferences, write in journals to a wider audience, etc. etc. And he said, very simply,

> "I actually asked the Lord to keep me small. Because if I got too big, I'd probably fall away from Him."

Which then leads us into the final point—*The leaven.*

As is clear from Holy Scripture, the leaven is the Holy Spirit working silently and steadily in a hidden fashion in the souls of His saints to bring the Kingdom of God more fully into the structures of This Fallen Age. Christ makes this explicit in his parable in Matthew 13:33.

The remaining uses of leaven in the NT refer to it in a negative sense—as the "leaven of the Pharisees, which is hypocrisy" (Luke 12:1) or the "leaven of Herod" (Mark 8:15). Though we could say much more, this leaven is the hypocritical hyperstructure of religion, on the one hand, or the power structures of the fallen world systems, on the other, that ultimately seek to replace the working of the Holy Spirit with their own power and authority.

My father's discipline in weekly preaching (when he was in full-time ministry, thrice-weekly preaching) combined with his daily discipline in Scripture reading and prayer, have been the means by which the Holy Spirit has been working in him to fulfill the work to which He has called him.

This is neither a system, per se, nor a technique that will "guarantee" spiritual productivity. Rather it is a life lived before God in humility and dependence. It is letting, in his own words,

> "all your prayers and actions be the outflow of a life hidden with Christ in God."

And with that I offer two final preparatory remarks before presenting Dr. Kelly's seven-fold synthesis of fasting. The first is that fasting is not something very often preached on in evangelical circles; nevertheless, it is a practical discipline enjoined on us by Christ Himself in His threefold synthesis of the Christian life given in the central section of the Sermon on the Mount.

And the second is, very simply, Christ-centered spirituality must be practiced before it can be understood. If so done then the understanding becomes rooted in the practical experience, which is to say, not in the theoretical realm of the *pneumatika* but in the flesh and blood, incarnate realities of life. And this is exactly where Dr. Kelly can direct us.

The Synthesis

From the biographical background of my father we now move into his Scriptural synthesis, which offers us a seven-dimensional view of the spiritual discipline of fasting, drawn from both the NT and OT and applied by the leaven of the Spirit down to the level of experience.

To summarize, fasting:

1. Brings down the Resurrection power of Christ;
2. Accomplishes the Promises of God;
3. Defeats Satan;
4. Hastens Repentance;

5. Opens the Door for Salvation;

6. Helps Christian Marriage; and

7. Furthers Christian Ministry

Now, as I was only able to scribble down a few notes in real-time, I unfortunately do not have the full text of the sermon to present to you. What I can do, however, is direct you to the Scriptural references for each of the aspects of fasting, then ask that you work through their particular application as time goes on. In the first point, I'll add quotations from prior, recorded sermons on these subjects. Later on, I will offer only the Biblical references themselves and their sermon links, if available.

To begin,

1. Fasting brings down the resurrection power of Christ

Dr. Kelly (or as a gas station attendant and longtime member of Reedy Creek, marked by a practical spirituality, profound humility and self-denying generosity, would often call my father, "Preacher Kelly") directs our attention first to Mark 9. Here, the disciples are coming down from the Mountain of Transfiguration and they meet a man "with a dumb spirit" who "seizes him and throws him down" to such a degree that he "gnashes his teeth and becomes rigid" (9:17-18). (As an aside, I have dealt with this very thing while working in Trujillo, Peru prior to starting medical school, and then during Medical School in the South, then Residency in New England, then in Tugela Ferry, South Africa, and in Addis Ababa, Ethiopia, as well as in South Carolina, North Carolina, New York, Connecticut, Georgia ... basically everywhere I've ever practiced medicine.)

When his disciples are powerless to "cast him out," Jesus reveals to his disciples that "this kind goes not out but by prayer and fasting" (9:29).[1]

---

1. For a medical case bearing witness to such a reality—a striking instance of both the interrelation of the physical and spiritual dimensions with the expulsive, healing power of prayer and fasting—see "Ehetnesh: Headaches, Left-sided Paresis & Severe Insomnia: Could the Spiritual realm be operating in all of this?" at https://

Andrew Murray on Fasting

"This kind goes not out but by prayer and fasting." This word takes us to Murray, who had a deep influence on my father to the degree that he carried with him for many years – together with his Bible and a list of prayer requests – an old copy of Murray's *Waiting on God*. In another of Murray's works that my father referred to often, *With Christ in the School of Prayer*, Murray, in the "Thirteenth Lesson", makes the following point first on how a life of prayer must be centered in Christ Jesus, then on how such a life is worked out practically in faith and self-denial—both key dimensions of fasting:

> Christ Jesus is our life and the life of our faith. It is His life in us that makes us strong and ready to believe. The dying to self which much prayer implies allows a closer union to Jesus in which the spirit of faith will come in power. Faith needs prayer for its full growth.

Then he offers us an image which my father often returned to both in lectures and in preaching:

> Prayer is the one hand with which we grasp the invisible. Fasting is the other hand, the one with which we let go of the visible. In nothing is man more closely connected with the world of sense than in his need for, and enjoyment of, food. It was the fruit with which man was tempted and fell in Paradise. It was with bread that Jesus was tempted in the wilderness. But He triumphed in fasting.

And finally, as to the eminent practicality of fasting (which may be why it is not so often preached on), as that which has been suited to our natures as "creatures of the senses", Murray continuing in this same "Thirteenth Lesson", writes:

> We are creatures of the senses. Our minds are helped by what comes to us in concrete form. Fasting helps to express, to deepen, and to confirm the resolution that we are ready to sacrifice anything, even ourselves, to attain the Kingdom of God.

---

careofthewholeperson.org/medicine-spirituality-paradigm-shifting-patient-cases/mns9l5fryo24pcuojlzrwlcwgtxlv8.

(On this, read and meditate on Mark 2:18-22 & Luke 5:33-39.)

And as to our pathway to "attain the Kingdom of God," we return to the Scriptural synthesis. From Mark 9, Dr. Kelly takes us back to Mark 2:18-22 and its parallel passage in Luke 5:33-39 (the full exposition of which can be heard in a recently released sermon series on the newly created DFK Archives from the Gospel of Luke in 1979-1980).[2] Jesus in these passages reveals how the resurrection power of our Lord works in us to transform our personalities such that we can begin to receive and bear witness to the Gospel of the eternal Kingdom.

First, Jesus is asked the question of "why the disciples of John fast often and make prayers and likewise those of the Pharisees" but the disciples of Jesus "eat and drink." Or to put it more another way, "Why do the disciples of Jesus not follow our system of spirituality?"

And Jesus said to them, "Can the friends of the bridegroom fast while the bridegroom is with them? As long as they have the bridegroom with them they cannot fast" (Mark 2:19; cf. Luke 5:34).

The reality of our union with Christ, the Bridegroom, is present to the disciples such that they can "eat and drink" and rejoice in His bodily presence with them. The "invisible", in Murray's conception, has become "visible."

Not always, though:

> "But the days will come when the bridegroom will be taken away from them, and then they will fast in those days" (Mark 2:20; cf. Luke 5:35).

And here Christ draws back the curtain, as it were, revealing to us what is happening when we fast the true fast in the Lord:

> "Then He spoke a parable to them: 'No one puts a piece from a new garment on an old one; otherwise the new makes a tear, and also the piece that was taken out of the new does not match the old'" (Luke 5:36).

---

2. The DFK Archives, containing the complete sermons of Douglas F. Kelly, may be found at http://www.dfkarchives.org

Or, as "Preacher Kelly" commented in his sermon on Mark 9 in 1979,

> And Jesus is saying the salvation I come to bring is not a "patching up" affair. It's not that you take some of the religion of the Pharisees, and some of Jesus' religion, and some of the religion of the Buddhists, and some of the religion of the Muslims, and some of the liberal humanitarian philosophers—and you mix it all together in a pot and make a soup and then you drink it and then you have the essence of all human religions.

> Jesus says, I have nothing to do with that because there would be death in that pot, like in the days of Elijah.

> The Christian religion, Gospel salvation, conversion and eternal life, is not a patching up affair, of taking some ideas from the Bible, and some ideas from philosophy, and some ideas from here and from yonder, and cutting out some things from the Bible so that it will fit in with what is current in any one generation—and then offering that up as a mess of pottage that you are to eat.

> Jesus says there is nothing in that but destruction. What I have come to give you is something entirely new.

Then back to Christ's next image:

> "And no one puts new wine into old wineskins; or else the new wine will burst the wineskins and be spilled, and the wineskins will be ruined. But new wine must be put into new wineskins, and both are preserved. And no one, having drunk old wine, immediately desires new; for he says, 'The old is better'" (Luke 5:36–39, cf. Mark 2:21–22).

This is to say, fasting is like we are paradoxically eating and being nourished by the living *epiousios* (daily) bread of the New Creation.

As Christ in the wilderness, as Moses on Mt. Sinai, as Elijah on Mount Horeb.

> "I have food to eat which you know not of" (John 4:32).

"My food is to do the will of Him who sent Me, and to finish His work" (John 4:34).

And this bread and this new wine cannot be contained in the pre-*metanoia* (pre-repentance) modes of thinking of the "old man" without bursting them open (ῥήξει).[3]

Or to put it another way, the bread that we moment-by-moment consume will sustain us "but for a moment"; but the bread of Christ Jesus, the living bread of the coming Kingdom will nourish us for all eternity. For in the process of our ingesting it, this bread begins to transform our entire person so as to receive and bear witness to the Gospel of the Kingdom. We are no longer trying to put new wine into old wineskins: we are, in the words of Paul, a new creation.

As new creational men and women, it is into the fullness of the New Creation that Jesus beckons us to come:

> Behold, I stand at the door and knock. If anyone hears My voice and opens the door, I will come in to him and dine with him, and he with Me.
>
> To him who overcomes I will grant to sit with Me on My throne, as I also overcame and sat down with My Father on His throne.
>
> He who has an ear, let him hear what the Spirit says to the churches (Rev. 3:20–22).

And with that I will bring this to a close.

The remaining points with their Scriptural references are below (as I've already exceeded my book chapter length ... but return to the DFK Archives as more sermons are being added by the day).

Blessings.

---

3. See "*metanoéō*: The Transforming Word of JHWH unto New Creational Life or Eternal Judgment," at https://careofthewholeperson.org/the-life-of-words-hebrew-greek-word-studies/-me-t-no-e-o-amp-me-t-noi-the-transforming-word-of-jhwh-unto-new-creational-life-or-eternal-judgment.

Fasting:

1. Brings down the resurrection power of Christ

2. Accomplishes the Promises of God: Daniel 9 and Jeremiah 9 (esp v. 3, 10:2, 10:12ff)

3. Defeats Satan: 2 Chronicles 20:1–30; Esther 4 & Esther 5[4]

4. Hastens Repentance: Joel 1:6, 14; 2:12–14

5. Opens the Door for Salvation: Acts 10:29–33[5]

6. Helps Christian Marriage: 1 Corinthians 7:3–5

7. Furthers Christian Ministry: 2 Corinthians 6:5, 7; 11:27

---

4. See Dr. Kelly's sermons on these passages at www.dfkarchives.org/2-chronicles and www.dfkarchives.org/esther.

5. See Dr. Kelly's sermons on this passage at www.dfkarchives.org/acts.

17

The Psalms and Prayer
in the Life and Disciple-Making
of Douglas F. Kelly

Taylor Ince

It is a high honor to have the opportunity to write on the importance of prayer and the Psalms in the life of Douglas F. Kelly. I have for years now seen the vital role both play in his life, so vital that it is hard to imagine Dr. Kelly apart from prayer and the Psalms. Similarly, it is hard to imagine Dr. Kelly's prayer life apart from the Psalms, just as it is hard to imagine the role the Psalms play in his life apart from his life of prayer.

This stands to reason, since the Psalms are the sung prayerbook of God's people. No one has taught me this with greater clarity and force than Dr. Kelly. And he has done it not only in the classroom, but also with his life and by bringing me into that life. To live alongside Dr. Kelly for any amount of time is to be enveloped in a life whose pace is set by, and whose marrow has for well over half-a-century soaked in, the Psalms and prayer. To know Dr. Kelly is to know that, for him, prayer and the Psalms are like eating, breathing, and sleeping—they are vital.

Dr. Kelly's Discipleship

Gino Wickman begins his book *Traction* by giving readers an insight into his success as a business leader and systems developer: he had a mentor who shared his life with Gino. Gino says his mentor, Sam Cupp, was "one of the best businessmen I've ever met. I was blessed to have him take me under his wing at a young age and teach me everything he knew."[1]

This is what good mentors do. And this is how lives change. When someone doesn't just give you lots of information or teach you in a class but pours his life into yours over the course of years, you cannot help but be changed.

Of course the Christian word for this is *discipleship*. Christ calls every follower of his to make disciples, but so few obey. I hesitate to say it, but my guess is that perhaps even fewer seminary professors follow this commission when it comes to their students. But thank God Douglas Kelly has followed this call and pattern of life-on-life ministry for over forty years with the result that dozens of lives—including my own—have been changed by Dr. Kelly's obedience, humility, kindness, and care in pouring his life into theirs and in pointing them constantly to the life of the One who gave Himself for us.

I came to RTS-Charlotte because Dr. Kelly offered for me to live with him and his wife my first year. I knew I wanted more than just classroom education—I wanted a mentor in the mold of Luther and Calvin, a pastor-teacher who would pour his love for God into my soul. Dr. Kelly did exactly that for the three years I was at RTS-Charlotte. And after those three years, the discipleship continued.

Following seminary, my wife Robin and I went on to Edinburgh to study Hebrew Bible at New College. In God's perfect and kind providence, Dr. Kelly and his wife Caroline were on sabbatical in Edinburgh that same year. How delighted we were to discover this! Doug and Caroline had studied and met in Edinburgh forty-

---

1. Gino Wickman, *Traction: Get a Grip on Your Business* (Dallas: BenBella Books, 2011), 5.

five years earlier, returning regularly for his writing sabbatical. Robin and I had stepped into this postgraduate adventure with our first child, Seth, who was only three months old at the time of our departure across the wide waters of the Atlantic. No fear: Dr. and Mrs. Kelly were waiting to greet us. Weekly prayers and constant fellowship continued and enriched our already rich friendship. They became like second parents to us.

A dozen years have passed since that time, and hardly a week goes by that I don't find myself drawing on what I learned from Dr. Kelly's life so generously shared with me. "What would Dr. Kelly do?" is a question I've often asked in times of crisis. Invariably the answer leads me to Jesus. And that owes, in no small part, to the formative influence of having spent hours upon hours, year after year, praying and reading and singing the Psalms (sometimes in Scots Gaelic!) with Dr. Kelly. The Psalms, which have been the prayer book of God's people for three millenia, have carved such a deep channel through Dr. Kelly's thinking and praying over his nearly eighty years of life that no one can spend much time in conversation with him, and certainly not much time in prayer with him, without finding himself in the flow of biblical currents.

Prayer and the Psalms in Dr. Kelly's Life

Prayer and the Psalms in the Kelly Home

In the time since my three years with the Kellys in Charlotte and my wife's and my additional year with them in Edinburgh at the outset of my doctoral studies, I have made it a priority to make an annual pilgrimage from my home in Houston to Dr. and Mrs. Kelly's home in Carthage, NC. When there, I enjoy the old, familiar rhythms as much as anything. In the morning, typically after a breakfast of eggs, cheese, yogurt, and strong coffee, we remove to the den where we sit on the bradded, brown leather couches, opposite one another. Books are encased and piled here and there. A fire usually warms the room. Dr. Kelly reads a psalm aloud and then we pray. Though in King James English, his prayers are never stilted. They are simple, direct, at times plaintive, always thankful—like those of a child, the child of God that Dr. Kelly knows he is. His prayers and life flow from a seemingly constant and grateful awareness of his privileged position as an adopted child of the heavenly Father, an incomparable gift received through faith in Christ.

During a recent visit, I found Dr. Kelly hard at work on his upcoming sermon for that Sunday. What was his text? Psalm 104, part of his series (at the time of writing this chapter) on the Psalms. I was there as part of a fellowship gathering that included seven or eight middle-aged men, all brought together by his youngest son, Patrick. At one point during our time together, Dr. Kelly called us all into the den for a time of Scripture reading and prayer—the Scripture reading coming from the Psalms, of course. Then we all prayed, one by one with Dr. Kelly closing.

Was this a surprise to any of us? Quite the contrary. If Doug hadn't called us in for this very thing at some point over those few days, *that* would have surprised us. This is normal practice in the Kelly household, and if you are with the Kellys in their home for any decent amount of time, you find yourself simply folded into their regular rhythms of prayer, Scripture reading, Psalm reading, together with thrice weekly congregational worship, farm road walks, table fellowship around a meal, extended conversation on the back porch, and even cemetery visits to ancestors long dead but many (even most, if not all) of them alive in the Lord and with the Lord.

Prayer and the Psalms on the Seminary Campus

One of the staples in Dr. Kelly's life on campus during the school term was the weekly brown bag lunch prayer meeting in his office. It was not only a time for weekly prayer; it was also an hour that served as a discipleship funnel. Who was hungry for prayer and for time with this godly professor? If you wanted a shot at being among the handful of young men Dr. Kelly would bring under his wing every few years, you had to start by showing up to that meeting.

Dr. Kelly would open our time by reading a Psalm aloud from his tattered, black Bible. Then, one by one, each student would share a thing or two he wanted prayer for. We prayed for all manner of things. More than once, a student came with a report of some unruly, proud, and, on occasion, even vituperative church officer. More than once Dr. Kelly directed, "Don't do or say a thing. Let's pray him out." We did pray, and more than once we found, weeks or months later, that the ruling elder of concern had been removed from office. Nothing is too small—or too nasty—to bring to God. The Psalms tell us this in clear and sometimes harrowing tones (e.g. Ps. 69:22-28, 73:18-20, 137:9). We learned it in this weekly prayer circle as well.

Prayer and the Psalms in Sermons and Systematics

I was helped just last week by listening to a sermon Dr. Kelly recently preached on Psalm 109. "They attacked me," the Psalmist says, "but I give myself to prayer" (v. 4). This past year my wife and I walked through perhaps the most painful experience of our lives. Good friends took actions that felt like betrayal, and our church split. Friendships were lost, as was a good deal of sleep. Months later, we are still working through the pain. In his unpacking of the text, Dr. Kelly reminds his hearers to take our travails to God—to cry out to him honestly, to not give ourselves to bitterness, or to wishing ill on those who hurt us. If those who have hurt us need to be brought down, let God do it, to the end that he might save and sanctify them, heal and mature them, and, if it please him, to mend the breach (vv. 6-20).

Elsewhere, in a similar vein (and of equal help to me personally), Dr. Kelly unpacks Psalm 143 in volume three of his *Systematic Theology*:

> David asks God to hear his prayer (v. 1). He is all but overwhelmed by enemies (vv. 3, 4), but then he turns his heart towards God: "I remember the days of old; I meditate on all thy works; I muse on the work of thy hands" (v. 5). Then he spends the rest of this brief Psalm stretching up his hands to God in prayer (v. 6) and calling on the help of the Spirit (v. 10); and he is

confident that the Spirit will "quicken" him (v. 11). Hence, true meditation moves into prayer, and into desires for obedience (v. 10).[2]

Farther along in his sermon on Psalm 109, Kelly comments on the first part of verse 21—"Do Thou for me" (KJV)—by stating, "We remain in bad shape when we keep focusing on what we ourselves can do. But once we turn to God, everything changes, for the better."[3] As many times as we may have heard this truth, we can never hear it too often. And the application is vintage Kelly: helpful, clear, profound, and personally lived.

In a sermon on Psalm 90, Dr. Kelly notes that the title tells us that this song is a prayer (a prayer of Moses).[4] Kelly goes on to comment that over the years young people have come to him to confess that they have a hard time praying for more than five or ten minutes. "After carefully listening to them," Kelly says, "Well, why don't you take one of the psalms and turn it into prayer? I have never known that to fail helping people." Long before Donald Whitney's little gem *Praying the Bible* was published, I and many others had experienced the help in prayer that comes from praying the Bible—and from praying the Psalms in particular—thanks to Dr. Kelly's example and instruction.[5]

Lessons Learned

First Lesson Learned: Prayer is for Everything

Dr. Kelly shared a story with me about a time he was in Edinburgh studying for his Ph.D. under T.F. Torrance. He may have been attending a midweek prayer meeting at Holyrood Abbey Church. Somehow it was discovered that his alarm clock had quit working. An elderly saint asked, "Have you prayed about it? Have you asked

---

2. Douglas F. Kelly, *Systematic Theology: The Holy Spirit and the Church* (vol. 3 of *Systematic Theology: Grounded in Holy Scripture and Understood in Light of the Church*) (Geanies House; Mentor, 2021), 168.

3. Douglas F. Kelly, "Psalm 109 – A Prayer Against the Wicked," n.p. [cited 27 April 2023]. Online: https://www.sermonaudio.com/sermoninfo.asp?SID=25231603682.

4. Douglas F. Kelly, "Psalm 90 – Our Brief Life," n.p. [cited 27 April 2023]. Online: https://www.sermonaudio.com/sermoninfo.asp?SID=88221759405523.

5. Donald S. Whitney, *Praying the Bible* (Wheaton: Crossway, 2015).

God to fix it?" Kelly's immediate impulse was to think this silly, as if it were beneath God.

But as he examined this reaction, within seconds he realized how silly *it* was. The woman's follow-up comment helped these thoughts along. Seeing his reaction to her question, she asked another, something like, "If God cares about big things like the stars and rulers of nations, why not little things like our alarm clocks?" So they prayed for his alarm clock.

When Dr. Kelly returned home, he found his alarm clock working again. And it continued working for the remainder of his time in Edinburgh. Perhaps he brought it back home with him to the Carolinas! I don't know. What I do know is that he told me that story, more than once if memory serves. The incident made an impression on him that lasted.

Years later he would write, "There is no area we should not bring before Him in prayer ..."[6] Maybe he had that prayer for his alarm clock in mind as he wrote this line. I can say that Doug has leaned into this lesson these fifty-five years since, praying for all manner of things, big and small and in-between.

As a result of his emphasis on praying even for the smallest things, I have never hesitated in the slightest to bring a small matter to Dr. Kelly for prayer. He cares because He knows God cares. He prays because He knows God listens and acts upon the prayers of His children in Christ Jesus. After all, what good parent scoffs at his child's small concerns, especially when brought to him with a furrowed brow or tear-stained cheeks? The loving parent naturally responds, "Come here sweetheart. Sit in my lap and tell me your troubles. Pour it out and let's work through it together. Let me comfort you. Let me help." If this is the spirit and tone of a loving parent, though evil, how much more our heavenly Father (Matt. 7:11)? Dr. Kelly has six children (one in heaven) and knows well that he is a child of the Most High, the Father of lights who is tender with us thanks to Jesus.

---

6. Douglas F. Kelly, *If God Already Knows, Why Pray?* (Geanies House: Mentor, 1995), 49.

Every time I have come to Dr. Kelly, I have come not only to a caring father but have been ushered by him into the loving embrace of our perfect Father who cherishes us so, who listens, who cares, and who acts, even when He does not grant our request. And when He doesn't grant our request, that too is because He cares.

Dr. Kelly taught us this in his classroom, but he also taught it with his life—in the way he prayed for himself, for us, for others. The lesson of his example was more powerful by far than even the lesson in his rich teaching. I have his notes to go back to, to pull off the shelf at times and to crack open when I need to look something up. But more precious still are the years I have of his fatherhood, friendship, and example to draw from with my mind and heart. What more could I have asked for from a professor of systematic theology? He was an outstanding classroom professor but has been, and remains far more to me and to many men now in their middle age and older.

Thanks in large part to Dr. Kelly's tutelage, having myself now "journeyed half of our life's way," I have not, with Dante, "found myself within a shadowed forest ..."[7] Dark have been some of the years that followed my formative ones with Dr. Kelly—my wife and I have lost children, lived and led through a worldwide pandemic, and endured a split in the church we planted—but while I have found myself at times disoriented, I have not been disillusioned or despairing: I never did lose "the path that does not stray."[8] I can say most truly—and not simply to honor him here in print—that Dr. Kelly's prayers for me and faithful teaching on prayer and personal example as a praying son of the Father helped pull me through some deeply shadowed and dark days, weeks, months, and years.

Second Lesson Learned: Prayer Strengthens and Settles Us

In 1 Kings 17, Elijah appears out of nowhere. He steps onto the scene fully formed, full of zeal for the Living God. Dr. Kelly's

---

7. Dante Alighieri, *The Divine Comedy: Inferno*, trans. A. Mandelbaum (New York: Bantam Books, 1980), opening lines (I.i-ii).

8. Ibid., I.iii.

colleague at RTS-Charlotte, John Currid (professor of Old Testament who contributed a chapter to this *Festschrift*) once asked us in class, "This man stands up to ancient near-eastern kings, fearless in his rebukes. Where did his courage come from?" He directed us to "look at verse 1," and read, "Now Elijah the Tishbite, of Tishbe in Gilead, said to Ahab, 'As the LORD, the God of Israel, lives, before whom I stand, there shall be neither dew nor rain these years, except by my word.'" Currid then emphasized to us, "Elijah stands before the Living God. Why should a mere man like Ahab, even if a king, frighten him?"

In a similar way, I can honestly say that I have never seen any indication of the fear of man in Dr. Kelly's mien or person. Like Elijah, he has long stood before the Living God, and there is a peaceful strength, resolve, and quiet that bear constant witness to that fact.

In *If God Already Knows, Why Pray?* Kelly writes of the Pharisees in Jesus's day: "They acted as though what people thought of them in the community was the final reality, whereas Jesus showed that was not the case at all. What matters is how we stand with God."[9] Kelly believes this in the depth of his being, and his prayer life—or rather his life of prayer—testifies powerfully to that belief.

In Psalm 63 we encounter David driven by deep hunger and thirst to a vision of His Maker and Redeemer. Gazing on God, David is sated. We see this in a more intimate way in Psalm 131. Like an infant full of mother's milk, David is content to just be with God. *Coram deo*, David is calm and quiet. Psalm 27:8 springs to mind: "You have said, 'Seek my face.' My heart says to you, 'Your face, LORD, do I seek.'" And again, Psalm 73:28, "But for me it is good to be near God." Moses opens the sublime yet trenchant Psalm 90, his prayer to the God he knows so well, by calling the Almighty his dwelling place, a truth the Son opens up fully for us in his incarnation, articulating it richly and astoundingly in John 15. Jesus is the God of Moses: our abode, our dwelling place,

---

9. Kelly, *If God Already Knows*, 16.

our home. And in Psalm 127, Solomon speaks of sleep as a gift God gives to his beloved children. In all these passages and so many more we learn that God not only gives us rest but is our rest—a rest that is in and through Jesus Christ. Prayer taps into this reality, hiding in God, enjoying his beauty, and drawing on his comfort, rest, power, and peace.

In more than twenty years of knowing Dr. Kelly, I have never seen him in a hurry. I have long known but never articulated this, and it is astonishing to reflect, as I write these words, how true this is of him. It takes my mind to the recent book *The Ruthless Elimination of Hurry* by John Mark Comer.[10] Comer reflects on the fact that in the Gospels, Jesus never seems to be in a hurry. It is not that Jesus doesn't have important things to do. He is in fact saving the world. But he is never out of step with His Father and His Father's agenda and timetable. So Jesus is just not in a rush.

This is such a Christ-like characteristic, one that stands out in the frenetic, breakneck, diffuse technopoly we have both created and succumbed to.[11] One can feel perennially, unceasingly caught up and spread thin by screens and spreadsheets and events and deadlines. Not Dr. Kelly. He doesn't own a T.V. and never watches one (with the exception of the once-a-year State of the Union Address). He is deliberate, purposeful, focused—what some have called "a non-anxious presence."[12] When you are with him, he is with you. True, he may also be contemplating a line from St. Gregory of Nazianzus in Greek or from St. Thomas's *Summa* in Latin—or something by John Owen or John Murray—but still, he is with you. He is present.

To take from missionary and martyr Jim Elliot, wherever Doug is, he is "all there." He is patient. He is calm. He is full of peace,

10. John Mark Comer, *The Ruthless Elimination of Hurry: How to Stay Emotionally Healthy and Spiritually Alive in the Chaos of the Modern World* (Colorado Springs: Waterbrook, 2019).

11. Neil Postman, *Technopoly: The Surrender of Culture to Technology* (New York: Knopf Doubleday, 1992).

12. Mark Sayers, *A Non-Anxious Presence: How a Changing and Complex World Will Create a Remnant of Renewed Christian Leaders* (Chicago: Moody, 2022).

a man of peace, because he is a man of prayer. He is unhurried, settled, grounded, humbled, resolved, quiet, thoughtful, incisive, perceptive, kind.

Where does this come from? It comes from the unhurried one Himself, the One who is our rest and home. It comes from Christ. To be with Dr. Kelly is to be with a man who has been with Jesus in prayer, who has gazed on Him in the sanctuary, beholding his power and glory, who is quiet and content. His heart has found that rest of which St. Augustine so memorably spoke: "Thou hast made us for thyself, O Lord, and our hearts are restless until they rest in thee" (*Confessions*, I.1).[13]

In *If God Already Knows, Why Pray?* Kelly reflects on Paul's conversion as recorded in Acts 9. He points out that when God tells Ananias to go to Paul and lay hands on him so his sight can be restored, God reassures Ananias of Paul's new birth with this comment: "for behold, he is praying" (Acts 9:11). Prayer from the heart is a hallmark of the child of God.[14] This is why it is at the heart, one might even say is the beating heart, of Doug's way of life. Under and around and above all, Doug's life flows from his understanding that he is a child of God, an adopted son through his union with the only Son, received with the open hand of faith, that faith a gift God graciously gave to Doug some seventy-five years ago.

God Himself is the Point of Prayer

It seems right to close this chapter with Dr. Kelly's own words on prayer from the Psalms, words that help close the third and final volume of his *Systematic Theology*. The passage is apt since it is characteristic not only of Dr. Kelly's thought but also of his life, owing not only to its focus on prayer but also to its focus on the point of prayer: that is, the beauty of God, the "light of the

---

13. Augustine, *Confessions*, trans. R.S. Pine-Coffin (New York: Penguin Classics, 1961), 3.

14. Kelly, *If God Already Knows*, 31.

knowledge of [His] glory," beheld truly, savingly, and captivatingly "in the face of Jesus Christ" (2 Cor. 4:6):

> In prayer, we are face to face with Christ, the One who commanded long ago through David: "[When thou saidst], Seek ye my face; my heart said unto thee, Thy face, LORD, will I seek" (Ps. 27:8). If it takes burdens of life and aspirations to see fulfilled holy promises in the Word to keep us seeking His face, so much the better. Seeing Him means being progressively transformed into His image, and that is the goal of our lives: "But we all, with open face beholding as in a glass the glory of the Lord, are changed into the same image from glory to glory, even as by the Spirit of the Lord' (2 Cor. 3:18)."[15]

---

15. Kelly, *Systematic Theology*, 3:345.

A Tribute to Douglas F. Kelly
on the Occasion of His
Retirement Banquet
April 28, 2016

Matthew S. Miller

DR. Kelly, this week I wrote pages of funny stories from the 18 years that I've known you, beginning with the day we first met in Edinburgh, Scotland, in the fall of 1998, after morning worship service at Holyrood Abbey. While your accent got my attention, it was your Bible of choice that morning that raised my eyebrows. We had each just worshipped in a conservative congregation of the Church of Scotland—I, with my New International Version, and you, with your *Biblia Sacra Vulgata*, the prized Latin Bible of the medieval Catholic church. Ever since that day, I've been trying to figure you out, and I can say that your life makes no sense at all apart from the person of Jesus Christ, but in his light, your life makes more sense than any I have ever known.

But this evening, I have an easier task than that of explaining you. I have simply to thank you. The obvious focus of thanksgiving would be the fruit of your life and ministry. For we have been privileged partakers of that fruit—the fruit of your mind, the fruit of your character, the fruit of your unconditional love. But in any man's life, the roots precede the fruit. And tonight I want to thank you for roots.

Now, with a man of your genealogical awareness, a proper focus on roots would start with Noah through the line of Japheth. That would take us back, according to Archbishop Ussher's chronology, to the year 2,348 B.C. But permit me to fast forward just a bit and begin here.

Thank you for following the Lord's call on your life, which you discerned at a very young age, to become a preacher and theologian.

You could have made a lot of money with your extraordinary mind. But you chose the path fed by manna. For riches, you toiled at the University of North Carolina—Chapel Hill, to master Latin and Greek, and thus to gain unfiltered access to the treasures of the patristic, medieval and Reformation eras, and for the sake of adorning the church in our day, *to bring forth out of this treasure things new and old.*

Thank you for working hard in the cotton fields in the summers of your youth, rising early on humid mornings to commit to memory lines from Pascal's *Pensées*, which you turned over in your mind as your hands labored. Thank you for forging in those fields a work ethic that would bear heavy loads and not break. Thank you for finding in those fields the nearness of heaven, as you sang psalms, hymns, and spirituals, to the One in whom you live, move, and have your being.

Thank you then for laboring in the libraries of Union Theological Seminary in Richmond, and then of New College Divinity School in Edinburgh. At Union, you read everything the liberals assigned you, and then beyond that, burned the midnight oil to refresh your soul in the pages of orthodoxy. You graduated unshaken in your faith, and equipped to engage its challengers, and through firsthand knowledge of their sources, not only defend the truth, but win them to it.

In the New College library, with your photographic memory, as you turned page after page, of volume after volume, you often lifted your eyes toward the towering windows a few minutes at a time, before returning to the pages, only to stare out the windows a few minutes more, as you worked your way through patristic sources.

This caught the attention of an observant young English woman, a divinity student, who wondered what you were doing, before she perceived correctly that you were praying your way through these ancient texts. Thank you for making prayer the atmosphere of your learning, so that it could be, for us, your students, the atmosphere of ours.

Thank you for submitting to the interruption of your doctoral studies to come back home and serve one year as the interim pastor in Raeford, NC.

You preached, you counseled, you married, you buried sometimes several members each week, you shepherded a large flock at a critical time. Most men would have turned down such a call, for the sake of their theological studies. You prioritized the church, and cemented the truth in your soul that theology is for the church.

Your teacher, John Leith, said this about John Calvin: "One of the most striking characteristics of Calvin's work as a theologian is his synthesis of the work of the exegete, the systematic theologian, and the preacher. This synthesis was rooted in Calvin's conviction that all theology stands under the Word of God and also in his insistence that theology is a practical science."[1] This synthesis is one of the most striking characteristics of your work as well. It was borne of personal and practical sacrifice for the bride of Christ. And we are thankful.

Thank you for asking our heavenly Father that he would give you that observant and remarkable young English woman to be your wife. Thank you, Mrs. Kelly, for having the keenness of mind to understand that when, in Edinburgh, Dr. Kelly asked if you

---

1. John Leith, *Introduction to the Reformed Tradition* (1991), 97.

would "come back to Dillon with me," that was his way of asking, "Will you marry me?" And thank you for saying "yes".

Thank you for your nine years of hard, but fruitful, pastoral ministry in Dillon, after which, at the right time, God called you to what would become more than three decades of teaching systematic and historical theology at RTS. Before giving your first lecture in 1983, you had gone through refining fires and engaged in spiritual warfare in the unseen world. Many men can get ordained, and earn a PhD, and receive a position on a faculty. But you followed Jesus along a much harder route, the kind that produces the rare doctor ecclesiae: a doctor of the church.

And from these roots, and many more known only to you and Mrs. Kelly, have come all of this fruit. The fruit of a generation of thousands of students on nearly every continent who love the doctrine of the Holy Trinity, who prize the doctrine of union with Christ, who hold fast to the doctrine of Scripture, and who defend the doctrine of creation. The fruit is a generation of thousands of students on nearly every continent who believe in the power of intercessory prayer (and led or attended a prayer meeting last night!). The fruit is a generation of thousands of students on nearly every continent who believe that Jesus is not only true, He is also exceedingly beautiful—and they believe that in no small measure because they have seen His beauty in your life.

Thank you for teaching us that "this is eternal life, that they may know You the one true God, and Jesus Christ whom You have sent."

And perhaps most remarkably, thank you for doing all of this without taking yourself very seriously. G. K. Chesterton wrote somewhere that angels can fly because they take themselves lightly. To know you is to know the sound of your laugh, and more often than not, the sound of you laughing at yourself. I love that old leather jacket, tattered and torn from when you fell off your motorcycle.

Thank you for your immeasurable influence on me, and your immeasurable influence on us. The fruit of your life is very visible. But thank you for what is less visible—all the sacrifice and all the surrender that extended the roots of your life deep into the soil of reality of God. You have known God, and that is why you have been so powerful in making Him known.

And on this night, and in the years to come, those of us who have been privileged to know you as a father of the faith can say, with the Psalmist:

> The lines are fallen unto me in pleasant places,
> yea, I have a goodly heritage.

May God bless you as you continue to know Him, and make Him known, in the years of fruitful writing, teaching, and preaching, that, Lord-willing, lie ahead.

Bibliography of Douglas F. Kelly's Works

Books

Calvin, John. *Sermons on 2 Samuel: Chapters 1-13*. Translated by Douglas F. Kelly. Edinburgh: Banner of Truth, 1992.

Gerstner, John H., Douglas F. Kelly, and Philip B. Rollinson. *A Guide to the Westminster Confession of Faith: Commentary*. Signal Mountain: Summertown Texts, 1992.

Kelly, Douglas F. *Creation and Change: Genesis 1:1-2:4 in the Light of Changing Scientific Paradigms*. Geanies House: Mentor, 2017.

———. *Deuteronomy. A Mentor Expository Commentary*. Geanies House: Mentor, 2022.

———. *If God Already Knows, Why Pray?* Geanies House: Christian Focus, 1995.

———. *New Life in the Wasteland: 2 Corinthians on the Cost and Glory of Christian Ministry*. Geanies House: Christian Focus, 2003.

———. *Preachers with Power: Four Stalwarts of the South*. Edinburgh: Banner of Truth, 1992.

———. *Revelation. A Mentor Expository Commentary*. Geanies House: Mentor, 2015.

——. *Systematic Theology Volume One: Grounded in Holy Scripture and Understood in the Light of the Church: The God Who Is: The Holy Trinity.* Geanies House: Mentor, 2008.

——. *Systematic Theology Volume Two: Grounded in Holy Scripture and Understood in the Light of the Church: The Beauty of Christ: A Trinitarian Vision.* Geanies House: Mentor, 2014.

——. *Systematic Theology Volume Three: Grounded in Holy Scripture and Understood in the Light of the Church: The Holy Spirit and the Church.* Geanies House: Mentor, 2021.

——. *The Emergence of Liberty in the Modern World: The Influence of Calvin on Five Governments from the 16th through 18th Centuries.* Phillipsburg: Presbyterian & Reformed, 1992.

——. *The Scottish Blue Family in North America.* Dillon: 1739 Publications, 2007.

Kelly, Douglas F., and Graham Dickson. *The Lord's Day in a Secular Society.* Edinburgh: Rutherford House, 1999.

Kelly, Douglas F., and Caroline S. Kelly. *Carolina Scots: An Historical and Genealogical Study of over 100 Years of Emigration.* Dillon: 1739 Publications, 1998.

Kelly, Douglas F., Hugh McClure, and Philip B. Rollinson. *The Westminster Confession of Faith: An Authentic Modern Version.* Signal Mountain: Summertown Texts, 2004.

Kelly, Douglas F., and Philip B. Rollinson. *The Westminster Shorter Catechism in Modern English.* Phillipsburg: Presbyterian & Reformed, 1986.

Book Chapters

Kelly, Douglas F. "Family Worship: Biblical, Reformed, and Viable for Today." In *Worship in the Presence of God: A Collection of Essays on the Nature, Elements, and Historic Views and Practice of Worship*, edited by David C. Lachman and Frank J. Smith. Fellsmere: Reformation Media and Press, 2006.

————. "Robert Lewis Dabney." In *Reformed Theology in America: A History of Its Modern Development*, 208–31. Grand Rapids: Eerdmans, 1985.

————. "The Beneficial Influence of Stoic Logic and Epistemology on Early Christian Theology: With Particular Reference to Novatian of Rome." In *Sprache Und Erkenntnis Im Mittelalter*, 817–25. Berlin: De Gruyter, 1981.

————. "The True and Triune God: Calvin's Doctrine of the Holy Trinity." In *A Theological Guide to Calvin's Institutes: Essays and Analysis*, edited by David W. Hall and Peter A. Lillback, 65–89. Phillipsburg: Presbyterian & Reformed, 2015.

————. "Varied Themes in Calvin's 2 Samuel Sermons and the Development of His Thought." In *Calvinus Sincerioris Religionis Vindex*, 209–23. Sixteenth Century Journal, 1997.

Articles

Kelly, Douglas F. "Review of Feld, Helmut. *Opera Exegetica: Commentariorum in Acta Apostolorum: Liber Primus.*" The Sixteenth Century Journal 33, no. 2 (2002): 510.

————. "1 Peter 2:13–15 – The Duty of the Christian to the Civil Government." Banner of Truth, 3 July 2015. https://banneroftruth.org/us/resources/articles/2015/1-peter-213-15-the-duty-of-the-christian-to-the-civil-government/.

————. "Adoption: An Underdeveloped Heritage of the Westminster Standards." *The Reformed Theological Review* 52, no. 3 (1993): 110–20.

————. "Afraid of Infinitude." Christianity Today 39, no. 1 (1995): 32–33.

————. "Classics of Personal Devotion." Banner of Truth Magazine, January 1987.

————. "Evangelical Reformulations of the Doctrine of the Trinity and Calvin on the Full Equality of All Persons of the Trinity." *Unio Cum Christo* 4, no. 1 (2018): 65–81.

———. "Hints from Cotton Mather on the Rearing of Children." Banner of Truth Magazine, August 1976.

———. "John Calvin's Teaching on Guidance as Expressed in His Sermons on II Samuel." *The Reformed Theological Review* 46, no. 2 (1987): 33–42.

———. "One to Four Things Which Cannot Be Shaken." Banner of Truth Magazine, January 2000.

———. "'Our Southern Zion': Old Columbia Seminary." Banner of Truth Magazine, November 2012.

———. "Prayer and Union with Christ." *Scottish Bulletin of Evangelical Theology* 8, no. 2 (1990): 109–27.

———. "Reflections on Four Great American Preachers." Banner of Truth Magazine, November 1992.

———. "Response to the Decision of the Church of Scotland 23 May 2011." Banner of Truth Magazine, September 2011.

———. "Review of Berthoud, Jean-Marc. *L' Alliance de Dieu À Travers l'Écriture Sainte: Une Théologie Biblique*." *The Westminster Theological Journal* 76, no. 1 (2014): 221–22.

———. "Review of Calvin, Jean. *Commentariorum in Acta Apostorum Liber Posterior*." *The Sixteenth Century Journal* 35, no. 2 (2004): 557–58.

———. "A Rehabilitation of Scholasticism: A Review of Muller, Richard A. *Post-Reformation Reformed Dogmatics Volume One: Prolegomena to Theology*." *Scottish Bulletin of Evangelical Theology* 6, no. 2 (1988): 112–22.

———. "Review of Ziolkowski, Jan M. Obscenity: *Social Control and Artistic Creation in the European Middle Ages*." *Speculum* 75, no. 4 (2000): 998–1000.

———. "The Sabbath vs. the Liturgical Calendar." *The Confessional Presbyterian* 11 (2015): 68.

———. "The Triune God." *Reformed Faith & Practice* 2, no. 2 (2017): 90–93.

Contributors

Jon Balserak (PhD, The University of Edinburgh; ThM, Reformed Theological Seminary, Jackson) is Senior Lecturer in Early Modern Studies at University of Bristol. He is the author of *Calvinism: A Very Short Introduction, John Calvin as Sixteenth-Century Prophet,* and *Divinely Compromised: A Study of Divine Accommodation in the Thought of John Calvin.*

Bill Bradford (ThM, Reformed Theological Seminary, Jackson) is Senior Pastor at Lawndale Presbyterian Church in Tupelo, MS. Previously he served for ten years with Peru Mission in church planting, leadership development, and mercy ministry.

John D. Currid (PhD, The University of Chicago) is Professor of Old Testament at Reformed Theological Seminary, Dallas. In addition to several commentaries on Old Testament books, he is the author of *The Case for Biblical Archaeology: Uncovering the Historical Record of God's Old Testament People, Why Do I Suffer?: Suffering & the Sovereignty of God,* and *Against the Gods: The Polemical Theology of the Old Testament.*

Gerrit S. Dawson (DMin, Reformed Theological Seminary, Charlotte) is Senior Pastor of First Presbyterian Church, Baton Rouge. He is author of *Raising Adam: Why Jesus Descended into Hell, Jesus Ascended: The Meaning of Christ's Continuing Incarnation,* and *Called by a New Name: Becoming What God has Promised.*

J. Ligon Duncan III (PhD, The University of Edinburgh) is Chancellor & CEO of Reformed Theological Seminary and John E. Richards Professor of Systematic and Historical Theology at Reformed Theological Seminary, Jackson. He is author of several books, including *Does Grace Grow Best in Winter?*, *Proclaiming a Cross-Centered Theology, Fear Not, Women's Ministry in the Local Church,* and general editor of *The Westminster Confession in the 21st Century: Essays in Remembrance of the 350th Anniversary of the Westminster Assembly.*

Sinclair B. Ferguson (PhD, University of Aberdeen) is Chancellor's Professor of Systematic Theology at Reformed Theological Seminary and Preaching Associate at Trinity Church, Aberdeen. He is author of several books, including *Some Pastors & Teachers, Devoted to God, The Whole Christ, The Big Book of Questions & Answers about Jesus, The Holy Spirit, The Sermon on the Mount,* and *The Christian Life.*

Christian D. Finnigan (PhD candidate, McGill University; J.D., Antonin Scalia Law School, George Mason University; MDiv, Reformed Theological Seminary, Charlotte) is Assistant Professor of History and Politics at Colorado Christian University.

Jonathan Gibson (PhD, Cambridge University) is Associate Professor of Old Testament at Westminster Theological Seminary. He is co-editor of *From Heaven He Came and Sought Her: Definite Atonement in Historical, Biblical, Theological, and Pastoral Perspective, Reformation Worship: Liturgies from the Past for the Present,* and author of *Covenant Continuity and Fidelity: A Study of Inner-Biblical Allusion and Exegesis in Malachi, The Moon is Always Round,* and *Be Thou My Vision: A Liturgy for Daily Worship.*

Taylor Ince (PhD, University of Edinburgh; MDiv, Reformed Theological Seminary, Charlotte) is Pastor at Sojourn Galleria Church in Houston, TX.

Caroline Kelly (MSc, BD [Hons], The University of Edinburgh) has been teaching Latin for over 30 years. She is a consultant and author for the *Ecce Romani* textbook series, and has written several articles on Latin pedagogy. Caroline also co-authored *If God Already Knows, Why Pray?* and *Carolina Scots* with her husband, Douglas Kelly.

Patrick Kelly (MD, The Medical University of South Carolina; BA Classics, The University of North Carolina at Chapel Hill) is a primary care doctor with Christ Community Health Services in Augusta, GA. After medical school Patrick attended Yale University-Yale New Haven Hospital for a residency in internal medicine. In addition to practicing medicine, he carries out research on the intersection of flourishing and the experience of suffering with a core team of theologians, pastors, poets, scientists, psychologists and philosophers.

Mark Ian McDowell (PhD, University of Aberdeen, MDiv, Reformed Theological Seminary, Charlotte) is Executive Director of Reformed Theological Seminary, Dallas and Houston campuses and Assistant Professor of Systematic Theology, Dallas. Previously he served as Associate Pastor at First Presbyterian Church, Columbia, SC. Mark has written on covenant theology, Christology, and political theology.

Alex Mark (MDiv, Reformed Theological Seminary, Charlotte) is Senior Pastor of First Scots Presbyterian Church of Beaufort, SC. He served as Douglas Kelly's Teaching Assistant from 2010–2013.

Mark Miller (ThM student, Westminster Theological Seminary; MDiv, Reformed Theological Seminary, Charlotte) is Senior Pastor of Clover ARP Church. He served as Douglas Kelly's Teaching Assistant from 2006–2007.

Matthew S. Miller (PhD candidate, University of Bristol; DMin, Erskine Theological Seminary; MDiv, Reformed Theological Seminary, Charlotte) is Associate Professor of Pastoral and Historical Theology at Erskine Theological Seminary and City

Director of the C. S. Lewis Institute in Greenville, SC. He has translated Pierre Courthial's *A New Day of Small Beginnings* (2018) and *The Bible: The Sacred Text of the Covenant* (2023). Matt served as Douglas Kelly's Teaching Assistant from 2000–2004.

Mantle Nance (PhD, University of Aberdeen; MDiv, Reformed Theological Seminary, Charlotte) is Senior Pastor of Ballantyne Presbyterian Church and Visiting Lecturer in Pastoral Theology at Reformed Theological Seminary, Charlotte. He is author of *The Adorable Trinity: Standing for Orthodoxy in Nineteenth-Century America.*

D. Blair Smith (PhD, Durham University; MDiv, Reformed Theological Seminary, Charlotte) is Associate Professor of Systematic Theology at Reformed Theological Seminary, Charlotte, and Academic Dean of RTS, Dallas and Houston. He is also Adult Education Coordinator at Christ Covenant Church in Matthews, NC. Blair has written on patristics, Trinitarian theology, theological retrieval, and confessionalism.

Kirk M. Summers (PhD, University of Illinois; MA Reformed Theological Seminary, Jackson) is Professor of Classics and Director of the Classics Program at The University of Alabama. He is author of *Morality after Calvin: Theodore Beza's Christian Censor and Reformed Ethics,* editor and translator of Peter Martyr Vermigli's *On Original Sin,* and co-editor of *Theodore Beza at 500: New Perspectives on an Old Reformer.*

Scripture Index

391

Subject Index

Christian Focus Publications

Our mission statement —

STAYING FAITHFUL

In dependence upon God we seek to impact the world through literature faithful to His infallible Word, the Bible. Our aim is to ensure that the Lord Jesus Christ is presented as the only hope to obtain forgiveness of sin, live a useful life and look forward to heaven with Him.

Our books are published in four imprints:

CHRISTIAN
FOCUS

Popular works including biographies, commentaries, basic doctrine and Christian living.

CHRISTIAN
HERITAGE

Books representing some of the best material from the rich heritage of the church.

MENTOR

Books written at a level suitable for Bible College and seminary students, pastors, and other serious readers. The imprint includes commentaries, doctrinal studies, examination of current issues and church history.

CF4•K

Children's books for quality Bible teaching and for all age groups: Sunday school curriculum, puzzle and activity books; personal and family devotional titles, biographies and inspirational stories — because you are never too young to know Jesus!

Christian Focus Publications Ltd,
Geanies House, Fearn, Ross-shire,
IV20 1TW, Scotland, United Kingdom.
www.christianfocus.com